Abner Ralph Small

The Sixteenth Maine Regiment in the War of the Rebellion

1861-1865

Abner Ralph Small

The Sixteenth Maine Regiment in the War of the Rebellion 1861-1865

ISBN/EAN: 9783337116507

Printed in Europe, USA, Canada, Australia, Japan

Cover: Foto ©ninafisch / pixelio.de

More available books at **www.hansebooks.com**

APPOMATTOX C. H., PLACE OF LEE'S SURRENDER.

THE
SIXTEENTH MAINE REGIMENT

IN THE

WAR OF THE REBELLION

1861=1865

BY MAJOR A. R. SMALL

With an Introduction written by GEN. JAMES A. HALL

FREDERICKSBURGH, CHANCELLORSVILLE, GETTYSBURGH, MINE RUN, WILDERNESS, SPOTTSYLVANIA, NORTH ANNA, TOLOPOTOMY, BETHESDA CHURCH, PETERSBURGH, WELDON R. R., HATCHER'S RUN, GRAVELLY RUN, FIVE FORKS, APPOMATTOX.

PUBLISHED FOR THE REGIMENTAL ASSOCIATION
BY B. THURSTON & COMPANY
PORTLAND, MAINE
1886

COPYRIGHT BY A. R. SMALL,
1886.

ILLUSTRATIONS.

	Page
APPOMATTOX COURT-HOUSE	Frontispiece.
COLONEL A. W. WILDES	34
GENERAL CHARLES W. TILDEN	44
COLONEL AUGUSTUS B. FARNHAM	75
MAJOR ARCH D. LEAVITT	101
MAJOR A. R. SMALL	175
CAMP TILDEN	162
CAMP LEAVITT	208

CONTENTS.

	Page
INTRODUCTION	1
PREFACE	5

CHAPTER I.
RECRUITING 9

CHAPTER II.
ORGANIZATION AND MUSTER-IN, FROM AUGUSTA, ME., TO ARLINGTON, VA. 15

CHAPTER III.
THE MARYLAND CAMPAIGN 32

CHAPTER IV.
FROM SHARPSBURGH, MD., TO FREDERICKSBURGH, VA. . 48

CHAPTER V.
FREDERICKSBURGH 59

CONTENTS.

CHAPTER VI.
Winter Quarters, 1863 84

CHAPTER VII.
The Chancellorsville Campaign 101

CHAPTER VIII.
Gettysburgh 111

CHAPTER IX.
On the March 136

CHAPTER X.
Mine Run Campaign 150

CHAPTER XI.
Outpost Duty at Mitchell's Station, Va. . . 162

CHAPTER XII.
Wilderness Campaign 175

CHAPTER XIII.
Closing Campaign of the War 209

APPENDIX.
Biographies of Officers 224
Statistical Tables 253

Company A, pp. 254-259; Company B, pp. 260-263; Company C, pp. 264-267; Company D, pp. 268-271; Company E, pp. 272-276; Company F, pp. 277-280; Company G, pp. 281-284; Company H, pp. 285-288; Company I, pp. 289-292; Company K, pp. 293-296. Officers and enlisted men detached, pp. 297, 298. Enlisted men transferred to 20th Maine Volunteers, pp. 299-306; Enlisted men transferred to Invalid Corps, pp. 307, 308; Enlisted men transferred to United States Navy, p. 308; Enlisted men transferred to Veteran Reserve Corps, pp. 309-311; Burial places, pp. 311-314; Roll of deceased, pp. 315-322; Summary, p. 323.

INTRODUCTION.

DAMARISCOTTA, June 7, 1886.

MAJOR A. R. SMALL, *Oakland, Me.*

MY DEAR COMRADE:—The story of the Sixteenth Maine Regiment from your pen surely requires no introduction from any one; but I gladly improve the opportunity kindly extended, to pay my humble tribute to the memory of the noble dead, and to cordially extend greeting to the gallant ones now living, of that illustrious organization which so signally honored the State of Maine by its distinguished service in the late war. The faithfulness with which you have produced the record, and the completeness of the tabulations, give the work a value not often found in such productions. The biographical allusions, the personal reminiscences, and the delineation of camp, march, bivouac, and battle, are so correctly drawn, that every member of the regiment must take great satisfaction in possessing the book. I think you have hit upon just the idea of such a work, and bespeak for it the highest place among regimental histories. Every one who feels a pride in their own State ought to read it, and undoubtedly they will.

Having been associated with the Sixteenth, in the same division, for a long time, having been cognizant of its many hardships, privations, and sufferings in the common cause, at the same time having been an eye-witness to some of its many heroic deeds and splendid actions, I may be pardoned for departing from the regular order of a formal introduction, to say a few words which the author, from a sense of modesty, has omitted, but which are due to the gallant officers and men of one of the most gallant commands ever marshaled in war.

Recruited in the summer of 1862, the opportunity offered the highest grade of material for the organization. It is a well-known fact, that, when recruiting stopped in 1861, there were thousands of gallant sons of Maine not enrolled, and they had been anxiously waiting for the chance which the call for the Sixteenth Regiment gave them to enlist.

It had among its officers many who had already seen much service in the field. Conspicuously so, Lieutenant-Colonel Tilden and Major A. B. Farnham, who had been captains in the Second Maine, and several others from different commands. This fact added materially to the early efficiency of the regiment.

The first colonel, A. W. Wildes, by reason of poor health, was obliged to leave the field early in October, 1862, and for the same reason, to resign January 7th, 1863, when Lieutenant-Colonel Tilden, who had been in command from October 7th, 1862, was promoted to be colonel, and Major Farnham became lieutenant-colonel, and Captain Leavitt was made major.

It is no exaggeration to say that no regiment in all the army had a more soldierly commander than Colonel Tilden, nor was there one braver, more skillful, or cooler under all circumstances. Modest and unassuming, quiet, and always generous and kind to subordinates, he resolutely grasped the situation in action, and fought with intrepidation that became the admiration of all around him; at the same time displaying a judgment for maneuvering, of the highest order.

With a much larger command he would have proved the equal of any in similar positions. In Lieutenant-Colonel Farnham he had a support in keeping with himself; while the entire organization, officers and men, one and all, were well worthy of their gallant leaders, and from their baptism at Fredericksburgh, December 13th, 1862, to Appomattox, the conspicuous service rendered on every field where engaged, might well have been expected.

The quality of the men is well known to me, from the fact of having had a large detail from its ranks to my battery in November, 1862, where they served with me, while I remained in command of said battery, until the middle of July, 1863, and where they remained with my successor until the battery was mustered out, and the detachment was transferred to the Fifth Maine Battery. It affords me much pleasure to testify to the intelligent manner in which they served as artillerymen. They were splendid soldiers.

Having carefully studied much of the history of the various organizations which composed the grand old army, I fail to find any regimental record superior to the Sixteenth Maine, especially at Fredericksburgh, and at Gettysburgh, July 1st, 1863.

So long as Maine shall have a place in the States of the American Union, so long as her people shall remember anything pertaining to the great struggle for human rights, so long as deeds of valor performed for great principles shall be cherished, so long will the praises of the grand old Sixteenth Maine Regiment be chanted, and children not yet born will imbibe devotion to their country from the story of its service, and those descending from the noble men who filled its ranks and were its officers will tell to their posterity, with commendable pride, how their ancestors were soldiers in that glorious organization.

To have been permitted, under the providence of God, to be a member of that command, with its illustrious record, with the results achieved, was a blessing and a favor Heaven has seldom vouchsafed to bestow upon citizens of the republic.

I congratulate you upon the completion of the work, and I congratulate the regiment upon having it so admirably performed.

JAMES A. HALL.

PREFACE.

The "Story of the Sixteenth," were it all told from individual experience, would fill volumes, but as told by me must necessarily be short and incomplete.

History wants the actual personal experience of participators in the events and incidents of the war, and calls for both the tragic and humorous phases of army life.

The brigadier-generals and other officers give coloring to the tapestries of history being woven; but the non-commissioned furnish the warp, and the privates the filling for the web. To the latter classes I appealed unceasingly for material, but, unfortunately, too many comrades would shield themselves behind modest deprecation.

If I have given undue prominence to a few, it is because the matter was furnished me, not that they alone are especially deserving; and because, further, their acts of bravery honor the regiment, and reflect a luster upon every member.

I did not receive the prompt and general response to my circular which was promised me, and some, from whom I had reason to expect most valuable aid, gave me no assistance whatever, either from a false sense of modesty, or too much faith in my ability to gather facts from other sources. I am especially indebted to General Tilden, to Major Aubrey Leavitt, and to Charles W.

Waldron of the *Lewiston Gazette*, who kindly sent me letters written in the field by his distinguished father. Captain Davies, Lieutenant Chapman, Lieutenant Wiggin, and comrade Thomas S. Hopkins aided me materially. To Sergeant Bradford I am more than grateful for his valuable assistance and sympathy.

The roster of the regiment is full and complete, and as correct in every particular as that of any volunteer troops who served in the war of the rebellion. This is due to the faithfulness of the officers in making their returns, and to Adjutant-General Hodsdon, whose untiring devotion to the individual interests of the citizen soldier is without a parallel in history. As adjutant I had occasion to learn how determined he was that no soldier should in the future suffer from any neglect of his to record the full name and history of every man correctly.

Any member of a regiment, officer or private, can have but little knowledge of movements outside his immediate command. He must draw upon his imagination, or from the experience of others. In all engagements with the enemy, every one has a specific duty to perform, and no time to look with a critical eye upon his comrade's conduct; he has all he can do to obey orders and keep from running — many failed even in this. Almost the first thought that comes home to a brave man is one of self preservation, and the second, the safety of his honor, when pride comes in as a powerful auxiliary, and, oftener than courage, keeps him to the front.

The idea that a soldier, whose simple duty it is to remain in the ranks and move in geometrical lines, has an opportunity to view a Gettysburgh as he would a panorama, is simply absurd. After the first volley of musketry, he is a rare man who theorizes, or speculates on the action of his comrade, or of his regiment, much more on that of the commanding general, three miles distant.

The inequalities of the ground, the wooded slopes and deep ravines, the fog, the dense smoke, and the apparent and often real confusion of troops moving in different directions under different orders, utterly precludes the possibility of a correct detailed observation of a battle of any magnitude. Hence I have drawn material from all sources considered reliable.

The long marches made by the Sixteenth are rich in material of substantial value to the gleaner of reminiscences. But however exquisite in suffering, and interesting as examples of heroic endurance, they may become stale to the general public by too frequent repetition — too high coloring.

The intrinsic value which attaches to the daily life of a soldier is modified by a look at the general balance-sheet for the campaigns which divides and sub-divides the experience among a half million men. No one action stands out prominent and clear among so many. One overshadows another in some peculiar quality. It is well that the exceptional cases of bravery and suffering are noticeable in battalions, especially so in companies where its prominence is justly recognized, and its memory cherished by comrades of the squad thus honored. The company refers to it with pride, the regiment shares in the glory and appropriates it; but the brigade, if it ever hears of it, forgets it.

The Sixteenth sends up a rocket; the Ninetieth sends up one, perhaps not so high, but more brilliant; the Ninety-fourth makes a gorgeous display; and the Thirteenth comes out with a regular aurora, when we all subside, and thenceforth look upon every meritorious act as an adjunct of a great whole. When one hero compares himself individually with other heroes around him, he swells with pride that his act makes him equal with any one of them, but when he comes to hear of a hundred brave acts, and places his record beside the grand total, his insignificance astonishes him. Each soldier stands apart in solitary weakness, but the army, as a whole, may in truth be said to be invincible.

I presume other regiments marched as long and as hard as the Sixteenth, and doubtless were just as lousy, and hunted as diligently for wood-ticks, but somehow there is a feeling of proprietorship in one's own performances, whether marching, fighting, cooking an elaborate dinner in a tin quart, or suffering torments in rebel prisons. I do not claim for the Sixteenth any patent on army life; simply claim its own, and as a constituent part of the grand old Army of the Potomac, expect it to share in that army's imperishable glory and renown.

The honorable record of the Second and Fifth Maine Batteries is a source of pride to the Sixteenth, which furnished details for service in both organizations.

Every item of interest clinging to our regiment is the property of its members, and to them is beyond all price. He who is not exalted with joyous gladness that he was both a soldier and a "Sixteener" is not worthy of the name "veteran."

A. R. SMALL.

Sixteenth Regiment Maine Volunteers.

CHAPTER I.

RECRUITING.

Our story opens in the dark days of the war, when the government, panic stricken by the fearful disasters at the front, — a sequence of timidity, exasperating procrastination, and poor generalship, — called earnestly for more volunteers.

The "Sixteenth Regiment of Infantry,"[*] for three years' service, was authorized by the following order, under direction of the War Department of May 21st, 1862. At that time there were no intimations of an immediate call for additional three years' troops from Maine; but within a few weeks a requisition was made upon the State for its quota, upon the call of July 2d for three hundred thousand volunteers for three years' service under the general government, and this regiment, with others subsequently authorized, was in satisfaction of this requisition.

HEADQUARTERS, ADJUTANT-GENERAL'S OFFICE,
Augusta, Me., May 22, 1862.
General Order No. 12.

Pursuant to authority and request from the War Department, the Commander-in-Chief orders and directs that one Regiment of

[*] Adjutant-General's Report, 1862.

Infantry, the Sixteenth of Maine Volunteers, to consist of not less than eight hundred and sixty-six, nor more than ten hundred and forty-six men, in the aggregate, be forthwith raised for the service of the United States, by voluntary enlistment, to serve for three years, or during the war, if sooner ended, and to be entitled to all the pay, allowances, and bounties provided for other troops raised for the United States.

Individuals to whom enlisting papers may be issued to recruit for this regiment, will receive *none but able-bodied men* of the age of eighteen years, and under forty-five years, nor minors without the written consent of their parents or guardians. . . . . The utmost caution is enjoined upon recruiting officers to receive none but able-bodied men, and to secure a *full, correct and legibly written description* of every man enlisted, with the *Christian* name written in full. . . . .

By order of the Commander-in-Chief,

JOHN L. HODSDON,
Adjutant-General.

From every part of the State recruits came forward slowly during the months of May and June. Governor Washburn, fully alive to the fact that the call was imperative, and the necessities of the service admitted of no delay, was nervously impatient at the apparent want of patriotism in the Pine Tree State, and issued the following Proclamation:—

EXECUTIVE DEPARTMENT, July 4th, 1862.
To the People of Maine!

An additional number of troops is required by the exigency of the public service, and if raised immediately, it is believed by those who have the best means of knowledge, that the war will be brought to a speedy and glorious issue. Of this number the President of the United States desires and expects that Maine should furnish her proportion or quota. Our gallant and patriotic State has done her whole duty in the past, and she will not falter nor fail in the present nor the future.

That her natural interests may be protected and advanced; that tranquility and peace may be restored throughout the land; that the constitution and the Union which have been to us all the source of unmeasured blessings may be preserved; that liberty, of which they were the inspiration and are the selected guardians, may be saved; and that the light of one great example may shine brighter and brighter to guide, to cheer, and to bless the nations; — to aid in all these, I invoke of the people of this State, a prompt and hearty response to this new demand upon their patriotism. And may they all unite in the work that is before them, each laboring in his own sphere, doing what he can by his example, influence, and sympathy — proffering his treasure, his time, his strength, his heart, and his highest hopes to the cause of his country! . . . .

ISRAEL WASHBURN, JR.,
Governor of Maine.

July 7th, Adjutant-General Hodsdon promulgated General Order No. 17, from which I make the following extract:—

CITIZEN SOLDIERS!— Remember you have a country to save, and you are the men who can render most efficient aid in this holy and patriotic work. To render success speedy and certain, and to alleviate and abridge calamities of war, the President of the United States has requested this call to be made.

By order of the Commander-in-Chief,

JOHN L. HODSDON,
Adjutant-General.

These and other appeals were promptly published at length by all the loyal press of the State, with editorial comment full of patriotic ardor.

They were read from the pulpit, posted on barns, on the cross-road fences; were discussed in cities and villages, declaimed from school-house steps, and found their way into every hamlet, where, long into the night, fathers and mothers pitted duty against inclination, and duty won.

Latterly men were so anxious to enlist that deception was often practiced on Examining Surgeon Briggs. One morning I found waiting at the door of number nine, regimental headquarters, two anxious civilians of decided mold. Patriotism oozed from every pore, and found utterance in voices heavy with war thunder and poor whisky. They could hardly wait the opening of the door, and growlingly said, "This govmunt can't be so damned hard up for trupes or the boss would be round airlier in the mornin'." A close scrutiny of the embryo heroes revealed some striking peculiarities of a recent make-up. One was about forty years old. The other anywhere from twenty to eighty. Stripped of his clothing, and the mysteries of hair coloring and whisker dye, he would present a type of the resurrection.

The regulation inquiries developed the case, and the afternoon train saw the young man, with his swagger, and the old man, with his war paint and hair dye, going to the rear. The visions of large bounties and an early discharge on a comfortable pension had vanished in the mists of a new determination to aid the cause by voting "agin the war."

Governor Washburn's appeal awoke a spirit of patriotism in the breast of a young man away in Piscataquis County. He came to the camp towering above all his comrades, and, Apollo-like, he was the personification of manly beauty. His curled hair betokened neatness; his step, confidence; and a new-born scowl and close mouth denoted firmness and courage. He bristled all over with fight, and was spoiling for a scrimmage. We picked that man out for a model soldier, and a successful competitor in the race for shoulder straps. We waited upon him graciously, for his superiority impressed us; and were flattered by his order to carry a valise and two large trunks to his quarters.

There is nothing like the stern realities of war as exemplified in rations of hard-tack, bacon, and salt pork, for the development of a "I-want-to-go-home" feeling. Only five days, and came into number nine our model soldier, who demanded a discharge. Asking a few questions, Major Gardiner referred him to the terms of his enlistment, and told him he was for three years at the option of the government.

"But, don't you never discharge a man?"

"Only for disability."

A few moments he stood, then drawing down the corners of his mouth, planted both hands over his bowels, fetched a fearful groan and went for the surgeon. In just five minutes that six-footer — our model soldier — came bounding into the office and shouted, "I can't go! I'm *busted!*"

Notwithstanding the order that "none but able-bodied men" should be received, many invalids crept in; and there were others who were essentially timid. They put on uniforms, hung a sword or bayonet on one side, a pistol on the other; and hung tales of heroism on the other sides, and on various places were pinned artificial records of campaigns. They sang patriotic songs, appeared on parade, and thought how they would figure in history. The Sixteenth was pretty well plucked of such poor material before it left Maine, yet there was enough left to cause an occasional halting in its progress toward a character for courage and patriotism.

Visitors came daily to camp and brought words of good cheer. Some said good by carelessly, fully believing that we should never leave the State. Others hung about the necks of loved ones, and only after embraces and kisses repeated over and over again, would they tear themselves away. Heavy with a precursor of coming sorrow, an untold intuition of a great loss, they looked for the last time upon the loved ones, and went away to mourn and question for years to come, the terrible necessity for their sacrifice.

CHAPTER II.

ORGANIZATION AND MUSTER IN. FROM AUGUSTA, ME., TO ARLINGTON, VA.

1862
Aug. 13.

THE additional stimulus of bounties offered in some localities, pensions promised, and bulletins of defeats of the boys in blue in the field, soon filled the ranks, and August 13th saw duly enlisted for the war nine hundred and sixty men. The Governor commissioned thirty-nine officers, thus completing the organization of the regiment, as follows:—

FIELD AND STAFF.

Asa W. Wildes,	Skowhegan,	Colonel.
Charles W. Tilden,	Castine,	Lieutenant-Colonel.
Augustus B. Farnham,	Bangor,	Major.
Abner R. Small,	Waterville,	Adjutant.
Isaac N. Tucker,	Gardiner,	Quartermaster.
Charles Alexander,	Farmington,	Surgeon.
Joseph B. Baxter,	Gorham,	Assistant Surgeon.
George Bullen,	Skowhegan,	Chaplain.

NON-COMMISSIONED STAFF.

Francis A. Wildes,	Skowhegan,	Sergeant-Major.
George W. Brown,	Augusta,	Quartermaster-Serg't.
Charles H. Parlin,	Skowhegan,	Commissary-Sergeant.
William W. Eaton,	Brunswick,	Hospital Steward.
William H. Palmer,	Calais,	Drum-Major.

COMPANY OFFICERS.

COMPANY A.

Charles A. Williams,	Skowhegan,	Captain.
S. Forrest Robinson,	Skowhegan,	First Lieutenant.
Isaac A. Pennell,	New Portland,	Second Lieutenant.

COMPANY B.

Charles K. Hutchins,	Augusta,	Captain.
Eleazer W. Atwood,	Gardiner,	First Lieutenant.
George W. Edwards,	Gorham,	Second Lieutenant.

COMPANY C.

Daniel Marston,	Phillips,	Captain.
Hovey C. Austin,	Presque Isle,	First Lieutenant.
Marshall S. Smith,	East Livermore,	Second Lieutenant.

COMPANY D.

Moses W. Rand,	Waterford,	Captain.
Humphry E. Eustis,	Dixfield,	First Lieutenant.
Henry P. Herrick,	North Yarmouth,	Second Lieutenant.

COMPANY E.

Arch D. Leavitt,	Turner,	Captain.
William E. Brooks,	Skowhegan,	First Lieutenant.
William A. Stevens,	Waterville,	Second Lieutenant.

COMPANY F.

Thomas E. Wentworth,	Gorham,	Captain.
Oliver H. Lowell,	Gorham,	First Lieutenant.
George A. Deering,	Saco,	Second Lieutenant.

COMPANY G.

S. Clifford Belcher,	Farmington,	Captain.
Joseph H. Malbon,	Skowhegan,	First Lieutenant.
Isaac H. Thompson,	Anson,	Second Lieutenant.

COMPANY H.

John Ayer,	Bangor,	Captain.
Ira S. Libby,	Limerick,	First Lieutenant.
Israel H. Washburn,	Orono,	Second Lieutenant.

COMPANY I.

William H. Waldron,	Lewiston,	Captain.
William Bray,	Turner,	First Lieutenant.
Charles A. Garcelon,	Lewiston,	Second Lieutenant.

COMPANY K.

Stephen C. Whitehouse,	New Castle,	Captain.
Augustus T. Somerby,	Ellsworth,	First Lieutenant.
Augustus C. Peters,	Bluehill,	Second Lieutenant.

With the exception of Captain Marston, promoted from private Ninth Maine, none of the line officers had done military service. Of the staff, Quartermaster Tucker was but recently lieutenant-colonel Third Regiment. A long and successful business life eminently fitted him for his new position. Adjutant Small was also from the Third Regiment. Lieu-

1862 tenant-Colonel Tilden and Major Farnham were fresh from active military service. The regiment was more fortunate than it knew in having the benefit of their experience in the gallant Second, under one of Maine's ablest and most distinguished colonels. General Hodsdon, in his Report for 1862, says: —

"Lieutenant-Colonel Charles W. Tilden of Castine and Major Augustus B. Farnham of Bangor made a record for themselves in the Second Regiment, which, with Colonel Wildes' well-known ability, will ensure the service all the military talent and energy in the field officers of the Sixteenth that can be required for its efficiency under all circumstances."

Company A was raised in Somerset and Kennebec Counties, mostly in Somerset.

Company B principally from cities and towns on the Kennebec River, from Waterville to Richmond.

Company C came from Franklin, Oxford, and Aroostook Counties. Company D from Oxford and Cumberland. Company E from Androscoggin, Kennebec, and Penobscot. Company F, York and Cumberland. Company G, Somerset and Franklin. Company H, Waldo and Penobscot. Company I, Kennebec and Androscoggin. Company K, along the coast, and from Hancock and Lincoln. Men from all parts of the State were scattered throughout the regiment.

Lieutenant Chapman says of Company K: —

"The men composing Company K came mostly from Castine, Bluehill, and the eastern section of the State, who were familiar with all the hardships of life as endured at sea and in the logging swamps of

Maine, which early training especially fitted them for the exposure of camp-life and arduous duty in the field. I heard it said when the regiment marched through Washington, on its way to the front, that it was made up of larger men than any regiment that had passed through the city. This remark was certainly true of Company K, for its members were all stalwart men, averaging by weight more than one hundred and fifty pounds. During the long marches it was seldom that any of the men fell out.

"Captain Whitehouse, the father of the company, often remarked that his company 'could beat any men under the sun for marching or foraging, and if they did straggle, it was to forage in front of the advance guard.'

"For cheerfulness in adversity, no company in the regiment could excel it. To illustrate, I recall the reply of Sergeant Dunbar to General Robinson, when the latter expressed the opinion 'that it must be very hard to march without shoes or stockings.' 'I do it,' said the Sergeant with a grim smile, 'for my country, for sixteen dollars a month, and *clothes*.'

"Very many of the men of Company K should be named for good conduct generally, but looking back over a space of twenty years, it is impossible to recall only the names of those connected with some unusual incident. Let me say, no better soldiers or braver men served under the flag of our country during the rebellion than those of Company K, God bless them!"

The closing remarks of Lieutenant Chapman are applicable to the other companies.

MUSTER IN.

1862
Aug. 14.

August 14th the regiment was formed in line and formally mustered into the service of the National Government by Major J. W. T. Gardiner of the regular army.

One moment we were free men to go and come as we pleased, and the next saw us amenable to all the arbitrary and despotic rules of the war department. In fact we were machines to be perfected and used as men like ourselves, holding commissions of authority, saw fit for the good of the service.

During the war this authority was at times shamefully abused. While green and unskilled, the "General" and "Special" orders were rained down upon the rank and file so persistently that the real intent and object of the commanding officer of a department or corps was as vague and obscure as Bible texts in the hands of commentators.

Boys of today may think it fun to be a private soldier, but it is n't. The picturesque blue and scarlet uniform and jaunty laced cap, or symmetrical helmet, seen in cuts, are very deceptive; and the whole soldierly make-up of a picture is misleading.

The "raw recruit" of '62 was suggestive of Falstaff's model private, and when foraging, a tramp.

Be a man never so much a man, his importance and conceit dwindles when he crawls into an unteaseled shirt, pants too short and very baggy behind, coat too long at both ends, and a cap shapeless as a feed bag. And the brogans! were n't they just lovely, with soles six inches wide and heels like firkin covers.

The ideal picture of a soldier makes a veteran smile. He knows the knapsack, which is cut to fit in the engraving, is an unwieldy burden with its rough coarse contents of flannel and sole-leather and sometimes twenty rounds of ammunition extra. Mixed in with these regulation essentials, like beatitudes, are photographs, cards, "housewife," Testament, pens, ink, paper, and oftentimes stolen truck enough to load a mule. All of this crowned with a double wool blanket and shelter tent rolled in a rubber blanket. One shoulder and the hips support the "commissary department"—an odorous haversack, which often stinks with its mixture of bacon, pork, salt-junk, sugar, coffee, tea, desiccated vegetables, rice, bits of yesterday's dinners, and old scraps husbanded with miserly care against a day of want sure to come.

Oh, the perfume of that haversack!

Loaded down, in addition to the above, with a canteen, full cartridge-box, belt, cross belt, and musket, and start on a gunning tour was n't fun. No, it was n't.

A graduate of West Point in his nobby uniform is a thing of beauty, made to inspire a boy's admiration. His carriage is superb. His posing in the position of a soldier makes an unfledged aspirant for military honor green with envy. Under the most trying circumstances he preserves an immobile face. No amount of abuse or insult will cause him to forget himself. But the recruit in his baggy contract suit, practicing "eyes right," is an object of both pity and ridicule. He has lost his identity, and all his claims to equality with even a fife-major are ignored. He finds it harder to hold his temper than to hold his little fingers on the seams of his trousers; hence, the first day's drill usually ends with solemn promises to "lick seven or eight corporals and a lieutenant, when the war is over"— and a night in the guard tent for calling the drill-sergeant offensively arbitrary, and needlessly particular in rehearsing such d—d nonsensical gyrations.

A "private" is anything but *private*. There is nothing in or about him that is respected as exclusive. The day that he is enlisted sees his whole person exposed to the critical eye of the surgeon — his lungs sounded, bowels manipulated, limbs bent, joints cracked, teeth examined, eyes tested, while he undergoes the closest scrutiny, in search of cutaneous eruptions and varicose veins.

After a few short months the lice claim close acquaintance, and the wood-ticks explore the second and third cuticle.

In camp, his tent is ransacked. His knapsack opened every Sunday morning to the view of some inspector. His gun, equipments, and all there is on or about this private, is made conspicuously public. Although the United States Army Regulations guarantee him the exclusive privilege of keeping his opinion of officers and measures as his private property, he is tortured into expression, and then is published throughout the army as "prejudicial to good order and military discipline," and he gets into the guard-house.

There was no aristocracy among the "privates." They were thoroughly democratic.

A graduate from Harvard and an illiterate from the wilds of Maine were often seen affectionately picking lice together.

Polished scholars and ex-convicts, Christians and heathen bounty jumpers from the slums of New York, would cheat each other at "seven-up." All would bathe in and drink from the same stream, whether prior or subsequent to the watering of the brigade mules.

None of us had a gluttonous appetite for a scrimmage, or a morbid desire to fill the last ditch; but when, on the afternoon of August 17th, we were told that the Sixteenth was ordered to the front, and must go the 19th instant, cheer after cheer rent the air. Every order published called for cheers and "tigers."

August 18th saw us getting rid of surplus baggage, packing up and sending home the temporary conveniences of "Camp Jamison." The amount allotted us was fearfully small, we thought, but long afterward, when we carried with us simply a quart pot, did we appreciate the bountiful measure of everything.

We left Augusta quietly, without ostentation or parade, for the days of masquerading had passed. We neither expected or received any marked expressions of profound gratitude or boundless enthusiasm to cheer us on our way to the seat of war.

Fresh as we were from civil life, we had a keen realizing sense of the situation and of the future, which promised no boys' play and held out no special inducements for "girding on an armor."

1862

The past year had demonstrated the cruel necessity for further sacrifice.

Aug. 19.

We are *en route* for the front; and how much is due to patriotism, how much to momentary enthusiasm, kindled by overwrought tales of heroism, how much to large bounties and prospective pensions, is for future critics to determine.

We shall not all return. Many lives will have gone out, and with them the light of many homes and the hope of many hearts, ere the war closes. But there comes home to us the thought that these will not have died in vain.

The regiment arrived in Boston at three in the afternoon, and was taken in charge by the authorities and bountifully served with coffee and sandwiches.

Left Boston at six P.M., by Old Colony Railroad, for Fall River, where the regiment embarked on steamer Commonwealth, and reached Jersey City at one P.M. Wednesday.

Aug. 20.

Left Jersey City at half-past four P.M., arriving in Philadelphia at one A.M., 21st, marched to "Cooper Shop" refreshment rooms and partook of a splendid collation.

At three P.M. left the city for Washington, passing through Baltimore at three in the forenoon, reaching the capital in the evening.

The regiment left Washington, under orders from General Casey, at eleven A.M., August 22d, crossing Long Bridge, marched about six miles to Camp Casey, and, in the words of Captain Waldron, "camped that night on the dirtiest soil that could be found in the dirty State of Virginia."

This was the first march of the Sixteenth Maine, and the hot, sultry weather caused some dozen men to fall out, and come straggling into camp late in the evening.

August 24th, broke camp and marched two miles to "Camp Whipple," near Fort Tillinghast. Assigned to First Brigade, Whipple's division, R. A. C.

The Massachusetts Fourteenth, one thousand eight hundred strong, marched past our camp in quick time to take part in the battles near Bull Run. They were met by the rebel cavalry at Fairfax Court House, and Friday night saw them marching back, weary, hungry, minus all their overcoats, and one surgeon, who was subsequently paroled and sent into our lines with a message from Lee, that he "should stop at his mansion that night." True or not, the report spread, and many of the men passed a sleepless night, planning and fighting imaginary battles in which every member of the to-be-bloody Sixteenth figured conspicuously as a hero.

Three companies were detailed for defence of Forts Cass, Woodbury, and Tillinghast.

Who of the command can forget the shock given his nervous system at the unmusical sound of the long-roll at half-past two A.M., and how, in ten minutes, the regiment was in line of battle for the first time, where it remained until sunrise? As we had not been taken into the confidence of the commanding general, our blissful ignorance was more manifest than that of the garrison flag waving above us. The thousand and one conjectures and surmises were indulged in until told that poor Pope was being terribly whipped

1862 within a few miles, and we were in danger of a rebel cavalry dash.

Aug. 29. Cannonading heard all day in our front.

Aug. 30. Captain Waldron, Company I, detailed "officer of the day." Companies H and K sent out on picket duty. Companies E and I ordered in the direction of Fairfax Court House, to watch for guerrillas. Established an advanced picket line near Falls church, and succeeded in capturing a lost black pig, several hens, and some leaf tobacco. These companies, which had solved the mysteries outside our picket line, and came marching into camp bringing mud and "something to eat," were for days the envy of the regiment. Company H had solved the problem of paramount interest to all soldiers, and henceforth rations of salt horse and hard-tack were flanked with roast pig and chicken.

Aug. 31. Sergeant Stevens of Company H, sergeant of picket guard, reports, arrested a spy who had worked himself through the outposts to the infantry line, in a farmer's cart, of which he was ostensibly the owner. The sergeant sent him to division headquarters, and received the thanks of General Whipple.

Since August 20th, McClellan's army had been marking time and apparently indulging in a mud-turtle strategy as the most effectual method of showing resentment for Pope's initiatory order, which so unjustly reflected upon McClellan's role as an artist-in-dirt. History says: At a quarter before three, August 29th, McClellan telegraphed President Lincoln: "I am clear that one of two courses should be adopted. First, to concentrate all of our available forces to open communication with Pope. Second, to leave Pope to get out of his scrape, and at once use all our means to make the capital perfectly safe." "He stayed Franklin at Annandale, and sent Sumners northward toward Chain Bridge instead of toward the enemy," thus fully demonstrating either the timidity of the government, or that neither McClellan nor his lieutenants desired the success of Pope as a general. If the former, then McClellan has been most unjustly accused, and Pope and his army were most cruelly and wickedly abandoned. Hence the fated 30th which sent his army retiring to the defences of Washington, defeated, humiliated, and discouraged.

The very attitude of the troops as they marched past us was one of mortification and rage, tempered slightly with disgust. Raw and inexperienced as we were, the contemplation of the column passing with its ragged banners; the long ambulance train, with its terrible freight of torn and crushed humanity; the wounded limping painfully in the rear, and all the evidences of war, carried home to our hearts a crushing sense of the business we were engaged in. And yet grim jokes and criticisms were indulged in at the expense of poor Pope and the authors of the on-to-Richmond policy. I can see "Ike" Thompson now, as he then stood with his back bent to an angle of fifteen degrees, hat on one side, with blanket thrown gracefully across his shoulders, one eye closed and the other critically inspecting Pope and staff as they rode wearily by on their retreat from Bull Run. As they passed from sight, like a funeral procession, Ike, assuming a tragic attitude, facetious-

1862 ly remarked, "Great God! what could you expect of a man who will persist in wearing his shirt wrong end up!" Pope wore a huge stand-up dickey.

Sept. 2. Notwithstanding McClellan's disasters, there seemed an almost imperative demand for his recall to the command of the army, which was done September 2d. Somehow a halo of glory which precedes great expectations encompassed his person with a superficial brilliancy, and whenever or wherever he appeared, a perfect ovation welcomed him. The Sixteenth was as enthusiastic and extravagant in their adulation of the young Napoleon, as were the older troops. He was modest and retiring, and apparently as unconscious of his fine person and superb horsemanship as he was of the enthusiastic greetings.

Details were made daily to work on a line of breast-works connecting the forts. The boys went at it with a will. Many of them, reared on farms, had a natural propensity for digging holes and shoveling dirt, which had not been fully satisfied by details to dig "sinks" and tent drains. They had read about the breast-works and redoubts of George Washington's day, and were glad of a chance to exhibit their artistic qualities on something less degrading than a camp sink. They were not at first impressed with the fact that army sinks are a government institution, duly recognized in the "Regulations," and led off in all sanitary measures, and were as necessary as they were objectionable.

Men questioned how digging a hole in Virginia mud would redound to their credit, and add to the laurels of a soldier. General orders won't say anything about them, unless demanding five to a regiment. Army correspondents, safely seated behind a redoubt, with a pipe and some rum, will write all about the forts, the long line of breast-works, how strong they are, how many bastions and angles, how much repelling power, and charmingly congratulate some pioneer corps on the splendid engineering qualities of — their general. But they never dilate on a line of army sinks, or compliment a regiment for the masterly, ingenious manner in which they cover up their unfaithfulness in the discharge of an irksome duty required of all good soldiers in camp.

Time brought experience, and experience stimulated a desire to please the colonel, and establish a reputation for the regiment. Men and officers soon performed all disagreeable camp duties. Orders, which were at first called hard knots in a long string of red tape, and were denounced as arbitrary, were cheerfully complied with as for the best interests of the regiment.

The adjutant used to call it part of a "d——d military despotism," and was about as unreconciled to "Orders" and restraint as any member of the command, until a shadow of insubordination brought in Colonel Tilden's authority.

"Fall in for letters!" The response to this command was always instantaneous. It was to the boys like the echo of voices from home calling to them.

1862 If an officer had been possessed of a magic wand he could not have called his men around him quicker than by the utterance of those magical words.

It was amusing to watch the men as they clustered around their company officers while the names of the recipients were rapidly called. Expectation was written on every face, changing to exultation as one heard his name, and eagerly reached for the precious missive. Others less fortunate returned to their tents with slow steps, and an air of disappointment illy concealed.

The letters for the Army of the Potomac were all sent to Washington, and from thence to army headquarters. They were again assorted and distributed to the different divisions, and so on down through brigade and regimental headquarters to the commanding officer of each company.

Great care was taken by the government in regard to the delivery of soldiers' letters. A soldier was sure to get his letter, no matter if the postage was a little short. Almost anything was allowed to go through the mails, even to pairs of boots; and clothing, packages of tea, pepper, etc., were very common.

When in winter quarters a mail was received every day; but when on the march, weeks sometimes passed without any. If men were on picket duty, the officers always endeavored to send their letters out to them.

Early in the war, Congress passed an act allowing soldiers' letters to pass through the mails without prepayment of postage, that being collected of the person receiving it. Members of Congress franked envelopes by the thousand, which were furnished the men at a nominal price, through the regimental postmaster. It was a great convenience to the boys, whose postage stamps would persist in sticking together. The "franking" of a letter by a commissioned officer was sufficient to insure its carriage and delivery by the United States mails.

Correspondence engrossed a large share of the leisure time of the soldiers, especially when in winter quarters. And in the number of papers and letters received and sent, the Sixteenth was not a whit behind the other regiments.

The Sixteenth again reported as "all cut up," but not by fighting. With the exception of the color company, C, the regiment was detailed for artillery service in the chain of forts from Fort Corcoran, opposite Georgetown, to Fort De Kalb, north of Alexandria, by the following order: —

1862

Sept. 4.

HEADQUARTERS 1ST BRIGADE,
WHIPPLE'S DIVISION,
Near Fort Tillinghast, Va., Sept. 2, 1862.

General Orders No. 3.

The 16th Regiment Maine Volunteers will be distributed in the forts of this command as follows: —

2 companies, Fort Corcoran, (D and F).
2   "   " Albany, Maj. Buxton, Mass. 14th, commanding.
1 company,   " Craig, Capt. Day, Mass. 14th, commanding.
1   "   " Tillinghast, Capt. Sargent, Mass. 14th commanding.
1   "   " Cass, Capt. Langworthy, 1st Wis. Ind. Co., commanding.
1   "   " Woodbury, Capt. Draper, 14th Mass., commanding.

1862   1 company, Fort De Kalb, Capt. Shutswell, 14th Mass., commanding.

And one company* will perform the guard duty at Division Headquarters, Arlington.

Lieutenant-Colonel Tilden, 16th Maine Volunteers, will command Fort Corcoran.

The commanding officers of the forts will give every facility to the companies of the Maine Regiment attached to their forts for instruction in artillery.

By command of WM. B. GREENE,
Colonel Commanding Brigade.

(Signed,)   F. W. TAGGARD,
1st Lieutenant and A. A. D. C.

Sept. 5.   Various rumors are current that our army is moving rapidly northward toward Frederick, Maryland, and that **Whipple's** division is ordered to join the main army.

    * Company C.

CHAPTER III.

THE MARYLAND CAMPAIGN.

In compliance with orders, through division commander, received at eleven o'clock P.M., the detached companies were directed to rendezvous at Fort Tillinghast, and be in readiness to move at one hour's notice. 1862
Sept. 6.

Company I, from Fort Cass, our extreme left, reported to Colonel Wildes at half-past twelve, and by four o'clock Sunday morning the Sixteenth was in line, with two days' rations and forty rounds of ammunition. Sept. 7.

Henceforth Washington and its defences would know us no more as a "heavy artillery regiment."

To the timid ones, this was a grievous disappointment; but to the regiment as a whole, the order to move at half-past four was not an unwelcome one.

The faces of the chicken-man, and the milk-woman wore a look expressive of something more than regret as the boys bid them an affectionate "good by."

The sick remained in charge of Surgeon Alexander for a few days, and were then sent to some general hospital in Washington.

1862   Great dissatisfaction was felt at leaving our tents, knapsacks, and overcoats behind. In our greenness, we expected they would follow us in a few days, as a matter of course.

With the swinging gait peculiar to Maine, we took up our line of march, crossing the Potomac over Aqueduct Bridge at sunrise; through Georgetown and Washington, and that night bivouacked under the stars and pines on the estate of Montgomery Blair, having marched fifteen miles.

Sept. 8.   The regiment was in line at four A.M., and *en route* north, until it reached the Baltimore and Frederick Turnpike; thence, northwest in the direction of Frederick City, and encamped near Leesboro'.

Sept. 9.   Assigned to Hartsuff's brigade (composed of the Eleventh Pennsylvania, Ninth New Hampshire, Twelfth and Thirteenth Massachusetts), Rickett's division, Hooker's corps.

Sept. 11.   The rapid marching continued, with short halts, Tuesday and Wednesday, and on Thursday the regiment went into camp at Ridgeville, Maryland, where it remained until the seventeenth.

The officers' tents followed the regiment, but the men sheltered themselves, as best they could, with fence rails and cornstalks.

Ridgeville was a sleepy looking town of one hundred inhabitants of a rebellious tendency. They were extremely solicitous of their gardens and haystacks, which were guarded with fidelity, and did not scruple to charge six cents per canteen for water.

The rebel officers who quartered here a few days previous were received with open doors and feted

with the fatted calf. Company H can testify that 1862
there was one calf and several pigs less when the
Sixteenth left.

The few loyal people in the vicinity visited the
camp daily, and left baskets of luxuries, and words
of encouragement. There was noticeable a lack of
refinement and womanly delicacy in the feminine
chivalry of Maryland. There was a coarseness, an
indifference to remarks, an absence of that degree of
cultivation one had reason to expect in one of the
oldest States in the Union. The young men looked
and appeared like the greenest rustics of New England, and exhibited a reckless indifference to dress
and manners, as well as of any opinion we might form
of them.

The terrific cannonading at Antietam, distinctly
heard by us for the past two days, kept us in anxious
expectation of orders to move, notwithstanding the
protest of the officers, and their frank acknowledgment
of deficiency in instruction, and their well grounded
fears that, if brought into action, their utter ignorance of commands and movements would endanger
a whole division, bring disaster to it, and disgrace to
the regiment.

"Colonel Wildes made known to General Hooker
the circumstances under which the regiment had
been raised, and its deficiency in instruction, occasioned through causes already named. The protest
and statement were without effect, and Colonel
Wildes, unwilling to command under the circumstances, tendered his resignation, which was accepted,
and he was honorably discharged in 'special order

COLONEL.

1862 No. 254,' Headquarters Army of the Potomac, September 13th, 1862."

Subsequently, Colonel Wildes was restored to the command of the regiment in the following order:—

HEADQUARTERS ARMY OF THE POTOMAC,
Near Sharpsburgh, Md., Sept. 25, 1862.

Special Orders, No. 262.

EXTRACT.

3. So much of Special Orders No. 254, of Sept. 13th, 1862, from these Headquarters, as accepts the resignation of Col. A. W. Wildes, 16th Maine Volunteers, is revoked, and Col. Wildes will resume the command of his regiment.

. . . . . .

By Command of MAJ.-GEN. MCCLELLAN.
"Signed."   S. WILLIAMS,
                                Asst. Adjt.-General.

Sept. 17. Orders were received to report to General Hooker on the field of Antietam.

Broke camp, and marched to Frederick City, eighteen miles, and halted two hours. No mail for two weeks, it having gone forward with the brigade.

Sept. 19. Continued the march ten miles, through Middletown, and bivouacked near the battlefield, the nineteenth instant.

Reported to General Williams, and learned from him that it was not intended that the Sixteenth should leave its former quarters, near Washington, it being a new and undrilled regiment, but official approval was expressed to Colonel Wildes, of the promptness and zeal of the officers and men, in marching under orders which had originated in mistake or ill judgment.

Crossed the battlefield, and went into camp near Sharpsburgh, joined the brigade, now in command of Colonel Richard Coulter. ^{1862 Sept. 20.}

After various changes in location, camped near the Potomac River, three miles west of Sharpsburgh.

Lieutenant Lowell detailed acting quartermaster, Quartermaster Tucker having remained at Arlington, under instructions to secure and bring up tents and baggage.

Captain Waldron says: "On Saturday, 28th, pickets from our brigade found ninety dead rebel cannon buried near the river, with neat headstones, bearing a name, and the regiment to which they belonged, so as to be identified by the affectionate relatives, should they be fortunate enough to make another raid into Maryland."

The condition of the regiment was most deplorable. The exposure to cold night air, after being heated by long and rapid marching, frequently through drenching rains, sowed seeds of disease in the system of many noble fellows, and sent to the hospital, and to death, scores of our best men.

Our sister regiments, well clothed in flannel and overcoats, and supplied with rubber blankets, when they fastened down their shelter-tents, dark and stormy nights, seemed to forget the suffering of their half-clad neighbors, whose only shelter was made from cornstalks and boughs, through which the rain would drip long after the storm was over.

Surgeon Alexander and his assistants were untiring in their attempts to succor the sick. But little medicine was furnished them until the middle of

October, hence the fatality of many cases. The only shelter, for those sick in camp, was furnished by flies from officers' tents.

A division hospital was established at Smoketown, to which the worst cases were sent; and in a little field beside the road rests a majority of them, — victims to inefficiency, neglect, and red tape.

October 15th the corrected "morning report" showed six hundred ninety-eight men present. Of these two hundred fifty-six were on the sick list, sixty-eight being in the regimental hospital.

Hospital Steward Eaton, who was unremitting in his care of the sick, says: "It is not strange that under such influences, uncleanliness, despondency, and gloom prevailed. Some fell victims to homesickness, a disease so fearful in its severer types. The very contrast with their former life of ease and comfort made this state of privation and exposure more unbearable. Weaker constitutions succumbed at once, the stronger bore up for a while, but the full fruits of those days were yet to be gathered."

Clothes help make history, hence the name the Sixteenth won at Sharpsburgh. Through the inefficiency and neglect of the quartermaster's department, at Washington, (and the corps, division, and brigade quartermasters were not blameless), the men were made to feel mean and despicable, and felt as does a poor boy at school, when the well-dressed student resents the contact of blue jean with broadcloth.

How those men suffered! Hunger, daily felt, was nothing compared with it. Men of education, of refinement, and wealth, who willingly and cheerfully gave up home, with all its love and comfort, for country, made to feel degraded for want of proper clothing!

September, October, and then the long march, in November, to the Rappahannock, through storms of sleet and snow; without shelter, without overcoats, shoeless, hatless, and hundreds with not so much as a flannel blouse, many without blankets; and through all that long, sad, and weary tramp, we were jeered at, insulted, and called the "Blanket Brigade!"

It may seem improbable, but it is nevertheless a fact, that the transition from fastidious neatness to heedless indifference, to filthy condition and habits, changed some men beyond recognition. High-spirited, opinionated, accustomed to advise and direct, they could illy brook the insolent contempt of their claims by a commissioned ignoramus, and so practically became subordinate in every sense. We remember a college graduate, a royal good fellow, too, who gradually lost his self-respect, and was only brought to himself and obedience by the free use of a corn broom and brook water.

Comrades may have accused their immediate commanders of neglect and inefficiency; and cursed them as the authors of their miserable condition, but could they have assembled at regimental headquarters, and heard the true history, known all the insults and reprimands borne by Colonels Tilden and Farnham; could have heard their sobs, which found response in every heart present, they would have felt that there was suffering almost as deep as theirs.

1862   All the applications of the colonel and quartermaster for a return of clothing and shelter, left at Tillinghast; all the requisitions for something in substitute; all the earnest appeals, and letters of explanation are on file, many of them bearing the endorsement, "disapproved."

Requisitions for shelter and clothing lay in pigeonholes for weeks, but requisitions for whisky were signed forthwith. Perhaps to the latter can be charged our non-recognition, as well as three-fourths the disasters which befell the Army of the Potomac.

Out of all this suffering grew a grand resolve which nothing ever after caused to waver. Out of it came a lasting patriotism and courage that no privation, no danger could abate. The few short months developed a new set of men, and what *kind* of men let Fredericksburgh tell. All that time God was busy making heroes.

Following are the orders and correspondence relating to the necessities and suffering condition of the regiment:—

HDQ'RS 16TH REG'T MAINE VOLS.,
Camp Near Sharpsburgh, Md., Oct. 2, 1862.

CAPT.:—

You will proceed at once to Washington, D. C., and obtain, immediately on your arrival, company books and papers of the 16th Me. Vols. Said books and papers are stored in the city, having been left at Arlington, Va., and since forwarded to Washington. You will also look up absentees from the regiment, and, if possible, obtain a correct and complete account of the sick belonging to the 16th Me. Vols., now in various hospitals between this point and

Washington. You will rejoin your regiment at the first practical moment.

By order of A. W. WILDES,
Col. Com'dg 16th Me. Vols.

(Signed), A. R. SMALL,
Adj't.

To CAPT. S. C. WHITEHOUSE,
Co. K, 16th Me. Vols.

HDQ'RS 3D BRIGADE, 2D DIV.
Oct. 6, 1862.

Approved and respectfully forwarded.
(Signed), R. COULTER,
Col. Com'dg 3d Brigade.

HDQ'RS 2D DIVISION,
Oct. 6, 1862.

Disapproved.

By command of
BRIG.-GEN. RICKETTS,
Com'dg Division.

(Signed), JOHN W. WILLIAMS,
A. A. G.

HDQ'RS 16TH REG'T. ME. VOLS.,
Camp Near Sharpsburgh, Oct. 13, 1862.

GENERAL:—

I would earnestly request that the within order may be forwarded with your approval, as men in my command are suffering for the want of a change of clothing, (some are without shirts to their backs, and many without underclothes). The clothing can be had with knapsacks.

The books and rolls of the companies are indispensable.

I have the honor to remain, General,
very resp'y, your ob't serv't,

(Signed), CHAS. W. TILDEN,
Lt.-Col., Com'dg 16th Me. Vols.

To BRIG.-GEN. TAYLOR,
Com'dg 3d Brigade, Ricketts' Division.

HDQ'RS 16TH ME. REG'T VOLS.,
Near Sharpsburgh, Md.,
Oct. 13, 1862.

CAPT.:—

You will proceed at once to Washington, and obtain immediately on your arrival, books and papers belonging to the companies of 16th Me. Reg't; also knapsacks packed with clothing, issued to this command, which is now stored in the city, having been left by command of Brig.-Gen. Whipple, Sept. 6, at which time the reg't left Arlington, Va.

You will rejoin your regiment without delay.

(Signed), CHAS. W. TILDEN,
Lt.-Col., Com'dg 16th Me. Vols.

To CAPT. STEPHEN C. WHITEHOUSE,
Com'dg Co. K.

HDQ'RS 3D BRIGADE, RICKETTS'
DIVISION, Oct. 13, 1862.

Respectfully forwarded, with the request that Capt. Whitehouse be authorized to proceed to Washington on the business within suggested.

(Signed), NELSON TAYLOR,
Brig.-General.

HDQ'RS 2D DIVISION, Oct. 13, 1862.

These articles can be telegraphed for from Sharpsburgh.
By order of
BRIG.-GEN. RICKETTS, Com'dg Division.
(Signed), J. W. WILLIAMS, A. A. G.

HDQ'RS 16TH REG'T ME. VOLS.,
Camp Near Sharpsburgh, Md., Oct. 18, 1862.

GENERAL:—

Herewith I have the honor to hand you copy of order from Gen. Whipple, to proceed to Leesboro', Md., and report to Gen. Burnside for assignment to his corps. At the time this order was received by Col. Wildes, then in command, the regiment was stationed at the different forts in front of Washington, extending from Fort Albany to Fort De Kalb. We were immediately called together at Fort Tillinghast, and left there in compliance with said order, at three o'clock on the morning of the 7th of September. On reporting to Gen. Burnside we were assigned to our present position. The trunks of the company officers, containing all their company books and papers; also the knapsacks and clothing belonging to the men, were left at the different forts, under guard, afterward taken to Washington by our quartermaster and stored. My command is suffering for the want of the knapsacks and clothing. Many of the men have neither shoes to their feet or shirts to their backs, and none of them have had a change of underclothing since leaving Fort Tillinghast. The absence of the company books is exceedingly annoying to my officers, as their accounts are necessarily behind.

In view of the above, I would very respectfully ask that my order, enclosed, may be approved and forwarded.

Very resp'y, your obd't serv't,

(Signed), CHAS. W. TILDEN,
Lt.-Col., Com'dg 16th Me. Vols.

To GEN. NELSON TAYLOR,
Com'dg 3d Brig., 2d Div., 1st A. C.

HDQ'RS 16TH REG'T ME. VOLS.,
Near Sharpsburgh, Md., Oct. 18, 1862.

CAPTAIN:—

You will proceed at once to Washington, and obtain immediately on your arrival, books and papers belonging to the companies of the 16th Me. Reg't; also knapsacks and clothing issued to this command, and now stored in the city of Washington by our regimental quartermaster.

You will rejoin your regiment without delay.

(Signed), CHAS. W. TILDEN,
Lieut.-Col. Com'dg 16th Me. Vols.

To CAPT. JOHN AYER, Com'dg Co. H.

INDORSEMENTS.

Hdq'rs 3d Brigade Ricketts' Division,
Oct. 19, 1862.

Respectfully forwarded, with the recommendation that Capt. John Ayer be authorized to proceed to Washington City, and superintend the transportation of the regimental and company property of his regiment to this place, or wherever the reg't may be encamped.

(Signed), NELSON TAYLOR, *Brig.-Gen.*

Hdq'rs 2d Division, Oct. 19, 1862.

(E. B. 264.)
Approved and submitted.
(Signed), JAMES B. RICKETTS,
Brig.-Gen., Com'dg Division.

Hdq'rs 1st Army Corps, Oct. 19, 1862.
Approved and respectfully forwarded.
(Signed), JOHN F. REYNOLDS,
Brig.-Gen., Vols., Com'dg.

Hdq'rs Army of the Potomac,
Oct. 21, 1862.

The above order is confirmed. Capt. Ayer to return in five days.

By command of MAJOR-GEN. McCLELLAN.
(Signed), JAMES A. HARDEE,
Lt.-Col. & A. D. C., A. A. A. G.

Headquarters Sixteenth Maine Volunteers,
Camp near Rappahannock Station, Va.,
Nov. 11, 1862.

GENERAL:—

I have the honor to make the following report, relative to the present condition of the regiment under my command, and the causes of the same. On our arrival at Washington, Aug. 21, 1862, we were ordered to report to General Casey, some two miles from Washington, on the Virginia side of the Potomac. We remained under his command until Aug. 24, when we were ordered to report to Gen. Whipple, at Fort

Tillinghast. On our arrival at Fort Tillinghast, a part of the regiment was employed in digging rifle pits, and the remainder were ordered to drill at heavy artillery in the different forts in front of Washington. On the 3d of September, by order of Col. Greene, commanding the brigade composed of the 14th Mass. Vols., and 16th Me. Vols., companies were detached to garrison the forts extending from Fort Albany to Fort De Kalb. On the night of the 6th of Sept., orders were received from Gen. Whipple to proceed with all possible dispatch to Leesboro', Md., and report to Gen. Burnside, a copy of which I herewith enclose. In addition to this order, was a verbal order from Gen. Whipple for the regiment to move in light marching order, and that all our property would be left in charge of our regimental quartermaster, with orders for him to arrange our camp between Forts Tillinghast and Craig, as the regiment was to return within two or three days. On reporting to Gen. Burnside, we were assigned to Gen. Hartsuff's brigade, Ricketts' Div.

Our quartermaster, learning that we were not to return, was ordered by Gen. McClellan, to whom he applied, to turn over all property not issued, and have the knapsacks and other articles stored at Washington.

On the 2d of Oct. an officer was detailed by Col. Wildes, then in command, to proceed to Washington, and obtain the company books and papers in store, and the same was sent up for approval, the copy of which I herewith enclose.

A third application was made, which was approved, and Capt. Ayer detailed for the business; copies of which I have also the honor to enclose.

Capt. Ayer proceeded immediately to Washington, and forwarded the property to Hagerstown, the nearest point by rail to our camp at Sharpsburgh, at which place we were encamped at the time of his departure, and at which place it arrived the day after our leaving Sharpsburgh.

Our quartermaster proceeded to Hagerstown, to look after the property, and have it sent to the regiment, but was refused transportation by the post quartermaster.

COLONEL AND BREV BRIGADIER-GENERAL

1862

I would very respectfully ask that steps be immediately taken to have the property transported to the regiment; also the subsistence and tents left at Berlin, Maryland, by our quartermaster, as per his report herewith enclosed.

I will here state that my command is destitute of clothing sufficient to make them comfortable, many of them being without a shirt to their backs, and none of them having had a change of clothing since the 7th of Sept.

I would also state that one cause of so much sickness in my command is for the lack of clothing, and the want of a change of diet.

  I am, Gen., very respectfully, your ob't servant,
(Signed),   CHAS. W. TILDEN,
       Lieut.-Col., Com'dg 16th Me. Vols.

To Gen. Nelson Taylor, Com'dg Brigade.

   HDQ'RS 1ST ARMY CORPS, November 13, 1862.

Special Orders, No. 51.

   . . . . .

II. Lieut. Lowell, 16th Me. Vols., will proceed to Hagerstown, and forward to his regiment all property stored there, belonging to it. He will then proceed to Berlin, and take charge of all public property left there, and return, without delay, to his regiment.

   By command of BRIG.-GEN. REYNOLDS,
      Com'dg 1st Army Corps.
(Signed),   C. KINGSBURY, JR., *A. A. G.*

     HDQ'RS 16TH ME. VOLS.,
 Camp Near Stafford Court House, Va., Nov. 21, 1862.

COL.:—There being some uncertainty about the officer detailed to procure the knapsacks and clothing of my command being able to obtain them, and as the regiment is suffering for the want of proper clothing, I would respectfully request that Capt. Crandall, Brigade Quartermaster, be authorized to proceed to Washington, and in case the property is lost, take the necessary steps to obtain a full supply for its immediate wants.

     Very respectfully, your obedient servant,
(Signed),   Chas. W. Tilden,
         Lt.-Col., Com'dg Reg't.
To Col. A. R. Root,
 Com'dg 1st Brigade.

     INDORSEMENT.
    Hdq'rs 1st Brigade, 2d Div.,
      1st Corps, Nov. 21, 1862.

I have today applied for permission for Capt. Crandall to go to Washington for supplies for the Brigade. The answer will arrive to-morrow, and will be made known to Col. Tilden in order that he may see Capt. Crandall in regard to the wants of the 16th Maine Vols.

(Signed),   Adrian R. Root,
  Col. Com'dg 1st Brigade, 2d Div. 1st A. C.

   Hdq'rs 16th Reg't Maine Vols.,
  Camp near Brooks Station, Va., Nov. 24, 1862.

Col.:—I would respectfully request that Maj. Farnham, 16th Me. Vols., may have permission to proceed to Aquia Creek, for the purpose of telegraphing to Lieut. Lowell, the officer detailed from my command to procure the clothing, etc., of this regiment, now at Hagerstown, Md., informing him of the location of the regiment, that the articles may reach us at the earliest possible moment.

   I have the honor to remain, Col.,
    very respectfully, your ob't serv't,
(Signed),   Chas. W. Tilden,
     Lieut.-Col. Com'dg 16th Me. Vols.
Col. Root, Com'dg 1st Brigade, 2d Div. 1st A. C.

     INDORSEMENT.
   Hdq'rs 1st Brigade, 2d Div. 1st A. C.
  Camp near Brooks Station, Va., Nov. 24, 1862.

Approved. Lieut.-Col. Tilden, 16th Me. Vols., has permission to take this communication to Division Headquarters in person.

(Signed),   Adrian R. Root,
  Col., Com'dg 1st Brigade, 2d Div. 1st A. C.

1862

HDQ'RS 2D DIV. 1ST A. C., Nov. 24, 1862.

Approved,
By command of GEN. GIBBON.
(Signed), FRANK A. HASKELL, *A. D. C.*

(Telegram).

AQUIA CREEK, Nov. 24, 1862.

LIEUT.-COL. J. W. HATHAWAY,
273 F Street, Washington, D. C.

Has Lieut. Lowell left Washington with the clothing for this Regiment? If not, send him to this place. Quartermaster-Sergt. Geo. W. Brown is at Alexandria with the property left at Berlin. Have the same sent forward with knapsacks and clothing. Reg't in camp near Brooks Station. Am waiting your answer by telegraph.

(Signed), CHAS. W. TILDEN,
Lieut.-Col. Com'dg 16th Me. Vols.

Extract from the report of inspection as to sanitary condition of the Sixteenth Regiment Maine Volunteers, made by Charles J. Nordquist, medical drector Second Division, November 13th, 1862: —

"I find the mean strength of the Regiment to be six hundred and ninety-three men, one hundred and eighty-one of whom are under treatment by the regimental surgeon. The prevalent diseases are diarrhœa, dysentery, bronchitis, rheumatic affections, and a few cases of intermittent fever. To the insufficiency of clothing I ascribe the unhealthy condition of the command, as of the whole number inspected, thirty-four were without underclothing of any description. The men are without overcoats; few have more than one blanket, and their clothing unclean and almost useless. . . . The Hospital under charge of Surgeon Alexander, is in excellent order, and cleanliness and comfort surround the sick."

CHAPTER IV.

FROM SHARPSBURGH, MARYLAND, TO FREDERICKSBURGH, VIRGINIA.

THE First Corps reviewed by President Lincoln, and General McClellan. The regiment numbered, on parade, four hundred and forty-five. When taking our position in line, for review, a rail fence was found to be much in the way. Colonel Coulter, after jumping it several times, turned to Sergeant-Major Maxfield, who wore a Burnside blouse, and said, sharply, "Here! Chaplain, make yourself useful, and tear down this 'rip-gut' fence."

1862
Oct. 2.

"Beg pardon, Colonel, I am not one of that useful class. I am Sergeant-Major of the to-be-bloody Sixteenth."

"Good God! I took you for a chaplain. Where are they?"

"That group on the knoll," pointing to some dozen or more, "are spoiling for the chance," replied Max.

Riding pell-mell into the squad, he ordered them to "pull down that fence!" "But, Colonel, *we* are chaplains."

"I don't care a G— d—n! Double-quick! By G—, you will do something to earn your salary, as

1862 long as I command this brigade." The chaplains took down the fence.

Oct. 3. Brigade reviewed by General Taylor.

Oct. 6. Palfrey says: "By the 6th of October, the President had become impatient, so much so, that Halleck, the commander-in-chief, was instructed to telegraph McClellan as follows: "The President directs that you cross the Potomac, and give battle to the enemy, or drive him south." This did not move McClellan, but a rumor that such a telegram had been received, reached us, and we were again in a state of suspense.

Oct. 8. General Taylor succeeds Hartsuff in command of the brigade. Drew full rations for the first time since the regiment left Arlington Heights.

Oct. 11. Brigade reviewed and inspected by General Taylor.

Oct. 12. One A.M., called out under arms. Two regiments of brigade ordered to strengthen picket line against raiders. Lieutenant Bisbee returned to Company I, bringing to Captain Waldron a pair of "new trousers," which were the envy of the line.

Oct. 16. Heavy cannonading heard in the direction of Harper's Ferry.

Oct. 17. Captain Waldron, Company I, brigade officer of the day. Mail arrived. Sutlers reaped a rich harvest among the troops, who, suffering with want and hunger, paid any price asked for food and clothing. Many assigned their pay in advance. The cornfields on our flanks were gleaned to the surface for man and beast. The enlisted men "bought" corn on the ear, picked up sardine boxes in rear of brigade headquarters, which, with a nail, they converted into graters; and on these rubbed the corn until enough was prepared to make a genuine Maine hasty pudding, singing all the while, "John Brown's body lies moldering in the ground." An enlisted man from Company —, for various charges, was sentenced by court-martial to pace around his regimental camp eight hours, with his head through a barrel. Some of the veterans mashed the barrel and set him free.

Oct. 20. Battalion drill, for the first time since we were mustered in, under Lieutenant-Colonel Tilden. Full rations issued, of good quality — a rare occurrence.

Oct. 21. Marching orders received, and cancelled, October 22d, on account of the severe storm.

Oct. 13. Captain John Ayer, Company H, sent to Washington to bring up our overcoats and blankets. The men are suffering terribly, and we muster but three hundred and fifty on parade. We pay as follows for supplies: two dollars per bushel for potatoes, forty cents per pound for butter, eleven cents for sugar, and ten cents per quart for milk.

Oct. 26. Sunday. Marching orders received. The right wing of the army is now crossing the Potomac at Berlin. At four o'clock struck tents, and marched through the village of Sharpsburgh in a torrent of rain — on, through mud ankle-deep, through Rhorersville, over South Mountain, through Thornton's Gap, and came to a halt about eight P.M., in the road, nearly an hour, when the regiment, by common consent and instinct, found its way into the woods on the west side of a bleak mountain. In a furious storm of

1862 wind and rain, Taylor's brigade passed a dismal night. Captain Williams, Company A, taken sick on march, and left at a citizen's house in Rhorersville, where he died a few days later.

Oct. 27. Marched to Birkettsville, and bivouacked.

Oct. 28. Reveille at five A.M., marched at six, and camped at Berlin. Shoes and shelter-tents issued.

Oct. 30. Crossed the Potomac on pontoons at four P.M.

Oct. 31. About fifty sick. The severest cases were sent to Washington. Marched to Lovettsville, and camped, where we were mustered for pay.

Nov. 1. Continued the march through Waterford and Hamilton.

Nov. 2. Regimental inspection.

Nov. 3. Marched through Middleburgh and White Plains, reaching Warrenton on the 7th, in a blinding snow storm. During the march water froze in canteens. Captain Whitehouse, of Company K, was here left sick. November 5th, halted near the residence of a rebel, Colonel Delainia, and, before the usual order to guard property was published, some of the boys discovered supplies. In spite of threats and muskets, arms were stacked, and a rush made for the outbuildings, boards were torn off, and out poured corn, potatoes, and salt in abundance. As well try to stem the Mississippi, as that torrent of hungry men, who, regardless of discipline and rank, went through the buildings, bringing to light, not only food, but ammunition, and hogsheads of salt, stored for the rebels.

Nov. 8. Company H all reported on the sick list. Left Warrenton at about four o'clock P.M., led by a stupid guide, who marched us six miles out of our way, arriving at Rappahannock Station at one o'clock, Sunday morning, November 9th, in a blinding storm of snow and hail. Notwithstanding the worn and forlorn condition of the men, they are cheerful and plucky; seemingly oblivious to the fact that they are less than two hundred for duty, ragged, dirty, half fed, half clothed, and sheltered only by the blue heaven, and the clouds, above the blanket of snow. The long march from Sharpsburgh was rich and varied, and invaluable to him whose heart was in the cause; for experience only perfects in any calling. We learned obedience, we were taught patience through suffering, courage came to us by exposure to danger; and, somehow, we were better men for these weeks of vicarious atonement. Our hearts, though brave and strong, were not, however, proof against ridicule. The appellation of " Blanket Brigade " still clung to us, in spite of heroic effort to establish a reputation which should compel the respect of a regiment whose paper " dickies " were supposed to cover all deficiencies in looks or demeanor.

General Bayard, in camp a short distance from us, sent Colonel Tilden half a sheep this forenoon. The Colonel hung it up in front of his quarters on the branches of a tree, and many hungry eyes measured the number of mouthfuls that carcass would make. Mouths watered until only the gambrels remained. I can testify that headquarters had but a small part of " Mary's little lamb." Captain Waldron made a pilgrimage to General Bayard's headquarters for " some more sheep," and, after being bluffed off by

1862 Captain Jones, succeeded in *drawing* a fat mutton, whose advent into camp set Company A wild. Their foraging propensities were duly exercised, and in a few short hours a bonanza was struck. Roast mutton, baked lamb, and boiled sheep sent up a delicious odor from every company. Blankets and boughs here and there hid suspicious looking boxes, with busy bees buzzing around, and a *sweet*, satisfied look crept over the whole command.

Lieutenant Chapman credits four members of Company K with a successful foraging of two hives of honey, and a brood of chickens. He says:—

"The funny part of this incident is that the foragers with their plunder came suddenly upon General Taylor and staff at a bend in the road in the midst of a dense wood. The General took in the situation at a glance, and, with grim humor, with his staff and guard faced to the front, and allowed the boys to 'pass in review' in single file, without breaking their formation. Not a word was said, nor a salute given by either party, but visions of the guard-house arose vividly in the minds of the marauders, as a hasty glance was given to the stern face of the brigade commander, as they filed past. As they hastened to camp an orderly followed, who went to the colonel with instructions from the general to send the honey and chickens to the division hospital for the use of the sick. The honey was disposed of, however, before the order reached the boys."

We reported so many on the sick list that General Gibbon sent Surgeon Nordquist to investigate. A well-fed and sheltered division commander and staff could not appreciate our destitute condition, and gratuitously insulted us by censuring the colonel and quartermaster. The Dutch beer guzzler added to insult injury by remarking to Colonel Tilden: "Your regiment are poor soldiers, but tam goot foragers." Calling me out, he said: "Ad-ju-tant, py Got, your men tey all pe det pefore night unless you dake dose honeys dose tam tiefs got mit 'em. You shust take some names of dose and send me, or I reports you to the sheneral." "All right, Surgeon, your order shall be obeyed. Boys, I am going for paper, and expect the names of every man who stole honey.' So, in obedience to orders, names were demanded, but I failed to find the "tam tiefs" (as I expected and desired). On returning to my tent I passed some Company E boys, whose smiles shone through streaks of grease and honey, as they courteously touched their hats. On a rubber in my tent I found about ten pounds of as delicious honey as Virginia could afford.

The rebels had a small force on the south bank of the river, which was quickly dispersed, and their camp destroyed. The Third Brigade, the advance infantry of the Army of the Potomac, was ordered to hold the position, and went into camp near the bridge. At two forty-five regiment ordered under arms, and remained so until daylight. Shelter is now sufficient and rations abundant, but some companies are so destitute of clothing, especially underwear and overcoats, that they are excused from duty. The sick list is frightful. The military commission, ordered by division commander to investigate the

1862

Nov. 11.

1862 condition of the regiment, in their report exonerate its officers, and declare that everything possible has been done by them for the welfare of the regiment.

Nov. 16. Being assigned to Duryea's brigade, struck tents and marched three miles up the O. & A. R. R., and joined it at Bealeton. Lieutenant Libby, Company H, left sick.

Nov. 19. Colonel Adrian R. Root assumed command of First Brigade, composed of Ninety-fourth and One Hundred and Fourth New York, One Hundred and Seventh Pennsylvania, and Sixteenth Maine. Second Assistant Surgeon Warren Hunter reported for duty. First Sergeant Conley in command of Company H.

Nov. 20. Reveille at half-past five A.M., marched at eight, and bivouacked at Morrisville, where we remained
Nov. 22. until 22d, when the march was continued to Stafford Court House.

Nov. 23 and 24. Continued the march, and camped at four P.M. near Brooks' Station, on the Acquia Creek and Falmouth Railroad, about four miles from the creek.

Nov. 26. Put up shelters, rested, and speculated on the "cause" of the cannonading heard in the direction of Fredericksburgh.

Nov. 27. November 27th was both the national and State "Thanksgiving Day," and as if to make it the more joyful and memorable to the regiment, Lieutenant Lowell, of Company D, arrived from Washington with knapsacks and overcoats. Seldom have men greater cause for gladness. The overcoats gave warmth and respectability, while the knapsacks supplied underclothing in place of that worn eleven long weeks. There, too, were the little conveniences

brought from home, pictures of loved ones, "house- 1862
wives," paper and envelopes, and many cherished
things that a soldier clings to as mementos of absent
friends, or relics of his former peace-life.

The pioneer corps of the regiment detailed today
consists of one sergeant and ten privates, as follows: Company A, Moses W. Cook; B, Joseph W.
Richardson; C, Archibald Finney; D, Benjamin F.
Foster; E, Ivory W. Riggs; F, Eben I. Walker; G,
Jacob T. Hodgkins; H, George W. Wilson; I, Benjamin F. Garcelon; K, Ira Page; R. E. Brann, Company E, acting sergeant.

Despondency gives place to a buoyancy hitherto Nov. 28.
unknown. Shelter, food, and clothing have done
their perfect work, and a feeling of satisfaction and
contentment envelops the command, which does
itself credit on parade, now held every night. Regimental and company drills take place daily.

CONSOLIDATED MORNING REPORT, DECEMBER 1, 1862.

	Present.											Absent.					
	Fit for Duty.				Sick.			Speci'l Duty.		In Arrest.		Ag. Prs.	Sick.		Special service.		Aggregate Absent. Agg'te pres'nt & absent.
F'ld & Staff.	Com. Officers.	Non-Com. O.	Privates.	Aggregate.	Com. Officers.	Non-Com. O.	Privates.	Aggregate.	Com. Officers.	Non-Com. O.	Privates.	Com. Officers.	Non-Com. O.	Privates.	Total.	Com. Officers.	Non-Com. O.	Privates.	Com. Officers.	Non-Com. O.	Privates.		
F & S	7	2		9								4				9	1	1				2	11
A	2	8	46	56		2	12	14			4					74		3	13		5	21	95
B	2	10	43	55	1	1	11	13								68		2	9		12	23	91
C	3	9	45	57		1	9	10			2					69		2	20	1	6	29	98
D	1	9	38	48	1	1	23	25			3					76	1	3	10		3	17	93
E	3	8	47	58		2	13	15			2					75		3	11		6	20	95
F	3	5	60	68		4	7	11			6					85		2	6		4	12	97
G	2	3	43	48		3	15	18			5					71		7	9	1	5	22	93
H	2	12	31	45		1	12	13			8					66	1	1	18	1	8	29	95
I	2	6	40	48			14	14			1					63			26	1	5	32	95
K	2	7	36	45		1	11	12			3					60	1		19		3	23	83
	29	79	429	537	2	16	127	145			34					716	4	24	141	3	57	230	946

1862 Dec. 3.	Brigade drill in the afternoon. Regiment complimented by Colonel Root. Aggregate strength of regiment present, seven hundred and fifteen; for duty, five hundred and ninety-eight; sick and on detail, one hundred and seventeen. Ordered to change camp to-morrow.
Dec. 5.	Fall of snow and rain. Line officers' baggage reduced to one piece of shelter and a gripsack. Surplus baggage all packed and sent to Washington, and supposed to be "stored."
Dec. 6.	Mail received. Paymaster arrived.
Dec. 7.	Three deaths have occurred during the past week. Three times has our garrison flag covered the remains of a "volunteer" as they passed in procession to a spot soon to be grown over with bushes, and forgotten.
Dec. 8.	Trousers issued to the men. Orders received to send all sick to Washington, and be in readiness to move at an hour's notice. The First and Third Divisions of our corps are now facing the enemy on the Rappahannock, and everything points to a great battle within a few days. Captain Waldron writes to a friend as follows: "You may be curious to know how a man feels at the prospect of going into battle within a few days. I am free to confess that for one I do not hanker after the job, but as my duty plainly lies in that direction, I think I conscientiously admit to you that I never felt lighter hearted or more buoyant in spirit than at the present movement of our troops upon the enemy's position; and could I have my choice to be detailed for some service which would

shield me from exposure to the enemy's bullets, I would prefer to take my chances with my company."

Preparing for battle.

Broke camp and marched to the river below Falmouth. The following order was handed to the colonel just as we left camp:—

1862

Dec. 9 and 10.

Dec. 11.

HEADQUARTERS 1ST BRIG. 2D DIVISION,
December 11, 1862.

General Order No. 15.

Adjutant A. R. Small, 16th Reg't Me. Vols., and Adjutant J. B. Thomas, 107th Penn. Vols., are appointed acting aids to the brigade commander, until further orders, and will be respected accordingly.

By command of COL. ADRIAN R. ROOT,
Com'dg 1st Brigade.
C. E. SCOVILL, *A. A. A. G.*

Crossed the river with division, and took up position on the left center of Franklin's grand division, just before sunset. The stars shone above us as we bivouacked for the night. Men wrapped their blankets around them, and lay down to sleep as if unconscious of their surroundings; of the missiles of death within short range; of the fact that this is their last sleep on earth. Arms were stacked, horses tethered, and gradually there stole over this valley of the shadow of death, a peaceful calm that gave no sign of the coming storm that would make desolate thousands of homes, north and south. Gradually the dew fell, and as silently as night cometh, crept the fog, until its density covered the plain, and hid from sight batteries, caissons, and fifty thousand men.

Dec. 12.

CHAPTER V.

FREDERICKSBURGH.

1862
Dec. 13.

THE world seemed so lovely, and life so precious and dear, and our hearts so hopeful and brave, yet in a few short hours were sown anguish and grief broadcast; only the burning of a little powder, and lives went out by scores — literally were snuffed out like candles.

The morning was brilliant with promise, but the night brought darkness and despair to thousands of hearts, and discouragement to the Army of the Potomac. When the fog lifted the Sixteenth wore a grim look of satisfaction as they viewed the entertainment to which they had been invited. The past, with its censure and ridicule, seemed ages back, and the future as far hence, when the ominous silence was broken by the terrific explosion of a shell through a space in the fog. In a moment, as it were, the battle opened along the whole line.

Colonel Tilden makes the following official report: —

COL. ADRIAN R. ROOT, *Com'dg 1st Brigade,*

COL.: — I have the honor to submit the following report of the Regiment under my command in the late engagement near Fredericksburgh: —

In compliance with your orders, my command, numbering 21 line officers, and 406 enlisted men, was in line at 5 o'clock the morning of the 11th instant, for the purpose of crossing the Rappahannock, as it was understood we were to cross at daybreak. We commenced our line of march with the 1st Brigade at 5.15 A.M., and proceeded some three miles toward the river, a short distance below Fredericksburgh, when it was ascertained that we could not cross, owing to the engineer's being unable to complete the bridges. At this point I brought my command to a rest, and remained through the day and night. On the morning of the 12th instant, orders being received from headquarters of the Brigade to be under arms at 5 o'clock, I had my command in line at the appointed time, and took up the line of march, crossing the river about 12 o'clock M. After crossing and resting for a short time, we formed a line of battle in the rear of the 107th Pennsylvania and 105th New York Volunteers, near the stone mansion occupied as a Hospital, which position we maintained through the remainder of the afternoon and night, with the exception of changing slightly, from time to time, to avoid the fire of the enemy's batteries in position on the Heights at our right.

1862
Dec. 13.

On the morning of the 13th instant I had my command under arms at 8 o'clock, and received orders to move by the left flank to the left about a quarter of a mile. Here we were obstructed in our passage by a thick growth of bushes and a ravine. Our pioneers soon cleared the bush, and we were again on the march. While waiting at the above place, two of my command were slightly wounded by pieces of shell from the enemy's guns, they having complete range of this point. After crossing the ravine, we moved by the right flank beyond the county road, and formed in line of battle. We remained here for a short time, and were then ordered to retire to the road, where we remained until about 1 o'clock P.M. At this time I moved my regiment, in compliance with your orders, to the front in the open field, and then by the right flank to the right, unmasking the 105th New York, and forming in line of battle on the right. We

1862
Dec. 13.
immediately opened fire upon the enemy, who were covered behind the enbankment of the railroad in front of us. Finding his fire very disastrous, and seeing that our fire was doing little or no execution, the order was received from you, through Lieut. Scovill, to fix bayonets, charge, and drive him from his breast-works. My regiment being some fifteen paces in advance of those on my right and left, I waited some few moments for them to come up, but finding they did not, I gave the order to charge, which was obeyed with promptness and firmness equal to that displayed by veteran troops, driving the enemy from his breast-works, and capturing some sixty prisoners, sending the same to the rear.

After crossing, I advanced into the woods a short distance. My lines being somewhat broken, I ordered a new line formed for the purpose of advancing still farther. But finding that we had no support, I immediately gave the order to fire into the woods, where it was evident the enemy were in ambush. I was hoping that support might be sent to us. None being received, however, my ammunition being nearly exhausted, and finding the enemy had gained possession of the point of woods making out on our left, which I supposed was held by one of the other regiments of the brigade, I gave the order to retire. We retired under the crest of the hill back of the county road, where we remained until 2 o'clock in the morning of the 14th inst. We then moved to the left some mile and a half, and remained until daylight, at which time we advanced, and formed a second line of battle at this point. We remained in this position Sunday and Monday. In obedience to your orders, I got my command into line at 7 o'clock Monday evening, and crossed the river without any casualty.

I should be doing injustice to mention the names of any of my command as worthy of mention in this engagement, as all performed their duty like true soldiers.

My loss of line officers was fully equal to the percentage of enlisted men, being eleven killed, wounded, and missing. Among the number were Capt. Hutchins of Company B, and Lieut. Herrick of Company D, who fell while gallantly leading their commands.   1862 Dec. 13.

I should be remiss did I fail to mention the bravery and heroic conduct of the 12th Massachusetts, Col. Bates commanding, which regiment we were ordered to relieve. It was with difficulty we gained their front, so determined were they in doing their whole duty. Herewith I hand you a list of casualties.

    I have the honor, Col., to remain very resp'y your ob't serv't,
                CHAS. W. TILDEN,
                Lt.-Col., Com'dg 16th Me. Vols.

The adjutant-general's report says: "At ten o'clock A.M., Colonel Root moved the brigade to the left about four hundred yards, and then changing direction to the right, advanced to the front across a deep, wooded ravine, and over an adjacent elevation of ground to the Bowling Green Turnpike. In effecting this movement the brigade was exposed to a severe fire of shell from the enemy's batteries, planted upon the wooded heights to the front, and in order to avoid this fire, a considerable *detour* was made to the left before the position was reached to which it was assigned. The Sixteenth, under the command of Lieutenant-Colonel Tilden, with the Ninety-fourth and One Hundred and Fourth New York, and One Hundred and Seventh Pennsylvania regiments, were then deployed in parallel lines to the right and left of Hall's battery, (Second Maine). The men were ordered to lie down, and for several hours the brigade remained, without loss, under a severe and constant fire from the enemy's batteries. At quarter to two o'clock Colonel Root was ordered

1862
Dec. 13.
to charge with his brigade to the front, storm the enemy's breast-works, and occupy his position. The Sixteenth sprang to the work with a will, at double-quick, advancing to the front with the rest of the brigade, under a severe fire of the enemy's artillery and musketry. The approach to the enemy's position, which consisted of the embankment and ditches of the Richmond railway, was rendered extremely difficult by several parallel ditches or rifle pits, and its rear protected by thick woods, sheltering infantry supports. As the brigade arrived upon the ground previously occupied by the Second and Third Brigades, the fire of the enemy became so incessant and galling, and so many of our men fell, killed or wounded, that a portion of the first line of the brigade slackened its pace, and the men, without orders, commenced firing. By the strenuous exertions of the regimental commanders, and the other officers, the firing was nearly discontinued. The brigade renewed its advance, and as the men recognized the enemy their movement increased in rapidity, until, with a shout and a run, the brigade leaped the ditches, charged across the railway, and occupied the woods beyond, driving the enemy from his position, killing a number with the bayonet, and capturing upward of two hundred prisoners. Of this number the Sixteenth captured between fifty and sixty, and sent them to the rear. The men fired with coolness and precision, until they exhausted the sixty rounds which they carried. Finding that the enemy had rallied in superior force, and were rapidly pressing the front and flanks of the brigade, and that the

position, which, with a supporting brigade, would have been tenable, was, by the absence of any infantry support whatever, rendered simply murderous to his command, Colonel Root * ordered the brigade to fall back. The officers and men received the order with surprise and grief, and retired so reluctantly the enemy were enabled to close up on the rear of the brigade, and inflict a loss exceeding that incurred during the charge itself."

1862
Dec. 13.

Colonel Root, in his official report, after speaking of the gallant conduct of the New York and Pennsylvania regiments, says: "I am sure that these brave regiments and their gallant commanders will not deem it invidious in me to make especial mention of the Sixteenth Maine Volunteers, Lieutenant-Colonel Tilden commanding. The regiment is a new one, and here fought its first battle, and I felt some apprehensions lest the terrible fire from the enemy's concealed rifle pits would be too severe a trial for its men. But the gallant manner in which the regiment charged the enemy's position excited my surprise and admiration, and reflected the highest honors upon its officers and men. Previous to the action, thirty-eight men of the regiment had volunteered to do duty with Hall's battery, and I am assured by Captain Hall that their conduct was creditable in the highest degree. Lieutenant Abner R. Small, Sixteenth Maine Volunteers, A. A. D. C., rendered me valuable and efficient

---

* Colonel Root, seeing the charge successful, went to the rear for support. The One Hundred and Seventh Pennsylvania, on the left, first noticed the enemy, in increased numbers, moving on his left flank, and ordered a retreat. The Ninety-fourth and One Hundred and Fourth New York had already fallen back from the woods, and the Sixteenth had no alternative but to follow.

1862
Dec. 13.

service, and bore himself with a cool intrepidity worthy of his regiment."

Captain Waldron, Company I, writes under date of December 20th: "The enemy occupied a range of hills well wooded in the form of a crescent, the center of which might have been from a mile and a half to two miles from the river, while their right and left rested on or near the river, thus precluding the possibility of our turning either flank. In addition to the situation which nature had so admirably fortified for the rebels, the F. & R. Railroad ran for a distance of three miles or more at the foot of the hills, and within a few rods from the edge of the wooded slope, affording by its embankment a safe position for their skirmishers and sharpshooters, from which they most effectively and destructively harassed and murdered our light artillerymen. In addition to these natural and artificial defenses of the enemy, for a great distance along the line were plowed fields, which during the heat of the day were converted into quagmires, so that our infantry were obliged to wade ankle deep in mud in almost every charge made. The distance to the railroad was about half a mile, in traversing which we had to face a galling and incessant fire from behind the railroad embankment in our front; while on our right flank was a battery of two guns, located in a spur of woods, which made sad havoc in our right companies.

"Our division occupied a place a little to the left of the center of Franklin's grand division. We had been somewhat exposed to the rebel batteries during our march to a comparatively safe place in front, where we remained until half-past twelve, at which time we were ordered into action. Our brigade was ordered to relieve Tower's brigade which had been maintaining a fire upon the rebels for an hour or more, who were comparatively secure from harm behind the railroad embankment. We unslung knapsacks,—not, however, until some of our men had been shot down,—took up a double-quick, and, as soon as the horrible condition of the ground would admit, relieved Tower's brigade. The practiced eye of our lieutenant-colonel (Tilden), at once detected the hazardous nature of the position we had been ordered into, where the effective was all upon one side, and called upon the colonel commanding the brigade to order a charge. This was done, and never did men respond with a more hearty will. They came to a right-shoulder-shift and rushed fearlessly on to the enemy, who lay concealed, as they supposed, secure from Federal bullets, but not from Federal bayonets. A ditch this side of the embankment for a moment retarded our progress, when we crossed bayonets with the foe, and all who did not yield either took to the woods, or were killed upon the spot. We captured between fifty and sixty prisoners, who were sent to the rear; and then commenced a return of the fire from behind the trees, a few rods distant. While the Sixteenth was busily engaged returning the fire, the other regiments of our brigade had retired, leaving us either to advance alone, or make the best retreat we could. The line officers called upon Colonel Tilden to order an

1862
Dec. 13.

1862
Dec. 13.

advance, but he, seeing that our support had left us, would not hazard being sacrificed or captured, and at once ordered a retreat, during which our greatest losses occurred, the regiment being completely at the mercy of the rebel infantry. It was our only resource, in which we lost from thirty to forty per cent of all that went into battle. Had the rest of the brigade been able to hold their ground as long as we did, a portion of the rebel fire would have been diverted from us. Out of four hundred and seventeen men who went into the fight, but one hundred and fifty-four answered to the rollcall that night. Of the missing enough have turned up so that we now have nearly two hundred men of those who were in the battle, for duty. Captain Hall's Second Maine Battery was ordered to support our charge by shelling the woods, which could have been done anywhere on the field, but he was ordered to move up within a rifle-shot distance of the enemy. He lost fifteen horses, beside the killed and wounded men, and was so much crippled that he had to leave one gun on the field." This gun men from the Sixteenth brought off under a galling fire.

An eye-witness of the battle writes to the *Whig & Courier* as follows: "During the conflict, so great was the admiration of Colonel Tilden for the coolness and soldierly conduct of his men, that he cried out, in a stentorian voice, 'Men of the Sixteenth! I wish to take every one of you by the hand, and thank you personally for your gallant bravery.' The wish was answered by a hearty cheer, and a request to be allowed to charge the enemy again, but the

Colonel saw by a glance to the right and left, that the regiments which should support the Sixteenth were hardly up to its enthusiastic attitude, and gave the order to give them a few more rounds, and then retire. The order was executed to the letter, as the whole sixty rounds carried into battle were exhausted. The officers of this regiment set the men a noble example, and by their courage and soldierly bearing did all that brave men could do to reassure and give confidence to the raw troops under their command. Colonel Tilden and Major Farnham were conspicuous everywhere along the line, and by their coolness inspired the men with a spirit which seemed utterly regardless of danger. Had the word been given by Colonel Tilden to charge the rebels into the woods and up the hill, so great was their confidence in his skill and leadership, every man would have applied himself with irresistible energy to the work. The noble conduct of the field officers on that memorable day has bound the hearts of the men of the Sixteenth to them with chains which cannot be broken. The clear, commanding voice of Colonel Tilden was heard above the din of battle, cheering on and stimulating the men to unsurpassed deeds of valor, while Major Farnham was personally active from one end of the line to the other, in saying an encouraging word to every one he passed."

General W. F. Palfrey says: "After all of Lyle's brigade, and all of Taylor's, except the Ninety-seventh New York and Eighty-eighth Pennsylvania, had given away, Root's brigade was ordered up. The Twelfth Massachusetts and some remnants

1862
Dec. 13.

1862
Dec. 13.
joined it, and the force advanced gallantly and took the embankment, and some prisoners."

The rebel troops engaged in our immediate front were a part of Talliaferro's, formerly Jackson's. That they fought with their accustomed ferocity, the loss of the First Brigade proved by its list of killed and wounded. Even when the Sixteenth sprang over the works, they showed a brave front, and only after a score or more were bayoneted would they yield to a more determined courage than theirs. Otis Libby, of Company II, crazed with pain from a wound in the head by a clubbed musket, ran two rebels through with his bayonet, and heedless of the fact that his enemies had surrendered, would have continued his ferocious work had not Colonel Farnham pulled him away. Monroe Lyford, of Company E, rushed over the embankment with the fury of a madman, and, running his bayonet through a rebel, yelled, "Curse you, you killed my brother!" which, alas, was too true. Charley Lyford, one of the handsomest and best boys of his company, had yielded up his young and hopeful life early in the charge. Captain Hutchins' presentiment was verified, for he fell shot through the heart. Lieutenant Herrick, of Company D, was killed. Lieutenant Edwards, a young graduate of Bowdoin, gave up his life with all its promise. The patriotic Heath, of the *Gardiner Home Journal*, fell shot through the head. Captain Ayer, of Company H, was mortally wounded. Young Beecher, and scores of brave fellows, went down, adding glory and honor to the regiment, and suffering to the hearts at home. I will not say "we fought as no other troops fought that day." It is not true of this, nor of any other regiment, but it should, in justice and honor, be recorded through all time, that unskilled and untrained though we were, to us belongs the credit of bull-dog fighting, until fifty-four per cent of our number were killed or wounded. The statistics fully revised from records to recent date, are as follows: —

	Killed.		Mort. Won Wounded.				Missing.		Total.
	Offrs	E.M.	Offrs	E. M.	Offrs	E. M.	Offrs	E. M.	
Company A		9			1	12		2	24
" B	1	4	1	2		10		1	19
" C		7		6	2	18			33
" D	1	5		2		12		1	21
" E		2		7	2	11		1	23
" F		6		1		10			17
" G		5		6	1	16			28
" H		5	1	4		17		1	28
" I		5				7			12
" K		6		4	1	14			25
	2	54	2	32	7	127		6	230

The six missing men rejoined the regiment.

The past was redeemed, the voice of insult and reproach was forever silenced. The regiments, which had hitherto ignored our claim to an honorable name, joined heartily with the Second Division in three cheers and a tiger for the Sixteenth, whose casualties were half the loss of the First Brigade. Thomas S. Hopkins, of Company C, contributed the following to The Youth's Companion: —

"The following narrative is strictly true, even to the minutest particular. I was but seventeen years of age when I enlisted in the Sixteenth Regiment, Maine Volunteers. Though our regiment suffered many privations in the summer and fall of 1862,

1862
Dec. 13.

we were not brought face to face with the enemy until December when the great battle of Fredericksburgh was fought. For weeks before the engagement we were constantly drilling and preparing for the conflict, having been assigned to the Left Grand Division of the Army of the Potomac, commanded by General Franklin.

"The morning of December 12th found us opposite Fredericksburgh, which is situated on the south side of the Rappahannock River. We spent the whole day in watching our batteries throwing shells over the river into the burning city. With the aid of a field-glass, we could see the enemy's works stretching a long distance down the river. That night their camp fires were plainly visible and we could sometimes hear their loud cheers. The engineer corps was endeavoring to lay pontoon bridges for the army to cross on. They were made of long flat-bottomed canvas boats, placed side by side in the water, and fastened together, and upon which was laid a plank walk. The enemy's sharpshooters hotly contested the laying of these bridges and many a poor fellow lost his life. But at last they were ready, and on the morning of the 12th, in a dense fog, we crossed about two miles below the city. As we climbed the banks we passed an aristocratic stone mansion, which soon became a hospital. That whole day and evening the entire army lay within easy range of the enemy's guns; but they fired not a shot, and some of us were unwise enough to think they were afraid. We knew that the next day we were to make the attack. Our supply of cartridges was better than our supply of food, and that day I husbanded my resources by dining and supping on parched corn. I slept soundly upon the frozen ground that night, and before light the next morning, we were all up and had cooked and eaten a hearty breakfast. Up and down the plain as far as the eye could reach, the camp fires lighted the wintry sky and around them were gathered groups of men muffled in their long blue overcoats, eagerly discussing the situation. There was no outward sign of fear or doubt over the terrible struggle we were about to engage in, but many of us I know thought of our loved ones at home and in our hearts bade them a silent farewell.

"The Rappahannock River, upon whose banks we lay, runs in a southeasterly direction. Back a distance of about a mile, rise the heights of Fredericksburgh, at the foot of which runs the railroad to Richmond. Behind the railroad embankment, and upon the heights, were intrenched the enemy. About halfway between the heights and the river, nearly parallel with the latter, runs the Bowling Green Turnpike. The right of our line of battle extended above the city. We were on the extreme left, two miles below. At sunrise our brigade began to move toward the turnpike. We had scarcely gone a dozen rods before the enemy opened on us with shot and shell. I could not help laughing aloud to see the captain of my company dodge the shells as they came over our heads, but I soon learned to do it myself. We double-quicked to the turnpike, where we found shelter by lying flat upon our faces, while the

1862
Dec. 13.

1862
Dec. 13.
shells went bursting over us with such horrible noises that I hugged the ground for dear life. It was a wild scene. The sharp rattle of musketry, the almost continuous booming of cannon, the neighing of horses, the yells of the drivers, and the sharp commands, mingling with the cries of the wounded, were enough to strike terror to the hearts of our boy soldiers. Our batteries replied to the fire of our foes with a promptness and energy that excited my admiration, and the sharp rattle of musketry told us that the battle was in progress. Aids and mounted orderlies went dashing hither and thither in hot haste, to the various commands; and generals and their staffs were gathered in groups, anxiously seeing the enemy's movements through field-glasses. Great clouds of smoke rolled over us like a burning city. and half obscured the columns of men who were marching with quick step in various directions, "swiftly forming in the ranks of war." Bugles blared and drums beat, and high above the awful din arose the shrill cry of some poor soul who had received a mortal wound. I know of no sound so horrible as the fiendish singing of the pieces of bursted shell, — and the wounds they make are usually fatal. The first one killed in our regiment was a noble young fellow in my company. He was struck in the back by a spent cannon-ball. We had time to give him a hasty burial before we moved forward.

"About half-past one P. M., came the word to advance. Between us and the enemy, a distance of half a mile, lay an open field where corn had been planted the preceding summer. The ground, frozen the night before and thawed again at noon, was miry and treacherous, and we often sank half-way to our knees. At intervals deep ditches had been dug for drainage. Just before the order came for us to advance the brigade commander rode down the line and spoke words of encouragement to us. 'Boys, don't dodge when ——,' but before he could finish the sentence, a shell whizzed so close to his head that he himself dodged very emphatically. He added with a laugh, 'But you may dodge big ones like these!' And we gave cheers for our commander, who, if he would dodge shell, was a brave man. Now our line moved forward a dozen yards, when the order came: 'Halt! Unsling knapsacks! Fix bayonets!' Then I knew that we were to fight the enemy with cold steel. Before we had time to execute the order to unsling knapsacks, one man in my company was divested of his by a movement not found in any book of military tactics. A piece of shell struck his blanket which was closely rolled and strapped on the top of his knapsack, just behind the back of his neck, and the momentum of the missile was such that for a moment man and knapsack revolved around each other and then they parted company. Again came the order — 'Forward!' The bullets now began to sing angrily about our ears, and our men began to fall. The one with whom I touched elbows on my left was among the first victims. The ball entered his leg with a sickening thud which I shall never forget, and he fell to the ground with a cry of 'I'm shot!' The company to which I

1862
Dec. 13.

LIEUT. COLONEL AND BREVET COLONEL.

1862
Dec. 13.

belonged was the color company, and the two brave fellows who carried the flags, as soon as the order to move forward was given, stepped out of the ranks in advance of the others, and maintained that position during the charge. It was a daring deed, for the enemy's sharpshooters always seek to pick off the color guard. They were soon made commissioned officers for gallantry. Down to this time I had felt nervous, and my knees trembled and legs felt weak. I acknowledge that I was afraid, but being afraid and yielding to fear are two different things. When my mother bade me good by the day my regiment left for Washington, she put her hands upon my head and said: ' My son, never let me hear that you turned your back to the enemy.' The remembrance of that pale face and her command were of themselves enough to make one brave, but I needed no such incentive, for when I saw my comrades falling on either side, fear left me and all my angry passions were aroused. The tears trickled down my cheeks, and I believe I could have fought a whole army.

"We had traversed about half the distance between the turnpike and the enemy, when we were obliged to pass through a line of our troops who were firing. We halted and fired a dozen or more rounds ourselves. I remember that while I was reloading, my orderly sergeant, who was in rear of the company, discharged his rifle. The muzzle was so near my ear that it stunned me for a moment. I clubbed my rifle, turned to him, and above the din of battle I cried, 'George B——, if you dare do that again I'll ——.' Here a bullet whizzed so near my nose that

I did not finish the sentence. Now came the order, 'Cease firing!' And then, 'Charge bayonets! Forward double-quick!' We had now a quarter of a mile of muddy ground to traverse, and deep ditches to leap down into and clamber up out of, in the midst of a terrible fire. With each advancing step the fire of the enemy increased. The air was filled with bursting shells, grape and canister, and minie bullets. So thickly did they fall around us that the dirt was constantly spattering in my face. Instinctively we bowed our heads to this fierce storm as we swept on. There were great gaps in our ranks as one after another fell under the awful fire, but there was no flinching, no hesitation, as with swift steps and stern faces we moved across the few remaining yards of ground toward the long row of leveled rifles from which were belching forth smoke and death. With one wild, determined cry our regiment leaped upon them. There was only a brief conflict,—the enemy fled up the hill, followed a short distance by our troops.

"But I never reached the intrenchment myself. When we were almost upon it, and I was grasping my rifle tight, and hoping that in a moment my good bayonet should revenge some comrade's blood, I found myself flat upon the ground, and heard Captain M., as he passed over my body, shout out to me, 'Lay low, boy!' And then I realized that I was wounded. For a few moments I lay perfectly still, but soon the pain in my groin told me where I was hit, and I determined to make a desperate effort to get off the field, for I thought it very likely our

1862
Dec. 13.

men would be driven back again. I dared not examine my wound for fear I should faint. Finding I could make some progress by using my rifle as a support, I slowly and painfully dragged myself to the rear.

"The battle was still raging behind me with unabated force, and the shot and shell from our own batteries, as well as the enemy's, were passing over my head, making deafening noises. On every side lay the dead and wounded, and the groans and appeals for help were pitiful to hear. I reached the turnpike at last, and, beneath the sheltering enbankment, I examined the nature of my injury. I was overjoyed to find that the supposed wound was only a very severe bruise! An army cup which I carried on the outside, and a tin plate carried on the inside of my haversack had saved me. The force of the bullet was such that it had taken a piece clean out of the cup, which was made of very thick material, passed through the plate and the hard-tack in my haversack — it would not take *much* hard bread of the kind to stop a cannon-ball — and stopped just short of my flesh. I have the piece of cup now. I was sent to hospital for a few days, until I could march again. I was sorry that necessity compelled me to go, for some rascal stole my blanket, and for the next week I slept out of doors on the frozen ground with nothing but my ordinary clothing and overcoat on. Some of my young seventeen-year-old readers would think it quite hard to do that in December, and I fear neither they nor their mothers, if they knew it, would sleep much. As I expected, the remnant of our regiment was driven back from the position they had so bravely, and at such fearful cost, won. When the sixty rounds of ammunition had been fired away and no fresh cartridges were sent them, they could only fall back. What a grave mistake for a general to charge an enemy and then send no support to his victorious legions; not even ammunition; while the river's bank was lined with fresh troops. From the time the regiment left the turnpike on the charge until it returned was, I think, less than an hour. In that brief time it lost more than one half its numbers in killed and wounded.

1862
Dec. 13.

"The following are incidents of the battle which came under my personal observation: Before the charge and while we were lying on our faces a piece of shell struck one of our boys' knapsacks, tore it open and lifted a pack of cards, intact, high into the air, when they suddenly spread apart and fell to the ground like a shower of autumn leaves. One of our boys — now in the United States Treasury — mounted the enemy's works. A stalwart fellow sprang up and thrusting the muzzle of his gun full in his face fired it. His face was burned and blackened by the discharge, but otherwise he was uninjured, and in an instant he thrust his bayonet through the man's breast. Probably the man had neglected to put his bullet in after charging his rifle with powder.

"Numerous instances came to my notice when, in the excitement, some would put in the bullet end of cartridge first. In some cases men were known to load their guns three or four times before firing. Unless one has had great experience and is very cool,

1862
Dec. 13.

he will fire too high. Nine out of ten bullets go over the heads of the enemy, and that is why the officers are always shouting, "Fire low, boys, fire low!"

"Lieutenant A—— of my company was saved by a tintype picture in his breast pocket, which caused the bullet to glance off; another by a pocket knife. There were few in the whole regiment who did not receive a bullet-hole through their clothing somewhere.

"Some years ago I revisited the battle-field. The bodies of the fallen had been gathered into the soldiers' cemetery just back of the city, near the deadly stone-wall where the right of our army fought. I walked down the turnpike to where we charged. Nature had obliterated nearly every sign of the conflict; and the miry field, across which we charged that eventful December day, was covered with waving corn. The sun shone as clearly, the birds sang as sweetly, and the flowers bloomed as brightly, as if that field had never been plowed with shot and shell, and fertilized with the blood of the brave."

An officer writes generously of his comrades as follows: "Lieutenant Peters, commanding Company K, proved himself among the bravest. Sergeant Ned Davis, who carried the national colors, distinguished himself as a gallant soldier, and paved the way to promotion. ''T was the proudest moment of my life,' said Davis, as he caressed the flag saved by his coolness and pluck. Charley Choate's conduct attracted attention, and he won a corporal's warrant by his bravery."

A sergeant of Company E writes: "Benny Worth, a mere boy of fifteen — the youngest in the command — won the admiration of his comrades by his brave and determined manner, worthy a veteran. While crossing the ravine, and just before reaching the turnpike, the enemy's shot and shell found their way into our midst, giving us a taste of that which was in store for us. Young Worth was struck in the head by a fragment of iron, shedding the first blood of the Sixteenth. Stunned and bleeding, heedless of advice to go to the rear, he went through the fight, and at its close, smilingly said, while rubbing his bruised head, 'This is what I came for.' Worth was among the number never sick, or off duty."

1862
Dec. 13.

Corporal Bradford, of Company E, was the first one struck by a bullet, which lodged in his hand and remained for two days. The ball is kept as a "pleasant" souvenir of the battle. Sergeant Warren Seaward, Company E, carried the State flag, and did himself and his State credit by his coolness and intrepidity. Among those who volunteered to bring off the wounded under fire was Sergeant Lamb, of Company E, and through his efforts the body of Captain Hutchins was recovered. Some ludicrous incidents blunted the keen edge of fear in this our first battle. Private Trask, of Company E, was naturally a nervous and excitable man, and at the sharp command, "Fall in, Sixteenth!" he began running wildly up and down the line in search of his place in the ranks. Great drops of perspiration stood out on his face in his anxiety to obey orders and escape censure and ridicule. His place was found,

1862
Dec. 13.
and no man kept it better than he. He was generally liked, and won high esteem by his good fighting qualities. The brave fellow was mortally wounded, May 5th, 1864, and died in the hospital at Fredericksburgh.

In Company F, was a private named Oliver Creddiford, a large, powerfully built man, but like many of us somewhat lacking in physical courage. A fellow private named Levi Baker had fallen wounded, and Creddiford, who was only too willing to go anywhere else than longer endure the fire under which his comrades were forced to stay, picked up Baker, and with the wounded man upon his back, between himself and the enemy's bullets, started for the rear. The captain of his company said, "Creddiford, come back into the ranks." Creddiford without stopping replied, "Captain, you must think I am a damned fool to let Baker die here on the field." And no more was seen of Creddiford during that battle.

Dec. 14. The day was spent in skirmishing and in dodging an occasional shell, thrown at random by the rebels for a feeler.

Dec. 15. Was quietly passed and nothing of interest occurred to disturb a retrospect of the past few days, and the sad reflection of what "might have been." Of all the mental suffering in the Army of the Potomac, none could have been keener than that which cut through and through the heart of Burnside, as the sun went down on that huge Golgotha. The day waned, and in the darkness and gloom that settled like a pall over that square mile of "Tophet," we silently obeyed the whispered orders to sling knapsacks, and, without the slightest noise, be in readiness to move. So quietly and skillfully were orders executed that not until we had crossed the pontoons did we know that ours was the last division to leave the field. The wind and rain were extremely favorable to the retreat and nothing betrayed to Lee the movement executed in his front. That he expected a renewal of the fight the 14th, General Hood in his book "Advance and Retreat" writes: "The following morning [13th] after the fog had disappeared and at about ten o'clock, the heavy lines of the enemy advanced upon our right and against Jackson's forces but were driven back. Again at about one P.M., the attack was renewed and the *Federals penetrated into a gap left in Jackson's front line. They were, however, speedily repulsed by his brigades held in reserve. I received instructions through an officer of Jackson's staff to join in the movement on my right as soon as A. P. Hill's division advanced. The order was accompanied with a message from General Jackson, that he intended to drive the enemy into the river. These orders were countermanded. About ten o'clock that night, I rode back to my encampment to procure a cup of coffee. General Lee's quarters being within a few hundred yards, I presented myself at his tent. He immediately asked me what I thought of the attack by the enemy, during the day. I expressed my opinion that Burnside was whipped; that no good general would ever make an assault similar to that upon my right and left, without intending it as his main effort. He

* Root's Brigade.

1862 then remarked that he did not think Burnside had made his principal attempt, but would again attack the next day, and that we would drive him back, and follow him up to the river.

"The morning of the 14th, both armies still lay face to face, when about noon Generals Lee and Jackson invited me to accompany them on a reconnoissance, toward our right. We soon reached an eminence, not far distant from Hamilton's Crossing on the railroad, and upon which some of our batteries were posted. From this point we had a magnificent view of the Federal lines on their left, some seven in number, and each, seemingly, a mile in length. . . . . The two armies stood still during this entire day, and the following morning we awoke to find the enemy on the north side of the Rappahannock."

The First Brigade marched in a northerly direction about a mile and a half, and bivouacked for the night.

Dec. 16. The regiment moved in a southerly direction about five hundred yards, and went into camp.

Dec. 27. Captain Waldron, Company I, detailed as officer of the picket, which is stationed on the estate of James Talliaferro, about one and a half miles from the Rappahannock River.

1863
Jan. 1. Visitors in camp. Among them is the father of Captain and Lieutenant Leavitt, from Maine. Officers all busy making up muster-rolls for pay.

Jan. 2. The sick were sent to general hospital, in Washington.

CHAPTER VI.

WINTER QUARTERS.

THE regiment moved about half a mile, and went into "winter quarters." The location was near Fletcher's Chapel, in the lower part of Stafford County, with a base of supplies at Belle Plains. The chapel was occupied as a hospital, and filled with sick, the victims of former exposure and want, the fell effects of which were also seen in the unusual mortality of the cases of amputation, eight cases in nine proving fatal. A general hospital was established at Windmill Point, near Acquia Creek. A row of headstones near the chapel and on the point marks the last resting place of the heroic dead of the Sixteenth. _{1863 Sunday Jan. 3.}

This A.M. the following order regulating camp duties was issued: — _{Jan. 4.}

HDQ'RS 16TH REG'T ME. VOLS.,
Jan. 4, 1863.

General Orders.

In order to classify and properly systematize the respective duties and general responsibilities of the Field and Line Officers of the 16th Reg't Me. Vols., it is ordered: —

That the 2d Lieut. of each company shall have the charge and personal supervision of the Co. rollcalls. He shall oversee and properly regulate everything pertaining to the

1863 sanitary condition and affairs of the company such as the laying out and proper trenching of the company streets; the pitching, striking, and proper arrangement and ventilation of the tents; the quality of the food used by the men, and its proper cooking; the location and use of the company sinks; the cleanliness, health, comfort, and general welfare of the men.

The 1st Lieut. of each company shall have the charge and personal supervision of everything pertaining to the discipline of the camp. He shall personally supervise the instruction, and conduct the drills of the non-commissioned officers and soldiers of the company. He shall personally attend to the care and condition of the arms, accouterments, ammunition, clothing, and discipline of the company. He shall see that all such punishments for misconduct in the company as may be ordered by the Captain or Colonel are duly carried into effect. Upon a march it shall be the particular duty of the 1st and 2d Lieut's to see that the men do not leave the ranks without permission from the captain, and that strict order and discipline are maintained in the company.

The Captains shall at all times exercise a vigilant and constant supervision over all matters pertaining to the welfare and good condition of their companies. They will maintain daily drill in the schools of the soldier and of the company without special orders from the Colonel. They will promptly order needful punishment for evil-doers and those who neglect their duties.

The Major of the Reg't shall oversee and personally direct the matters pertaining to the sanitary concerns and condition of the Reg't in camp and on the march. He shall personally direct and supervise the formation and order of the camp and bivouac; the location, pitching, striking, and proper arrangement of the tents of the Regiment, assigning proper locations to the tents of the Field, Staff, and Line Officers, the Band, Drum Corps and Pioneer Corps, Hospital and Quartermaster's Dept's; the kitchens, sinks, stables, etc., of the Regiment. He shall personally supervise the quality and cooking of the food provided for the men, and the proper drainage of the camp. Upon a march the Maj. will maintain good order and strict military discipline in the left wing of the battalion. He will keep the officers and soldiers in their places and prevent useless straggling, depredating, and misconduct of any kind at all hazards. The Maj. will be held strictly responsible for the conduct of the officers and soldiers of the left wing of the battalion.

The Lieut-Col. shall oversee and personally supervise all matters pertaining to the drill and discipline of the Reg't. He will see that the several Capt's maintain daily drills in their companies. He will attend to the care and condition of the arms, accouterments, clothing, and ammunition of the Reg't, the posting of the guards, sentinels, and patrols for special duty. He will attend to the care and disposition of prisoners, captured or stolen property that may come into possession of the Reg't, exercising under the direction of the Col. the duties and functions of a Provost Marshal. Upon a march the Lieut-Col. shall maintain good order and strict discipline in the right wing of the battalion. He will keep the officers and soldiers in their places and prevent useless straggling, depredating, and misconduct of any kind at all hazards. The Lieut-Col. will be held strictly responsible for the conduct of the officers and soldiers of the right wing of the battalion.

The Chaplain of the Reg't shall have the personal charge, control, and supervision of the postal affairs of the Reg't, attending to the receipt, delivery, and prompt transmission of the regimental mails. He shall receive letters at all times from the officers and soldiers of the Regiment, and shall be supplied with postage stamps to sell to the officers and soldiers who may desire to purchase them. The Chaplain shall have the charge of the religious concerns of the Reg't, visiting the sick in camp or hospital at least once daily and conducting the public religious services of the Regiment. He shall also be an assistant to the Maj. in the sanitary department, reporting promptly to the Maj. all matters requiring attention.

1863 The Officer of the Day in addition to reporting daily to the Col. for orders will also report to the Lieut.-Col. and Maj. for directions in regard to matters concerning their respective departments.

Company commanders will immediately furnish themselves with copies of this order.

By command of CHAS. W. TILDEN,
Lieut.-Col. Comd'g the Reg't.

Captain Waldron on picket. Sergeant Doe, of E Company, was instantly killed by a falling tree. He was a brave and faithful soldier, and deserving the military honors observed at his funeral. Colonel Wildes rejoined the regiment today, and at dress parade signified his intention of resigning his commission, owing to his continued disability. He complimented Colonel Tilden for his success in establishing the enviable character of the regiment, and feelingly bade farewell to his old command. The men were much attached to their first colonel, and in many ways expressed their sorrow for his disability.

Jan. 5. Colonel Wildes left camp for Washington.

Jan. 9. January 9th the camp of the Sixteenth was completed. The grounds were policed, and a general appearance of thrift and home comfort characterized the encampment. While in winter quarters we were sometimes bored with unwelcome visitors — unwelcome, because, although no doubt intentionally kind, they brought upon us more trouble and annoyance than comfort. The ground for our winter home was a narrow gorge, with a brook of good water running through the center. Quite a grove of trees had to be felled, which were all utilized for houses and firewood. Headquarters were established on a side hill, into which we digged for the foundation and first story. In the back end was scooped a neat fireplace, with a hole leading up through the ground, surmounted by a pork or lard barrel for a chimney, which, when thoroughly dry, often took fire and illuminated the whole camp. The quarters were finally finished, bedsteads made, nice pine boughs laid for a mattress, and covered with a counterpane, ornamented in the center with U. S. We had slept on the ground, between knolls, to keep from rolling down hill, in all kinds of weather, and now congratulated each other on the opportunity for a heavenly rest two feet from the ground. We longed for night, and measured the going down of the sun with impatience. Even Ben's silvery voice, announcing that tea was ready, failed to move us from our rapt contemplation of that fine feather-bed. Just as the sun began hiding itself behind the hill, there hove into sight a horse, then an ambulance, and in the ambulance, two women. "O Lord!" said I. "O hell!" says Max — (never mind what the colonel said), and we went out and cried. That night we lay in the frosts, under the stars, shivering under one poor blanket, and near enough to hear our visitors remark, "What splendid beds the soldiers have." These two patriotic ladies ate up what cost us five dollars, — some things sent from home, that we could not duplicate; cost two of us severe colds, and left nothing, — hardly an acknowledgment of our courtesy, — rather conveyed the idea of conferring a favor upon us! What they came for, the Lord only knows. Max says they did leave a ten-cent Testament, and a calico blouse which our colored cook, Ben, embellished with some red tape and wore as an undress uniform until the starch was out, then he used it for a dish-cloth.

While at this camp one female did us some service. She came with an extra polonaise and spirited away from Company C one Brown, who has never been heard from since — as Brown. A comrade gives us the following version: "This corporal was visited by a wealthy sister, who claimed to reside in New York City. She was cordially received by the officers and men, who did everything to make her stay as pleasant as possible. Everybody envied the corporal. She remained but a few days, and on the morning of her departure, an ambulance was provided to take her to the landing, which was some miles away, and permission given to her brother to go with her. He went, but the ambulance came back without him. Strange to say, this corporal's record, down to this time, had been of the very best, and promotion awaited him. He was universally liked for his quiet, dignified demeanor, and careful attention to his duties. But he must have been bad at heart, for a few moments before his departure with his sister, he stepped back into his tent and borrowed his messmate's watch, which he never returned."

The members of the Sixteenth were not all of the masculine persuasion. Company I boasted of the presence of one of the gentler sex in the ranks, who did good service at Fredericksburgh. She is thus spoken of by the *Richmond Whig*: —

Yesterday a rather prepossessing lass was discovered on Belle Isle, disguised, among the prisoners of war held there. She gave her real name as Mary Jane Johnson, belonging to the Sixteenth Maine Regiment. She gave as an excuse for adopting her soldier's toggery, that she was following her lover to *shield* and *protect* him when in danger. He had been killed, and now she had no objection to return to the more peaceful sphere for which nature, by her sex, had better fitted her. Upon the discovery of her sex Miss Johnson was removed from Belle Isle to Castle Thunder. She will probably go north by the next flag of truce. She is about sixteen years of age. — 1863

Regimental inspection. — Jan. 11.

Orders received relative to having five days' cooked rations on hand. — Jan. 12.

Men are ordered to be in camp, and all surplus baggage and camp furniture disposed of, which means "destroyed for want of transportation." This includes all the handy things for housekeeping, constructed ingeniously from the bark and roots of trees. From bread boxes and barrels grew center tables, chairs, desks, and even cake trunks. Dice, chessmen and checker-boards abounded in every company, and to abandon all these was "cussid." One man in Company C dug a grave, and, piling in his little treasures, read service over them, and preached a sermon from the text, "And Ephraim fed upon the east wind three days and hungered not." A neat headboard marked the resting place of his jewels. On his return from the mud march, the grave was opened, and the numerous corpse resurrected without ceremony. — Jan. 14.

Owing to the heavy storm, the order to move was countermanded, and camp duties resumed. — Jan. 15.

1863 Jan. 18.   Divine service was held by Chaplain Bullen.

Jan. 19.   At nine o'clock A.M. orders were issued to pack up and march at twelve o'clock M., precisely. Then followed the usual bustle and hum of activity. Every man comprehended the situation, and the accumulated, improvised, and stolen housekeeping utensils were again, amid tears and groans, "destroyed for want of transportation." Headquarters was on a level with the line, and embodied the kitchen and parlor departments in the person of one Tibbetts, who, with his head and shoulders hid behind a huge frying pan, led us in Burnside's famous mud march. God bless Tibbetts! Why not? He was the boss forager, the king of cooks, and the chiefest of liars where the rations of headquarters were concerned. He was like an *ignis fatuus* when the patrol went for him, but as come-at-able and innocent as an infant after he had unloaded, which he often did in unheard of hours and places. Two o'clock in the morning would see him near the picket line, and, meekness personified, he would creep into camp, and crawl under his old army blanket. If he snored in the course of twenty minutes, we knew his conscience was clear, and somebody's "critter" was born into another life. Breakfast proved the correctness of our conclusions. The colonel and adjutant, *en route* for division headquarters one forenoon, when about midway Mud Creek, heard a half-strangled voice saying, "How aire ye, kurnel! Ye don't speak to common folks, do ye?" "Why, Tibbetts, old fellow, how are you; what are you doing?" asked Colonel Tilden, "bathing?" Pulling up into sight the head of a half-drowned mule, he commenced pouring water into his ear, and confidentially remarked, "I'll tell you, kurnel, if ye want to cure a damn balky mule, just pour water into his off ear."

A long, wearisome march was before us. The threatening rain now came down in torrents, and now in a soaking, aggravating drizzle; and nothing could have reconciled the field and staff to the prospect but the disappearing behind the hill of the faithful Tibbetts, and the heaving into sight of Captain Ike, with four canteens slung to his person. Ah! Ike always knew just what the exigency of the service required, and a requisition "duly signed," with his persuasiveness, bridged over many little discrepancies in the United States Army regulations. At twelve M. we took up the line of march in the direction of Falmouth, crossed the railroad in rear of the town, and continued up the Rappahannock until nine o'clock P.M., when we bivouacked for the night. The storm had increased in power, and torrents of rain drenched us through and through. In the darkness regiments and brigades became separated, companies went astray, and whole divisions of troops were in hopeless confusion. Regardless of orders or discipline, men camped where they best could,— some in bed of a brook, which, before morning, became a stream of sufficient force to carry away knapsacks and shelter-tents. Cuss-words were at a premium.

Marched about three miles and remained stuck in the mud until the 22d, when we commenced our

Jan. 20.
Jan. 22.

1863 return to old camp. Met commissary teams with rations for men. Continued march through Falmouth, past General Sumner's headquarters, and went into camp on our grounds of December 10th, *ultimo*. Length of march ten miles.

Jan. 23. Marched four miles to our old camp, through mud from six to twelve inches deep. Pitched tents and spent the remainder of the week in policing grounds.

Jan. 24. Mail arrived.

Feb. 1. Paid to November 1st. Divine service in the afternoon.

Feb. 2. The regiment was inspected by Captain Fisher, who gave the Sixteenth the best report of any regiment in the division. Captain Leavitt, Company E, sent out on patrol in command of a large detail. Marched eight miles and bivouacked for the night in the woods.

Feb. 3. Captain Leavitt continued his march until eight A.M., when he concealed his reserve and sent out a small patrol. They captured one musket and twelve soldier's uniforms abandoned by deserters. Captain Leavitt returned to camp 5th instant.

Feb. 7. Adjutant Small left the regiment for Maine, on fifteen days leave of absence.

Feb. 8. Captain Leavitt "officer of the day." Captain Waldron "officer of the picket." Our brigade picket line is about two miles from camp — the outer line on the extreme left of the A. P. near the Rapidan River.

Feb. 15. Captain Leavitt receives his commission as major.

Feb. 17. Major Leavitt, field officer of the picket. Captain Waldron with Company I, ordered on patrol duty for three days.

1863

Captain Marston obtains leave of absence for fifteen days, and starts for Maine. — Feb. 18.

Major Leavitt moves to regimental headquarters. — Feb. 21.

Adjutant Small rejoins regiment from furlough. — Feb. 22.

Colonel Tilden detailed "division officer of the day." William E. Brooks, recently commissioned captain Company E, left camp at five o'clock P.M., having been discharged for disability. His resignation received the willing indorsement of Colonel Tilden. — Feb. 27.

Regiment mustered for pay by Major Tomlinson. — Feb. 28.

Snow-storm and heavy wind. The men's quarters were nearly all stripped of their canvas roofs. Chimneys were blown down, and books, papers, and clothing scattered in all directions. The camp had the appearance of a laundry drying yard. — Mar. 4.

The officers are all happy, having just received by teams from Third Brigade, thirty-six boxes and five barrels packed and sent by friends at home. — Mar. 7.

Regimental inspection found the command in excellent condition. — Mar. 8.

Major Leavitt mustered under his commission by Lieutenant Baldwin, Fifth United States Battery. — Mar. 9.

Colonel Tilden goes home on leave of absence. He carries with him the kindest wishes of the whole regiment, who hold him second to no regimental commander in the army. Lieutenant-Colonel Farnham assumes command. — Mar. 11.

Thunder-storm accompanied with hail. Regimental inspection. Sergeant Rowe, Company I, receives a furlough of fifteen days. — Mar. 15.

1863
Mar. 16.

Brigade guard mounting. Major Leavitt as adjutant. At eleven o'clock A.M., the line officers held a meeting and unanimously elected Rev. Uriah Balkam of Lewiston, chaplain.

Major Leavitt, field officer of the picket.

Under this date Captain Waldron writes of his men: "About O'Neil, he is a very fine man, and I am sorry to lose him. He always did his duty faithfully, and beside was a gentleman, hence he got kind and gentlemanly treatment from his commanding officers. I am down on *'bummers'* and have got quite a reputation in the regiment, for the manner in which I make them do their duty." Captain Waldron was a humane man, and a believer in the United States Army Regulations, in the abstract, but no amount of red tape would hold him, or friendship for brother officers bottle him up, when he was requested to "report." He would do it in his peculiar way, as in the following "weekly report of sick sent to hospital."

To LIEUT. A. R. SMALL, *Adj't 16th Me. Vols.,*

SIR: — I have the distinguished honor to submit for your consideration and approval, the following statement respecting the departure from Co. I, 16th Me. Reg't, of sick men and *bummers*, since my last weekly report. I very much regret the necessity I am under of stating that the bummers far exceed in numbers the genuine sick. I will add in this connection that the bummers, in my opinion, have been very materially aided and abetted in their nefarious practices through the overflowing (but mistaken) kindness of heart which our two amiable and esteemed surgeons exhibited toward this rascally set of men who are drawing sustenance from Uncle Sam's plethoric purse, but who persistently refuse to render any aid in crushing the infamous and cussed rebellion. 1863

Sent to General Hospital sick, 4.

Sent to General Hospital bumming, 6.

I have the honor to be very truly yours,

W. H. WALDRON, *Capt. Co. I.*

Captain Marston returned from leave of absence. Mar. 26.

Colonel Tilden returned from leave of absence. David Perry died at division hospital. He was one of Captain Waldron's best men, never off duty until taken sick. Mar. 27.

The action of the line officers, in nominating Parson Balkam, of Lewiston, for chaplain, received the approval of Colonel Tilden, who forwarded his name to Governor Coburn for commission. Very cold and windy. Mar. 28.

Brigade drill in the afternoon. Headquarters have invested in a span of native mules and a condemned ambulance. Mar. 30.

General orders and circulars are as thick as snowflakes, all indicating active service in the near future. Extra baggage has been sent to the rear, and the regiment daily inspected and drilled preparatory to another campaign. We are ordered to move without wagons, and carry ten days' rations. This means that every man will be as a pack mule and carry by actual weight, ten days' rations — twenty-six pounds, four ounces; arms, equipments and sixty rounds of ammunition, twenty-eight pounds, one ounce; total, fifty-four pounds, five ounces. Ordered in line for a review of the division by Major-General Hooker. The Sixteenth was one of the first regiments in posi- Apr. 2.

tion, and had a fine opportunity, to take in the moving panorama of blue and scarlet, as the different brigades and batteries took the positions assigned them. The neatly clad men with burnished guns, the brilliant uniforms of officers, the gorgeous decorations of the general staff, the loved ensigns fluttering in the breeze, and the measured tramp of the veterans to the inspiring music of bands and drum corps as they marched in review, the evident satisfaction of Hooker and the conscious power so plainly shown in his finely cut, but rather too rosy face, all combined to set at rest our fears of another defeat. Winter quarters, with the wearing inactivity and irksome routine duties, seemed more distasteful than ever, and every indication of a move toward the enemy was joyously welcomed by the regiment. We had a few — very few — pessimists among us, constitutional growlers, who were, on the opening of every campaign, attacked with a dyspeptic foreboding that defeat and disaster would follow us. While under the influence of this malady, which was happily not contagious, the ruin revealed to them as being stored for the first brigade was enough to unbalance a healthy mind. With them we always marched too long and marched too fast, but never fast enough to get ahead of their dismal prophecies. They had an ingrained hatred of discipline, cursed red tape by the great gross, and itched with a desire to "see a live Johnnie and draw a bead on him." Their desires were never gratified, for the Johnnies seemed to have had an intuitive perception of these ferocious fighters' intentions, and kept out of sight, hence the few casualties in the immediate front of these rascally bummers.

Brigade drill by Ninety-fourth New York and Sixteenth Maine. <small>Apr. 3.</small>

Major Leavitt officer of the picket. <small>Apr. 5.</small>

Chaplain Bullen obtains leave of absence. <small>Apr. 7.</small>

Major Leavitt left for Maine on a leave of fifteen days. <small>Apr. 8.</small>

The First Army Corps reviewed by President Lincoln. <small>Apr. 9.</small> The regiment never looked finer than when it joined the march of the brigade at six A.M., *en route* for Belle Plains. We were reasonably proud of our appearance, which elicited a marked compliment from the brigade commander. The officers had been untiring in effort and unrelaxing in discipline, during the winter months. Rations had been good, clothing well supplied, and the last lingering memory of the "Blanket Brigade" vanished forever. I hardly think it will be counted against us in the great hereafter that we could not muster a paper collar or a "biled shirt" for review. A sister regiment filed past us with a stunning toilet. Turning their heads as much as possible in paper dickeys and stocks, they looked in vain for the old lousy Sixteenth, and greeted us with, "Hallo, 'roostooks! Where's yer blankets?" Not a yip from a Sixteener. The colonel's eyes seemed to see every man, and they loved him too well to reflect the slightest upon his discipline. It was our second victory. The sun, as he came up in the heavens, grew hotter and hotter, and every paper collar by the roadside, marking the progress of the —— regiment on its

1863 way to Belle Plains, caused a numerous yell of delight. Our boys picked them up on their bayonets and left them in a pile near the Plains, and set up a board on which they inscribed, "Sacred to the memory of ———— State pride."

Apr. 12. Captain Waldron, with nearly all the regiment, detailed for three days' picket duty. We participated in a division drill in the forenoon, Colonel Tilden commanding the brigade. Grand guard mounting on brigade parade ground.

Apr. 13. The cavalry pickets in our front have been reduced one-half, and this forenoon, about three o'clock, the brigade reserve post was increased to two hundred and fifty men. Regiment relieved and returned to camp at five P.M.

Apr. 15. Orders to march were promulgated this forenoon. Heavy rain-storm. The regiment sent home five thousand eight hundred and forty-five dollars by express.

Apr. 22. Broke camp this forenoon, and moved about half a mile in a drenching rain, to harden us, the boys said.

Apr. 23. Major Leavitt and Chaplain Bullen rejoined the regiment from leaves of absence. During the winter the musicians organized a band under the lead of John Shea, principal musician, and today a complete set of instruments came as a donation by the officers. Captain Waldron, who had not a remarkable ear for that kind of music, — had rather hear a bullet whistle, or a shell explode, — says, "And now, in addition to other afflictions, we are doomed to a constant succession of toots from fifteen beginners on wind instruments." Long afterward we blessed the Lord, every one of us, for the inspiring music of the best band in the division.

Was published a stereotyped order: —

Regimental commanders will have their command in readiness to move at a moment's notice, with eight days' rations, and forty rounds of ammunition.

MAJOR

CHAPTER VII.

THE CHANCELLORSVILLE CAMPAIGN.

1863
Apr. 28. STRUCK tents and moved at ten A.M. Continuing the march for six miles, we bivouacked near the Fitzhugh House.

Apr. 29. Formed in line at three o'clock A.M. Stacked arms and rested until noon in the edge of the woods. Early in the morning, the Sixteenth Michigan crossed the river in boats, under a galling fire of musketry, and captured about one hundred rebels, driving the rest from their rifle-pits. Pontoons were laid, when the First Division of our corps crossed over. Amid the booming of cannon and the noise of an indiscriminate firing from sharpshooters and infantry pickets, our boys are playing poker, chasing rabbits, swopping lies, apparently indifferent to the sharp demands of a near future.

Apr. 30. Made history down on the Rapidan. In easy range of the rebel guns, we were mustered for pay. At four o'clock P.M. it was proposed by a congress of chaplains, to hold divine service in the brigade, preparatory to the general slaughter anticipated during the next forty-eight hours. Everything was quiet over the river, and not a sign betrayed to the innocent twelve hundred dollar shepherds, the gathering storm, as they collected in the center of a hollow square, and fervently pleaded the cause of the Lord and the country. They were eloquent in their appeals to our patriotism, and pictured in glowing colors the halo of glory that would enfold the martyred dead, and the armfuls of shoulder straps that would find resting places upon the blue coats of the surviving heroes. Counseling all to stand firm, to shrink not from the terrible ordeal through which we were called to pass, to be brave and heroic, and God being our shield we would have nothing to fear, — when came a slight puff of smoke, followed by another, and yet another, in quick succession, just across the river, and then a rushing sound like trains of cars and terrific explosions all around us of "whole blacksmith shops." The explosion of shells, the neighing of horses, and the sharp commands were almost drowned by the shouts and laughter of the men, as the brave chaplains, hatless and bookless, with coat-tails streaming in the wind, went madly to the rear over stone-walls, through hedges and ditches, followed by, "Come back and earn your twelve hundred dollars!" "Stand firm! Be brave and heroic and put your trust in the Lord!" The scare was soon over, but no persuasions could induce the chaplains to come back and speak in meeting, so it was never known what the Lord had done for them. I'll not say that these men were other than good Christian men trying to discharge their duties under peculiarly trying circumstances. They failed simply for want of preparation. But I will say, in addition to the noble Christian men, the army was cursed with

1863 a lot of scalawags, who fitted themselves for chaplains how, when, or where, nobody knows. Surely they were never drilled in the army of the Lord. The brigade moved half a mile to the rear, and occupied a comparatively safe position behind a stone-wall and hedge until after dark.

May 1. The regiment took up a line of march early in the morning, and was under fire of rebel artillery until it passed Fredericksburgh. Greeley says, "The First Corps moved leisurely up the river." The march of twenty miles was a rapid and most exhausting one. The heat of the sun was intense. At half-past seven P.M. we crossed the river at United States Ford, on pontoons, and bivouacked. In thirty minutes we were again marching rapidly to the front. The right of our lines was in extreme peril, for Howard's corps had stampeded, and the tide of exultant foes must be stemmed to save a general disaster. On at double-quick, through burning woods, over dead and dying, amid a terrific cannonading and an incessant rattle of musketry, we pushed. Exhausted and panting, the Sixteenth took the extreme right and front of the Army of the Potomac at half-past ten P.M., and remained in line of battle until three A.M., when we threw up breastworks and posted videttes about thirty rods in front, which were advanced one-quarter of a mile at daylight. The Twenty-ninth and Thirty-second New Jersey took position on our right and rear, and extended the line, as was supposed, to the Rapidan River. The Sixteenth lay on their arms all day, listening to the terrific fighting on the center, and hourly expecting an attack, for which they were fully prepared. At half-past four P.M., Colonel Tilden handed the adjutant the following order:—

HEADQUARTERS 2D DIV., 1ST CORPS,
May 3, 1863, 4½ o'clock P.M.

COL.:— You will please send an intelligent officer to the right of your line to ascertain and report upon the condition of affairs on the Rapidan. Observe particularly whether the enemy is making any movement in that direction. The information is wanted this evening.

JOHN C. ROBINSON, Brig.-Gen. Com'dg.

COL. A. R. ROOT,
  Com'dg the Brigade.

Respectfully referred to Adj't Small, 16th Me. Vols., who will execute the duty, and report thereon.

A. R. ROOT, Col. Com'dg Brigade.

In obedience to this order, Adjutant Small mounted his horse, and with an orderly leaped the breastworks and proceeded down the road toward Ely's Ford. Passing our picket line half a mile out, and the cavalry videttes but a short distance beyond, he slackened pace and moved cautiously some three miles, and drew rein at the edge of the wood, where the road made a sharp bend to the left, in the direction of the ford. The quiet hush of the woods and the stillness of the air betrayed no presence of a living thing. The Adjutant at once left the road, and meeting a probable owner of the house directly in his way, bade him good evening, and asked if he objected to his crossing the yard and field. He was a most villainous-looking and shabbily-clad tramp. The Adjutant felt uneasy at leaving him at large, but time was precious, the orderly unarmed, and he could

1863 not invest in a rebel and proceed, so, politely thanking him, he rode out some mile or so to a bend in the river, on an elevation of some fifty or seventy-five feet, and rapidly noted all of interest for future use. Directly across the river, and from one to three miles to the left, fires from deserted camps and several buildings were still burning. Two long columns of infantry with artillery were rapidly moving from our front in the direction of Fredericksburgh. He saw no other signs of the enemy, and believing the information valuable to an army waiting behind breastworks for an attack from a force, who, unseen, were withdrawing to fall upon Sedgwick, he started on his return, elated with success secured with so little danger. Leaving the field by the way he came, he reached the house yard, and was startled to see the rebel picket line across the road, and following the woods both ways. The reserve was one hundred yards to the left, lying on the ground near their stack of arms. There was but one alternative; it was either prison or the Union lines. The Adjutant had escaped notice thus far, and burying his spurs in his horse's flanks, shot across the yard into the road, followed by the orderly. The first plunge of the horses alarmed the picket, and with the command, "Halt! Halt!" came three shots which passed harmlessly by. On across the road and into the woods, when again came the shout, "Halt, you damned Yanks!" They were in for it, and reckless of the bullets from the rebels, who now crowded the road in the rear, they went madly on out of range, and none the worse for the scare. Luckily for them, carbines were used instead of rifles. Nearly a mile out from our lines was General Reynolds, our corps commander, with staff, anxiously waiting for the intelligence requested through General Robinson. Meeting the Adjutant, he said, quickly, "Well?" Receiving the information with cordial thanks, the General rode rapidly to Hooker's headquarters. Some one knows what was said by the corps commanders assembled there within thirty minutes, — I don't. But I firmly believe that had General Reynolds' suggestion, referred to in Doubleday's "Chancellorsville and Gettysburgh," been adopted, our defeat would have been a victory. The facts obtained by this reconnoissance, added to the result of a reconnoissance said to have been made by General Webb a few hours earlier, were such as to warrant Hooker in acting up to his intentions, as indicated in his dispatch to General Sedgwick at twelve o'clock M.: "If the necessary information can be obtained today, and if it shall be of the character the commanding general anticipates, it is his intention to advance upon the enemy to-morrow." He could anticipate but one thing favorably to his advance, and that was the withdrawal of a portion of the enemy's forces from his front. The reconnoissances alluded to gave him the necessary information.

During the afternoon Hall's battery advanced toward Ely's Ford, losing one killed and fifteen wounded, in a short yet sharp engagement. About nine o'clock P.M., out of the quiet in our vicinity came a single shot which brought every man to his feet, musket in hand, instantly, and just in

1863

May 4.

1863

season to receive a whole broadside from the Twenty-ninth and Thirty-second New Jersey, stationed in our rear. Fortunately for us, their lack of good training — having been in service but a few months — made targets of the tree tops instead of us. Captain Waldron, who was stationed with the pickets in our immediate front, writes of the scare:

About nine o'clock in the evening volleys of musketry were heard on our right which led me to suppose that the rebels had got between our pickets and our intrenchments; and I began to think I had received a ticket for Richmond, and immediately made arrangements to get back to our intrenchments with my command. I caught my haversack and blankets, and was making my way thitherward, when the line of fire rapidly extended to the left. By the time I reached the edge of the woods, the sleepy-heads — or those who had been asleep — caught their muskets and blazed away at us. I kept on my way until near enough to make the blunderheads hear when I ordered them to cease firing, which was at once obeyed. The most of my men fell to the ground, and the balls passed over them harmlessly.

May 6. The regiment remained in the intrenchments until three o'clock A.M., 6th instant, when, with the division as rear guard, it quietly withdrew and re-crossed the river in a drenching rain. Marched twelve miles, and bivouacked in the mud on a bleak hill near Falmouth. The men suffered severely. No wood being obtainable for fires, they alternately chewed the cud of discomfort and dry hard-tack, and saved their coffee for the morrow, when they had a reasonable hope of confiscating somebody's front yard fence or the favorite fence rail.

Marched four miles, and bivouacked in a grove of pines, near the Fitzhugh House, and remained until the 10th, when we moved about half a mile, and went into camp near White Oak Church, where we remained until June 10th, drilling early mornings and late nights to avoid the heat at midday. Lieutenant L. C. Bisbee, who was left behind sick, the last of March, rejoined his company at this camp. The mail comes quite regularly, and beside the encouragement in letters comes an occasional bit of good cheer in the newspapers. But the intelligence that President Lincoln pardons a large number of deserters has a most depressing effect upon the brave boys at the front, and the indignation aroused at the disapproval of the sentence of a court-martial passed upon Vallandigham is above all discipline. *1863 May 7. May 10.*

A fine old Virginia mansion furnished the regiment with material for good comfortable quarters. The streets were finely graded and policed, and at the head of each was an evergreen arch, from the center of which hung a large wreath of evergreens and flowers, containing the letter of the company. The garrison flag floated proudly above us, the regimental flags were unfurled at headquarters; bands were playing, men were singing merrily, and a holiday aspect met the eye of the looker-on. Only two weeks since the terrible battle in the woods, and not the shadow of a recollection of the awful results was apparent to a superficial observer. The mail arrived and a schoolboy scramble took place. We didn't all receive letters, but the man with three, one from his best girl, was the envy of the camp. *May 20.*

1863
May 25.   The whole corps is cheering wildly over the reported capture of Vicksburgh.

May 26.   Regiment detailed for picket. While lying in camp and enjoying misery, the trials were, as was often the case, accompanied by some grotesque incidents. Chenery, armed with a pass, went out of camp about seven P.M., to "make a call." Returning after taps with a hive of honey, and finding the adjutant asleep, aroused the sergeant-major, who got a tub and received for headquarters a liberal donation of the delicious luxury. "George, are there any *bees* in this?" asked Max. "O, only a few, and they are too cold to sting," replied Chenery. With a peculiar chuckle, Max quietly deposited the tub close up and partly under a corner of the adjutant's blanket, and waited. Directly the heat warmed up the bees, which crawled over the sleeping officer. The uncomfortable sensation made him "thrash round," which stirred up the insects, and they just wreaked vengeance for the theft. He thought of enormous lice, of bedbugs, of fire, and danced around the tent like a lunatic. Honey always makes him sick.

May 29.   The Ninety-fourth New York has been detached from our brigade for guard duty at Acquia Creek. The Thirteenth Massachusetts joins the brigade, and Colonel S. H. Leonard, the ranking colonel, assumes command. Rumors reach us that Lee is about to invade Maryland. William H. Hatch and William P. Blake, of West Waterville, Maine, came into camp unexpectedly, taking us so completely by surprise, that for hours we could simply look with glad eyes upon these most welcome visitors from home. It was their rare good fortune to see a line of rebel pickets, and to witness the grand review of the First Army Corps on the 30th, by Major-General Reynolds. <small>1863</small> <small>May 30.</small>

The strength of the First Corps was greatly reduced by the discharge of troops whose term of enlistment had expired, compelling a reorganization of its divisions and several of its brigades. In reorganizing Robinson's division the three brigades that formerly composed it were consolidated into two brigades. The One Hundred and Fourth New York, One Hundred and Seventh Pennsylvania, Thirteenth Massachusetts, and Sixteenth Maine formed the First Brigade, under command of General Paul.

Messrs. Hatch and Blake leave camp to visit other Maine regiments. <small>June 1.</small>

Two o'clock in the morning received orders to be in line at daylight, with three days' rations in haversacks. Orders to march countermanded at quarter past eleven A.M. Pitched tents and resumed camp duties. <small>June 4.</small>

Struck tents at half-past three o'clock A.M., and formed in line, ready to march. Guns remained in stack nearly all day. At sunset, tents were pitched, and we were at home to callers. <small>June 6.</small>

Brigade and battalion drills, and the usual order of camp filled the time. <small>June 7 to 12.</small>

CHAPTER VIII.

THE GETTYSBURGH CAMPAIGN.

1863
June 12. At half-past five A.M., struck tents, packed up, and bade a last good by to camp near White Oak Church. The regiment began its march with two hundred eighty-one men, thirty-two officers, and two hundred sixty-three guns. Marched until dark and bivouacked at Deep Run, a distance of twenty miles. Regiment detailed for picket.

June 13. Slung knapsacks at six o'clock A.M., marched twelve miles, and bivouacked between Bealeton and Rappahannock stations. Strength of regiment in the morning, two hundred and fifteen guns, two hundred and one men, twenty-eight officers, — at night, two hundred and thirty-seven guns, two hundred and eighteen men, thirty-two officers.

June 14. Marched at eight A.M., reached Warrensburgh one P.M., and Manassas Junction at half-past three, June 15, with two hundred and eighteen guns, two hundred and twenty-six men, thirty-two officers. Length of march twenty-six miles.

June 15. Left at nine o'clock A.M., and marched seven miles to Centerville, and remained until 17th. Number of guns two hundred and twenty, men two hundred and thirty-two, officers thirty-two.

Left Centerville at half-past five A.M., with two hundred and fifty-two guns, two hundred and sixty-six men, and thirty-two officers. Marched twelve miles to Herndon station. **1863 June 17.**

Marched to Guilford station, a distance of five miles, where the regiment remained until 25th, sending out pickets some six miles south of Leesburgh. Strength of regiment, two hundred and forty-five guns, two hundred and ninety-five men, and thirty-two officers. The march from W. O. C. has been a rapid and exhausting one. Water extremely scarce. The men gladly filled their canteens from the muddy brooks and sluggish runs of Virginia. No member of the Sixteenth suffered from sunstroke, a casualty which occurred in many regiments of the division. It was reported that the "blanket fellers" brought into camp every night a larger percentage of guns and more forage than any troops in the division. Some mile or more back from our camp, we passed a plantation, the house and grounds undisturbed, except by time. Crowning a dilapidated fence, which showed, between innumerable dusky legs, spots of ancient whitewash, were darkies of all shades, sizes, and ages, from a bullet-headed baby to a centenarian. The indescribable attitudes struck and the grimaces of astonishment that spread over the faces of that dark collection, as regiment after regiment massed in a field and batteries parked beyond, would have driven a circus crowd wild. One old nigger, with a face like parchment, crowned with white wool, doffed his rimless hat, and stretching out his long, bony fingers as if to cover us with a bless- **June 19.**

ing, shouted in a cracked voice, "Tank de Lord fer de glory ob dis yer 'casion! Hebbenly massa bress de Linkum sojers, an' show dese yer eyes de golden chariot fo' I die!" Old hats, jackets, and shoes went high in the air and shouts of "Glory hallelujah!" went along that color line. An aged darky came limping to the road, exclaiming, "Gret King! how many moe you 'uns comin'? Specs forty millions toted by hyer since mornin'." "Well, uncle," said Corporal F., "you can stand here three weeks and see the Yanks go by." "Fo' God I dun reckon so. Massa Linkum mighty sojer, I reckon. Is he a-gwine by hyer too?" "O yes, uncle, he is at the rear of our corps, forty miles back — be along in his chariot tomorrow." Limping back to the fence now fairly covered with shining faces, the old patriarch yelled, "Chillun, cotch off yer hats and jine in de chorus." Swaying from side to side, in grotesque attitudes, they sang in a way peculiar to southern negroes:—

"Don' yer see um comin', comin', comin'—
  Milyuns from de oder sho'?
Glory! Glory! Hallelujah!
  Bress de Lord forebermo'.

"Don' yer see um goin', goin', goin'
  Pass ole massa's cabin do'?
Glory! Glory! Hallelujah!
  Bress de Lord forebermo'.

"Jordan's stream is runnin', runnin', runnin,—
  Milyuns sojers passin' o'er;
Linkum comin' wid his charyot,
  Bress de Lord forebermo'.

"Don' yer hear him comin', comin'?
    Yes, I do!
Wid his robe an' mighty army?
    Yes, I do!
Want ter march wid him to glory?
    Yes, I do!"

Long into the night would I seem to hear, "Glory! Glory! Hallelujah! Bress de Lord forebermo'."

June 21. Major Leavitt left for Washington, sick.

June 25. At half-past eight A.M., broke camp, and marched fifteen miles to Boonesville and bivouacked.

June 26. Reveille at half-past four A.M. At half-past five, marched. Halted at Jefferson six P.M.

June 27. Marched at half-past eight A.M., and at half-past one bivouacked near Middletown. Distance, five miles. Regiment sent on picket. The Ninety-fourth New York assigned to First Brigade.

June 28. General George G. Meade relieves Hooker. After two hours' sleep, fell in at half-past seven P.M., and marched to Frederick City, where we rejoined brigade at two P.M., 29th, having marched thirty-eight miles in twenty-five hours. Number of guns, two hundred and thirty; men, two hundred and sixty-seven; officers, twenty-five.

June 29. Bugle call at five o'clock A.M. Fell in and marched via Lewistown Furnace to Emmitsburg, and waited orders, at quarter of six P.M.

June 30. Regiment left Emmitsburg at nine o'clock A.M., and marched to Pennsylvania line and bivouacked. "The First Corps, although ordered to Gettysburgh, was halted by General Reynolds at Marsh Creek, as the enemy were reported to be coming from the

1863 direction of Fairfield." They were within six miles of us. If we had any lingering doubts about the probability of a battle in the near future, which would call us into action, they were promptly dispelled by General Meade's address to the army, published to each regiment.

July 1. "In June the Army of Northern Virginia, divided into three corps, under Longstreet, Ewell, and A. P. Hill, commanded by General Lee, crossed the Potomac at Williamsport and Shepherdstown, and marched into Pennsylvania; a part going as far as Carlisle, the remainder halting at Chambersburgh. The Union Army, under Hooker, had, in the meantime, crossed the river at Edward's Ferry, and headed toward Frederick City, Maryland. June 27th, Hooker, having been refused the use of ten thousand men not needed at Harper's Ferry, tendered his resignation, which was accepted, General George G. Meade succeeding to the command. On the morning of July 1st, Hill, whose corps was in the advance, six miles from Gettysburgh, learned that the place was occupied by a Union force. Sending back to urge Longstreet to hasten his march, he moved on. In the meantime, General Reynolds, who was in command of that portion of the Union Army, had sent out a cavalry reconnoissance, and the forces came into collision about two miles northwest of Gettysburgh. Reynolds sent Wadsworth's division of the First Corps to the support of the cavalry under Buford, and thus opened the great historical battle of the war."

Although early under arms, the Sixteenth did not

leave camp until nine o'clock A.M., when it marched rapidly in the direction of Gettysburgh, and halted southeast of the seminary. The heavy cannonading broke upon our ears, and gave elasticity to weary legs, and steps increased to the double-quick as we were met with the intelligence that General Reynolds was killed, and the First Division desperately fighting double its numbers. As the regiment left the Emmitsburg road, and followed the track of the First Division, the men insisted that they could hear the sharp bark of Hall's guns in the direction of Willoughby Run. Doubtless this was true, for at this moment the Second Maine Battery was in a perilous position on the first ridge in the rear of Willoughby Run, between the old railroad cut and the Chambersburgh Turnpike, where it remained, sustaining a fearful loss, until the whole line was forced back. General Hall says, "No artillery of our army ever went back to the spot." (For the exact location of this superb battery, see Batchelder's "Isometrical View" of the Gettysburgh battle-field, in which he locates Califf's where Hall's should be.) By command of General Robinson, the First Brigade hastily threw up a redoubt of earth and fence rails, in a circular form, just in front of the seminary. Stevens' Fifth Maine Battery, which, under its commander, Captain G. T. Stevens, did such notable service between Culp's Hill and the cemetery, on the 2d and 3d, was in echelon in the rear and to the right of the seminary.

While here in line, and momentarily expecting the order to "go in," Captain Whitehouse, with a

1863 pitiful smile, said to me, "Adjutant, I wish I felt as brave and cool as the colonel appears." "Why, Captain," I replied, "he is as scared as any of us. Cheer up, 't will soon be over." "Well, the colonel may be scared, but he *looks* as happy as though we were to have an old-fashioned State of Maine muster." "I know that, Captain. No man ever saw him appear differently in a fight. Notice, the men just idolize him. They would be perfectly happy if Colonel Farnham was here too." About one o'clock rang out the command, "Fall in! Forward, Sixteenth." "Good by, Adjutant, this is my last fight," cried Captain Whitehouse. He turned, repeated the command to his company, and I never saw him afterward. We double-quicked to the right, and took position behind a rail fence, in a piece of woods, and nearly parallel with the Chambersburgh Turnpike, and were at once engaged with the enemy, who were also in rear of a fence, and some two hundred yards distant. Corporal Yeaton, of the color guard, was the first man killed. While cautioning his men to keep cool, and aim low, Captain Waldron, of Company I, was struck, a ball entering just back of the jugular vein, and penetrating to the lung. Colonel Tilden, the only mounted regimental officer in the brigade, had his horse shot from under him. Now came the order to charge bayonets. Color Sergeant Mower was the first to jump the fence, and the regiment followed with a ringing cheer, and in the face of a galling fire, went double-quick, scattering the rebel line, they going pell-mell to the rear into the woods. Our boys would have followed them, but were recalled and moved with the division still further to the right, fighting until overpowered by numbers pressing upon our right flank, which had been fully exposed by the skedaddling of a part of Howard's Eleventh Corps.

"Ammunition being nearly all expended Baxter's brigade was withdrawn, Paul's brigade relieving it." Yes, Paul's brigade did relieve it, and when the whole force was falling back, General Robinson, in order to save as much of the division as possible, personally ordered Colonel Tilden to again advance the Sixteenth, and hold the hill at any cost. The regiment advanced, took position behind the stonewall, and broke the right wing to the right parallel with the Mummasburgh road, the color company holding the apex —(the identical spot where the Eighty-eighth Pennsylvania have since placed a tablet. They held the position bravely against fearful odds, but the Sixteenth Maine was the last regiment that left the extreme front, July 1st, if four officers and thirty-eight men can be called a regiment). The intrepid color bearers, Mower and Thomas, waved defiance to the foe, as they closed around the regiment. Although conspicuous marks, they gallantly held aloft the loved emblems until capture was inevitable, and then by advice and consent of the colonel and other officers, broke the staff and tore in shreds the silk banners, the pride of the regiment, and divided the pieces. Today away down in Maine, can be found in albums and frames, gold stars and shreds of silk — cherished mementos of the critical period.

1863

Lieutenant Chapman writes: " Company K went into the fight with twenty-three men. Its position in regimental line was between Companies E and B. Frank Devereaux was killed early in the fight. A moment after he fell, Lieutenant Thompson of Company G, noticed a stranger to the regiment, standing about fifteen paces in rear of line, loading and firing independently. Thinking the man might do mischief to his comrades, Thompson went to him, said something in his low, peculiar tone, and, receiving a reply, immediately knocked him down, and then raising him from the ground by the collar, kicked him rapidly to the rear, much to the merriment and satisfaction of the men, who did n't care to be shot in the back. Lieutenant G. A. Deering, of Company G, sheathed his sword, and seizing a musket from a fallen man, went into the ranks. He was evidently excited, and every once in a while would forget to return his rammer after loading, hence would send it over to the enemy. The peculiar swishing noise made by the rammer, as it hurried through the wood was laughable to the boys, and must have been a holy terror to the rebels."

The brigade loss was officially reported as follows:—

July 1.	Killed.		Wounded.		Missing.	
Regiment.	Off.	E. M.	Off.	E. M.	Off.	E. M.
13th Massachusetts..	....	5	3	71	3	110
107th Pennsylvania..	....	5	5	57	7	102
104th New York.....	....	8	9	57	9	75
94th New York......	....	4	4	37	10	300
16th Maine..........	2	8	7	29	11	148
Total...............	2	30	28	251	40	735

The claim of General Robinson that his division 1863
held the ground, after all the other troops had fallen
back, has never been disputed. Colonel Coulter,
commanding First Brigade, (after Paul,) says in his
official report, "Not a single case of faltering came
to my notice." Nine P.M. Lieutenant Davis detailed
for picket.

Captain Marston in command of regiment. Ewell July 2.
occupied the city, posting his line within half a mile
of cemetery. General John Newton assumed command of First Corps, and placed it in reserve in rear
of the cemetery, and within thirty minutes march of
any part of the Union line. The regiment changed
position from time to time as ordered; with brigade
was ordered to the left center of line, late in the
afternoon. While moving by the right flank past
General Meade's headquarters, a rebel shell exploded in the regiment, severely wounding Lieutenant
Fred. H. Beecher and seven enlisted men. Moving
eight hundred yards, the command was given, "By
the right flank! March!" and in line of battle the
brigade dashed on through the smoke, over the
boulders, in sight of a battery with only two men
working the guns against the rebel troops advancing to capture it. With a wild yell the brigade
charged beyond the battery, and returning brought
off the guns. Early in the morning, the brigade was
reorganized, Colonel Richard Coulter commanding.
The following order was announced:—

HDQ'RS 1ST BRIGADE, 2D DIV., 1ST A. C.
July 2d, 1863.

General Order, No. 44.

I. Adjutant A. R. Small, 16th Me. Vols., is hereby detailed as Acting Assistant Adjutant-General of this Brigade. . . . He will be obeyed and respected accordingly.

By command of COL. R. COULTER,
Com'dg Brigade.

Colonel Coulter established his quarters in an "A" tent, pitched by his orders on the brow of the hill at the left of cemetery, in the edge of a grove, just in rear of the brigade's last position on the second day, and planted in clear view of the rebels the brigade flag. From this point I took in nearly the whole line from the cemetery to Weed's Hill. The position of the national line of skirmishers was clearly defined by a streak of curling smoke that lazily faded into thin vapor. The sky was clear, and a quiet aspect pervaded everything — 't was a moment of rest before a battle. The lazy attitude of men and horses, the apparent indifference of all the army appointments, as the sun went down, afforded but slight indication to a looker-on of the terrible storm gathering for the morrow — a day ever memorable in American history. During the night eighty thousand men concentrated behind the rocky ridge in Lee's front.

July 3. The morning opened with some artillery practice, principally from the rebel side, and continued for a few hours, when a terrible struggle took place for a new position on Culp's Hill. Before eleven o'clock A.M. the Twelfth Corps had regained their position on the eastern slope of the hill. As if by mutual desire, the rain of lead and iron ceased after a few spasmodic discharges. At noon, the hot summer sun beat relentlessly upon the heads of the waiting infantry. The silence was as oppressive as the heat, and time was counted by moments, and moments seemed hours, as we watched, with a terrible intentness, the wheeling into position of batteries in our front. Directly, the silence on Cemetery Ridge was broken by the rapidly-moving artillery, which took positions all along the line from the cemetery to Little Round Top. Guns were sighted, caissons passed to the rear, and men posted for action. In terrible suspense, moments crept by until one o'clock, when the stillness of the air was suddenly broken by an explosion in the wheat field on Oak Hill, and a huge Whitworth shell, with lightning quickness, came crashing through the Union lines. But ere the iron missile crossed the valley, one hundred and fifty guns were discharged as if by electricity, and tons of metal parted the air, which closed with a roar, making acres of earth groan and tremble. The hills and the huge boulders take up the sound and hurl it back, to add its broken tones to the long roll of sound that strikes upon ears thirty miles away. For two hours the air was filled with a horrible concordance of sounds—a roar, echoing the passions of hell loosed among men. The air, thick with sulphurous vapor and smoke, through which comes the sharp cry of agony, the hoarse command, and the screaming shell, almost suffocated those supporting the batteries. Men cover the ground in fragments, and are buried in detail beneath the iron hail. Guns are dismounted, and rest their metallic weight upon quivering flesh. Caissons explode, and wheels and boxes strew the ground in every direction. Horses by the score are blown down by the terrible hurricane, and lie shrieking in agony almost human in its expression. One battery in our immediate front lost forty horses in twenty minutes. In the vicinity of Meade's headquarters shells exploded at the rate of sixty per minute. Solid shot would strike the ground in our front, cover a battalion with sand and dirt, ricochet, and, demon like, go plunging through the ranks of massed men in the rear. For a mile or more a lurid flame of fire streams out over the heads of our men in long jets, as if to follow the tons of metal thrown through the murky air, which parts to receive it, and shudders as if tortured by screaming furies. Roar answers roar, and, meeting in the valley, doubles the awful din which reels into the Devil's Glen, and holds high carnival for hours.

During the fusillade, Colonel Coulter, who has been tearing up and down the line to cool his impatience, suddenly exclaims, "Where in hell is my flag? Where do you suppose that cowardly —— —— has skedaddled to? Adjutant, you hunt him up and bring him to the front before the color is missed." Away the adjutant went, but returned in season to see the colonel snake him out from behind a stone-wall, where he had lain down with the flag folded up to avoid attracting attention. Colonel Coulter shook out the folds, placed the staff in the poor fellow's hand, and double-quicked him toward the front line. Just then a shell exploded in a low wall, killing a horse, and sending a blinding shower of gravel and dirt broadcast. Again seizing the staff, he planted the end where the shell had burst, and said, "There, orderly, hold it in position, and if I can't get you killed in ten minutes, by G—! I'll post you right up among the batteries." Riding away, he laughingly remarked, "The poor devil don't know that I could n't put him in a safer place. Two shells rarely explode in the same spot, and if he obeys orders he will be safe, and I'll know where my headquarters are." He dashed recklessly down the line to return in a few minutes with a bullet in his shoulder. Looking pale, I asked if he would dismount. "No, no, not now. Who in hell would suppose a sharp-shooter would hit a crazy bone that distance?"

Our ammunition was reduced to a few rounds, and there came a signal from Little Round Top that the dense smoke afforded a screen for the enemy, behind which they were rapidly massing for the charge. Notwithstanding Hancock's lines are weak at the center, the order is issued and the firing ceases. The rebels jump at conclusions and send up a wild yell, which echoes the length of the valley. We had heard it too often to lose heart or courage, but nerves were at their extreme tension, as we watched the splendid lines of infantry stretched for miles in our front, as if for parade, and a second and yet in the rear a third debouch from the woods into view. Such a sight is given only once in a life-time, and once seen never to be forgotten. The veterans of Virginia, the flower of the rebel army, under its

1863 idolized commander, were writing another bloody chapter in the history of the rebellion. History says that Lee's ammunition was nearly exhausted and there was no time to replenish it, so the attacking column of eighteen thousand men move silently and swiftly down the slope and across the plain toward the left center of our line, the weakest point. Pickett's division leads the front on the right with Pettigrew's on the left. In their rear marches Anderson's and Trimble's commands, whose right was covered by Perry and Wilcox, and left by McGowan and Thomas. Down the slope into the valley they come and now it is our turn, and from the black muzzles of one hundred cannon pour round shot, spherical case, and canister, in an incessant torrent which cuts great swaths of living grain. Men go down by scores but others fill the gaps, and the resistless tide sweeps on in perfect order into the Emmitsburg road, when from behind the stone-wall our boys pour in a shower of hissing bullets, carrying death and destruction to those brave but mistaken men. They go down like jack-straws — they lie in windrows. The rich carpet of white clover and daisies is dyed in crimson figures, by the hot blood of southern sons. With a desperation born of madness, they force their way through a shower of leaden hail. Hot with passion born of war, stained and blinded with blood, the living fail to see the terrible harvest of death in their rear, and, utterly reckless of personal results, they press on and on and, with a yell of victory, plant their tattered flags of rebellion in our breast-works, and brain gunners at their posts. They

turn to beckon on the next line. The next line!— *1863*
where is it?—exultation is drowned in despair and
defeat, for from both flanks the Union boys are
giving a deadly fire, while shot and shell enfilade
their rear. Thousands fall to the ground, and hold
up their hands in token of surrender, and others flee
only to be swallowed up in the flood-tide that reach-
es the Emmitsburg road. A brave man can but pity
the victims of such a terrible disappointment. Looking down upon all this, I could see, shorn of all
wordy description, simply a square mile of Tophet.

The remnant of the Sixteenth is sadly depressed. *July 4.*
The loved colonel on his way to Richmond — to the
prison-pens of the South; the brave lieutenant-
colonel at the point of death; our valued surgeon,
Alexander, wounded and a prisoner; all the line officers but four either killed, wounded, or missing, and
a fearful list of casualties among the men. We
thought of the brave fellows started on a pilgrimage
worse than death. There is said to be an average
time in every man's life, when he learns to cry. I
believe many of us graduated in this accomplish-
ment that night. Among those captured was Benny
Worth, of Company E. He was kept busy in the
unwelcome task of carrying United States muskets
from the field, July 2d. He quickly discerned that
the rebels were being worsted, and shrewdly worked
his way into the hospital. Procuring some bloody
bandages, he bound up an imaginary wound in his
ankle, and hence was left behind, while the well and
unharmed were marched toward Richmond. Worth
rejoined the regiment on the morning of the fourth.

1863 Corporal Bradford with others, rendered timely aid to many of the wounded inside the rebel lines. He found Captain Lowell of Company D, where he fell mortally wounded, a short distance from the Mummasburgh road, and near the stone-wall. Although conscious, he was speechless. He was carried to a vacant room in the seminary, on the first floor. Before Bradford could find a surgeon, he, with others, was marched to the rear some two miles. Corporal Bradford adds, that when he found Captain Lowell he had been robbed of all valuables, and the absence of papers, and a small diary torn up and scattered, made it impossible for strangers to identify the body, hence his burial place is unknown. While in the slough of despond, and trying to assist as skirmishers in the front line, Major Leavitt joined the regiment, and assumed command at ten o'clock P.M. The heavy rain could not put out our enthusiasm, or dampen our joy at his coming. While lying here, Sergeant Morrill, of Company A, was mortally wounded in the breast, by a sharp-shooter. Among the incidents of the battle, is one written by Adjutant Small for the *Richmond Enquirer,* brought out by the following letter published in the *Petersburgh Appeal:* —

Mr. Editor: — Please send me the paper for another year. I don't know how I could do without seeing a paper every day. It may be an old woman's fancy, but somehow I am not yet hopeless that I shall yet hear something to cheer my last days. My bright, manly boy, William, left in '61 to join the Confederate Army. He was then seventeen — my only boy — and from then till the battle of Gettysburgh, I saw him twice, and heard from him often. In that dreadful battle he was left wounded on the battle-field. His fate I know not, but I read the papers every day, hoping that I may gain some tidings of him. I hope on, and still hope that he may be alive. The shadows are growing longer, and the dark river is rolling nearer and nearer to me; but beyond the light grows brighter and brighter. William may be there. I am waiting for my Master's call.

Yours, etc.

I have just been reading the sad story of bereavement, and it brings vividly before me the battle of Gettysburgh and its attendant incidents. This sadly patient mother tells her story and brings to mind, distinctly, a spot in the grove at the left of Cemetery Hill, nearly in front of General Meade's headquarters, where were lying a number of wounded, in grey suits, fallen in the last brave charge on the 3d of July. Sadly I made my way among the dead and dying, proffering such assistance as sympathy dictated. One poor fellow, about twenty-five years of age, was shot through the body. His wants were few — " Only a drink of water. I am so cold — so cold! Won't you cover me up?" And then his mind wandered, murmuring something about " Dear mother. So glad 't is all over." Then a clear sense of his condition, and would I write to his father and tell him how he died; how he loved them at home? "Tell them all about it, won't you? Father's name is Robert Jenkins. I belong to the Seventh North Carolina troops — came from Chatham County. My name is Will ——," and tearfully I covered his face. Perhaps he was this mother's boy; perhaps not, but he was some mother's darling.

1863 A little further on my attention was attracted toward a young man, of Kemper's brigade, I think. Kneeling down by his side, I looked at his strikingly handsome face some few moments, when he unclosed his eyes and looked steadily into mine with such a questioning, hungry look, an appeal so beseeching, so eloquent, and I had not the power to answer — could only ask where he was wounded. "Don't talk to me, please," he said. A moment after he touched his breast, and I saw there was but a chance for him. Asking if he was afraid to die, he replied, "No; I am glad I am through. Oh! I hope this will end the war; will it?" I asked him if he was a Christian, and I think he told me he was not a professor, "but tried to be good," when a spasm of pain closed his eyes. I could not bear to leave him, and, putting my face close down to his, he suddenly opened his eyes. I shall never forget their unearthly beauty, and the sweet, trusting expression which overspread his whole face, as he said to me, with a motion as though he would throw his arms around my neck, "I am going home — good by!" I did weep; I could n't help it. I do not recollect his name; he might not have told me. I only remember that boys from the Sixteenth Maine carried him to the field hospital because they wanted to, although they, too, saw it was nearly over.

It may seem out of place, in the history of a regiment, to treat of matters outside its own guard, yet a little skirmishing through the division and corps lines may be allowable, where it seems necessary to confirm facts which concern and interest the regiment as a part of the army.

The First Army Corps, although absorbed by the Fifth, preserves its identity in the hearts of veterans, and is today as much a fact, a reality, as when in line of battle, or performing one of its masterly feats of marching, which won for it the title of "Lightning Corps." General Newton, in an eloquent farewell address, said of the First Corps, "In relinquishing command, I take occasion to express the pride and pleasure I have experienced in my connection with you, and my profound regret at our separation. Identified by its services with the history of the war, the First Corps gave at Gettysburgh a crowning proof of valor and endurance in saving from the grasp of the enemy the strong position upon which the battle was fought. The terrible losses suffered by the corps in that conflict attest its supreme devotion to the country. Though the corps has lost its distinctive name by the present changes, history will not be silent upon the magnitude of its services."

Its participation in the battle of Gettysburgh is always referred to with pardonable pride by the rank and file, and any detraction, directly or indirectly, from its record, or from the merits of its eminent commander, is promptly resented. Every member of the First Corps considers it a personal matter whenever the memory of the gallant Reynolds is called up by the cool assumption of Howard. His voice is silent, but thousands consider it an honor and a duty to speak for him. History is unmistakable in its verdict, which cannot be *anticipated* by any "act of Congress," or revised by the newspaper staff of any commander. It is written that as early as the 29th of June General Pleasanton directed General Buford to "occupy Gettysburgh" the 30th, and hold it until the Army of the Potomac came to his relief. He fully realized the importance of the position. It is also an established fact that it was Reynolds' determination to "advance rapidly and hold Gettysburgh." His home was in Pennsylvania, and both State and personal pride were aroused to spur him on to a victory for the national forces. The lion in his nature was thoroughly awakened, and, putting the First Corps in rapid motion, "he directed the Eleventh, Howard's, to hasten to the support of the First."

The battle was opened at nine A.M., by Buford's cavalry. Ten o'clock saw Cutler's brigade, of Wadsworth's division, followed by Meredith's, filing into the field south of the seminary, from the Emmitsburg road. An hour later the remainder of the corps came up, followed by the Fifth Maine and other batteries. Robinson's division, composed of Paul's and Coulter's brigades, halted in front of the seminary. Meanwhile "Reynolds, from his position in the belfry, saw at once the military advantage of Cemetery Ridge," and directed Howard's aide, who had reported to him for instructions, to "bring his corps forward, and form them on Cemetery Hill, as a reserve." This order was given in the presence of Rosengarten, of Reynolds' staff, who states positively as to its promulgation. General Howard's memory is conveniently defective, as it would otherwise conflict

with his claim to the championship of Gettysburgh.
The First Corps will never forgive the astounding
news, sent by Howard's special messenger to General
Meade, that the First Corps fled from the enemy at
the first contact. Two regiments of Cutler's brigade, overpowered by a division of rebel troops,
retreated a short distance in obedience to orders.
Howard, losing his usually calm balance, saw the
whole corps fleeing to the rear (like the Eleventh in
the wilderness) when only one division had reached
the field. Afterward, learning of Reynolds' death,
he assumed command by virtue of his rank, and
then, forced to notice that the First Corps was fighting three to one, ordered up the Eleventh, which
hove in sight at quarter of one. In informing
Meade that Reynolds was killed, he omitted to can-
cel, or modify the message sent earlier in the day.
There was a feeling of satisfaction throughout the
corps, on the immediate supersedure of Howard by
Hancock, which was intensified on learning of the
unjust dispatch. When the Eleventh Corps reached
the field, hardly a field officer had escaped, and nearly
half of the First Corps lay dead and wounded. In
view of the uncontrovertible facts that General
Pleasanton, August 29th, saw the importance of
Gettysburgh; that the profound sagacity and generalship of Reynolds made it possible for the Union
Army to win a victory on the Heights; that he
ordered Howard, who was four miles in the rear, to
hasten forward and form on Cemetery Ridge; that
Hancock saw the advantages of the position, and at
his suggestion (which any soldier of intelligence

1863 would have made) Meade concentrated the army there; is it a wonder that the First Corps resent Howard's assumption? or that students of history reverse the premature verdict of a Congress made in a moment of elation, and recognize Reynolds as the conspicuous figure in the first day's fight, and the grand central character of the greatest battle of the war?

July 5. Lee retreated last night, leaving his dead and many of his wounded on the field. The regiment was relieved from picket at ten minutes of one P.M., marched to the left and rear about one mile, and bivouacked for the night. Lieutenant Lord, of Company K, who had escaped from the rebels, and Lieutenant Plummer, of Company D, who had partially recovered from the stunning effects of a shell, reported for duty.

July 6. Lieutenant Plummer, Company E, rejoined the regiment, and reported Lieutenant Aubrey Leavitt wounded in both thighs. Ordered to move at five o'clock A.M. Marched at seven, and camped near Emmitsburg. Distance, eight miles.

July 7. Broke camp at half-past three A.M. Marched through Emmitsburg, Mechanicstown, by the Catoctin Iron Works, over the Catoctin Range, and camped on its western slope, four miles north of Middletown, Maryland. Length of march, twenty-five miles.

July 8. Reveille at daybreak. Broke camp in a heavy rain. Marched through Middletown, and halted at eleven A.M., one mile west of village. Marched again at four P.M., and bivouacked for the night, in line of battle, on western slope of South Mountain. Threw up breast-works of stone. Length of march, ten miles.

Remained in line. Heard firing near Boonsborough. *July 9.*

Marched at five o'clock A.M. Passed through Boonsborough, and halted three miles north of the town, near Beaver Creek. Threw up breast-works in line due north and south. Changed direction about eighty rods south, and built breast-works at right angles with the first line. Distance marched, seven miles. *July 10.*

Remained in line near Beaver Creek until three o'clock P.M., when the regiment went on picket. *July 11.*

Relieved from picket at ten A.M. Moved through Funkstown, and formed line of battle on the north side of Antietam Creek, facing Hagerstown at four P.M. Remained in line about two hours, when the regiment changed direction to the front by the left flank, and faced Williamsport. Again moved thirty rods and built breast-works. Regiment on the left of division and joined the Fourth Maryland. Hon. Henry Wilson at brigade headquarters. Shoes were issued. They were much needed, some of the men having marched barefoot for the past week. Length of march six miles. *July 12.*

Regiment in line. There was some skirmishing by the pickets, about one hundred rods in our front. The rebels had a small gun stationed about half a mile distant, which made some noise but did no damage, and was soon withdrawn. The men were *July 13.*

1863

1863 impatient to advance and freely discussed the unaccountable delay.

July 14. The regiment was in readiness to move at five A.M., but did not leave the works until one P.M., when it moved leisurely toward Williamsport, some three miles, and halted to learn that the rear of the rebel army crossed the Potomac at ten A.M. Camped one mile east of Williamsport.

CHAPTER IX.

ON THE MARCH.

1863

FORMED in line at half-past five A.M., and marched toward Sharpsburgh. Passed through Smoketown, over the Antietam battle-field, across the stone bridge, through Keedysville, Rhorersville, and camped at the base of the Catoctin Mountains, on the west side near Crampton's Gap, which is filled with sad memories of war — the unmarked mounds of the heroic dead. An old stone breast-work is a silent witness of the numerous struggles for the possession of this gateway of the valley. The regiment moved just west of Birkettsville, and camped near Berlin. Distance marched eight miles. *July 15*

Rested in camp. Since June 30th, the company commanders have made their morning reports to the adjutant in person, who consolidated them and regularly forwarded to brigade assistant adjutant-general. This forenoon blanks were furnished, and the clerical machinery was again running in the regular channel, in accordance with regulations. Captain Marston, of Company C, Lieutenant Plummer, Company D, and Hospital Steward Eaton, were sent to the general hospital at Frederick, Maryland, sick. *July 17.*

1863
July 18.   Marched at six o'clock A.M. Crossed the Potomac on pontoons at Berlin. Passed east of Lovettsville, and bivouacked near Waterford, Virginia. Length of march, ten miles.

July 19.   Reveille at five A.M. Marched at six, through Waterford, past Harmony Church, through Hamilton, and camped half a mile west of village. Length of march, six miles. The regiment was now so small, that we all hailed with pleasure the following order: —

                HEADQUARTERS 1ST A. C., July 21, 1863.
Special Order No. 167.

The following named officers and enlisted men will, under circular of July 3, 1863, W. D. A. G. O., proceed to rendezvous in their respective States, and nearest to where their regiment was enrolled, for the purpose of conducting to their commands, the drafted men to fill them up. . . . .

        Captain John D. Conley, 16th Me.
        Lieutenant A. R. Small,   "
        Sergeant W. H. Chapman,   "
        Sergeant Jones Whitman,   "
        Private J. Donnell,   "
        Private George Peabody,   "

        . . . .

        By command of MAJ.-GEN. NEWTON.
        E. C. BEARD, *Capt. & A. A. G.*

July 20.   At seven A.M. took up line of march for Middleburgh, and tramped fifteen miles to advance ten. Moseby's guerrillas left this notably sesesh town as the head of the corps entered, taking with them the corps quartermaster and two officers, who had ridden in advance of the column. Went into camp just outside the village limits at half-past five P.M.

1863
July 21.

Rested. Sent out a large picket, which captured some bushwhackers. They were numerous and daring. Some of our venturesome men were captured by them in the afternoon. In company with Lieutenant Mathews of the brigade staff, I rode into the village to make some "necessary purchases." Scarcely a building that was not shuttered and barred, and no visible sign of life except on the corner of a street, where lounged a single contraband.

July 22.
July 23.

Broke camp at seven P.M., and marched slowly in rear of trains until eleven o'clock. At twelve o'clock, midnight, continued the march until four A.M., July 23d, and halted at White Plains. Distance, ten miles. Left White Plains at seven A.M., and passing between Besant and Pignut mountains, reached Warrenton at five P.M., and bivouacked southwest of town. Length of march, fifteen miles. Since we struck the Loudoun Valley, good water has been abundant.

July 24.

Rested in camp. A portion of the regiment was detailed to build breast-works. Another detachment went on picket. Sent company histories to the ordnance office, Washington.

July 25.

Reveille at half-past six A.M. Marched at seven. The weather was extremely hot. A member of Company E was sun-struck. Arrived at Warrenton Junction at twelve o'clock M. Lieutenant-Colonel Farnham rejoined the regiment from sick leave, and assumed command. At eight P.M. fell in and marched to Bealeton Station in a heavy thunderstorm. Length of march, fifteen miles.

1863
July 26. The detail, under special order number one hundred and sixty-seven, July 21st, left camp for Maine. Lieutenant Broughton, Company D, detailed as acting adjutant. Broke camp at midnight and marched about three miles to Rappahannock Station. Halted at four A.M., and formed line of battle near the bridge. Remained in line all day. At night pitched tents behind the hill. Our forces threw up a line of works along the bank of the river, facing the rebels, who are intrenched on the opposite bank, and remained until the arrival of pontoons, the bridge having been burned.

July 30. One of our men swam half-way across the river, and met a rebel with whom he exchanged papers. The pickets ceased firing and watched, with evident interest, this interchange of courtesies.

Aug. 1. At half-past two the regiment broke camp, and moved into the breast-works at the end of the old bridge. Our cavalry crossed in boats at six A.M., and drove the rebels from their position. At two o'clock the infantry crossed on pontoons, and advanced in column by battalion, with the Thirteenth Massachusetts deployed in front. Moved past the Paine House, halted, and formed line. Threw up breastworks.

Aug. 3. The men pitched their tents, and would have been comparatively happy but for the intense heat.

Aug. 4. Major Leavitt, officer of the picket. Lieutenant Davis, Company K, with twenty-two men, detailed for picket. Colonel Davis, Thirty-ninth Massachusetts, in command of brigade.

Paymaster present. We crossed the Rappahannock, and camped on the eastern bank, about one hundred rods above the railroad bridge. 1863
Aug. 8.

Sunday, August 9th, was fully appreciated as the first day of general rest the regiment had had since June 12th. Aug. 9.

Mrs. Fogg, one of the brave and self-sacrificing women of the war, visited our camp today, and added to her former popularity among the men, by distributing a liberal supply of delicacies to the sick, towels and shirts to the needy, and kind and cheering words to all. Aug. 10.

Camp duties were resumed, and the usual propensity for foraging indulged in by those who are constitutionally uneasy when they suspect there is a stray hen within a day's march. Company and regimental drills. Aug. 12.

Major Leavitt detailed on corps court-martial. Aug. 14.

Sergeant Charles C. Small was today drowned in the river while bathing. His body was recovered by divers. He was interred with military honors. The band played a dirge for the first time over the remains of one of its members, a promising young man of good habits and sterling worth. The shock of his death was felt more keenly than would have been the loss of a dozen men in battle. Aug. 16.

Major Leavitt made a visit to the famous White Sulphur Springs, a few miles distant. He reports that the Goddess of Liberty, who once so proudly occupied a niche in a marble facade, has *lost her head*, which fact, Belcher says, accounts for our presence in Virginia. Aug. 19.

1863 Aug. 20.	Robert Funston, our new purveyor, arrived in camp today. A council of administration fixed a scale of prices for his wares.
Aug. 23.	Received one hundred and sixty-eight conscripts and substitutes, and receipted for them to Lieutenant-Colonel Rider, Thirty-third Massachusetts.
Aug. 24.	Moved camp to the left of brigade.
Aug. 25.	The recruits were examined by the surgeon, and five were rejected.
Aug. 28.	There was a brilliant assemblage at General Crawford's headquarters to witness the presentation of a superb sword to General Meade. Governor Curtin, Generals Heintzelman, Pleasanton, French, and Meiggs, and the President's son, were present. The surroundings of the camp were tropical, and beautiful to the eye beyond description — almost oriental in display. The pillars of the stately arches were tastefully festooned with evergreens, wild flowers, flags, and guidons, in all their bewildering variety of emblems and colors. The streets were enchanting, the officers gorgeous in brilliant uniforms and decorations; the national colors floated from the roofs of rebel houses, and numerous bands enlivened an occasion that must have been exquisite torture to the five deserters, sentenced to be shot on the morrow. While the delicious sensations of a rare gala day were traveling down the backs of men, while the officers hung up their swords in a dreamy maze, and just as men were forgetting where they were, orderlies rode down those same streets, and scattered throughout the corps compulsory orders for every command to be present and witness the execution.

Received muskets for our recruits.   1863 Aug. 30.

Regiment mustered for pay by Lieutenant-Colonel Farnham.   Aug. 31.

Sergeant J. S. Stevens, with a squad of Company H convalescents, rejoined his company.   Sept. 2.

Lieutenant S. H. Plummer, of Company D, reported for duty.   Sept. 3.

Three men deserted from Company E.   Sept. 6.

Regiment paid for four months' service, by Major Burt.   Sept. 11.

Received orders to be in readiness to march at a moment's notice.   Sept. 12.

"General" at five A.M. Marched at eight. Crossed the Rappahannock, and moved past Brandy Station, just west of Stevensburgh. Took the road leading from Culpeper to Stevensburgh, and went into camp near Pony Mountain, at four o'clock P.M. Cannonading heard in the direction of Raccoon Ford. Length of day's march, twelve miles.   Sept. 16.

Camp duties resumed. While encamped here, a sergeant of Company K, and a friend of his, of the Ninety-fourth New York, happened to be in a negro shanty, conversing with the wench in charge, when an orderly, attached to General Robinson's headquarters, came in with a large and choice roast of beef, which he gave to the negress, with the remark, "General Robinson desires you to have this nicely roasted by two o'clock this afternoon." With many courtesies, the wench replied, "I'll done gone cook it right up, massa," and the orderly departed with his saber dangling at his heels. The sergeant and his companion listened to the conversation with   Sept. 17.

1863 much interest, and immediately left the shanty for camp. "What a bully joke it would be on the general, if we should steal that roast," said the sergeant. The other laughed, and swore he would have it for a late dinner, or burst in the attempt. So, after reaching camp, he borrowed his lieutenant's saber, with the avowed intention of cleaning it, but he buckled it on, and, about half-past one, strode into the wench's presence, and demanded, "Is General Robinson's beef done?" "Lor' bress you, massa, I 'se just hooked it out de oben; here 't is," and she presented to the delighted soldier a beautiful loin of beef, cooked to a turn. His mouth watered, but having no time to lose, he gave her a twenty-five cent scrip, thanked her in the general's name, and left the house in quick time. Soon after, the real orderly came into the shanty, and demanded, as his counterfeit had done, "Is the general's beef done?" The negress looked at him in astonishment, and doubtless thinking him an impostor, gruffly replied, "Course its done cooked, an' de gineral's man come an' got it half hour ago, an' carried it away wid him." "The devil he did!" said the surprised orderly. "I 'm the 'gineral's man,' and if any one has stole that beef you 'll get hell." "I tells ye de gineral's man hissef come an' took it, an' dat 's all I knows." And this explanation was all she would condescend to make. The orderly was obliged to retire, and report the loss to the general, who immediately remarked, "O, the Sixteenth Maine."

Sept. 23. Division drill by General Robinson.

Sept. 24. Packed up and marched four miles to Raccoon Ford, and went into camp at four o'clock P.M.

Today the colonel's colored man, Ben, on "Lady Washington," and Chenery, on the major's "Winged Pegasus," had a hurdle race. The latter won, best two in three heats. _{1863 Sept.25.}

Broke camp at quarter past one P.M. and marched at half-past two. Camped at four o'clock, two miles north of the ford. _{Sept.27.}

Our regiment bivouacked one night in September, 1863, near an old mansion which stood a short distance south of Brandy Station on the Orange and Alexandria Railroad, and which General Robinson, Commanding Division, had chosen as his headquarters for the night. As usual the mansion was nearly surrounded by negro shanties, some of which Sergeant Dunbar, of Company K, concluded had been used for smoking ham and bacon; at least his suspicions were so strong that the building contained these two commodities that, accompanied by a comrade, he resolved upon a critical examination so soon as it became dark enough to pursue his investigations without fear of interruption by the headquarters guard, who occupied the veranda of the mansion and only a rod or two away. As soon as it became dark, therefore, Dunbar and his comrade slowly approached the suspicious shanty, and after smelling around to "make assurance doubly sure" that they were right in their conjectures, they commenced operations by cutting an aperture through the logs and in a comparatively short time it was large enough to admit Dunbar to the interior. Just at this moment a stranger put in an appearance from around the corner of the building, and upon being roughly seized, announced himself as the "Kernal's

1863 nigger, don't ye know me?" and being recognized was released and invited inside by the sergeant. The invitation was at once accepted, when he was told to feel around overhead until he found a pole, then to mount it and pass down the bacon and hams. The darky followed the instructions to the letter and all hands were soon busy at work "confiscating the subsistence." Dunbar passed the smoked hog to the comrade outside who carried it on a run to his shelter tent, covered it with blankets and returned for more. In this way a large quantity was collected in a short time, but in an unlucky moment, the darky dropped a ham which struck a box in its descent, thereby causing a thundering noise and arousing the guards. Dunbar jumped to the opening and easily escaped, but the unfortunate darky leaped from his perch on high and landed in a barrel of soft soap! He floundered around in the barrel several moments before he could extract himself from the slippery stuff, muttering to himself in the meantime, "Oh, de Lor! Oh, de good Lor!" which the guards, endeavoring to open the door in front, could plainly hear. When they finally succeeded in opening the door they found the bird had flown. The matter was duly reported to General Robinson in the morning by the planter, who was exceedingly indignant at his loss, and Lieutenant-Colonel Farnham, of our regiment, who happened to be field officer of the day, was ordered to trace up and punish the offenders. This was not hard to do, for the darky had left a trail of soft soap behind him in the grass which led the surprised officer to

10

his own quarters, where he found his servant *sick* 1863
and lying covered in blankets. Just what Colonel
Farnham reported to the general is unknown, but he
probably had ham for breakfast and "Jack" got a
reprimand.

Major Leavitt, division officer of the day. While Sept. 28.
encamped here Colonel Farnham and the Major
called upon Colonel Stringfellow of Kansas noto-
riety, who is true to his convictions and an ardent
rebel. Mrs. Stringfellow is an accomplished conver-
sationalist, a regular apostle of garrulity. In fact
she did most of the talking. Moved camp one mile
northwest.

Regiment had "dress parade" in the woods. Sept. 30.

Captain Belcher rejoined the regiment from fur- Oct. 2.
lough and reported for duty. The regiment with
division ordered out to see a deserter shot.

Major Leavitt, officer of the picket. At two Oct. 4.
o'clock moved camp from woods to the open field.

Captured a rebel on the picket line. Oct. 5.

Three hundred and thirty-eight conscripts joined Oct. 6.
the regiment.

Six conscripts received. Chaplain Bullen tend- Oct. 7.
ered his resignation, which was accepted and forwarded for approval.

The division camp is known as "Camp Nordquist." Oct. 8.
The lieutenant-colonel today had an experience with
one of the conscripts who declared himself a "Second Adventist" and a non-combatant, and refused to
do duty or obey any orders except to eat. He was
tied to a tree to learn by suffering that he was
human like his comrades, and must not hide his cow-

1863 ardly instincts behind a pretence. This man was of good physical and mental structure, and would have developed into a good soldier but for his shameless position. Men who willingly carried fifty pounds on long marches, stood guard in storms of sleet and rain, faced worse storms of shot and shell, had no patience with any man's conscientious scruples when they conflicted with one's duty to country and comrades. They called it a cowardly pretence, and no one was disposed to dispute the charge.

Oct. 9. Lieutenant Aubrey Leavitt rejoined his company. In the afternoon regiment changed position to the right of brigade. In the evening orders were received to be in readiness to move at short notice. It was reported that the enemy had left our front.

Oct. 10. Lieutenant E. F. Davies with fifty men detailed to guard division train. Broke camp at half-past one A.M. and marched rapidly to near Germania Ford, and halted at half-past ten. Marched again at eight o'clock, and bivouacked near Stevensburgh about midnight. Length of march, twelve miles. Company H detached and ordered to follow Fourth United States Battery.

Oct. 11. Regiment in line at three o'clock A.M. Marched at ten, through Stevensburgh to Kelly's Ford and crossed in three feet of water, at five P.M. The rebels were within a mile of our rear. Bivouacked. Length of march, ten miles.

Oct. 12. Rations issued to the division.

Oct. 13. Struck tents at half-past one A.M. Marched at two, and halted at Warrenton Junction at ten o'clock some four hours, for the trains to pass. Continued

the march and bivouacked at Broad Run at half-past 1863
eight. Length of march, thirty miles. The new
men stood the rapid marching remarkably well and
adapted themselves to their surroundings like veterans, and used less than their proportion of cusswords.

Left Broad Run at seven A.M. and marched past Oct. 14.
Manassas Junction, and crossed Bull Run at Blackburn's Ford. Arrived at Centerville at half-past
one and bivouacked. Marched fourteen miles. The
Second Division was sent on a reconnoissance at five
P.M. Major Leavitt went on picket with Thirtyninth Massachusetts.

Detachment from Company H, in charge of Sergeant Stevens, sent to picket "Salisbury Place." Oct. 16.
Regiment remained in line of battle along Cub Run.
The day has been rainy and the recruits suffered for
want of rubber blankets and overcoats. Lieutenant
Davis detailed for picket.

Still in line of battle and constantly on the alert. Oct. 17.
The men have not taken off their equipments since
the thirteenth.

Took up line of march at eight A.M., toward Oct. 19.
Thoroughfare Gap. Passed Gainesville, and bivouacked at Haymarket at five P.M. We had hardly
thrown off our equipments, when the booming of
guns in our front put us under arms. The rebels in
driving back our cavalry, came unexpectedly upon
our infantry lines and were repulsed. Today's
march, ten miles.

The regiment took arms at an early hour, and Oct. 20.
remained in line until four P.M., when it marched

1863 slowly through the gap. At nine P.M. bivouacked on a hill near the west end of the gap. Length of march, five miles.

Oct. 21. This morning moved to a better position and pitched tents. The headquarters' team came up, and the field and staff had tents for the first time for twelve days.

Oct. 22. Resumed camp duties and the usual drills.

Oct. 24. At half-past four A.M., the regiment received orders to have everything packed at five o'clock. At nine returned through the gap in a drizzling rain. The Sixteenth was detailed to protect the rear of the artillery. Moved through Haymarket and Gainesville. Forded Broad Run and bivouacked near Bristow Station, on the battle-field of 14th instant. Length of march, twelve miles.

Oct. 25. The sick call shows quite an increase in the list, consequent upon fording the runs, and exposure to rains, during the late marches. The Thirty-ninth Massachusetts and Ninety-fourth New York, ordered to Kettle Run last night. Nine exchanged prisoners returned to regiment.

Oct. 26. Camp duties and drills resumed. Regiment inspected by Captain Livermore, acting assistant adjutant-general, First Brigade. Three exchanged prisoners report for duty.

Oct. 29. Lieutenant-Colonel Farnham, division officer of the day.

Oct. 30. Major Leavitt, field officer of the picket. Regiment moved to Kettle Run.

Nov. 3. Brigade drill in the afternoon. Sutler arrived with goods in the evening.

CHAPTER X.

MINE RUN CAMPAIGN.

LIEUTENANT-COLONEL Bankhead, corps inspector, came to inspect and condemn some government property, when the regiment was ordered to pack up. Marched at four P.M., and halted at Catlett's Station at nine o'clock. Distance, six miles. Clothing, blankets, etc., were issued to the regiment. 1863
Nov. 5.

The command was alarmed by the cavalry discharging their carbines. During the day moved to a good camping ground. Companies E and F lost some property by fire. "No insurance." Nov. 6.

Reveille at six A.M. Marched at seven. Passed Catlett's Station, Warrenton Junction, Elkton, and Morgantown, and went into camp near Morrisville. Length of march, twelve miles. Fight at Kelly's Ford, and at Rappahannock Station. The Sixteenth not called into action. The Sixth Maine made one of the most brilliant and successful charges of the campaign. Nov. 7.

The regiment marched at seven A.M. Passed Holly Church, and crossed the river at Kelly's Ford, on pontoons. Moved up the river to near Rappahannock Station, and followed the railroad to Brandy Station, and camped, having marched ten miles. Nov. 8.

SIXTEENTH MAINE REGIMENT. 151

1863
Nov. 9. At ten minutes past five, took the road to Bealeton, thence northwest to Liberty, where we halted at midnight in a blinding snow-squall.

Nov. 10. In the morning moved to a good position and pitched tents. Sergeants Wilmot H. Chapman, Company K, Jones Whitman, Company E, and privates J. Donnells and George Peabody, rejoined the regiment from recruiting service. They brought two stands of colors, one from the State, and the other a present from the Merchants' Exchange, of Portland.

Nov. 11. Captain Conley and Adjutant Small returned from detached service, and reported for duty.

Nov. 12. After battalion drill, two officers and one hundred and fifty men were detailed to repair the Orange and Alexandria Railroad.

Nov. 15. Our artillery can be heard in the direction of Cedar Mountain. Orders received to pack up and wait.

Nov. 18. Regiment inspected by Captain Livermore, and afterward paid by Major Russell Erritt.

Nov. 20. Battalion drill in the afternoon. Aggregate strength of command, six hundred and fifty men.

Nov. 21. Today, about noon, a dragoon, with pistols in hand, and bareheaded, came dashing into camp, shouting, "The guerrillas are coming! The guerrillas are coming!" Colonel Batchelder, Thirteenth Massachusetts, division officer of the day, shouted, "Turn out! Turn out the regiment!" In five minutes the men were under arms, in line, and on their way double-quick. Major Leavitt was in command of Companies C and H, which were deployed as skirmishers. Moving half a mile, we reached a wagon-train which Mosby had swooped down upon. He captured the escort, detached the mules, set fire to the train, and rode away just as the Sixteenth came upon the ground and gave them a parting yell. Just as we were retiring, the Third New York Cavalry, mistaking us for rebels, charged upon Companies B and D, wounding two men before they discovered their error.

Nov. 23. The regiment broke camp at daylight, and marched at seven, and halted at Bealeton Station until the division was massed, when it rejoined the brigade and marched to Rappahannock Station, and camped southeast of bridge at eleven A.M., when ammunition and rations were issued to the brigade.

Nov. 24. Drizzling rain-storm. Major Leavitt examined applicants for promotion, under an order of Colonel Farnham that every man recommended must be qualified for the position sought.

Nov. 26. Colonel Leonard commanding the brigade, read a congratulatory order on the success of General Grant on the Mississippi. Took up line of march, and crossed the Rapidan at Gold Mine Ford, and bivouacked. Length of march, eighteen miles.

Nov. 27. The advance began at daylight. The regiment, being detailed to guard the wagon train, moved slowly through Culpeper Gold Mines, and struck the Fredericksburgh plank road, about four miles north of the Wilderness. Passed the Wilderness Church and took the plank road leading to Orange Court House. Halted several hours at Parker's store, and bivouacked for the night at Robinson's

1863   tavern. Length of march, sixteen miles. During the march several wagons were decoyed from the train and destroyed by bushwhackers.

Nov. 28. At half-past five A.M. moved forward about one mile and formed line of battle. Though raining heavily, an advance was made by the First Division, which drove the rebels about two miles to a fortified position just across Mine Run. The Union batteries opened fire and developed the lines of the enemy. Rested in line until sunset, then moved into the woods and bivouacked for the night. Length of march, six miles.

Nov. 29. Rested all day in the woods. Ammunition and three days' rations issued. Having cut loose from our base, we are cautioned to husband our food, as no more will be issued before December 5th. Orders received that an attack will be made on the rebel works at three P.M. The run had been dammed by the rebels (and damned by us) and widened in our front to two hundred yards, presenting a most disagreeable prospect for a scrimmage. The enemy from their secure position hoped it would prove a Red Sea to us, and not without good reason. To say that we rejoiced to have the order for a charge countermanded, was putting it mild. Later an order was issued for a general attack at eight A.M. to-morrow, on the discharge of a signal gun from the right.

Nov. 30. To-morrow came, and from daylight every man thought he heard the signal gun. The snapping of a twig would make men jump. At five A.M. the regiment moved to the right of the First Division. Knapsacks were unslung, and we took position in

second line and waited for the signal that would ring
out the knell of many thousand soldiers. At thirty-
five minutes past seven a young officer came dashing
madly up the line. Just in the rear of our regiment
was a slough-hole which the horse failed to clear,
and with a plunge went in to his shoulders, crushing
the officer beneath him as he fell. Some of the men
released him from his perilous position. Fearfully
pale and hardly able to breathe, he managed to say,
"I am General Meade's son. Send an officer quickly
to the right and say the order to attack is countermanded. Quick! Quick!" Lieutenant Davis, I
think it was, was immediately mounted and dis-
patched to General ———. Young Meade was true
grit and insisted upon going forward with the dispatch. Being assisted to mount he put spurs to his
horse and reeling in his saddle fled along the front
and reached General ——— in season to confirm the
advance courier and stop the mouth of the black
monster that in ten seconds would have pronounced
the doom of ten thousand men and perhaps that of
the Army of the Potomac. Since the countermand,
the prospect in our front could be studied with feelings less disagreeable. The skirmishers of the two
armies were about two hundred and fifty yards apart
on either side the run, partially protected by redoubts
of rails and earth, to which our boys had added
feather-beds and cane-seat chairs, and wasted ammunition trying to shoot each other. A flock of fine
sheep had been let loose from a barn just at our left,
and were running backward and forward between the
lines, marks for the bullets of either party. The

1863 rebels could n't reach them across the run, and vigorously opposed their capture by the Yanks. Our boys, although hungry and hankering for mutton, dared not risk it until two o'clock, when a squad of Sixteenth and Twentieth Maine men made a dash and an effort to drive the lambs into our fold, but the fire from the rebels was so incessant that they retreated amid the yells of the gray-backs and the cheers of the Union troops. One of the Twentieth Maine rose from his position on the skirmish line, coolly took aim and brought down a fine lamb. He laid down his rifle, went out and brought in the animal, took off his pelt and hung it up on a pole for a target for the Johnnies, amid the cheers of the brigade and the crack of the rebel guns. "What pleases the men, major?" asked the adjutant, who noticed the collective grin of the regiment about sunset. "Why, they saw an aide give a billet to Colonel Farnham." "What of it? They don't know its purport." "O, they caught the word 'picket,' and that's enough, for somehow they know that when he is in charge of the picket line in the night, we always move."

Dec. 1. And so we did, soon after, commence a retreat toward Germania Ford, over an exceedingly rough road. Reached the ford at eleven P.M., and bivouacked.

Dec. 2. At sunrise, again on the march. Crossed the river at eight A.M., and rested several hours near the ford, then continued the march to one mile north of Stevensburgh, and bivouacked for the night. Length of march, ten miles.

Marched at eight A.M., and went into camp about one mile southwest of Kelly's Ford, and immediately prepared to build winter quarters. I can't close the record of 1863 without special reference to the most abject, patient, long-suffering of God's creatures, — the army mule. He took no account of the oath and lash of the driver, but through the deep mud, often to his body, over rocks, stumps, and side hills, through ditches, brooks, and streams, he pulled the fuel of the campaign in the shape of salt pork and hard-tack. He literally went through fire and water, and submitted to the most inhuman and reckless treatment at the hands of brutal drivers, as if abuse was a condiment of army life, strictly in accordance with the regulations. We had one whole-souled fellow in particular, who duly appreciated this most useful animal. The only time we ever saw him thoroughly angry was at a creek ford, when a half savage driver was mauling a leader with a fence rail. There is no language in the army dictionary that will do credit to "Gideon's" voluntary literary effort in photographing a human jackass. When Ruskin said, "There is in every animal's eye a dim image and gleam of humanity, a flash of strange light, through which their life looks up to our great mystery of command over them, and claims the fellowship of the creature, if not of the soul," he possibly included the mule collectively, but this particular "critter" ignored it when his harness fell off, and he demonstrated an old theory without any "mystery," and photographed a "dim image" of his two hind feet on the body of that other brute, who, in

1863
Dec. 3.

1863 the "flash of a strange light," saw the "gleam" of a rapidly-moving mule who was ashamed of the kin. The average veteran has a green place in his memory sacred to the army mule, for, without him, many campaigns would have ended in defeat for want of sustenance. But for him many disasters would have been laid at the door of Providence, the convenient scapegoat for the result of jealousy, inefficiency, and too much spirit of a wrong distillation.

Dec. 4. The location for winter quarters was well chosen. The soil was sandy and easily drained, wood was plenty, springs of excellent water near at hand, and the rebel barracks of good lumber were still standing a short distance away. It was rare sport to see the men of the brigade race for a claim on a particular house. The first arrival established his title, and no one disputed it. There was an honor, a generosity among soldiers that is not shown anywhere else. In the space of half an hour, every barrack was spotted and owned, and yet away in the rear men were toiling from the extreme right of the brigade, to reach the camp only to find there was not a board left unclaimed. Invariably the man with two or more would divide, and night saw an equal distribution as though ordered by a quartermaster. The order issued in the morning, for us to be ready to move, was cancelled half an hour later.

Dec. 5. This was a day of annoyance and surprise, through the vacillating policy of some "superior." First came an order saying, "Colonel, you will have your regiment ready to move at a moment's notice." Soon after came an orderly with the welcome intelligence that the command to move was cancelled, and he rode away. Scarcely had the echo of his horse's hoofs ceased, when out of the woods, like a jack-in-the-box, sprang orderly number three who, with the air of a corps commander, placed in the hand of Colonel Farnham an order to hold the regiment in readiness to move at an hour's notice. Heavens! had there been a time since August, 1862, when we were not "in readiness to move"? The three orders were duly entered, quietly folded, and with a piece of red tape around either end laid gently away; and the men continued to put the camp into shape. In a few days it grew into an evergreen village, well ordered and attractive. A look of contentment spread over the collective face of the regiment, and peace reigned.

Dec. 7. Major Leavitt detailed officer of the picket.

Dec. 13. Orders having been published that all business be suspended on the Sabbath, except what is positively necessary, a general quiet prevailed throughout the corps.

Dec. 17. Rained all day.

Dec. 19. Regiment inspected by Captain Livermore, and its condition pronounced highly satisfactory.

Dec. 21. Major Leavitt froze three of his fingers while on battalion drill.

Dec. 22. Lieutenant-Colonel Farnham, and Captain ——— went home on leave of absence. Major Leavitt in command. Battalion drill in the afternoon.

Dec. 23. Again ordered to be in readiness to move.

Dec. 24. The night had been very cold, and in the early frost of the morning, the brigade bugler blew a blast

1863 long enough and loud enough to awaken the dead. We had heard it often enough to know what it meant. In an incredibly short period tents were struck, and the six hundred and fifty men of the Sixteenth were in line, and reluctantly marching away from a comfortable home, to the tune of "The Girl I Left Behind Me." The cold was so intense that in less than five minutes the band instruments froze up, and in silence we fell into line with the brigade, and speculated upon our errand, or destination. Marched past Brandy Station, through Culpeper, and came upon the rebel cavalry picket, near Mitchell's Station, on the Rapidan River, who retired before our advance. Length of march, twelve miles.

Dec. 25. In bivouac in a marshy forest. Applications for furloughs have been so frequent of late, that Sergeant-Major Maxfield sent up his application, based upon Deuteronomy, twentieth chapter, seventh verse: "And what man is there that hath betrothed a wife, and hath not taken her? Let him go and return unto his house, lest he die in battle and another man take her." If it is approved, he says he shall ask for an extension, referring to Deuteronomy twenty-fourth chapter, fifth verse: "When a man hath taken a new wife, he shall not go out to war, neither shall he be charged with any business; but he shall be free at home one year, and shall cheer up his wife which he hath taken." Much to his surprise, he obtained his leave, while the applications of two officers were disapproved.

At three o'clock P.M., marched two miles and bivouacked in the mud until 30th, waiting orders. <!-- Dec. 26. 1863 -->

Officers busy making muster-rolls. <!-- Dec. 29. -->

Major Leavitt mustered Thirty-ninth Massachusetts for pay. Lieutenant-Colonel Peirson mustered the Sixteenth. The last day of the year found us in an exposed and suffering condition, on the extreme outposts of the Army of the Potomac, the main line of our army being at Culpeper, some six miles in our rear. It found our sick list largely increased. Notwithstanding the frozen, muddy, and weary condition of the regiment, when it broke from column to the rear by companies, and stacked arms preparatory to "lunch," and although past sunset, an order was issued for the regiments of the brigade to hold dress parade! The Sixteenth believed in discipline, and had a natural hankering for "orders," and doted upon the "regulations" as second only to the Old Testament, but just at this moment, when the half ration of whisky began its work, swear words were at a premium again. The adjutant had the bugler make the call, but there was no response from the band leader. The call was repeated, and yet no reply. The adjutant went up to the right, saw the trouble, and could not resist the temptation. "Mr. Shea, did you hear the call?" Mr. Shea was always a gentleman, and doffing his hat, managed to say, "Ashtant, I'm puty d-r-r-runk, hope you'll skuse me." "How is the B flat, Mr. Shea?" "Hes-bad offsiam." "How is Locke?" "'Slaid down — dreffultired." "O nonsense, Mr. Shea," said the adjutant, "there is a cold spring of water down

1863 there; send for a pailful or two, bathe your heads, and drink a quart or so, and you will be O K. Hurry up." He returned to his quarters, thinking just how it would work when the water got warm. Before he was ready for parade, the call rang out, clear and correct, as he knew it would. The band took position, and played the companies into line. Ranks were opened, when the adjutant gave the command, "Troop — Beat off!" with some misgiving. The ground seemed very uneven and full of cradle knolls to the band, and now and then the leader would lose a note, and trying to catch it, would clash into the B flat, and sandwich in between the alto and bass, and somehow the bass drum would persist in coming down heavy on the up beat, and the cymbals forgot to clang when they should, and closed with a crash when they should have been still. Countermarching, they started on quick time; but alas! the water was warm, and somehow the leader's order was misunderstood, and when half the band struck up one tune, and the other half another, it was too much! Then rang out the colonel's voice, in tones that drowned the band, "Parade is dismissed!" Well — the adjutant received a reprimand, but it was worth it. The band enjoyed it, and I think all did, from the smile which went down the line. Certainly the Sixteenth was the most jolly regiment in the brigade. They laughed so loud and so long, that the other regiments took it up, and so the good nature spread, and the adjutant was forgiven.

CHAPTER XI.

OUTPOST DUTY AT MITCHELL'S STATION.

1864
Jan. 1.

AFTER a week of cold storms, the sun rose bright on New Year's morn and shed its welcome rays on as dirty, despondent, and disgusted a brigade as could be found on duty, and yet after rollcall, when men had drunk their hot coffee and thawed out, something like good humor began to prevail. Men took an inventory of their surroundings and the distant perspective, and settled at once into the belief that the regiment was located for the winter. The shrewd ones had already made requisitions for rails, and unsightly piles covered the camp-ground, and yet no order to camp. The brigade machine began to work about nine o'clock, and at ten the regiment was ordered to change direction to the left, in line running parallel to the Orange and Alexandria Railroad a few rods distant, and go into camp. Like magic tents went up, streets were policed, the parade-ground graded, and before night the Sixteenth was again at home. Cabins of logs were ordered to be erected as rapidly as possible for the whole brigade. Regrets at being compelled to abandon our fine quarters at Kelly's Ford were all banished, and later we fully appreciated our good fortune in being on an out-post

CAMP TILDEN, MITCHELL'S STATION, VA.

1864 of great strategic importance; for in all the movements made by the army, our brigade was not once ordered out. Our position was one of peril, and realizing it, the regiment daily excelled in discipline and improved in soldierly qualities. With regular duties the health of the command improved and the winter months passed pleasantly. Assistant Surgeon Eaton received leave of absence for sixty days, and left for Maine.

Jan. 2. Frank Richardson, of Maine, joined us to-day. He was engaged by the officers at a salary of one hundred dollars per month, to reorganize and drill the band. Mr. Richardson was an accomplished musician and had a thorough knowledge of his business. Under his direction the band improved rapidly, and subsequently was pronounced the best band in the division by General Robinson, and one of the best in the corps. Doubtless some of its members will recollect (I know Frank does) the invitation to serenade the division commander, and play for a ball at Culpeper. In anticipation of a supper or treat of some kind, the boys, armed with brass, walked six miles, stood outside an hour or two playing their best, when they were invited into an entry-way where they played as long until the entertainment closed, and then a little fellow with spectacles and high-top boots, told them they could go back to camp. I won't say he forgot to thank them, but he did n't. The band was indeed an honor to us. We were better men and slept sweeter for its presence and good music. Mr. Richardson organized it as follows (as nearly as can be recalled): Frank Rich-

ardson, Leader; John Shea, first E flat; P. Cool- 1864
broth, second E flat; Charles A. Locke, first B flat;
H. W. McKenney, second B flat; B. Johnson, first
alto; Wesley Webber, second alto; D. H. Thorpe,
first tenor; Samuel B. Geary, second tenor; Charles
H. Gould, baritone; James A. Barrows, tenor drum;
Robert C. Brann, bass drum; William A. Follett,
cymbals; Frank Jones, bass; Eben Curtis, bass.
The instruments were of the best quality, and cost
four hundred and twenty-one dollars. Of this sum
the officers gave one hundred and seventy dollars,
and the enlisted men, two hundred and fifty-one dollars. In March, 1864, the brigade commander, staff,
and line officers of other regiments in the brigade
contributed one hundred and twenty-five dollars for
the support of the Sixteenth Band.

Brigade guard mounting instituted. Jan. 3.

Heavy snow-storm. Surgeon Alexander's wife Jan. 4.
arrived in camp, with an atmosphere of "home"
about her, peculiarly pleasing to the surgeon, whose
face brightened and shone with a happiness which
spread all over the camp. The night shut in with a
heavy rain-storm.

Right wing of the regiment detailed as in-lying Jan. 5.
picket.

Captain Broughton and quartermaster rejoined Jan. 6.
the regiment. Adjutant Small detailed as adjutant
of the day.

Mail arrived. Colonel Farnham reported too sick Jan. 9.
to return.

The Ninety-fourth New York broke camp and left Jan. 11.
for Annapolis, Maryland. The Sixteenth band and
nearly all of the regiment were at the station.

1864
Jan. 13.   Four fine brass instruments, costing two hundred dollars, a gift from the officers, were received by the band.

Jan. 14.   Captain Marston left for home, on fifteen days' leave of absence.

Jan. 16.   Adjutant Small granted a leave of absence.

Jan. 17.   Lieutenant L. K. Plumer detailed as acting adjutant. Lieutenant-Colonel Farnham returned, and assumed command. Major Leavitt started for Maine on fifteen days' leave.

Feb. 11.   Adjutant Small returned. Colonel Farnham, Chaplain Balkam, and the Adjutant rode out to a Mrs. Fessenden's to see "Mose" and "Robert," old servants of Washington. Robert said he was one hundred and six years old, but not too old to forget Massa George, or sing. Blind, deaf, bald, and toothless, he sat in a cane-seat chair of the last century, facing the sun. His appearance would warrant a belief that he was five hundred years of age. "Robert, can you sing?" asked the chaplain. "O, yes, massa." "Well, sing some familiar hymn for us." Words would fail to do justice to Robert's attempt to sing. Sing! There was n't the most distant approach to anything like tune, time, or harmony. The voice was not even human; and they rode away and left him solemnly chanting the tenth verse of some darky song.

Feb. 14.   Regimental inspection. Evening prayer-meeting was held in the new chapel.

Feb. 15.   Captain Livermore inspected the regiment.

Feb. 17.   Lieutenant-Colonel Farnham issued an order forbidding the sutler bringing liquors into camp.

About two miles northwest from the Rapidan, and some three miles from camp, is Bald, or Lookout Mountain, which has been used alternately by Union and Rebel, for a signal station. The former hold it today. 1864
Feb. 20.

Chaplain Balkam delivered a touching eulogy in memory of the late Captain Lowell. Funeral of Private Dee, of Company D, at eight o'clock P.M. Feb. 21.

Regiment detailed for picket. Mail arrived. A number of F. A. M. visited "Army Lodge, No. 8," established by the Thirty-ninth Massachusetts. Some rebel deserters were brought in and sent to Culpeper. Feb. 22.

Corps reviewed by General Newton. Feb. 24.

The new chapel, of hewn logs, was completed today, and does credit to the mechanical skill of Maine men. Feb. 26.

Chapel dedicated by the chaplains of the brigade. The interior was tastefully decorated with evergreens, which were festooned, hung in crosses, anchors, and circles, upon the walls. Familiar texts of Scripture met the eye from over and around the pulpit. Feb. 27.

General U. S. Grant assumed command of the armies of the United States. Mar. 1.

Captain Belcher departed for Maine on fifteen days' leave. Mar. 5.

The Fourteenth Brooklyn Serenaders gave a complimentary concert, in our chapel, to Colonel Leonard. Mar. 8.

Regiment detailed for three days' picket duty. Mar. 9.

Rain-storm commenced, which continued ten days. Alarm on the picket line. Regiment under arms at five o'clock A.M. Mar. 10.

1864 Mar. 13.	Surgeon Alexander, accompanied by Mrs. Alexander, left camp for Maine.
Mar. 14.	Brigade drill.
Mar. 18.	The enemy reported to have crossed the river at Raccoon Ford. Regiment ordered under arms at half-past two P.M., in readiness to move, with four days' rations.
Mar. 19.	Snowing.
Mar. 20.	Paid by Major Erritt.
Mar. 22.	Very cold. Snow commenced falling at half-past two P.M., and increased to a violent storm by nine o'clock.
Mar. 23.	First Corps absorbed by the Fifth. General G. K. Warren relieves General Newton. The old brigade and division organizations are retained. The divisions are to be commanded respectively by Generals Griffin, Robinson, Crawford, and Wadsworth.
Mar. 26.	Fifth Corps reviewed by Grant, Meade, and Warren.
Mar. 28.	This was a gala day with the regiment. Every member had made his toilet long before reveille. The new men were as earnest as the old, in their efforts to give a fitting welcome to the colonel they had never seen. The forenoon was spent in adding touches of attraction here and there through the camp, such as would do credit to born artists. The band, resplendent in brass burnished like gold, assembled on the parade-ground, and played the regiment into line at two o'clock P.M. About four the train from Culpeper arrived, and directly the major and adjutant approached escorting Colonel Tilden, who was mounted on a superb black stallion. The regi-

ment presented arms, when the colonel acknowledged the salute by removing his cap. We knew not which the most to admire, his soldierly bearing and fine horsemanship, or the perfect discipline of the command. When Colonel Farnham rang out the commands, "Shoulder-arms! Order-arms! and now, boys, three times three for Charley Tilden!" the men were wild with enthusiasm and cheered to the echo, while the band played "Hail to the Chief." Parade was dismissed, guns stacked, when an informal greeting seldom seen outside the army, was given the much loved commander. Colonel Farnham, who had made generous preparation, gave a reception that evening in the chapel, to the officers. Chaplain Balkam in a letter to the *Lewiston Journal*, says of the supper, and of the evening's entertainment: —

The tables were spread with admirable taste, and in every respect well furnished, under the direction of Major Leavitt, chairman of the committee. The invited guests were the field officers of the brigade. Lieutenant-Colonel Farnham, who has omitted nothing in his power, to make the return of Colonel Tilden to his regiment, after eight months confinement in Libby Prison, a happy one, presided at the tables. He assigned to the chaplain, the duty of presenting in a few words, these festive boards to the Colonel, which his officers had prepared as some expression of their appreciation of him, and grateful sense of his return. To this address the Colonel replied briefly, thankfully accepting the honor, but declaring that he did not feel worthy of it. Talking was not his vocation, and he would only say that he hoped to show by his acts, how well he appreciated and wished to deserve their kindness. The divine blessing was then invoked and prayer offered, that while all was dark, and gloom, and storm with-

1864 out — naught but light, and calm, and happiness might reign within; for so dark, rainy, and tempestuous a night I have not known in Virginia, and seldom anywhere else. We trembled somewhat for our fly, but it stood well and we were made perfectly comfortable, though the rain poured and the wind raged. You will not think it strange that on such a night, it was difficult to find our cows, and they were late in, consequently the oysters were hurried and got a little scorched, otherwise they were perfectly delicious, and as it was, I think I never ate any that relished so well. Possibly some of our company, who had recently come from home, could not say so much. I noticed that my friend Captain Belcher, who had just returned from "a leave," had not entirely recovered from daintiness contracted at home. We had tea and coffee with genuine milk, though it must be confessed that Virginia milk is very poor; the cows get no hay and but little of anything else. Virginia turkeys well roasted, ham, tongue, pie, cake, apples, oranges, nuts, etc., etc., all this was excellent, though I believe in this instance they all came from Washington. In short it was a Washington supper transported to poor Mitchell's Station. When all had well eaten and drunken, of things permissible, came a batch of regular toasts from Adjutant Small, who acquitted himself on this occasion, as he always does, with distinguished credit. I can attempt to give you but very few of the toasts, regular or volunteer. The eloquence and wit which followed them, I must leave almost entirely to the imagination of your readers to supply. "Our colonel. He has been tried by the camp and the march, by battle and by prison. We are made happy to-night in welcoming his return, by daring escape from the toils of a dreary captivity, and know not which the more to approve, the nobleness of his manhood, or the superiority of his soldierly qualities; his country has need of both; may nothing but a just and glorious peace ever again deprive her of his services. Lieutenant-Colonel Farnham: the worthy representative of his superior. His happiness at the return of his commanding officer is only paralled by his earnestness and undivided efforts to maintain the reputation of the Sixteenth Maine, during his absence. Officers of the Sixteenth Maine who are not with us tonight: with some of them we shall be associated no more on earth; they are absent but not forgotten."

This toast was responded to in an excellent speech by Dr. Alexander. To a toast alluding to the tunnel through which our prisoners escaped, Dr. Whitney, brigade surgeon, — who took lodgings for a considerable time at Libby, — replied in an admirable speech. The Doctor found it so good to get out, that he was almost tempted to go in again, for the pleasure of coming out. Colonel McCoy replied in a speech that brought down the house, to a toast complimentary of the One Hundred and Seventh Pennsylvania. Colonel Davis, whose encampment is a paragon of neatness and comfort, replied in his calm and witty way to a toast complimentary of the Thirty-ninth Massachusetts. In the absence of Colonel Leonard, of the Thirteenth Massachusetts, commanding brigade, Captain Porter, assistant adjutant-general, was called up, and detailed Lieutenant Pradlee to make a speech, which he did greatly to the amusement of all. At about eleven o'clock the company broke up. Two or three hours had been well enjoyed, and most of us emerged into the pitch dark and rain of the night, to find our camps, and thankful, I trust, that they were still dry and comfortable. The occasion was a happy one, marked by good feeling and sobriety.

Tuesday forenoon, at nine o'clock, some four or five hundred men from the different regiments in the brigade assembled near regimental headquarters. Soon after, the battalion, in command of Sergeant-Major Stevens, led by the band, doubled on the center in front of the colonel's tent. Colonel Tilden made his appearance, and accepted as a gift from the enlisted men, the beautiful horse ridden by him yesterday, together with a complete set of equip-

1864 ments. The presentation was made by Sergeant-Major Stevens, in a feeling address. Colonel Tilden then took by the hand those captured with him at Gettysburgh. The remainder of the day was spent in field sports. In the evening, the officers, with their guests, the brigade commander and staff, and officers from other regiments, partook of a luxurious dinner in the chapel. The rain, which commenced drizzling in the morning, now came down in torrents.

Mar. 30. A complimentary dinner was given to the band, sergeants, and color guard.

Mar. 31. All quiet on Cedar Run, except that infernal horn of the One Hundred and Seventh Pennsylvania, which has volume enough to waken the dead. The health of the regiment greatly improved during the month of March, and no death was recorded, except at the division hospital.

The "army hospital" was an institution never to be forgotten by a patient. The "surgeon's call" at first suggested care for the sick, and certain remedies for nostalgia. Men were disinclined to heed the call, and shrank from the mysteries of that long, white tent, — its row of cots so close together that one patient could reach over and clasp the feverish hand of his neighbor. The whole interior arrangements were horrible in suggesting sickness, suffering, and death away from home, and only a thin canvas between one and eternity, which flapped restlessly in the wind as if impatient to open its loose seams and let some tired spirit through.

If one took pains to visit the sick, his impressions would be lasting. The row of fair, boyish faces drawn with suffering, — how eagerly they scanned each new face as it entered under the raised flap, as if, by some possibility, friends from distant home had come to them! Here and there would be seen the wrinkled face of an old man (more patriotic than wise) whose seams and lines of age were made more conspicuous by the fading of hair and whisker dye. If they lived through their first hospital experience, a few months saw them at home with a satisfied consciousness of having done what they could — and later in life enjoying a comfortable pension from a grateful government. It did seem strange that some men grew old so rapidly. A few months since they swore they were only forty-five, and now they are just as ready to swear that they are seventy-five. Early in the war, "bummers" were unknown. Only after one or two skirmishes did they develop a wonderful capacity for belly-aches. The favorite disease was "diarrhœa," which became *chronic* in a week. The general order for "three days' rations, and forty rounds of ammunition," was equal to croton oil in its effects; "winter quarters" was the only antidote, although "numbers six, nine, and eleven" were prescribed as a remedy.

Mingled with pity was a feeling of indignation to see so many able-bodied men fall into line at the head of each company street every morning, at the surgeon's call, and march to the hospital tent, and swallow, with evident relish, a blue pill, bitter morphine, or quinine, and whisky. Boys of seventeen

1861 would watch this funeral procession, so filled with disgust and anger, that no discipline could prevent the most scientific profanity. The regular prescriptions were numbered six, nine, and eleven, which were blue pill, quinine, and vinum. We soon learned that "vinum" meant either wine or brandy. I have seen men count from right to left, "six, nine, eleven," — "six, nine, eleven," — "six, nine, eleven," and step into the ranks just where eleven would strike. It was a sure thing, as the surgeon gave in regular order, as the men filed past him, something as follows: "Well, what is the matter with you?" "I don' know, doctor, I've got an awful pain in my bowels; guess I've got the chronic diarrhœa." "Let's see your tongue! Give him number six! Next, what is the matter with you?" "I was took with an awful griping in my bowels — guess I've got the chronic diarrhœa." "Give him number nine! Next, what ails you?" "I've g-g-got an almighty b-b-belly-ache, g-g-guess I've got the chronic d-d-diarrhœa." "Run out your tongue! Give him number eleven!"

April 1. All-fools-day was appropriately observed. It rained. The One Hundred and Seventh Pennsylvania left us. The only objection we had to this regiment, they could n't eat baked beans, but would persist in eating that abominable slosh called "swagin," by the boys.

April 3. The Ninetieth Pennsylvania joined the brigade, and took the barracks vacated by the One Hundred and Seventh.

April 4. Colonel Tilden assumed command.

Regiment detailed for three days' picket duty. **1864** April 5.
Cold rain-storm.

Reviewed by General Grant. It was amusing to April 8. notice how keenly every one looked at the new commander-in-chief. Many were disappointed in the appearance of the plain and unpretending general, and no enthusiasm was, or could be shown for the power that lay hidden beneath a modest exterior. Grant's face showed the energy of silence, of patience, and a consciousness of possessing the profound strategy which lies in unswerving persistence.

Heavy thunder-shower. Apr. 10.

Regiment detailed for three days' picket duty. Apr. 20.

Fifty men were transferred to the navy and Apr. 22. veteran reserve corps.

Broke camp and moved across Cedar Run, half a Apr. 26. mile up the railroad, in order to get rid of all surplus baggage, and accustom ourselves to sleeping on the ground, preparatory to field duty. The formation of the regiment during the campaign was as follows: C, H, B, D, G, I, A, K, E, F.

MAJOR.

CHAPTER XII.

WILDERNESS CAMPAIGN.

1864
May.

MAY, 1864, initiated a campaign of corduroy roads, bridges, and earth-works, and until September there was a smell of new earth about us, suggestive of planting time at home. We digged, we tramped; we tramped, chopped wood, and digged. It was shovel and shoot, shoot, shovel, and dig. We dug before reveille, and fought before noon; marched a short distance, and if it were n't good shooting, piled up the ground. Often the rebels objected; then we would have a fight, and appropriate their works — if we were the smartest. After supper, and half a ration of good (?) government whisky, and further stimulated by a wholesome respect for somebody in gray in front of us, we turned to the fresh air new earth, and the morning light showed the herculean labor of a few hours, just as a long line of tired boys shouldered their knapsacks and moved out, and so on through the Wilderness to Spottsylvania, North Anna, and Cold Harbor. Zigzag lines and parallels crossed the ground in every direction. Oftentimes the gray of the morning would find the gray of the rebellion but a few yards front of us, looking over works a foot higher than ours. Some-

times the presence of the enemy would be announced
by the whistling through the fog of a bullet uncomfortably near one's head, or the dull thud of a bullet,
as it put out the life of some mother's boy and the
light of a distant home. A bread box, often only
an army blanket, a few sad words of prayer, some
more digging, amid tears and sorrow, to be followed
daily by similar horrors, called "fortunes of war."
Accustomed to it as we were, every case brought
forth fresh words of sympathy for the wounded at
home. But we had no time for mourning. "Portable breast-works on the tramp" they called us. We
alternately shouldered spades and muskets, and saw
visions of Richmond and peace in the future.

The expected order to march was received, and at *May 3.*
two o'clock A.M., May 4th, the regiment broke camp *May 4.*
and took the road to Culpeper; thence to the right
through Stevensburgh to Germania Ford, and crossed
at four P.M. Bivouacked at night near Wilderness
Church, having marched twenty-five miles. The
men unused to marching and heavily loaded straggled far behind, and some of them, together with
thousands of blankets and overcoats, were picked up
by guerrillas who kept well up to our rear.

"Reveille at four A.M. Moved forward to the *May 5.*
Lacy House, halted and rested until noon, when the
engagement became general. The brigade formed
in line of battle, and advanced across the fields and
woods, and by the Orange Court House road about
one mile, when the rebels were found in force with
artillery commanding the road. Within short range
of this battery the woods terminated in an open

1864 field. The regiment advanced to the border of this, and held the point until about sunset; when a charge was ordered, but failed to obtain any advantage. We formed at edge of woods and repulsed every attack of the enemy, until relieved and sent to the rear at daylight May 6th.

May 6. "Coffee was made and breakfast eaten, when the brigade again advanced to nearly the old position; but was shortly withdrawn, and sent to the extreme left on the F. and O. plank road, where breast-works were built under active skirmishing. Thus far our loss was slight.

May 7. "The intrenchments were strengthened and the ground held, with slight skirmishing. At eight P.M. the regiment was relieved and massed with the division near the church, whence a rapid night's march was made, by the way of Todd's Tavern, to near Spottsylvania Court House. Halted at three A.M.

May 8. "May 8th near the rebel lines. An hour's halt was given to close up the division and rest. Thoroughly exhausted, the men threw themselves flat to the ground and slept. At nine A.M., the regiment was in line with the division, led by General Robinson on that famous charge of double-quick, for full two miles, nearly to the court-house, when the General was wounded and the exhausted troops, encountering fresh forces behind strong breast-works, were withdrawn a short distance and re-formed. Works were thrown up and the ground held until the army advanced. The loss in the regiment was nearly one hundred men. Captain Belcher, of Company G, and Lieutenant Fowler, of Company A, were so severely

12

wounded as to require their discharge. Lieutenant Richards, of Company H, was wounded and taken prisoner." The color-bearers won the admiration of all by their saucy intrepidity. Not once did the loved ensigns touch the ground. The flag was carried in the case for protection through the woods, but on reaching the enemy's lines the brave Corporal Palmer deliberately removed the case and flung the ensign to the air amid the cheers of the men. Almost instantly he was struck in the arm and received a bullet in the side. The brave fellow held the flag aloof until it was taken from his grasp by Corporal William Manchester, who gave the State flag to Corporal Robinson Fairbanks of Company C. Corporal Palmer crawled to the rear on his hands and knees' until exhausted. That night he was found by comrades and carried to the hospital where he died. At night five days' rations were issued to the brigade. Colonel Coulter of the Eleventh Pennsylvania assumed command of division. In his official report he says, "The disability of General Robinson at this juncture was a severe blow to the division and certainly influenced the fortunes of the day. The want of our commanding officer prevented that concert of action which alone could have overcome the enemy in front."

Skirmishing continued all last night and during today. The regiment changed position several times to the right, and each time threw up breast-works. *May 9.*

The battle of Laurel Hill was fought. The Sixteenth was in the breast-works built the night before, until eleven A.M. It was then ordered toward the *May 10.*

1864 left and center, and took part in the day's engagements that terminated in a general charge on the rebel works about seven P.M. Corporal Fairbanks, being wounded, gave the State colors to Corporal Bradford, of Company E. During the charge, Corporal Manchester was wounded, when Bradford, the only one of the guard left, seized his colors and carried both, until relieved by Barney Boyle, of Company G, who, mixing brogue and courage, stuck by Bradford, swearing by all the saints in the calendar that he would "stand by the ould flag as long as there was a gray divil in front." The regimental loss during the day was fifty men and four officers. At eight o'clock the regiment was relieved, and supplied with rations and ammunition. The First Brigade was temporarily assigned to the First Division, General Cutler commanding.

May 11. A slight change in position, and more or less skirmishing.

May 12. The men, thoroughly exhausted, would lie at length on the cool, fresh earth, some of the timid ones hugging the bottom of the trench, painfully expressing the dread of something to come. And yet these timid ones, at the first rebel yell, would over and "at them," or draw bead on some venturesome Johnnie, and shout with derision if he was made to dodge. If they dropped him, a grim look of satisfaction, shaded with pity, passed over their dirty faces. The quiet was almost unbearable, the heat in the trenches intolerable, and rain, which commenced falling, was most welcome. Time dragged. We had not the slightest hint of what was developing.

The rebels seemed very far off, and trouble ominously near.

From the right came an aide, and, quietly passing down the line of works, he dropped a word to this and that colonel; only a ripple, and all was again suspiciously still. "What was it, colonel?" asked the adjutant. The colonel made no reply, but simply pointed up the hill. Soon he took out his watch and looked anxiously to the right. Suddenly a commotion ran down the line, followed by the command, "Attention! Forward, double-quick!" On went the brigade with a yell which was echoed from thousands of throats in front, and thrown back by the double columns in our rear. Down from the rebel right thundered shot and shell, making great gaps in our ranks, while on swept the brigade, until suddenly loomed up in our front, three lines of works — literally a tier, one above another — bristling with rifles, ready aimed for our reception. There was lead enough to still every heart present, and yet, when sheets of flame shot out in our faces, scarcely a dozen men of the regiment were hit. Then men tore madly at the abatis, and rushed on only to fall back or die. Again and again did the brigade charge, and as often came those terrible sheets of flame in our faces, while solid shot and shell enfiladed our lines. The crash which followed the fearful blaze swept away men, even as the coming wind would sweep away the leaves from the laurel overhead. Our ammunition was reduced to three rounds, when Colonel Lyle directed me to hasten to General Cutler and ask for ammunition or release. Hastening

1864 to the rear, I found the General nervously watching the effects of the shell which came crashing through the trees over his head. He came immediately forward to meet me, and said, "What is it, lieutenant?" Taking the verbal dispatch from Lyle, he replied, "Don't know that I can get a round of ammunition to your brigade. Tell Colonel Lyle to hold his position until relieved."

I was absent scarcely ten minutes, yet long enough for death to do its harvest work. "Look here," said Colonel Farnham. Partly buried in leaves and dirt lay the form of a splendid officer of the Ninetieth Pennsylvania, his head entirely shot away. Piled against his body lay six dead and dying men, all silenced by one shell. While viewing the ghastly sight, a huge shell exploded in our midst, sending Colonels Pray and Farnham to the ground, and Adjutant Small whirling like a top, neither of whom were injured. Just as the last charge was rammed home, relief came, when the brigade retired to the works in the rear, to learn that "it was not expected of the brigade to carry the works, only to hold a strong force of the enemy, while Hancock carried the lines in his front, which were more favorably situated for a successful attack." "Maine in the War" thus truthfully says of Major Leavitt:—

> In this charge Major Leavitt was mortally wounded, the musket ball passing through his chest. He was carried to the field hospital and thence to Washington, where he died May 30th. Words would but feebly express the feelings of his brother officers as they parted for the last time with him, who by his noble virtues and manly qualities, had endeared himself to every heart. Ever will they fondly cherish the memory of one of earth's truest men and bravest soldiers.

Corporal James C. Foss of the color guard, while lying flat upon the brush had a solid shot go under him raising him bodily from the ground. A comrade spoke to him a moment after and receiving no reply touched him and found a lifeless body, with not a scratch or bruise upon it.

The regiment changed position several times during the day, and all the while with more or less skirmishing. At ten P.M. left Laurel Hill by a wide detour through the woods, and by roads to the Fredericksburgh and Spottsylvania Pike, one mile from the court-house, and occupied the breast-works thown up by the Ninth Corps, at daybreak.

From the 14th to the 21st, there were frequent changes in line of battle and continued skirmishing, but no engagements or movements of any importance. When the main line was withdrawn for a movement to the left, Corporal F. L. Tarbox, of Company F, was among the number left on the picket line, and they, hearing an unusual commotion both in front and rear, pushed back to join the regiment and approaching the works were astonished and alarmed to receive a cordial invitation from the line of rebels to "come in, Yanks." They quickly scattered, amid a shower of bullets, rather than again starve at Libby and Belle Isle. Tarbox went to the left, tearing through the thorns and laurel all night, losing gun and equipments and nearly all his clothing, and early next morning was challenged by a Union vidette and soon after joined his company, ready for duty.

1864
May 20.
The Sixteenth now numbered less than two hundred men — good and true, rugged and hearty, and ready for any duty. We lay within half rifle range of the enemy, and could see their dirty rags waving saucily in the breeze. The regimental loss since May 5th was as follows: eleven men killed, nine officers and one hundred and twenty-four men wounded, two officers and thirty-eight men missing. The regiment has been well supplied with rations and had access to plenty of good water. The army has been skillfully handled with none of the confusion and useless nervous hurry of the past.

May 21. Mail arrived for the first time since we left Mitchell's Station. Slung knapsacks at noon and made a rapid march to the left, and bivouacked near Guiney's Station, on the F. and R. Railroad.

May 22. Moved at one P.M., and went into bivouac at St. Marguerite's Church, twelve miles southwest of Bowling Green.

May 23. Broke camp at five A.M., and marched by the way of Gainesville and Mt. Carmel's Church, to Jericho Ford, on the North Anna River, and crossed at four P.M. with slight opposition. While the Second Division was getting into position on the right of the First, the enemy opened with shot and shell and some musketry, and for forty minutes made it very uncomfortable for us, as we were wholly unprotected. About six o'clock Hill's Second Division attacked Griffin's division, and being repulsed, turned and made a furious assault on Cutler's, with the evident intention of driving us into the river, but the skillful handling of our division, and the admirable disposition of our batteries, foiled the attempt, and hurled back the foe in wild confusion and heavy loss. Some of our men were wounded by fragments of shell from the depressed pieces in our rear. Sergeant George H. Fisher, Company H, had an artery severed, which was quickly taken up by our assistant surgeon, who was always present in a fight, looking as smiling as though in a camp hospital. This was a brief but brilliant engagement, and the troops received a complimentary order from General Meade. After the lead storm and terror of the day, when the hush of the great woods stole over our hearts with a soothing calm, we lay at length on the ground, or rested against the newly built works, some munching hard-tack, others whittling, and many improving the golden opportunity for writing letters; some peering into the sky through the trees overhead, as if to force the secrets of the morrow, and while all were in their own way busy, suddenly there came out of the silence a low moan, as if from the center of the earth. Men looked at each other and silently grasped their weapons. The moan grew into a cadence, into a song, and from our whole front swelled in mighty voice that grand old "Old Hundred."

Occupied and destroyed the railroad. A line of battle was advanced and extended to the left, and connected with the Second Corps, when breast-works were built, in which we remained until the 26th. *May 24.*

Recrossed the North Anna and continued the march down the river, and bivouacked at sunset on the 27th. Length of march, thirty miles. *May 26.*

1864 May 28.	Broke camp at five A.M. and continued the march down the Pamunky, which the regiment crossed at one P.M., near Hanovertown. Formed line of battle and built earth-works.
May 29.	Advanced two miles. In the evening the brigade was ordered to intrench and hold a position near Old Church, fourteen miles from Richmond.
May 30.	Returned to old position. General Lockwood, with a batch of green aides, was running the division in a feeble way. Advanced with the division two miles, and came upon the rebels near Bethesda Church. Our skirmishers were hotly engaged. Worked all night intrenching.
May 31.	The picket firing continued all day and night.
June 1.	The division advanced and drove the rebels over a mile, then halted and built a new line of works, in which the Sixteenth frequently changed position. Until June 5th, we were alternately in the trenches and the skirmish line, all the time exposed to severe shelling.
June 3.	The pickets of the division extended some two miles along the front of our line, but too near the works to afford much protection to the men from the incessant fire of the enemy. Colonel Tilden as division officer of the picket was ordered to advance the whole line. Every man in the regiment held his breath as this intrepid officer sprang over the works, and alone advanced to the front and down the picket line, rapidly issuing his orders under a most galling fire. It was a hazardous attempt successfully accomplished, with the loss of one captain wounded, four men killed, eight wounded, and six missing. Moving

still farther to the left, the Colonel and Captain Washburn of the Thirteenth Massachusetts, advancing beyond the line to reconnoiter in the edge of the woods, were met with a shower of bullets, one of which severely wounded the Captain. Expecting an advance by the enemy, the Colonel immediately ordered the picket forward to protect him in recovering the body of Captain Washburn.

In the night the regiment was quietly withdrawn from the enemy's front, and marched rapidly some five miles to Cold Harbor, where the corps was put in reserve. A part of the Sixteenth left on the skirmish line at Bethesda Church was captured. Some of the men escaped and rejoined us here. Clothing and shoes were issued. Lieutenant-Colonel Farnham was detailed as division inspector-general, and chief-of-staff to General Crawford.

The First Brigade was transferred to Third Division, under General Crawford.

Early in the morning the bugle rang out loud and clear the unwelcome notes to pack up. Marched at five A.M., and camped within two miles of Bottom Bridge on the Chickahominy river, at noon.

Under this date, Lieutenant Frank Wiggin, of Company II, writes to the press, as follows:—

I was taken prisoner on Sunday morning the eighth of May, near Spottsylvania, while our division was charging the rebel breast-works. On the ninth, myself with nearly four hundred other prisoners were started for Richmond, and after a hard day's march, and just as we reached Beaver Dam Station, up came Sheridan's cavalry, and in less time than it takes me to tell it, we were liberated and our rebel guards were skedaddling through the woods. At Beaver

1864 Dam we drew rations from rebel supplies, and helped ourselves liberally I assure you; then two long trains of cars well loaded with commissary stores were fired, the railroad track torn up, and then we camped for the night. On the morning of the 10th, we took up the line of march for Richmond, and pursued our course without incident, crossing the South Anna near night, and encamping in a splendid grove. On the 11th, we reached Ashland about noon, and there another destruction of railroad track, bridges, and depots took place. At two o'clock we again took up the line of march for Richmond, and after traveling about a mile, found Stuart's cavalry disputing our further progress; a severe action was the result, and in that action the great rebel cavalry general, Stuart, was killed. The rebels were severely whipped in this encounter, and were glad to get out of our way, but the wounded had to be cared for, and it was midnight before we were ready to start again. The night was dark and rainy. We were going directly toward the rebel capital. There was no talking and no unnecessary noise, and every one seemed to be impressed with a foreboding of great events to be soon developed, and two signal guns breaking the gloomy stillness of the night did not tend to lessen this impression. It seems that one division was conducted on to the wrong road by their guide, and had to fight their way out of a critical situation, but by sunrise the rebels had closed in around us and the fighting became general. A rebel force was also posted on the other side of the Chickahominy to prevent our crossing, so for a short time the prospect was rather gloomy, but the rebels cannot corner our cavalry. General Custer dismounted part of his brigade and plunging into the Chickahominy Swamp, they charged on the rebels and sent them flying in all directions. We then crossed, protected by our artillery, and at noon halted at Mechanicsville.

As we crossed the Chickahominy we could plainly see the outer defenses of Richmond. It is strong on that side whatever its other approaches may be. We had no trouble after crossing the river, but following the route of the famous seven days' fight, we proceeded leisurely to the James River, 1864 striking it at Haxhall Landing, some three miles above General Butler's headquarters, to which place the recaptured prisoners were sent, and from that time our journey partook more of the character of a pleasure excursion than anything else. We had a fine sail down the James River to Fortress Monroe, and also from Fortress Monroe to Alexandria, making in all about three hundred miles by steamer.

From Alexandria, as soon as we were clothed, armed, and equipped, we were sent again to the front by the way of Belle Plains, Fredericksburgh, and Bowling Green, finding our regiments in line of battle across the North Anna, having been absent from them eighteen days. We were treated well by the rebels while in their hands, and our guards seemed to be as good-hearted, intelligent, and well looking a lot of men as one often comes across.

This campaign has learned us what "carrying on war in earnest" means. For a month our tattoo has been the boom of cannon and the crack of musketry, and our reveille the same, while we became so accustomed to the sound of shells and bullets whistling over us and by us, that we would cook our coffee as unconcernedly as if in winter quarters, and I have often listened to catch the tone as a bullet went humming by. This is the first Sabbath we have had since the first of May. Our corps is lying now at Turnstall Station, not far from White House.

Took up the line of march at six o'clock P.M., crossed the river over Long Bridge, pressed forward three miles and halted at daylight. Then advanced to White Oak Swamp and formed line of battle. This demonstration was made by the Third Division, alone, while the remainder of the corps, with the army, moved farther down and crossed the James at Charles City Court House. From our position on the brow of a hill, the rebels could be seen less than a thousand yards away, getting into line. An officer

1864 on a white horse was a conspicuous mark for our sharp-shooters, but he went about his business unharmed. Our skirmishers were deployed, and until night kept up a constant peppering. The enemy opened with artillery. Our batteries although occupying commanding positions, were unaccountably silent after one discharge. Our loss was two men, both severely wounded. After dark, the division withdrew in silence and marched rapidly, with June 14. but two hours rest, until noon June 14th, when it encamped near Charles City Court House, where ammunition and rations were issued. The Sixteenth had a weakness for fence rails, and notwithstanding the ground had been canvassed, occasionally struck a bonanza. As the day's march drew to a close every "Sixteener" had an eye on either flank, and held himself ready for a dash, at the word "Halt." Knapsacks, canteens, and everything which would impede his progress were loosened ready to drop, and, with one eye on the colonel and the other on his particular rail, he waited for the order.

Sometimes an aide would come dashing down the line with "orders" about "holding the colonel strictly responsible" for all property, including fence rails, on his flanks. A peculiar expression would mingle with the color in the colonel's face, as he, in ringing tones, repeated the order, and added, "Now, boys, I don't want to see one of you touch a rail!" Giving his whole attention to a study of the landscape in his rear, there was the sound of many feet, and he was quickly relieved of all responsibility that was supposed to cluster around forty rods of split cedar. Whether this was "prejudicial to good order and military discipline" or not, it certainly improved the landscape, and enriched the slave-worn soil.

The commander of the regiment would wink at a reasonable amount of vandalism, when the health and comfort of his men were concerned, but there was a limit, as in the case of the poor woman who lost her all. Her rails were burned, her out-buildings stripped of boards, and her home intruded upon. When she came to Colonel Tilden, and, with a face full of suffering, told him that some one had taken the only kettle she owned, which was a tea-kettle, and killed the last poor calf left by those who preceded us, his anger was just. The advantage taken of his good nature could not be easily forgiven, and for a long time we felt the cords of discipline drawn closely about us. He immediately called the officers around him, and put the case before them in language that mantled every face with shame. Pulling his wallet he paid for the calf, restored the kettle, and forbade any one's approaching the house. The officers immediately pooled in, and I think left the old woman in better circumstances than she had been in for a year. I have often thought of that poor old woman, gray, wrinkled, and worn, bent with the cares of many years, alone on the edge of a clearing hardly large enough, if all cultivated, to bear food for three months, perhaps awaiting the return of a husband or son, and daily hoping against hope for the presence of either to shield her from insult, and keep her from starvation. Visited by

1864 first one army and then the other, who trampled into the earth her little all, alternating betwixt hope and despair, what a life she must have led! Who wonders that it takes time to heal the wounds and quiet the spirit of that man, be he never so much a rebel, who, if spared, found his mother's heart broken, or in vain hunted for her grave in a place changed beyond recognition.

June 16. Sergeant Wilbur F. Mower rejoined the regiment and again carried the national colors. Mower was soon after promoted, when the flag was returned to Sergeant Bradford. Brigade broke camp at dawn and marched to the James River and crossed in steamers James Brooks and Joseph Powell. Rested until afternoon, then marched rapidly to near Petersburgh, halting at three A.M., June 17th.

June 17. At daylight moved across swamp lands, through tangled underbrush, to the support of the Ninth Corps, and remained under fire all day. At night participated in the charge on the rebel works, which was but partially successful.

June 18. In the assault that was made, the brigade advanced nearly a mile, forcing back the rebels, and gaining position on the Norfolk Railroad, within a mile and a half of the city. Withdrew from railroad cut, and formed in line of battle in the county road, along the base of the slope overlooking and near the railroad. Here the men worked diligently all night, throwing up intrenchments.

June 19. The rebel sharp-shooters had an uninterrupted range of our whole front, and the men lay close to the ground all day, and at night deepened the trenches, and dug parallels and approaches to the wells and other works in the rear. The regiment remained here until the 24th instant within eighty yards of the rebels, and suffered a daily loss. Captain Stevens, of Company E, while reading a newspaper, inadvertently moving his head from cover of a tree behind which he was seated, was instantly shot through the neck. The carotid artery was severed, and he died in his brother's arms, vainly striving to finish a message of farewell. His brother was killed two months later, in the Battle of Weldon Railroad. Regimental headquarters were behind a monster oak six feet in diameter. A redoubt was thrown up some six feet either side and parallel with line of works. Here reports were made, rations eaten, and callers received. During the day-time, military etiquette was as a rule ignored. Visitors, orderlies, and aides, came in with a jump and "landed on all fours." Sergeant Mower, however, did stop to salute. The command of "Down, Sergeant!" was not quick enough, and he today carries a withered arm from a bullet lodged in the shoulder. His wound was dressed, and the brave fellow smilingly saluted, as he left for the hospital. In the rear of the brigade was an orchard, covering part of the slope. In spite of orders and friendly counsel, men would persist in risking life for the possession of a green sour apple. A number of brave but foolhardy men lie buried in Virginia, in consequence. An orderly handed the colonel a circular today. No sooner had he fixed his signature to it, than a rebel bullet scattered the sand thickly over the

1864 paper. "Never mind the blotter, Adjutant," coolly remarked the colonel, as he shook off the surplus dirt. The orderly took the paper, gave a quick glance over the redoubt, and jumped for the ditch — with an additional hole in his coat. The regimental loss while occupying this position was one officer and six enlisted men killed, and twelve men wounded, by sharp-shooters.

June 24. Moved to the left. The order was executed under a furious fire from the rebel batteries. Our new position was partially intrenched. The works were changed and strengthened. A large fort, subsequently called Fort Davis, in honor of Colonel Davis, of the Thirty-ninth Massachusetts, who was here mortally wounded, was built by the brigade and occupied by several regiments. The Sixteenth had the honor of holding a line of works several hundred yards in front of the fort, until August 15th.

July 3. This Sabbath was quiet, only an occasional shot on the skirmish line, and the booming of a sixty-four-pounder away up on the right of the line. The First Corps and the rebel troops in its front suspended hostilities as if by mutual consent. Guns were stacked, and many of the men lay around on the works, talking with the enemy just across the way. Occasionally a Yankee and a rebel would meet between the lines and exchange coffee and tobacco, and offer an *Enquirer* for a *Herald*. The Johnnies were careful to cut out the "news," and the Yanks, equally cautious, passed over a mutilated paper. When a rebel battery was about to open upon us, the skirmishers would shout, "Down, Yanks!" One day the range was low and our kitchen department was knocked up, and the rations distributed broadcast. When the Union batteries were to open, "Down, Reb!" went the cry, and not a grey-back was seen during the artillery duel which followed. The band was with the regiment, and for an hour in the morning, and just before sunset, would play some of its best selections, generally closing with some national air. Often would the enemy crowd up to their works and listen to "America," or the "Battle Cry of Freedom." None of the rebel bands had been heard since we left the North Anna. Sunday evenings, "Old Hundred," and "Pleyal's Hymn" would come rolling in over the works, from a thousand throats, to mingle harmoniously with thoughts of home and a better life. And this was war!

The following extract from a diary illustrates army life at this time:— *July 10.*

Let me tell you what is going on within eight hundred yards of my tent at nine P.M., Sabbath evening. A sutler selling whisky, a prayer-meeting, boys playing poker, band playing "Johnnie, Fill up the Bowl," four hundred men at work on fortifications, stimulated by half-ration of government whisky, profanity in all directions, violin and banjo quicksteps, and five horns sounding tattoo.

As early as three A.M., the regiment was under arms and nervously waiting for the explosion of Burnside's Mine, which was delayed until quarter of five. It was a miserable failure, and our divisions remained quietly behind their works. *July 30.*

1864
Aug. 15. The Fifth Corps was relieved and withdrawn to the rear, preparatory to an attack upon the Weldon Railroad, August 18th.

Aug. 16. Colonel Tilden, division officer of the day. Received orders to move at half-past two A.M., 17th. A large part of the command detailed for fatigue, and went on duty in a heavy rain.

Aug. 17. Packed up ready to move, and remained in position all day. Pitched tents at five P.M., during a heavy shower. Ordered to move at four A.M., August 18th.

Aug. 18. Struck tents at four A.M. Marched at half-past six. Lee was compelled to strengthen his forces north of the James, or risk the fall of Richmond. Immediately Warren struck out for the long coveted road, which was reached at a point called the Yellow House, about five miles south of Petersburgh. The Sixteenth was the extreme left of the division, which was supposed to connect with the right of the Second Division, resting upon the railroad. But a most unaccountable posting of the brigade, by a bewildered commander who moved it in all directions but the correct one, left it in an irregular line at an angle of forty-five degrees, one hundred and fifty yards from the road. Regimental commanders were informed that a strong line of skirmishers was posted thirty yards in their front, waiting orders to advance. Meanwhile, no firing of muskets must take place. Hardly had the men kicked the underbrush from their feet, when the rebels rose up fifty yards in front, with that half human, half animal yell, and poured a volley of bullets into our column. The Zouave skirmishers, of the Second Division, rushed through the brigade to the rear, without firing a gun. Meanwhile, the enemy, quick to discover the opening between the divisions, filed through and formed rapidly in rear of the regiment. The first intimation the right battalion had, was the melting away of the left. Some officer ordered the men to lie down and blaze away. Immediately the enemy charged the brigade in front and rear, and over one hundred of its numbers started, with a most willing escort, for Petersburgh — cursing the blundering stupidity of some one, they knew not who. The division, so much of it as remained in line of battle, was withdrawn from the woods and a new line established, less favorable to the rebels. The Sixteenth lost Sergeant-Major Edwin C. Stevens and Private James Fahey, Company A, killed; about twenty enlisted men wounded; Captain Conley, Lieutenants Broughton, Fitch, and Chapman, Adjutant Small, and thirty men prisoners. Intrenchments were thrown up during the night, and with one important omission (credited to General Crawford) we were prepared for the morrow's expected fight. Beyond the Third Division was only a skirmish line without breast-works, or support.

The enemy, reinforced, made a heavy attack along the whole line. The skirmish line alluded to gave way, and allowed a large force to advance unperceived, in the dense woods, to the rear of our lines, then hotly engaged in front. The First Brigade had repulsed two direct assaults, when the rebels appeared in their immediate rear. In the confused struggle that followed, less than one hundred men, with two officers, escaped. The regiment sustained the following losses in the two days' fight: —

KILLED.

Sergeant-Major E. C. Stevens, shot through the head; private James Fahey, Company A, do.

WOUNDED.

Company A — Sergeant D. A. Spearrin, elbow; privates Timothy Ford, chest, flesh wound; Joel B. Hurd, chest, dangerously.

Company B — Privates, Randolph Elbridge, thigh, flesh wound; Edward C. Folger, do., fractured.

Company C — Corporal Robinson Fairbanks, foot, slight; privates, Isaac N. Coombs, hip, do.; Otis Getchell, head, dangerous; Ambrose C. Davis, hip, deep flesh wound.

Company E — Corporal Luther Bradford, shoulder, severe; privates, Benjamin F. Worth, hand, slight; Elisha Coolley, foot, do.; Isaac H. Fairbrother, hip, bayonet wound.

Company F — Corporal E. H. Floyd, arm, fracture; privates, Warren Butters, hand, slight; M. B. Smith, face, arm, and arm fracture; Benjamin Dalton, chest, slight; Granville R. Jordan, forefinger amputated; Sergeant John McPhee, side, contusion.

Company G — Privates, Luke Emery, leg, slight; A. H. Sutherland, foot, slight; Harry Sullivan, hand, slight; David A. Scott, foot, slight; B. C. Robie, thumb, slight.

Company I — Private T. W. Folley, chest, contusion, slight.

Company K — Corporal Everard Thing, arm amputated, upper third; privates, George U. Fisher, thigh, severe; Ira Page, hip joint, severe.

MISSING.

Captains John D. Conley, Company H; J. O. Lord, Company K; Adjutant A. R. Small; Lieutenants William H. Broughton, Company D; Atwood Fitch, do.; W. H. Chapman, Company K.

Company A — Sergeants, James Parsons, C. C. Williams; 1864
Corporals, Freeman T. Knowles, Tilson T. Whitcomb;
privates, Freeman Brackett, S. H. Chamberlain, Hugh Conway, Timothy Ford, William H. Knowles, Albert J. Murch,
Simeon Tripp, Benjamin Carvill or Carver.

Company B — Privates, Charles D. Smith, Alden Turner,
Adin B. Thayer, Clinton A. Davis, Henry Maddocks, Henry
Mansfield.

Company C — Sergeants, William Farnhum, Henry Fiske,
Edwin C. Jones; Corporal M. C. Grindle; privates, John
O. Allen, John Emerson, Martin Butterfield, Ezekiel Cole,
George W. Evans, William Farrar, William D. Grant,
Charles H. Gilman, David H. Hines, Elias Humphrey,
Henry A. Sharp, A. W. Shorey, S. H. Scudder, Charles W.
Wright, Archibald Phinney.

Company D — Corporal Charles Couture; privates, S. T.
Robinson, Ezra S. Seavy, Austin Hobart, Timothy Butters.

Company E — Sergeants Joseph Lamb, Warren Seaward;
Corporals C. F. Blaisdell, H. F. Judkins; privates, Stephen
Buzwell, Mark Towle, John Hartwell.

Company F — Sergeant Charles W. Ross; Corporals Charles
H. Goodrich, Frank J. Leavitt; privates, Theodore T. Buzzell, Wilmot W. Dunton, Dennis Haley, Albert Powers, John
W. Chadbourne, Samuel Pierce, George W. Smith, John W.
Webster.

Company G — Sergeant J. H. Frain; Corporal S. T. Farnham; privates, W. H. Chamberlain, T. Coharn, M. Doyle,
Barney Boyle, Patrick Larry, L. M. Porter, B. S. Morgan,
H. J. Redd, F. S. Saunders, A. Treat.

Company H — Sergeants George W. Fisher, William Fennelly; Corporal Thomas Witherly; privates, Charles R.
Atkins, William Annis, Charles R. Dore, Henry Chandler,
Lewis F. Gilbert, Charles E. Hatch, Henry Shield, Lemuel
Hoyt, Dennis Jenkins, Danforth Lovely, Thomas Middleton, Jasper Nash, George W. Smith, Martin L. Whitten,
John Farly, Charles Crompton.

Company I — Sergeant George B. Haskell; Corporals A.
H. Briggs, William Davis; privates, George W. Anderson,

1864 Wesley Booker, William L. Blagden, Jeremiah Cornish, Thomas Campbell, Thomas Crosby, Benjamin D. Colby, James T. Dilling, James Dutton, William Frozer, B. F. Garcelon, Oliver Stover, Charles Thompson, Steward G. Holmes, John Worcester.

Company K — Sergeant Colon Mayo; Corporal Joseph Peacock; privates, A. B. Sanborn, H. Brown, Calvin Marks, E. G. Lyons, Charles A. Jordan.

SUMMARY.

Number of killed............................... 2
    "   " wounded 28
    "   " missing 115
                                              ———
Total loss 145

Colonel Tilden, in reporting the part taken by his regiment in the operations near the Weldon Railroad, says: —

My regiment, numbering eight line officers and two hundred and thirty-one guns, moved in column with the First Brigade on the morning of the 18th inst., and arrived at the Weldon Railroad at twelve M., halted and rested one hour, to the right and rear of the Yellow House. At one o'clock received orders to advance and form line at the edge of the woods, extending my left to the right of the railroad. Advanced into the woods to connect with the right of the Second Division. While forming my regiment, and before the remainder of the brigade on my right had formed, the enemy opened a sharp fire on my left and the right of the Second Division, causing the latter to retire somewhat, thus leaving my left flank exposed. We, however, held the enemy some minutes, when I discovered that he was close on my flank and rear, causing my men to retire to save capture. These were rallied and formed on the left of the One Hundred and Fourth New York, which position we held the remainder of the day. During the night we threw up breast-works in our front, extending to the railroad. This position was held by us until two o'clock P.M., the 19th inst., when we moved to the right one hundred and fifty yards, being relieved by a portion of General Hayes' brigade extending from my left to the railroad. At three P.M. the enemy attacked our line and was repulsed three times, when we were attacked in our rear, he having come around the right of our line. This attack in the rear, together with the fire from our own artillery, created a panic among the men, but not until the troops on my right and left had fallen back, did I allow my command to retire, feeling confident that if we were not attacked in the rear, we could take care of the force in our front. On retiring we found that we were completely surrounded and were compelled to surrender, not yielding however until several efforts were made to elude the enemy. At this time my loss was wholly in prisoners. I was captured, together with three line officers and eighty-three men. Lieutenant Davies and myself succeeded in making our escape from the enemy on the 20th inst. My colors were destroyed, thus preventing their capture by the enemy. My regiment was behind works, and the enemy being obliged to emerge from the thick woods in our front was very much in our favor in this day's attack, and must have caused severe loss to him.

Colonel McCoy, in reporting the action of the First Brigade, says: "This brigade advanced into the woods, with orders to connect with the right of the Second Division, which extended * across and to the right of the railroad, from fifty to one hundred yards. This was effected by the Sixteenth Maine Regiment (Colonel Tilden), that regiment being on the left of the brigade. While Colonel Lyle was exerting himself to bring up each successive regiment on the right of the Sixteenth Maine into line, it being very difficult to accomplish,

* Was supposed to.

1864 in the thick and tangled wood and underbrush, the enemy's column of battle advanced and made a furious attack on the Second Division, on our left and extending along the front of our brigade, then in course of formation. The Sixteenth Maine first came under the fire with the right of the Second Division. The troops on the right of that division retiring somewhat, left the left flank of this brigade exposed. This regiment, holding its ground for some minutes, soon discovered that the enemy was threatening its flank and rear, fell back some hundred and fifty yards, together with the other regiments of this brigade that had also become engaged, suffering a loss of some killed, wounded, and missing. The brigade again advanced under a brisk skirmish fire, and partially re-occupied the ground from which it had just retired." In his report of the engagement on the 19th instant, Colonel McCoy after referring to his losses by capture, thus speaks of Colonel Tilden: "I would not omit to mention that Colonel Tilden, of the Sixteenth Maine, a most worthy and esteemed officer, being deeply impressed with a vivid recollection of a former imprisonment in Richmond, after having been taken to Petersburgh, and while on his way under guard from that city to the Libby Prison, made a most daring and successful escape, and rejoined his regiment the third night after his capture. Considering the perils through which he passed in making his escape, it cannot be otherwise regarded than remarkably providential. He was accompanied by Lieutenant E. F. Davies, of the same regiment. Lieutenant Aubrey Leavitt, acting aide-de-camp of the First Brigade, was captured, but made his escape, bringing into our line a number of prisoners.

OFFICIAL LIST OF CASUALTIES IN FIRST BRIGADE, IN THE WELDON RAILROAD CAMPAIGN.

Troops.	Killed.				Wounded.				Missing.				Total.
	G.S.O.	F.O.	L.O.	E.M.	G.S.O.	F.O.	L.O.	E.M.	G.S.O.	F.O.	L.O.	E.M.	
Brigade Staff	..	..	..	..	..	..	..	..	1	..	2	..	3
16th Maine	..	..	..	2	..	..	..	28	..	..	6	116	152
39th Massachusetts	..	..	1	11	..	..	1	43	..	..	8	238	293
90th Pennsylvania	..	..	1	5	..	..	..	16	..	2	1	96	121
104th New York	..	..	..	..	..	..	..	8	..	2	10	126	146
107th Pennsylvania	..	..	..	4	..	..	..	3	..	..	..	145	152
			2	22			1	485	1	4	27	721	867

The prisoners were closely guarded by the rebels, but on their way to Richmond, Colonel Tilden and Lieutenant Davies escaped and rejoined the regiment on the morning of the 22d. A correspondent of the *New York Herald* thus describes the experience of Colonel Tilden: —

Having on a light-colored and broad-brimmed Kossuth hat and a rubber overcoat was unquestionably his salvation. The fact that it rained nearly all the time he was a prisoner gave no look of strangeness or ground of suspicion in his wearing a rubber coat, while his broad-brimmed beaver gave him the air and tone of a true Southerner "to the manor born." At all events, he walked through the streets and public places of Petersburgh, picking up much valuable information, which he has since imparted to the commanding general. When he first struck the rebel lines, with a view to get through them, he was fortunate enough, in his place of concealment and observation, to hear a rebel soldier remark to another, "The Yanks will have hard work

1864 getting through our three lines of battle here, but below, where there is only a thin skirmish line, it ain't so safe, I reckon." The Colonel thought he would take a look after that thin skirmish line, and he found it. The heavy storm and dense darkness of the night enabled him to get through the line. He did not get through any too quick, for two shots were fired at him while between the enemy's skirmish line and ours. He came upon the pickets of his own brigade — a piece of good fortune, pleasing, agreeable, and quite as remarkable as agreeable.

The correspondent omitted to compliment Lieutenant Davies in seconding all the Colonel's movements.

Aug. 21. The third and last assault of the enemy at this point was handsomely repulsed. Shortly after this, the Third Division was reorganized, when the Sixteenth was assigned to the Second Brigade, commanded by Brigadier-General Baxter.

Aug. 22. Colonel Tilden returned from capture, and reported to Colonel Lyle.

Aug. 23. Regiment employed in tearing up the track of the Weldon Railroad, until seven o'clock P.M.

Aug. 25. General Crawford, commanding division, called upon Colonel Tilden for his opinion as to the cause of our lines giving way on the 19th instant. The Colonel's explanation satisfied the General that not only the brigade, but the division, did its whole duty, and retired only when the enemy appeared in their rear.

Aug. 26. Received orders in the afternoon to be in readiness to move at short notice. Regiment in line at four o'clock, and stacked arms. At two P.M. struck tents and moved to the left to support Second Corps. At seven P.M. retired to the woods, in rear of corps headquarters, and bivouacked for the night. **1864**

Aug. 27. In line at eight o'clock A.M., and moved out just in front of corps headquarters, and formed in line of battle at right angles to Weldon Railroad. Threw up earth-works and remained quiet during the night.

Aug. 28. Went into camp. Ordered the band to report for duty. Regiment at work on fortifications. Chaplain Balkam's resignation accepted.

Aug. 29. Officers engaged on monthly returns. Large part of the regiment on fatigue duty.

Aug. 31. Regiment mustered at half-past one P.M. Received orders to be in readiness to move at a moment's notice. Soon after struck tents and changed camp to the woods, about three hundred yards in the rear.

Sept. 2. At half-past three A.M. went out on a reconnoissance. Held in support of the cavalry until eight o'clock, when the regiment returned to camp.

Sept. 3. Lieutenant Davies, with a portion of the regiment, detailed for fatigue duty.

Sept. 4. Weather pleasant. Thirty-five men detailed for fatigue, which interrupted arrangements for Sunday morning inspection. Chaplain held divine service in the afternoon.

September 5th and 6th large details were made for fatigue.

Sept. 9. Lieutenant Davies, brigade officer of the day. Clothing received and issued to the regiment.

Sept. 11. Railroad completed from City Point to General Warren's headquarters. First train arrived this P.M.

1864 Sept. 15.	The brigade made a successful reconnoissance in the direction of the South Side Railroad, its object being to ascertain the position and works of the enemy.
Sept. 16.	The regiment was assigned to garrison duty in Fort Wadsworth, on the Weldon Railroad. The unfinished fort was soon completed, and the regiment moved in and set up "housekeeping."
Sept. 28.	Colonel Tilden left for Maine to recover his health, which the hardships of the campaign, and more particularly his exposure while a prisoner, had materially impaired.
Oct. 6.	Lieutenant-Colonel Farnham rejoined the regiment, and took command.
Oct. 8.	Chaplain Balkam was discharged by special order of the War Department, but did not leave the regiment until the 14th. The whole brigade missed him, for he was one of the few brave Christian men who comprehended the situation, and adapted himself to circumstances in the faithful discharge of his duties. "Comrades all know how extempore pulpits and altars sprang up for the occasion — often a breadbox, and sometimes a beef barrel; the latter occasionally illustrating (as in the case of Chaplain ———, of the ———th Pennsylvania, whose avoirdupois assisted gravitation) how uncertain the *foundation* of a chaplain's *understanding* — how unstable are material things, and how exceedingly well a man of small brains can *fill a pulpit.*" Chaplain Balkam never made a mistake of that kind. Full of humor and good cheer, he carried sunshine and good-fellowship, as a good soldier carries his musket. He had a heart

as big as a bass drum, and grieved deeply over matters beyond his control.   *1864*

Ninety conscripts and substitutes arrived; also one company of eighty-four, in command of Captain Hildreth, of Gardiner. This detachment was officered, and subsequently known as Company A, new organization.   *Oct. 11.*

Eighty-seven recruits joined the regiment.   *Oct. 27.*

Surgeon Alexander was discharged for disability. A more efficient and faithful officer was not in the Fifth Corps.   *Nov. 8.*

Colonel Tilden returned from leave of absence, and took command.   *Nov. 29.*

On the morning of the 5th, the Sixteenth was relieved from garrison duty, and ordered to the rear, bivouacking near the Jerusalem plank road.   *Dec. 5.*

Broke camp at day-light, and took the road to Sussex Court House. Crossed the Nottoway River at Blackburn's Ford, and bivouacked two miles from the court-house.   *Dec. 7.*

The march was resumed at dawn, and the objective point of the expedition, the Weldon Railroad, reached that afternoon. In the work of destruction which was rapid and complete, the regiment was engaged until midnight, and a portion of the day following.   *Dec. 8.*

On the return, the brigade was detailed as rear guard, and covered by a small squadron of cavalry. They were attacked about noon by a mounted force of the enemy, and driven in confusion upon and through the brigade. Two companies of the regiment repulsed the charge without loss.   *Dec. 10.*

1864
Dec. 11.

Recrossed the Nottoway. The hardship and suffering incident to a campaign, and so hard to be borne, were often tempered by some ludicrous incident. Who of the Sixteenth has forgotten Lieutenant S., (now a celebrated divine), a fine, dashing fellow, but rather too fond of a nice uniform, or the grievous loss he met with during this campaign? One night, after a heavy day's marching and some fighting, Lieutenant S. lay down near a camp fire with a lot of the boys of his company, and as the day's duties had been exceedingly arduous to him, he was soon fast asleep. During the night he suddenly aroused his comrades by jumping up and, frantically seizing his coat tails, prancing around like one wholly daft, exclaiming, "Water! Water! Bring some water, for God's sake; I'm all afire!" Canteens were hurriedly brought, and the water poured down S.'s back, where the fire seemed to be. In the meanwhile nearly the whole regiment had been aroused by the excitement in Company —. By the time the fire had been "got under control" a large crowd had gathered around S., anxiously waiting to ascertain what damage had been done. A glance was sufficient, for as the unfortunate officer stood in the glowing light of the camp fire, it was noticed that the rear part of his fine dress coat had been burned away as high up as the buttons below his belt, then in a circular form on each side, down to the points of the skirts of the coat in front. Knowing the Lieutenant's fastidiousness in matters of dress, and observing his rueful countenance as he surveyed the result of the conflagration, the men roared with laughter. Some cried "Fire!" others,

"Water!" "Play away Six!" "Shake her down!" while others hammered on tin plates to represent a fire-alarm, and the rush of a hose carriage. All the cries resembled those usually heard during a big blaze in a civilized community. Fully an hour elapsed before the merriment ceased, and the camp became quiet.

Dec. 12.
Returned to old position near Jerusalem plank road, having been absent six days. Marched eighty miles, destroyed twenty miles of track and much valuable property, with a loss to the regiment of four men taken prisoners. The lateness of the season, and the continued inclemency of the weather, rendered it probable that no further demonstration by the Army of the Potomac would be attempted before another spring. We were immediately ordered to prepare winter quarters. Once more, and for the last time, the men fell to with a will, and built substantial barracks, and in a few weeks had supplied themselves with all the conveniences and home comforts of a settled camp. Company K, *as usual*, exercised its ever increasing propensity for foraging, hence an inspection of the quarters showed not only "conveniences" but some questionable luxuries. This camp was called "Camp Leavitt," in honor of the lamented Major. It would compare favorably with any cantonment in the army.

Dec. 19.
Eighty-five recruits joined the regiment.

Dec. 20.
Lieutenant-Colonel Farnham, who had served on the division staff as inspector-general, but had returned to the regiment during the absence of Colonel Tilden, was again detailed to the same position.

CAMP LEAVITT.

CHAPTER XIII.

THE CLOSING CAMPAIGN OF THE WAR.

1865
Jan. 1.
SINCE its organization in 1862, the Sixteenth has been debited with seventy-one officers and two thousand and ninety-seven men, and yet today its aggregate strength is but eight hundred and eighty-seven enlisted men and thirty-two officers. Of this number are absent, sixteen officers on detached service and sick, and three hundred and seventy-five enlisted men from various causes; leaving present for duty sixteen officers and five hundred and twelve men to consider the above, and coolly calculate probabilities for the coming year. The defeats sustained during the twenty-eight months, the terrible list of casualties and the hardships endured, had not disheartened or soured us. Roseate bulletins describing victories when we knew we were whipped, and general orders of congratulation for successful movements which covered up marches made in the dark, and inglorious retreats, did not deceive the rank and file. Men knew it all; knew that they stood with one foot in the grave all the while, and for this were better men and better soldiers. And better than all, they knew that faith was a beautiful trait in human nature, and exercised it. Grumble they did, and grumblingly

14

faced the music of bullet and shell, but beneath the grumble was a fixed principle that harmonized all discords and won for them imperishable laurels as patriots. Among the strongest and most lasting attachments formed by the Sixteenth for other troops during its term of service, was that for the Thirty-ninth Massachusetts, Colonel Davis commanding. I have no record of the date when it joined the First Brigade, but it was a day which marked an era of progressive good feeling, which ripened into warm personal attachments. This regiment was splendidly officered, and, under its able commander, was an ever present incentive for us to do our very best. We never quite reached its precision in the manual of arms. We doubt if in this particular qualification it had a superior in the army; certainly it had not an equal in the corps. Colonel Davis had a quiet way of coming into our hearts, and he came to stay. From this date up to February 5th the regiment remained in camp near Petersburgh, on the Jerusalem plank road.

On the morning of the 5th the regiment, numbering eight line officers and two hundred and twenty-three guns (the last detachment of recruits, camp guard, and sick, remaining in camp), broke camp at seven o'clock A.M., in light marching order, and supplied with four days' rations, moved out in the direction of Hatcher's Run via Vaughan Road; and on this road, about two miles southwest of Rowanty Creek, the regiment, with the brigade, bivouacked for the night.

1865
Feb. 6.

Moved out on the Vaughan Road about four o'clock A.M., and halted at eight on the east side of Hatcher's Run, where the regiment remained until two o'clock P.M., when the brigade was moved forward about two miles, and formed in lines of battle. The Sixteenth, having the center of the first line, advanced and engaged the enemy, and from this point, until late in the P.M., the regiment was kept under fire. Three successive charges were made by this line, and as many times we were forced back by superior numbers, and the last movement to the rear, late in the afternoon, being caused by operations of the enemy in strong force on our flank. The line was soon re-established, and the enemy, who were following up their success, were driven back in confusion. This ended the operations of the day, and the regiment bivouacked near Hatcher's Run, but a short distance from the scene of action. The casualties for the Sixteenth were as follows: One commissioned officer wounded, two enlisted men killed, thirty-four wounded, and eleven missing, — total, one commissioned officer and forty-seven enlisted men.

Feb. 7.

Moved at seven A.M. Marched two miles northeast on the Vaughan Road, and formed on the right of the first line of battle, in the open field west of the road. The line advanced about nine A.M., forced the enemy from his temporary works, and steadily drove him through the woods, giving us an elevated position in a belt of woods, some three hundred and fifty yards in front of his main line. About eleven o'clock the Sixteenth, in charge of Captain Davies,

Company C, deployed as skirmishers. Immediately the enemy opened his artillery on the right of our line, compelling it to retire. The regiment again advanced to within two hundred yards of the rebel works, and, from lack of support, and ammunition, once more retired to its first position.

About one o'clock, February 8th, the line was withdrawn, and bivouacked about two miles from the battle-field. The Sixteenth lost in the two days' engagement one officer and seventy-three men, killed and wounded. In his official report of the battle, Colonel Tilden says: "I desire to bring to the notice of the general commanding, the name of Color Sergeant Luther Bradford, who was wounded in the left arm, (causing amputation of the same,) while gallantly bearing the colors in advance of the line, urging the men on to their work. This is the third time he has been wounded since his connection with the color guard. Corporal J. M. Grindle, of the color guard, is also deserving of especial mention for his bravery in seizing the colors after Sergeant Bradford was wounded, and pushing forward in advance of the line, and placing them in the enemy's works. This act of bravery was performed in presence of the general, commanding brigade. The Corporal was also wounded. It is with great pleasure that I can speak in commendatory terms of the officers of my command, who were constantly with their companies from the time of our breaking camp on the 5th instant. I deem it worthy of remark, that, with two exceptions, the line officers present came out with the regiment as non-commissioned officers and

1865 privates, and gained their present positions by meritorious conduct on former occasions. Especial credit is due to Captain E. F. Davies, for his efficient aid in taking charge of the regiment while deployed as skirmishers on the 6th instant. I can also speak in high terms of the conduct of the non-commissioned officers and men, some of whom had never before been under fire. I should not forget to mention Corporal James Maloney, Company H, who bore the colors with honor and credit to himself, after two color bearers had been successively wounded and carried from the field."

Feb. 9. The regiment was on picket near Halifax Road and on the 10th returned to old camp, and on the 11th moved into camp near the Weldon Railroad above Ream's Station, where the regiment remained until March 29th.

Mar. 29. Broke camp and moved with the brigade at six o'clock A.M., marching toward the Boydton plank road, and formed line of battle at four o'clock P.M., one and a half miles from the road, and bivouacked for the night.

Mar. 30. Moved forward toward the Boydton plank road, which was reached and breast-works thrown up, in which the regiment bivouacked for the night.

Mar. 31. Moved out of the works, and after a few preliminary movements, participated in the battle of Gravelly Run, suffering the following casualties: one enlisted man killed, four wounded, and twenty-three men and one officer missing.

Apr. 1. Moved from position occupied March 31st, and halted near Gravelly Run Church until about one

P.M., when the regiment moved in a northwesterly direction some four miles, and formed line of battle facing the South Side Railroad. Advanced steadily until dark, driving the enemy, flanking and capturing his works. The regiment during the advance captured a train of wagons and ambulances upon the White Oak Road. So impetuous was the charge, so intent was the regiment upon its mission, and so determined to have the wagon train, that the right of the regiment deploying, charged through the second and first lines of the brigade much to the astonishment and merriment of the men. "How came you here?" demanded Colonel McCoy of Colonel Tilden. "Don't know," replied the Colonel. "We are after that wagon train. Forward, boys!" The casualties of the day were: Lieutenant-Colonel Farnham severely wounded, one enlisted man killed and twelve wounded.

Moved directly toward the South Side Railroad, which was reached about three o'clock P.M. Moving down the road about seven miles, turned to the left, marched in a northwesterly direction until about half-past six P.M., halted and stacked arms. At half-past seven the enemy opened with musketry from a piece of woods, but without effect. The firing soon ceased, and no further demonstration being made by the enemy, the regiment went into bivouac.

Lieutenant George D. Bisbee rejoined his company from Camp Parole. From this point the regiment followed the brigade on its direct route to Appomattox Court House, at which place on the 9th instant, the rebel general, Lee, surrendered the Army of Northern Virginia.

1865 It was late in the afternoon when it became known that General Lee had sent for General Grant to surrender to him. It was between two and three o'clock when we met in the little room in the house where the surrender of Lee's army took place. I know there is a belief that the surrender took place under an apple tree, where Grant and Lee met and exchanged a few words. The surrender took place in the left-hand room of that old-fashioned double house. The house had a large piazza, which ran along the full length of it. It was one of those ordinary Virginia houses, with a passage-way running through the center of it.

In that little room where the meeting took place sat two young men — one a great-grandson of the Chief-Justice Marshall of the Supreme Court, reducing to writing the terms of the surrender, on behalf of Robert E. Lee; the other a man with a dusky countenance — a great-nephew of that celebrated chief, Red-Jacket — acting under General Grant. The two were reducing to writing the terms of the surrender of the Army of Northern Virginia to the Army of the Potomac. Gathered around the room were several officers, of whom I was one.

At some distance apart sat two men; one, the most remarkable man of his day and generation. The larger and older of the two was the most striking in his appearance. His hair was as white as the driven snow. There was not a speck upon his coat; not a spot upon those gauntlets that he wore, which were as bright and fair as a lady's glove. That was Robert E. Lee. The other was Ulysses S. Grant, whose appearance contrasted strangely with that of Lee; his boots were nearly covered with mud; one button off his coat — that is, the button off was not where it should have been — it had clearly gone astray; and he wore no sword, while Lee was fully and faultlessly equipped. The conversation was not rapid, by any means. Everybody felt the overpowering influence of the scene. Every one present felt they were witnessing the proceedings between the two chief actors in one of the most remarkable transactions of this nineteenth century. The words that passed between Grant and Lee were few.

General Grant — endeavoring to apologize for not being fully equipped, and noticing Lee's appearance — while the secretaries were busy, said: "General Lee, I have no sword; I have been riding all night." And Lee, with that coldness of manner, and all the pride — almost haughtiness — which, after all, became him wonderfully well, never made any reply, but in a cold, formal manner bowed. And General Grant, in the endeavor to take away the awkwardness of the scene, said: "I don't always wear a sword, because a sword is a very inconvenient thing." That was a very remarkable thing for him to say, considering that he was in the presence of one who was about to surrender his sword. Lee only bowed again. Another, trying to relieve the awkwardness of the occasion, inquired. "General Lee, what became of the white horse you rode in Mexico? He might not be dead yet, he was not so old." General Lee bowed coldly, and replied, "I left him at the White House, on the Pamunkey River, and I have not seen him since." There was one moment when there was a whispered conversation between Grant and Lee, which nobody in the room heard.

The surrender took the form of correspondence; the letters were all signed in due form, by the chief actors, in the presence of each other. Finally, when the terms of the surrender had all been arranged, and the surrender made, Lee arose, cold and proud, and bowed to every person in the room on our side. I remember each one of us thought he had been especially bowed to. And then he went out and passed down the little square in front of the house, and bestrode that gray horse that carried him all over Virginia, and when he had gone away we learned what that whispered conversation had been about. General Grant called his officers about him, and said, "You go to the Twenty-fourth, and you to the Fifth," and so on, naming the corps, "and ask every man who has three rations to turn over two of them. Go to the commissaries, and go to the quartermasters, etc. General Lee's army is on the point of starva-

1865 tion!" And twenty-five thousand rations were carried to the Army of Northern Virginia. — *Gen. Geo. H. Sharp.*

General Robert E. Lee was visited at Richmond, after Appomattox, by Chaplain Pepper, of the Eightieth Ohio Regiment, who has published some reminiscences of his interview.

The General spoke admiringly of Grant. "I wish," he said, "to do simple justice to General Grant when I say that his treatment of the Army of Southern Virginia is without a parallel in the history of the civilized world. When my poor soldiers, with famished faces, had neither food nor raiment, it was then that General Grant immediately issued that humane order that forty thousand rations should be furnished to the impoverished troops. And that was not all of his magnanimity. I was giving directions to one of my staff officers, when making out the list of things to be surrendered, to include the horses. At that moment General Grant, who seemed to be paying no attention to what was transpiring, quickly said, " No, no, General Lee, not a horse — not one — keep them all! Your people will need them for the spring crops!"

Apr. 15. The regiment remained at Appomattox Court House until April 15th, when it broke camp, and with the brigade marched to Black and White Station on the South Side Railroad, and went into camp on the 21st, and remained until May 1st. Major Small, Captains Conley and Lord, and Lieutenant Chapman rejoined the command from Camp Parole, Annapolis. Colonel Tilden left camp for Maine on fifteen days leave of absence, drawn thither by the alarming illness of his wife. The prayers and sympathy of the men went with him. Major Small assumed command of the regiment. The last brigade drill in which the regiment participated, was had at this station. ₁₈₆₅

Our work was done. The bugle sounded the order to pack up and march, and without a regret the men saw the sacred soil glide under their feet and fade into the distant perspective. Manchester was reached on the 4th instant. _{May 1.}

The brigade camped that night within sight of the Libby Prison. Through its grated windows, the writer, with many others had often cast longing eyes upon the green field now occupied by our tents. _{May 4.}

On the 6th, continued the march, passing through the principal streets of Richmond, to Hanover Court House. Thence over familiar ground to Fredericksburgh, where the regiment bivouacked on the 9th. In the morning moved over the old battle-field where the regiment received its first baptism of blood. Many of the men passed the whole distance in silence with uncovered heads. Crossing the Rappahannock below the city, the march was continued without incident via Fairfax Court House to Arlington Heights. Went into camp at Balls Cross Roads and remained until June 5th. Of all the marches made by the Sixteenth, for rapidity and length, without rest, none would compare with that most inhuman tramp for display at the "Grand Review." It was the last ounce of suffering needed to break the health of thousands of veterans. It was indeed a magnificent spectacle. The vanity of that prince of military humbugs, Halleck, as well as that of President Johnson was fully gratified. _{May 6.} _{May 9.}

1865
June 5.

Captain Walter T. Chester mustered the Sixteenth Regiment of Maine Volunteers out of the United States military service, in compliance with the following order:—

HDQ'RS ARMY OF THE POTOMAC,
June 4, 1865.

Special Orders, No. 141.

Under the provisions of General Orders, No. 94, current series from the Adjutant-General's office, and General Orders, No. 26, current series from these Headquarters, and upon the certificate of the proper Commissaries of Musters that the following named Organizations have complied with the requirements of the first mentioned order, they will at once be mustered out of service and placed *en route* to the proper State rendezvous — viz.:—

16th Maine Vols., 30 Commissioned Officers, and 285 enlisted men — to Augusta, Maine. . . . . .

The men of the organization, not entitled to discharge, will be transferred to their respective Corps Commanders as follows . . . .

The Quartermaster's Department will furnish the necessary transportation.

By command of MAJOR-GENL. MEADE,
(Signed)   GEO. D. RUGGLES, *Asst. Adjt-Genl.*

HEADQUARTERS 5th ARMY CORPS.
June 5, 1865.

"*Official.*"

The transferred men of the 16th Maine Vols., will be sen with their Descriptive Lists, Clothing Account, and a copy of this order to the 20th Maine Vols. to which Regt. they have been assigned.

By command of BRVT. MAJ.-GEN. GRIFFIN,
(Signed)   FRED T. LOCKE,
              Brevet-Col. & A. A. G.

Transportation was furnished and the regiment placed *en route* for the State rendezvous, at Augusta, Maine, at which place it arrived on the morning of June 10th, and quartered in the cavalry barracks on the fair grounds, near the capitol. The regiment was immediately paid in full, disbanded, and with sad leave taking severed ties which had bound men together with an affection as strong as that of David and Jonathan.

1865
June 6.

DEATH OF THE OLD WAR HORSE.

BY REV. NATHANIEL BUTLER, D.D.

BRIGADIER-GENERAL Charles W. Tilden, formerly colonel of the Sixteenth Maine Regiment, after his capture at Gettysburgh and confinement in Libby Prison, from which he escaped, received from his old regiment the present of a noble horse, with all the usual accouterments. Lieutenant Frank Wiggin, of the Sixteenth Maine Regiment, says, "We followed that horse and rider through the Wilderness and during the rest of the war: and the noble steed was at Appomattox when Lee surrendered. I think every soldier of the command would have followed him and his rider wherever they might have led." The horse was tenderly cared for by his owner till a few weeks since, when he was buried under the direction of General Tilden.

> Farewell, my horse! thy work is done,
>   Thy splendid form lies low,
> Thy limbs of steel have lost their strength,
>   Thy flashing eye its glow.
>
> No more thy quivering nostrils snuff
>   "The battle from afar,"
> No more beneath thy flying feet
>   The plains with thunder jar.
>
> For thou wert born a hero soul,
>   In days when heroes fought,
> When men, borne by thy glorious strength,
>   Immortal laurels sought.

Seated upon thy nerve-strung form,
   Another life was mine,
And well I knew the same high thrill
   Ran through my soul and thine.

A throne thou wert to sit upon,
   And true as steel within,
Whene'er I felt thy brave heart beat,
   My own has braver been.

And when the bugle's call to *charge*
   Over the column ran,
Thy arching crest, " with thunder clothed,"
   Loved best to lead the van.

Upon the march with tireless feet,
   Through mountain, gorge, and plain,
When others strayed thy place was kept
   Through all the long campaign.

But now, thy last, long halt is made,
   Thy last campaign is o'er;
The bugle call, the battle shout
   Shall thrill thee never more.

Where art thou gone — old friend and true?
   What place hast thou to fill?
For it may be thy spirit form
   Somewhere is marching still.

Are there immortal vales and hills,
   And pastures living green,
And sunny glades and waters sweet
   For such as thou didst seem?

Here there are those whom we call *men*,
   Whose souls, full well I know,
Another life may not deserve
   One-half so well as thou.

And natures such as thine has been
 That other life may claim,
And God may have a place for them
 Within his wide domain.

His armies tread their glorious march
 O'er the eternal plain,
Their leader rides a snow-white steed —
 Who follow in his train? *

We may not ever meet again;
 But, wheresoe'er I go,
A cherished place within my heart
 Thou 'lt have, old friend, I know.

God made us both, and we have marched
 Firm friends whilst thou wert here;
I only know I should not blush
 To meet thee anywhere.

* Rev. 19: 14.

BIOGRAPHIES

OF THE

OFFICERS

OF THE

SIXTEENTH MAINE REGIMENT.

BIOGRAPHICAL SKETCHES.

COLONEL A. W. WILDES.

"Was appointed aid with the rank of lieutenant-colonel on the staff of Governor Washburn, in 1860. At the commencement of the war he was deputed by the Governor, to superintend the transportation of troops to the front, manifesting in this as in other important duties, the highest efficiency and zeal. In May, 1862, Colonel Wildes was appointed colonel of the Sixteenth Maine, and until the muster-in of the regiment served without pay, and made liberal expenditure of his own means to further the interests of the regiment. While encamped near Sharpsburgh, Maryland, for some weeks after the Battle of Antietam, Colonel Wildes was seriously ill from some organic disease, and, growing worse, was by the medical board granted leave of absence for a brief period. Before recovery he returned to Washington in order to rejoin his regiment at Fredericksburgh. After visiting the regiment, and it being deemed expedient by the medical director that he should delay joining it in consequence of continued illness, Colonel Wildes thought it unjust to his officers to hold a command which his ill health prevented him from assuming, and tendered his resignation which was accepted, and he was honorably discharged from service January 7, 1863."—*Adjutant-General's Report.*

BREVET BRIGADIER-GENERAL CHARLES W. TILDEN

Was commissioned first lieutenant Company B, State Militia, October 20th, 1858; commissioned first lieutenant Company B, Second Maine Volunteers Infantry, April 27th, 1861; promoted captain June 24th, 1861; commissioned June 23d, 1862, and mustered as lieutenant-colonel Sixteenth Maine Regiment, July 8th, 1862; commissioned colonel, January 8th, 1863, and mustered February 16th following. General Tilden was taken prisoner at battle of Gettysburgh, July 1st, 1863. He escaped from Libby Prison through the famous tunnel, February 10th, 1864, and rejoined his command March 24th, 1864. The General was again captured August 19th, 1864, at the battle of Weldon Railroad. He made his escape on the 20th, and entered the Union lines in front of his regiment. He was soon after assigned to the command of the Third Brigade. He was brevetted brigadier-general volunteers, for faithful and meritorious services during the war, March 13th, 1865.

The adjutant-general's report says, "During his connection with the Sixteenth, his military history was thoroughly identified with that of his regiment, an abstract of which may be found under its appropriate heading in this volume. Should that fail to do adequate credit to the superior efficiency of this distinguished officer, it is sufficient to know that his unwritten record awards him a high place, not only in the esteem of his comrades, but also upon the roll of honor."

COLONEL AUGUSTUS B. FARNHAM

Was commissioned first lieutenant, of Company H, Second Maine Regiment, May 13th, 1861; captain, September 14th, 1861; was commissioned major Sixteenth Regiment, August 9th, 1862; lieutenant-colonel, February 5th, 1863; mustered, February 16th following; May 8th, 1863, Lieutenant-Colonel Farnham was appointed by General Robinson, inspector general and chief of staff, Second Division, and subsequently to the same position on Third Division Staff, Fifth Corps, by General Crawford, which position he held until wounded at Five Forks, Virginia, April 1, 1865. He was brevetted colonel for gallant and meritorious services at battles of Gravelly Run and Five Forks, Virginia, April 1st, 1865. Mustered out, June 5th, 1865. Colonel Farnham, while leading the front line of his division in the charge of the Fifth Corps, at battle of Five Forks, received a bullet in the lungs about one and one-half inches from the heart, and fell from his horse; the latter was shot through the jaw, through both hind legs, and in the rump. The Colonel lay on the field until the next morning, when men carried him to the house of a Mr. Moody, the inmates of which rendered him such assistance and attention as was possible, for nearly a month, when a detachment of the Sixteenth, under command of Lieutenant George D. Bisbee of Company C, carried him six miles through the woods to the railroad station, whence he was conveyed by rail to Petersburgh, Virginia, thence to City Point and Washington, and placed in Armory Square Hospital under charge of Surgeon Bliss. He lay at the point of death for weeks; was finally carried to his home in Bangor, Maine, and months elapsed before he recovered a sufficient degree of health to resume business duties. During all his suffering and the severe hemorrhages, which occasionally have occurred to the present time, Colonel Farnham has shown the same quiet fortitude which won for him the love and esteem of his comrades in the field.

MAJOR ARCH D. LEAVITT

Was wounded at the battle of Laurel Hill, Virginia, and died in Douglass Hospital, Washington, May 30th, 1864. Having fitted for college at his home, without the aid of seminary or academy, he entered Waterville College in 1858, and held first rank in his class. In the summer of 1862, those dark days when the cry went up for more men, he, with two of his classmates, raised a company, of which he was elected captain, and was mustered into the United States service, at Augusta, Maine, August 14th, 1862, as captain Company E, of the Sixteenth Regiment. In the January following, he was promoted to be major (commissioned February 5th), and in that capacity participated, with his regiment, in the following engagements: Battle of Fitzhugh Crossing, April 30th, 1863; Chancellorsville, May 2d; Gettysburgh, July 4th; skirmish of Funkstown, July 12th; Mine Run, November 29th; battle of the Wilderness, May 5th to 7th, 1864; and battle of Laurel Hill, in which he was mortally wounded, May 12th.

At the commencement of the battle of Gettysburgh, he was at Washington, sick, but hearing of the battle, and impatient for the light, he applied for leave to join his regiment, and reached the field on the last day of the action, in season to take command of the small, uncaptured remnant, numbering two officers and fifteen men. At the skirmish at Funkstown, Major Leavitt was in command of the regiment, having been placed in that position on the 5th of July, and retaining it until November 1st. On the 14th of August, 1863, he was detailed a member in the corps court-martial, to convene at the headquarters of First Division, First Army Corps, for the trial of deserters, etc. On the 21st of September, he took charge of a school of instruction for commissioned officers, and drilled the battalion.

Extracts from his diary show that Major Leavitt was a young man of strong sympathies, and that he desired the best welfare of his comrades, whilst the testimony of all associated with him in camp or on the battle-field, proves that in the performance of duty he was prompt, active, and conscientious, giving his most earnest thoughts, labors, and prayers to advance the interests of his country. He died as he had lived, a pure patriot and a true Christian, leaving as his last message, "Tell my friends I have always tried to do my duty."

Of the estimation in which Major Leavitt was held by the regiment, Rev. Mr. Balkam, its chaplain, wrote: "His excellent character and amiable disposition had won our respect and affections. You know his reputation as a scholar, and his devotion to study; his studious habits did not forsake him in the camp. Especially did he strive to increase his military knowledge and capacity. He had a conscientious regard for every obligation, and for every duty, nor was he unmindful of the higher relations which connect us with God and another world."

His remains were brought to Turner and buried with Masonic honors.— *Adjutant-General's Report.*

MAJOR S. CLIFFORD BELCHER.

Samuel Clifford Belcher entered Bowdoin College at the age of fourteen, and graduated in course with the class of 1857. After his graduation he served for three years as preceptor of Foxcroft Academy, which position he resigned in 1860, to enter the office of Honorable Nehemiah Abbott of Belfast as a student at law. The following year he was admitted to the Franklin County Bar. Soon after the outbreak of the Rebellion, Mr. Belcher enlisted in the United States Service, and June 4th, 1862, was commissioned captain of Company G, Sixteenth Regiment of Maine Volunteers, immediately leaving for the front. This regiment was among the most gallant among the Maine regiments. It took part in the battle of Fredericksburgh, where Captain Belcher was slightly wounded; it also served in the Chancellorsville campaign, and at Gettysburgh. To this regiment at Gettysburgh was assigned the perilous task of covering the retreat of the First Corps, upon the first day of the battle. It heroically held the position, from which two regiments had been previously driven, until every man but forty was killed or taken prisoner. It was while performing this duty that the regiment cut its battle-flag in pieces and distributed it among the men, that it might not be captured by the enemy. This famous order was given by Captain Belcher. Captain Belcher commanded the left wing of the regiment, and with his comrades was taken prisoner of war. While the prisoners were marching to Libby Prison, Captain Belcher made his escape, and by clever stratagem gained the Union lines. His regiment being captured, he was assigned as *aide-de-camp* to General Heintzelman of the department at Washington. The following autumn he joined the soldiers at the front, and entered the "Wilderness" campaign. On the 8th of May, 1864, he received a bullet in the head, which pierced the skull and rested upon the brain. After seventeen days the ball was extracted, but Captain Belcher was not sufficiently recovered to rejoin his company before the cessation of hostilities. Governor Cony commissioned him Major June 1st, 1864. Upon recovering his health, Major Belcher resumed the practice of law at Farmington, and has remained actively engaged in his profession up to the present time.— *History of Farmington.*

MAJOR ABNER R. SMALL

Was first mustered into the United States service as a private in Company G, Third Maine Infantry, in June, 1861, and was speedily promoted to corporal, and then to sergeant. In May, 1862, he received further promotion by being commissioned first lieutenant and adjutant, Sixteenth Regiment. In December, 1862, he was assigned to duty as aide-de-camp on the staff of First Brigade, Second Division, First Army Corps, and whilst serving as such was complimented with well-deserved special mention for distinguished gallantry displayed in the battle of Fredericksburgh. In July, 1863, he was also appointed acting assistant adjutant-general of the same brigade, and again received special notice in general orders for his brave conduct in the battle of Gettysburgh. He also participated in all the battles in which his regiment was engaged, until taken and held a prisoner from August 18th, 1864, to February 22d, 1865. In the meantime, October 31st, 1864, he was commissioned major of the same command. Thus he was with the Sixteenth Regiment from the time of its organization until its muster-out, June 5th, 1865.—*Adjutant-General's Report.*

ADJUTANT CHERBURY F. LOTHROP.

Appointed sergeant Company C, June 9th, 1862; mustered into United States service, August 14th, 1862; promoted orderly sergeant, sergeant-major, September 9th, 1863; second lieutenant Company F, December 1st, 1863; first lieutenant, August 8th, 1864; adjutant, December 9th, 1864; mustered out, June 5th, 1865.

QUARTERMASTER ISAAC N. TUCKER.

Mustered as lieutenant-colonel Third Maine, June 14th, 1861; resigned, September 30th, 1861; commissioned quartermaster Sixteenth Regiment, August 16th, 1862; resigned and discharged, July 28th, 1864.

QUARTERMASTER GEORGE W. BROWN.

Appointed quartermaster sergeant, June 6th, 1862; mustered into United States service, August 14th, 1862; commissioned quartermaster, August 13th, 1864; acting assistant quartermaster, Second Brigade, Third Division, Fifth Army Corps, February, 1865; mustered out, June 5th, 1865.

SURGEON CHARLES ALEXANDER.

Appointed surgeon, July 10th, 1862; mustered, August 14th, 1862; wounded at battle of Gettysburgh, and prisoner, July 1st, 1863. Paroled on the field, July 2d, 1863, and rejoined regiment, October, 1863. Resigned and discharged for disability, November 9th, 1864. By special order number twenty-three, headquarters Third Division, Fifth Army Corps, July 11th, 1864, he was appointed surgeon-in-chief of the First Brigade, and subsequently surgeon-in-chief of Third Divison, Fifth Army Corps.

SURGEON WILLIAM W. EATON.

Appointed hospital steward, June 27th, 1862; mustered into United States service, August 14th, 1862; commissioned assistant surgeon, February 5th, 1863; commissioned surgeon, November 25th, 1864; mustered out, June 5th, 1865. Taken prisoner at Gettysburgh, July 1st, 1863; paroled.

ASSISTANT SURGEON JOSEPH B. BAXTER.

Appointed assistant surgeon, July 22d, 1862; mustered into United States service, August 14th, 1862; in charge of division hospital, Second Division, First Army Corps, August, 1863; mustered out, May 23d, 1865.

ASSISTANT SURGEON WARREN HUNTER.

Commissioned assistant surgeon, October 24th, 1862; joined regiment —— ——; resigned, January 24th, 1863.

ASSISTANT SURGEON DAVID P. BOLSTER.

Commissioned assistant surgeon, February 10th, 1865; mustered out, June 5th, 1865.

CHAPLAIN GEORGE BULLEN.

Commissioned, August 4th, 1862; resigned and discharged, October 3d, 1863.

CHAPLAIN URIAH BALKAM.

Commissioned, December 18th, 1863; resigned and discharged, October 8th, 1864.

CHAPLAIN JOHN MITCHELL.

Commissioned, February 8th, 1865; mustered out, June 5th, 1865.

CAPTAIN CHARLES A. WILLIAMS.

Commissioned captain Company A, July 9th, 1862; mustered into United States service, August 14th, 1862; died of disease at Rhorersville, Maryland, November 10th, 1862.

CAPTAIN S. FORREST ROBINSON.

Commissioned first lieutenant Company A, July 21st, 1862; mustered into United States service, August 14th, 1862; resigned and discharged, January 24th, 1863.

CAPTAIN ISAAC A. PENNELL.

Commissioned second lieutenant Company A, July 29th, 1862; mustered into United States service, August 14th, 1862; commissioned first lieutenant, November 19th, 1862; wounded at battle of Fredericksburgh, December 13th, 1862; commissioned captain, March 2d, 1863; detached for recruiting service in Maine, July 23d, 1864; discharged for disability, October 14th, 1864.

CAPTAIN CHARLES T. HILDRETH.

Commissioned captain Company A, September 15th, 1864; mustered out, June 5th, 1865.

CAPTAIN CHARLES K. HUTCHINS.

" From the commencement of the war, by word and deed, he sought to encourage patriotic action, and aid in the suppression of the rebellion. He made pecuniary sacrifices, he enlisted men; an eloquent speaker, his stirring appeals made in behalf of his country's cause will long be remembered in many towns of this State. In May, 1862, the governor tendered him a captain's commission in the Sixteenth Regiment, which was accepted. (Captain Hutchins was commissioned in Company B, August 9th, 1862, and mustered into the United States service August 14th.) As a commander, he received the respect and affection of his men, by uniform kindness and attention to their wants. At the time of the movement upon Fredericksburgh, he was suffering from the prostrating effects of a fever, which had so weakened him that he was scarcely able to keep with his command; but when the hour of battle came, it found him at the head of his company; and of the many brave men in the Sixteenth Regiment who fell on that bloody field, Captain Hutchins was one. The regiment was in the advance, and while encouraging his men, he was pierced simultaneously by two bullets; one entered his head, the other near his heart; either would have produced instant death. He fell a brave soldier, and though the glory of many battles, or the fame of proud position may not have sounded his name in the ears of nations, his country none the less lost a true and gallant hero, and his family and friends, a dear and much loved companion."

Comrade Brookings, a member of his company, writes: "I remember that just prior to the battle of Fredericksburgh, Captain Hutchins was sadly and strongly impressed with the belief that this was to be his first and last battle, and he so informed one of his company. But, notwithstanding his feelings, he addressed the company on the morning it started for the battle-field, asking them to sustain him fully as an officer and soldier, to which they replied with a cheer."

CAPTAIN ELEAZER W. ATWOOD.

Commissioned first lieutenant Company B, August 9th, 1862; mustered into United States service, August 14th, 1862; commissioned captain, December 31st, 1862; resigned and discharged, November 25th, 1864; taken prisoner at Gettysburgh, July 1st, 1863.

CAPTAIN JOSEPH H. MALBON.

Commissioned first lieutenant Company G, August 16th, 1862; captain company B, December 9th, 1864; in command of Division Ambulance Corps, Second Division, First Army Corps, from 1863 until mustered out, June 5th, 1865.

CAPTAIN DANIEL MARSTON.

Mustered into the United States service as private in Company D, Ninth Maine Regiment, September 22d, 1861; commissioned captain Company C, Sixteenth Maine Regiment, August 9th, 1862; mustered, August 14th following; wounded accidentally at battle of Fredericksburgh, December 13th, 1862; resigned and discharged, December 22d, 1864.

CAPTAIN EDWARD F. DAVIES

Was mustered into the United States service, August 14th, 1862, as fourth sergeant Company K. For bravery as color sergeant at battle of Fredericksburgh he was promoted to second lieutenant and commissioned May 22d, 1863; commissioned first lieutenant, December 1st, 1863; commissioned captain Company C, January 28th, 1865; mustered out, June 5th, 1865. He was taken prisoner at the battle of Weldon Railroad, August 19th, 1864, and with Colonel Tilden escaped and rejoined his company, August 20th, 1864. He was wounded at battle of Spottsylvania Court House, May 9th, 1864.

CAPTAIN MOSES W. RAND.

Commissioned captain Company D, August 16th, 1862; died in Portland, December 8th, 1862.

CAPTAIN OLIVER H. LOWELL.

Commissioned first lieutenant Company F, August 16th, 1862; commissioned captain Company D, December 31st, 1862; killed at battle of Gettysburgh, July 1st, 1863.

CAPTAIN SAMUEL H. PLUMMER.

Appointed first sergeant Company D, July 21st. 1862; mustered, August 14th, 1862; commissioned first lieutenant, December 31st, 1862; commissioned captain, December 1st, 1863; wounded and prisoner of war, July 1st, 1863; paroled and rejoined regiment, July 4th; discharged, October 20th, 1864.

CAPTAIN WILLIAM H. BROUGHTON.

Mustered as private Company D, August 14th, 1862; commissioned second lieutenant, December 31st, 1862; commissioned first lieutenant, December 1st, 1863; commissioned captain, November 9th, 1864; mustered out, June 5th, 1865. Captain Broughton was one of the youngest and bravest officers of the civil war. He was born in Naples in 1846, and removed to Portland when quite young. In fact, he was only sixteen years old when he enlisted. At the battle of Fredericksburgh, his intrepid daring was made the subject of special mention by a correspondent of the *Press*, who says: "One of the most gallant and meritorious deeds of the action was performed by Sergeant William H. Broughton of Company D, Sixteenth Maine. During the retreat of our brigade, the color sergeant of the 94th New York was shot down; he called for some one to carry off the colors; the call was unheeded by his own regiment, but being heard by Sergeant Broughton, he promptly obeyed the call, seized the flag, and carried it in triumph from the field, and delivered it to Colonel Tilden." The officers of his company being killed or wounded, he took charge. For these and other brave acts, he was made second lieutenant on the field. He was captured on the Weldon Railroad, August 18th, 1864; exchanged and rejoined his company in time to participate in battles of Hatcher's Run, Gravelly Run, Five Forks, and Appomattox Court House. He was a genial, kind-hearted man. His ready wit, his alert and vigorous mind, and the cordiality of his manners, made him a delightful companion. He died January 27th, 1882.—*Portland Press.*

CAPTAIN WILLIAM A. STEVENS.

Commissioned second lieutenant Company E, August 9th, 1862; mustered, August 14th, 1862; commissioned first lieutenant, February 5th, 1863; commissioned captain, March 26th, 1863; wounded at the battle of Fredericksburgh, December 13th, 1862; wounded and prisoner at the battle of Gettysburgh, July 1st, 1863; killed, June 17th, 1864. "Captain Stevens was a graduate of Waterville College, of the class of 1862, taking his diploma while dressed in Federal uniform. After graduation, he was appointed second lieutenant of Company E, Sixteenth Regiment, and was successively promoted to be first lieutenant and captain. He was wounded at Fredericksburgh, taken prisoner, and paroled at Gettysburgh. He was killed near Petersburgh by a rebel sharpshooter. When informed that he could not live, he told his brother that he died calm and happy. His remains were sent home, where appropriate religious services were held, June 29th, and a brief address pronounced by Rev. Mr. Pepper, his former pastor, in which appropriate mention was made of his character, and the events of his short life, so sadly and yet so gloriously ended. At the close of the services his remains were taken in charge by the members of the senior class of Waterville College, and, preceded by Waterville Lodge of Freemasons, were borne to the Pine Grove Cemetery, where 'the brothers of the mystic tie' performed the last offices for a deceased brother."—*Adjutant-General's Report.*

CAPTAIN WILLIAM E. BROOKS.

Commissioned first lieutenant Company E, August 9th, 1862; mustered, August 14th, 1862; commissioned captain, February 6th, 1863; wounded at battle of Fredericksburgh, December 13th, 1862; resigned, February 26th, 1863.

CAPTAIN AND BREVET LIEUTENANT-COLONEL LINCOLN K. PLUMMER

Was appointed first sergeant Company E, May 30th, 1862; mustered into United States service, August 14th, 1862; commissioned second lieutenant, March 2d, 1863; first lieutenant, March

26th, 1863; captain, August 8th, 1864. Was taken prisoner, May, 1864; recaptured by Sheridan, and rejoined company; appointed aide-de-camp on staff of First Brigade, Third Division, Fifth Army Corps, 1864; brevetted major and lieutenant-colonel, for faithful, meritorious, and gallant services, to date from March 13th, 1865.

CAPTAIN THOMAS E. WENTWORTH.

Commissioned captain Company F. August 9th, 1862; mustered into United States service, August 14th, 1862; captured at battle of Gettysburgh, July 1st, 1863, and paroled; discharged, July 1st, 1864.

CAPTAIN GEORGE A. DEERING.

Commissioned second lieutenant, August 16th, 1862; first lieutenant, December 31st, 1862; captain, August 8th, 1864. "Captain Deering, of Saco, received a recruiting commission from Governor Washburn in June, 1862, and at once proceeded to recruit men for the new regiments then being raised. In August of that year he was mustered into service at Augusta, by Major Gardiner as second lieutenant Company F, Sixteenth Regiment, Maine Volunteers. He participated in the first battle of Fredericksburgh under General Burnside, and for meritorious conduct on that occasion was promoted to first lieutenant. He also shared in all the battles of the Army of the Potomac up to the battle of Gettysburgh. In that battle he had command of companies F, D, and A, and late in the afternoon of the 1st of July, he, together with his entire command, was captured by the enemy and marched through the Shenandoah Valley to Richmond, where he was confined in Libby Prison for ten months. He was afterward sent to Macon, Georgia, thence to Savannah, and finally to Charleston, South Carolina, where, during the months of August and September, he, with other Union officers, was confined in the jail-yard under the fire of the guns from Gilmore's batteries on Morris Island. He was then removed to Columbia, South Carolina, where he remained until December 10th, 1864, when after having been subjected to rebel cruelty, imprisonment, and privation, he was so fortunate as to effect his escape by assuming the name of a commissary sergeant of an Ohio regiment, who had died or was not present to answer to his name at rollcall. During his imprisonment he was promoted to the captaincy of his old company (F), but his health had become so much impaired by his confinement in Southern prisons that he did not rejoin his regiment until May 1st, 1865, and was mustered out of service at Washington in June following."—*Adjutant-General's Report.*

CAPTAIN ISAAC H. THOMPSON.

Commissioned second lieutenant Company G, August 16th, 1862; mustered into United States service, to date from August 14th, 1862; commissioned first lieutenant Company I, December 18th, 1863; commissioned captain Company G, December 26th, 1864; mustered out, June 5th, 1865. Was wounded, June 18th, 1864, in front of Petersburgh, Virginia.

CAPTAIN JOHN AYER.

Commissioned captain Company H; mustered, August 14th, 1862; wounded at battle of Fredericksburgh, Virginia, December 13th, 1862; leg amputated, from which he died in Libby Prison, Richmond, Virginia, February 22d, 1863.

CAPTAIN JOHN D. CONLEY.

Mustered into the United States service as first sergeant Company H, August 14th, 1862; commissioned second lieutenant, December 13th, 1862; commissioned captain, May 22d, 1863; taken prisoner at battle of Weldon Railroad, August 18th, 1864; exchanged, February 22d, 1865, and rejoined his company April following; mustered out, June 5th, 1865.

CAPTAIN WILLIAM H. WALDRON.

Mustered into United States service as captain Company I, August 14th, 1862; wounded, July 1st, 1863, at battle of Gettysburgh; taken prisoner and paroled, July 4th; discharged for disability, September 27th, 1863; died, February 25th, 1881. "The leading characteristics which distinguished the subject of this sketch were the leading characteristics that distinguished his forefathers. Ever a fighter himself, both in a moral and physical sense, he came of a family of fighters, who generation after generation made themselves conspicuous in New England annals, wherever there was work of the heroic sort to be done. The war was the supreme crisis and turning point in the life of the country. It was equally so in the life of Captain Waldron, in common with thousands of his countrymen. When the integrity of the Union was attacked, all other considerations were swallowed up by his sense of duty to that Union. He believed that every able-bodied man should go to the front and fight when he got there—and he acted on that belief. This decision cost him more than his life. It cost him a prosperous business, a promising career, everything in circumstance and opportunity that goes to the making of a successful man. Animated by his uncompromising sentiments of loyalty, in the summer of 1862, he at once set to work raising a company, which he did on his own responsibility. He was then over forty years old, and the regiment to which he was assigned, made up mostly of young men from eighteen to twenty-four, looked upon him as a veteran, and affectionately called him 'Old Waldron'— for they had great regard for him from the first, a regard that the experiences of the terrible years following only served to increase. 'The first time I saw him,' says Captain Broughton, 'I was impressed with his soldierly qualities, his unassuming manner, and a firm, quiet, bull-dog tenacity which he seemed to possess. The opinion then formed was confirmed by further acquaintance.'

"Major Small, then adjutant, writes of Captain Waldron at Gettysburgh: 'The memory of his coolness and intrepidity at the battle of Gettysburgh is always fresh with me, and I can clearly picture him with a ghastly wound in his neck—supported by a tree—facing the enemy who was pouring shot and shell all around him, shouting encouraging words to his men. We repeatedly urged him to allow them to carry him to the rear, but without avail. Brave and true himself, he had no patience with timidity or shrinking in others.

"'Hospital bummers won his especial hatred and disgust, and he was not slow to anathematize all such who came under his observation. But a kinder and more humane man toward the deserving, I never knew. In battle his example was a tower of strength to his comrades, and in camp he left a broad path of sunshine wherever he went. Genial and social always, none went to him for a word of sympathy and encouragement and came away empty. There is not a member of his regiment who would not gladly add words of tribute to his worth.' With the battle of Gettysburgh closed his military career. What that career was, how honorably pursued, how faithfully and energetically persevered in to the end, the unwritten history of his regiment sufficiently attests. Throughout it all his purpose was single-hearted; his one sole aim was to help defend this Union from the attacks of its enemies, and in the cause he was ready, with the thousands of his brave comrades, to lay down his life, if need be — as finally he did. In life he asked no praise for doing his supreme duty. He needs none now he is dead. His faithful service, consecrated by death, stands apart and above all praise, and no weak speech of ours shall intrude upon its simple, silent heroism."— *Biography, Lewiston Weekly Gazette.*

CAPTAIN LEWIS C. BISBEE

Was mustered as private Company I, August 20th, 1862; commissioned first lieutenant, August 23d, 1862; captain, December 1st, 1863; wounded and prisoner at battle of Gettysburgh, July 1st, 1863. Captain Bisbee was confined in the famous "Libby Prison" at Richmond; also at Macon, Georgia; Savannah, Georgia; Charleston, South Carolina, and finally transferred to the stockade at Columbia, South Carolina, where he remained until released in the spring of 1865.

CAPTAIN STEPHEN C. WHITEHOUSE

Was mustered as captain of Company K, August 14th, 1862; was killed at battle of Gettysburgh, Pennsylvania, July 1st, 1863; while leading his men into action. "Captain Whitehouse was a brave, a patriotic officer, a generous whole-souled companion, and a Christian gentleman. He was dearly beloved by the company he commanded, and honored and respected by his brother officers."

CAPTAIN JOSEPH O. LORD

Was appointed first sergeant Company K, June 5th, 1862; mustered into the United States service with regiment, August 14th, 1862; commissioned first lieutenant, May 22d, 1863, to rank from March 31st, 1863; commissioned captain, December 1st, 1863, to rank from July 1st, 1863. He was wounded at battle of Fredericksburgh, December 13th, 1862; taken prisoner at battle of Gettysburgh, July 1st, 1863, and escaped the third day after his capture; prisoner at battle of Weldon Railroad, August 19th, 1864; was confined in Libby Prison, Richmond, Virginia. Salisbury Stockade, North Carolina, and Prison "No. 3," Danville, Virginia; exchanged, February 22d, 1865; rejoined his company in May, 1865; mustered out, June 5th, 1865.

FIRST LIEUTENANT NATHAN FOWLER.

Mustered a private, Company A, August 14th, 1862; commissioned second lieutenant, May 22d, 1863; commissioned first lieutenant, June 13th, 1863; discharged, October 26th, 1864. Wounded at battle of the Wilderness, May, 1864.

FIRST LIEUTENANT SAMUEL P. NEWMAN SMYTHE,

Class of 1863, Bowdoin College; commissioned first lieutenant Company A, September 15th. 1864; acting regimental quartermaster, 1864-5; mustered out, June 5th, 1865.—*Adjutant-General's Report.*

FIRST LIEUTENANT GEORGE W. EDWARDS.

Commissioned second lieutenant Company B, August 9th, 1862; mustered, August 14th, 1862; commissioned first lieutenant, December 31st, 1862; killed at battle of Fredericksburgh, December 13th, 1862. Lieutenant Edwards, class of 1862, Bowdoin College, was born in Gardiner, Maine, November, 1839; served in the

Maryland campaign; in December, 1862, acted as judge advocate of his brigade court-martial; was killed in action at Fredericksburgh, gallantly leading his men in a bayonet charge, at the age of twenty-three years.—*Adjutant-General's Report.*

FIRST LIEUTENANT FRED H. BEECHER.

Mustered into the United States service as second sergeant Company B; commissioned second lieutenant, January 24th, 1863; first lieutenant, March 26th, 1863; discharged, September 30th, 1864. Lieutenant Beecher, class of 1862, Bowdoin College, a nephew of Henry Ward Beecher, was a young officer of remarkable coolness and bravery, and distinguished himself at the battle of Fredericksburgh, where he was severely wounded in the knee. On the point of joining his regiment at the expiration of his leave of absence, he was thrown from the carriage, injuring the wounded knee so severely as to require an extension of his leave. While lame and unfit for duty, he joined his company in season to participate in the battle of Gettysburgh. His courage was undaunted and kept him to the front, when on the afternoon of July 2d he was again wounded by a shell in the same knee, and carried from the field. He seemed fated. He was appointed first lieutenant in the Veteran Reserve Corps; was sent out to Raleigh, North Carolina, by General Howard, on business connected with the bureau. Disliking the duties required, he was subsequently appointed second lieutenant regular infantry, and sent to the frontier, where he was killed in his first action with the Indians. His command was surrounded by superior numbers, and from the commencement of the fight until nearly all were sacrificed, Lieutenant Beecher was cool, courageous, and unyielding. His body was riddled with bullets, and he died fighting so long as he could grasp a sword or load a rifle. His was a noble, generous soul. Truly, he was one of the most loving and lovable of men.

FIRST LIEUTENANT JONES WHITMAN.

Appointed corporal Company E, July 12th, 1862; mustered, August 14th, 1862; promoted second sergeant, January 3d, 1863; commissioned second lieutenant, November 25th, 1864; commissioned first lieutenant Company B, December 9th, 1864; mustered out, June 5th, 1865.

FIRST LIEUTENANT HOVEY C. AUSTIN.

Commissioned first lieutenant Company C, August 16th, 1862; mustered, to date from August 14th, 1862; wounded at battle of Fredericksburgh, December 13th, 1862; discharged for disability, March 20th, 1863.

FIRST LIEUTENANT MARSHALL S. SMITH.

Commissioned second lieutenant Company C, August 19th, 1862; mustered, August 14th, 1862; commissioned first lieutenant, April 10th, 1863; missing in battle of Wilderness, May, 1864; discharged, May 15th, 1865.

FIRST LIEUTENANT HUMPHREY E. EUSTIS.

Commissioned first lieutenant Company D, August 16th, 1862; mustered to date from August 14th, 1862; resigned, December 8th, 1862.

FIRST LIEUTENANT ATWOOD FITCH.

Mustered into the United States service as sergeant Company K, August 14th, 1862; commissioned second lieutenant Company D, December 1st, 1863; commissioned first lieutenant, November 9th, 1864; prisoner of war at battle of Weldon Railroad, August 19th, 1864; exchanged and rejoined regiment; mustered out, June 5th, 1865.

FIRST LIEUTENANT AND BREVET MAJOR AUBREY LEAVITT.

Appointed third sergeant, Company E, July 5th, 1862; mustered into United States service, August 14th, 1862; commissioned second lieutenant, May 22d, 1863; commissioned first lieutenant, August 8th, 1864; mustered out, June 5th, 1865. Lieutenant Leavitt was assigned to duty by general order number thirteen, headquarters First Brigade, Second Divison, Fifth Army Corps, April 12th, 1864, as acting aide-de-camp on the staff of the general commanding; again by special order number ninety, Second Brigade, Third Division, December 6th, 1864. He was relieved from duty in the following well-deserved, complimentary order: —

HEADQUARTERS 2d BRIG., 3d DIV., 5TH A. C.
June 5th, 1865.

General Order No. 10.

Lieut. Aubrey Leavitt, 16th Me. Vols., is relieved from duty at these Headquarters on account of muster out of service.

The Brigadier-General commanding desires to express his thanks to Lieut. Leavitt for the able, efficient, and prompt attendance to duty, ever proving himself a most brave and gallant soldier on the battle-field, performing his duties with that ability, coolness, and decision that rendered his services most valuable.

By order of BRIG.-GEN. BAXTER, *Com'dg Brigade.*
JAMES B. THOMAS, *Capt. & A. A. A. G.*

Lieutenant Leavitt was brevetted captain and major, for faithful, meritorious, and gallant services, to date from March 13th, 1865. He was wounded at battle of Gettysburgh, July 1st, 1863.

FIRST LIEUTENANT LEWIS G. RICHARDS.

Mustered into United States service as corporal Company H, August 14th, 1862; promoted to fourth sergeant, December 1st, 1862; promoted second lieutenant,— not mustered; commissioned first lieutenant Company G, December 9th, 1864; prisoner at Gettysburgh, July 1st, 1863; paroled and rejoined regiment; discharged, February 4th, 1865.

FIRST LIEUTENANT FRANK WIGGIN.

Mustered into the United States service as private Company H, August 14th, 1862; appointed fifth sergeant, December 1st, 1862; subsequently reduced to the ranks to join the band; commissioned first lieutenant Company G, March 15th, 1865; mustered out, June 5th, 1865; captured, May 8th, 1864; recaptured by General Sheridan and rejoined regiment.

FIRST LIEUTENANT IRA S. LIBBY.

Commissioned first lieutenant, August 16th, 1862; mustered into United States Service, to date from August 14th, 1862; resigned, October 31st, 1862.

FIRST LIEUTENANT ISRAEL H. WASHBURN.

Mustered into United States service, second lieutenant, Company H, August 2d, 1862; commissioned first lieutenant, December 13th, 1862; appointed aide-de-camp on staff of Major-General H. G. Berry; resigned, June 12th, 1863. Lieutenant Washburn, of Orono, is one of the young men of Maine, who, from a conviction of duty, when enlistments did not keep pace with the requirements of the service, came forward and encouraged patriotic action by enlisting in the Sixteenth Regiment. He was appointed second lieutenant, and was afterward promoted to first lieutenant. The first battle of his regiment was at Fredericksburgh, in December, 1862, and his gallant behavior on that occasion coming to the notice of Major-General Berry, that lamented officer gave him a position on his staff. Resigning the service in June, 1863, he was subsequently appointed lieutenant in the United States Marine Corps. Recently he has been ordered to report on the United States Steamer Rhode Island, the flag-ship of the West India Squadron.— *Adjutant-General's Report.*

FIRST LIEUTENANT WILLIAM BRAY.

Commissioned first lieutenant Company I, August 16th, 1862— not mustered; resigned.

FIRST LIEUTENANT WILMOT H. CHAPMAN.

Lieutenant Chapman, the youngest officer in the regiment, was born in Nobleboro, Lincoln County, Maine, January 24th, 1846; enlisted in Company K, June 7th, 1862; mustered as corporal, August 14th, 1862; promoted sergeant, December, 1862; first sergeant, May, 1863; commissioned second lieutenant, December 1st, 1863; commissioned first lieutenant Company I, December 26th, 1864; mustered out, June 5th, 1865. He was in command of

Company K, from May 9th to 25th, 1864; Company I, from May 28th to June 18th, 1864; Company G, from June 18th to August 18th; taken prisoner at battle of Weldon Railroad, August 18th, 1864; paroled February 22d, 1865, and rejoined his company, April following. He was wounded at Spottsylvania Court House, May 10th, 1864. He took an honorable part in all the battles in which the regiment was engaged.

FIRST LIEUTENANT AUGUSTUS T. SOMERBY.

Commissioned first lieutenant Company K, August 16th, 1862; mustered into the United States service to date from August 14th, 1862; resigned, March 12th, 1863.

FIRST LIEUTENANT JABEZ P. PARKER.

Mustered into the United States service, corporal Company I, August 14th, 1862; promoted sergeant and first sergeant; commissioned second lieutenant Company K, November 25th, 1864; commissioned first lieutenant, January 28th, 1865; mustered out, June 5th, 1865; was severely wounded at battle of Wilderness, May, 1864.

SECOND LIEUTENANT FRANCIS A. WILDES.

Appointed sergeant-major, June 12th, 1862; commissioned second lieutenant Company A, December 3d, 1862; resigned, February 6th, 1863.

SECOND LIEUTENANT NATHANIEL W. COSTON.

Enlisted, July 8th, 1862, and appointed fifth sergeant Company A; mustered into the United States service, August 14th, 1862; promoted first sergeant; commissioned second lieutenant, June 13h, 1863; wounded in the Wilderness campaign, May, 1864; died of wounds, May 27th, 1864.

SECOND LIEUTENANT AND BREVET FIRST LIEUTENANT WILLIAM T. DODGE.

Mustered into the United States service, second lieutenant Company A (new organization), October 17th, 1864; acting quartermaster; mustered out, June 5th, 1865; brevetted first lieutenant for gallant and meritorious services during the war, to date from March 13th, 1865.

SECOND LIEUTENANT MELVIN C. WADSWORTH.

Class of 1866, Bowdoin College, was mustered into the United States service, fourth corporal Company B, August 14th, 1862; promoted first sergeant; commissioned second lieutenant, March 26th, 1863; mustered out, June 5th, 1864.

SECOND LIEUTENANT GEORGE D. BISBEE.

Was born in Hartford, Oxford County, Maine, July 8th, 1841; volunteered from Peru, June 17th, 1862; mustered with regiment, August 14th, 1862; appointed first sergeant, August 27th, 1862; wounded at battle of Fredericksburgh, Virginia, December 13th, 1862; discharged from service by reason of wounds, at Mt. Pleasant Hospital, Washington, District of Columbia, April 25th, 1863. He again entered the service, under commission as second lieutenant, dated April 10th, 1863, and joined his old company while on the march to Chancellorsville, April 28th, following; but on account of the active movements of the regiment, was not mustered as second lieutenant until May 2d, 1863. He was closely identified with his company during the campaign. Lieutenant Bisbee was captured at Gettysburgh, Pennsylvania, July 1st, 1863, and held a prisoner of war until December 9th, 1864, suffering confinement for ten months in Libby Prison, and the remainder of time at Macon and Savannah, Georgia; Charleston, South Carolina, and in the stockade at Columbia. He was paroled from the latter place, December 9th, 1864, being considered unfit for further duty, and sent to Camp Parole, Annapolis, Maryland, where he was specially exchanged, April 1st, 1865, and started for the front, rejoining his regiment, April 5th, in season to participate in the last scene at Appomattox. He was commissioned first lieutenant while a prisoner, but could not be mustered, and the commission was revoked. Mustered out with regiment, June 5th, 1865. Lieutenant Bisbee, and other officers of the Sixteenth, lost promotion by reason of long confinement as prisoners of war.

SECOND LIEUTENANT HENRY P. HERRICK.

Commissioned second lieutenant Company D, August 16th, 1862; killed at battle of Fredericksburgh, December 13th, 1862.

SECOND LIEUTENANT CHARLES H. PARLIN.

Enlisted as private Company K; appointed commissary sergeant, August 11th, 1862; mustered into United States service, August 14th, 1862; commissioned second lieutenant Company D, November 9th, 1864; mustered out, June 5th, 1865.

SECOND LIEUTENANT GUSTAVUS MOORE.

Enlisted as private Company B, and mustered into United States service, August 14th, 1862; commissioned second lieutenant Company E, December 9th, 1864; mustered out, June 5th, 1865.

SECOND LIEUTENANT DANIEL L. WARREN.

Mustered as first sergeant Company F, August 14th, 1862; commissioned second lieutenant, March 17th, 1863; discharged for disability, October 27th, 1863.

SECOND LIEUTENANT DANIEL A. SPEARIN.

Appointed corporal Company A, July 31st, 1862; mustered into United States service, August 14th, 1862; promoted to sergeant; transferred to Company K, and commissioned second lieutenant Company F, December 9th, 1864; mustered out, June 5th, 1865. Was wounded, July 1st, 1863, at battle of Gettysburgh.

SECOND LIEUTENANT ISAAC R. WHITNEY.

Mustered as second sergeant Company F, August 14th, 1862; promoted first sergeant; commissioned second lieutenant Company G, December 18th, 1863; discharged, December 17th, 1864; wounded at battle of the Wilderness, May, 1864.

SECOND LIEUTENANT JOHN H. FRAIN.

Mustered into United States service as corporal Company G, August 14th, 1862; promoted first sergeant; commissioned second lieutenant Company G, 1864; not mustered; captured at battle of Gettysburgh, July 1st, 1863, and paroled; prisoner of war at battle of Weldon Railroad, August 19th, 1864; discharged, September 4th, 1865.

SECOND LIEUTENANT CHARLES A. GARCELON.

Commissioned second lieutenant Company I, August 16th, 1862; mustered into United States service, to date from August 14th, 1862; detached to command Brigade Ambulance Corps, Second Division, First Army Corps, 1862; discharged, February 5th, 1864, to accept appointment as captain and assistant quartermaster volunteers.

SECOND LIEUTENANT WILBUR F. MOWER.

Mustered into United States service as corporal Company I, August 14th, 1862; promoted sergeant; commissioned second lieutenant, January 28th, 1865; discharged May 15th, 1865, for disability on account of wounds received before Petersburgh, June 19th, 1864. Sergeant Mower carried the colors at battle of Gettysburgh, July 1st, 1863, with conspicuous gallantry.

SECOND LIEUTENANT AUGUSTUS C. PETERS.

Commissioned second lieutenant Company K, August 16th, 1862; mustered into United States service, to date from August 14th, 1862; wounded at battle of Fredericksburgh, December 13th, 1862; discharged for disability occasioned by wounds, March 30th, 1863.

SECOND LIEUTENANT FRANCIS C. MAYO.

Mustered as private Company K, August 14th, 1862; promoted to sergeant, May 1st, 1863; commissioned second lieutenant ——— ———, 1864; not mustered; wounded and prisoner at battle of Gettysburgh, July 1st, 1863; paroled; wounded at battle of the Wilderness, May —, 1864; mustered out, June 5th, 1865.

NON-COMMISSIONED STAFF.

SERGEANT-MAJORS.

DATE.	NAME.	RESIDENCE.	REMARKS.
June 12, '62	Francis A. Wildes	Skowhegan	Prom. 2d Lieutenant Co. A.
'63	James D. Maxfield	Newport	Disc. for dis. Sept. 9, '63.
'63	Cherbury F. Lothrop	Chesterville	Prom. 2d Lieutenant Co. F.
'64	Edwin C. Stevens	Waterville	Prom. from Sergeant Co. E.
Sept. 1, '64	Hosea D. Manley	Auburn	Prom. from Corporal Co. 1.

QUARTERMASTER SERGEANTS.

DATE.	NAME.	RESIDENCE.	REMARKS.
June 6, '62	George W. Brown	Augusta	Promoted Quartermaster.
Dec. 14, '64	Charles E. Deering	Gardiner	Prom. from Sergeant Co. B.

COMMISSARY SERGEANTS.

DATE.	NAME.	RESIDENCE.	REMARKS.
Aug. 11, '62	Charles H. Parlin	Skowhegan	Prom. 2d Lieutenant Co. D.
Nov. 11, '64	Charles Plummer	Waterford	Prom. from Private Co. D.

HOSPITAL STEWARDS.

DATE.	NAME.	RESIDENCE.	REMARKS.
June 27, '62	William W. Eaton	Brunswick	Prom. Assistant Surgeon.
Jan. 25, '63	Joseph B. Dow	Farmington	Prom. from Private Co. G.
Sept. 1, '64	E. Payson Snow	Skowhegan	Prom. from Private Co. A.
	Royal L. Cleaves	Bridgton	Prom. from Private Co. F

PRINCIPAL MUSICIANS.

DATE.	NAME.	RESIDENCE.	REMARKS.
August, '62	William H. Palmer		Discharged.
Oct. 8, '63	John Shea	Anson	Promoted from Co. G.
Oct. 8, '63	Pelatiah Coolbroth	Standish	Promoted from Co. G.

STATISTICAL TABLES

OF THE

SIXTEENTH MAINE REGIMENT.

COMPANY A.

NAMES.	Age.	RESIDENCE.	Married or Single.	Mustered into the U. S. service.	REMARKS.
SERGEANTS.					
Emilus N. D. Small	21	Mt. Vernon	S.	Aug. 14, '62	Disc. for dis. Mar. 2, '63.
Howard W. Wells	24	Waterville	S.	Aug. 14, '62	Wd. Fred., Dec., '62. Disc. for dis., May 3, '63.
Ephraim M. Young	38	Fairfield	M.	Aug. 14, '62	Red. to Ranks for dis. Transferred to Co. I.
Plummer T. Haskell	23	Hartland	M.	Aug. 14, '62	Disc. for dis. Feb. 6, '63.
Nathaniel W. Costan	21	Athens	S.	Aug. 14, '62	Pro. 1st Sergt. and 2d Lieut.
Winslow A. Morrill	29	No. 4, R. 5	M.	Aug. 14, '62	
Daniel A. Spearin	21	Blanchard	S.	Aug. 14, '62	Transferred to Co. K.
James Parsons	36	Lexington	M.	Aug. 14, '62	Pris. Aug. 18, '64, tr. Co. D.
Phineas McCollar	24	Madison	S.	Aug. 14, '62	Wounded trans. to Co. B.
CORPORALS.					
Winslow A. Morrill	29	No. 4, R. 5	M.	Aug. 14, '62	Pro. Sergt. Wd. Aug. 12, '63.
Daniel A. Spearin	21	Blanchard	S.	Aug. 14, '62	Pro. Sergt. Wd. July 1, '63.
William S. Plummer	20	Skowhegan	S.	Aug. 14, '62	Wounded Dec. 13, '62.
James M. Foster	19	Canaan	S.	Aug. 14, '62	Disc. for dis. Feb. 14, '63.
John C. Turner	20	Moscow	S.	Aug. 14, '62	Wounded Dec. 13, '62.
James Parsons	36	Lexington	M.	Aug. 14, '62	Promoted Sergt.
Charles M. Baker	21	Moscow	S.	Aug. 14, '62	Disc. for dis. Dec. 23, '62.
Henry E. Dexter	29	Vienna	M.	Aug. 14, '62	Transferred to Co. B.
Phineas McColler	24	Madison	S.	Aug. 14, '62	
John W. Watson	21	New Portland	S.	Aug. 14, '62	Discharged July 24, '65.
Bray Wilkins	18	Fairfield	S.	Aug. 14, '62	Transferred to Co. E.
Clement C. Williams	19	New Portland	S.	Aug. 14, '62	Transferred to Co. E.
Hiram R. Brackett	21	Detroit	S.	Aug. 14, '62	
Tilson T. Whitcomb	27	Concord	M.	Aug. 14, '62	
MUSICIANS.					
Melville D. Brown	21	Harmony	S.	Aug. 14, '62	Transferred to Co. K.
Reuel S. Cummings	39	Brighton	S.	Aug. 14, '62	Disc. for dis. Nov. 25, '62.
PRIVATES.					
Achorn, Jacob B.	25	Washington	M.	Aug. 14, '62	
Adams, Philip C.	21	Carratunk	S.	Aug. 14, '62	Transferred to Co. H.
Adams, Samuel C.	19	Mayfield	S.	Aug. 14, '62	Transferred to Co. H.
Bailey, Albion	18	Cambridge	S.	Aug. 14, '62	Transferred to Co. G.
Berry, Levi	40	Embden	M.	Aug. 14, '62	Transferred to Co. F. Nurse in Hospital.
Bracket, Hiram R.	21	Detroit	S.	Aug. 14, '62	Wounded Dec. 13, '62. Pro. Corp. Trans. to Co. G.
Brown, Hiram	22	Harmony	S.	Aug. 14, '62	Trans. to Co. I.
Burdeen, George F.	19	Detroit	S.	Aug. 14, '62	Missing since battle Fred., Dec. 13, '62.
Butts, Isaac H.	20	New Portland	S.	Aug. 14, '62	Transferred to Co. I.
Carville Benjamin	36	New Portland	M.	Aug. 14, '62	Mis'g in act'n July 1, '63, prs. Missing in action Aug. 19, '63, Tr. to Co. G.
Chamberlain, S. A.	21	Mayfield	S.	Aug. 14, '62	Trans. to Co. I.
Clapp, Ai	26	New Portland	M.	Aug. 14, '62	Des. while on furlough.
Clark, Henry R.	18	Solon	S.	Aug. 14, '62	Wd. Dec. 13, '62, & Jly. 1, 63.
Clement, Charles W.	19	Palmyra	S.	Aug. 14, '62	
Clossen, Henry P.	20	Fairfield	S.	Aug. 14, '62	Disc. for dis. Mar. 28, '63.
Cook, Moses W.	30	Waterville	M.	Aug. 14, '62	Wd. July 1, 63, dis. Apr. 11, '64.
Costan, Samuel L. C.	18	Hartland	S.	Aug. 14, '62	Wd. Dec. 13, '62, disc. Dec. 29, '62.
Cunningham, Daniel C.	39	Augusta	M.	Aug. 14, '62	
Cunningham, Owen B.	18	No. 4, R. 5	S.	Aug. 14, '62	
Dexter, Henry E.	29	Vienna	M.	Aug. 14, '62	Pro. Corp. Pris. July 1, '63.
Downing, George A.	21	Skowhegan	S.	Aug. 14, '62	Trans. to Co. E.
Fowler, Nathan	21	Skowhegan	S.	Aug. 14, '62	Pro. 2d Lieut. and 1st Lieut.
Fox, James E.	18	Whitefield	S.	Aug. 14, '62	
Fuller, Horatio G.	44	New Portland	M.	Aug. 14, '62	Pris. July 1. Disc. for dis. Oct. 31, 63.
Fuller, William L.	18	New Portland	S.	Aug. 14, '62	Disc. for dis. April 14, '63.
Furbish, Jairus H.	36	Lexington	M.	Aug. 14, '62	Pris. July 1, '63. Tr. Co. G.
Getchell, Calvin	20	Anson	S.	Aug. 14, '62	

COMPANY A—Continued.

NAMES.	Age.	RESIDENCE.	Married or Single	Mustered into the U. S. service.	REMARKS.
Gifford, LaForrest F...	18	Harmony....	S.	Aug. 14, '62	Transferred to Co. G.
Goodrich, Ira H..........	27	Lexington...	M.	Aug. 14, '62	Disc. for dis. April 3, '63.
Goodwin, Lyman O....	21	Detroit......	S.	Aug. 14, '62	Pris. July 1, '63. Trans. to Co. G.
Grace, George W.......	44	Benton.......	S.	Aug. 14, '62	Disc. for dis. July 12, '63.
Gould Elisha P.........	22	Lexington...	S.	Aug. 14, '62	Missing in action Fred. Dec. 13, '62.
Gould, George H	18	Lexington ...	S.	Aug. 14, '62	Pris. July 1, '63. Trans. to Co. H.
Hacket, Alden T.......	18	No. 4, R. 5 ...	S.	Aug. 14, '62	Transferred to Co. B.
Hall, Cyrus............	40	Concord......	M.	Aug. 14, '62	Disc. for dis. Feb. 24, '63.
Hanks, Jason..........	40	Madison......	S.	Aug. 14, '62	
Holbrook, Abel C......	33	Embden.......	S.	Aug. 14, '62	Wd. July 1, '63. Tr. Co. K.
Hurd, Joel B...........	20	Harmony.....	S.	Aug. 14, '62	Wd. July 1, '63. Tr. Co. K.
Hussey, Buzzella L. C.	44	Hallowell.....	S.	Aug. 14, '62	
Kealiher, John	31	Moose R. Pl..	S.	Aug. 14, '62	Transferred to Co. B.
Knowles, Freeman T..	18	Skowhegan ...	S.	Aug. 14, '62	Transferred to Co. K.
Kyle, James S.........	25	Chester.......	S.	Aug. 14, '62	
Leavitt, James.........	19	Lincoln	S.	Aug. 14, '62	
Maxfield, James D....	24	Newport......	M.	Aug. 14, '62	Adj't's Clerk. Prom. Sergeant-Major.
McCollor, Phineas.....	24	Solon	S.	Aug. 14, '62	Promoted Corp.
McCollar, Michael.....	25	Hallowell.....	S.	Aug. 14, '62	Discharged for disability.
McKeen, John H......	18	No. 4, R. 5 ...	S.	Aug. 14, '62	
Merrill, Hiram A......	26	Lexington ...	M.	Aug. 14, '62	Transferred to Co. F.
Moore, George P......	34	Canaan.......	M.	Aug. 14, '62	Missing battle Fred. Dec. 13, '62.
Moore, Nelson.........	18	Anson........	S.	Aug. 14, '62	Disc. for dis. Nov. 19, '62.
Morrill, Stephen F.....	28	Chesterville..	S.	Aug. 14, '62	Disc. Feb. 22, '64.
Moulton, Randall......	19	Embden.......	S.	Aug. 14, '62	Missing battle Fred., Dec. 13, '62.
Murch, Albert J	24	New Portland	S.	Aug. 14, '62	Pris. July 1, '63, Par. Tr. to Co. E.
Neal, William..........	45	Richmond ...	M.	Aug. 14, '62	Disc. for dis. Jan. 24, '63.
Nelson, William H....	26	New York ...	S.	Aug. 14, '62	Wd. Dec. 13, '62.
Nutting, Josiah........	18	Canaan.......	S.	Aug. 18, '62	Disc. Nov. 10, '62.
Oliver, Seth...........	41	Appleton.....	S.	Aug. 14, '62	Transferred to Co. F.
Piper, Thomas B......	22	Mayfield.....	S.	Aug. 14, '62	Missing bat. Gettysburgh, July 1, '63.
Poor, Austin...........	22	Patten........	S.	Aug. 14, '62	
Pratt, Henry L........	20	Skowhegan...	S.	Aug. 14, '62	Wounded Dec. 13, '62.
Reed, William H......	24	Anson........	S.	Aug. 14, '62	Wd. Dec. 13, '62. Tr. Co. C.
Rowell, Haniff.........	34	New Portland	M.	Aug. 14, '62	Transferred to Co. F.
Sibley, John L........	21	Appleton.....	S.	Aug. 14, '62	
Smith, Ambrose.......	32	Brighton.....	M.	Aug. 14, '62	Missing act. Dec. 13, '62.
Smith, James..........	23	Harmony	S.	Aug. 14, '62	
Snow, Edward P......	20	Skowhegan ..	S.	Aug. 14, '62	Nurse in Hospital, '63. Pro. Hospital Steward, '64.
Stafford, John.........	22	Carratunk....	S.	Aug. 14, '62	
Stinneford, Oliver R...	32	Harmony	M.	Aug. 14, '62	Trans. to Co. C.
Sweat, Jacob..........	44	New Portland	M.	Aug. 14, '62	Disc. for dis., Apr. 20, '63.
Sweat, John...........	20	New Portland	S.	Aug. 14, '62	
Thompson, John F....	18	New Portland	S.	Aug. 14, '62	Wd. July 1, '63. Tr. Co. E.
Tripp, Alonzo..........	22	No. 4, R. 5...	S.	Aug. 14, '62	Disc. for dis. Aug. 10, '63.
Tripp, Simeon.........	27	New Portland	M.	Aug. 14, '62	Missing action Aug. 18, '64.
Warren, Harrison S...	34	New Portland	M.	Aug. 14, '62	
Watson, John W......	21	New Portland	S.	Aug. 14, '62	Promoted Corp.
Wells, Amos R........	35	St. Albans...	S.	Aug. 14, '62	Disc. Aug. 30, '63.
West, Aratus H.......	28	New Portland	M.	Aug. 14, '62	Prom. to Corp. Tr. to Co. C.
Whitcomb, Tilson T...	27	Concord......	M.	Aug. 14, '62	Prom. to Corp. Tr. to Co. G.
Wilkins, Bray.........	18	Fairfield.....	S.	Aug. 14, '62	Pro. Corp. Pris. July 1, '63.
Williams, Clement C..	19	New Portland	S.	Aug. 14, '62	Pro. Corp. Pris. July 1, '63.
Witham, James A	23	No. 3, R. 3 ...	S.	Aug. 14, '62	
Wyman, James R......	27	Wellington ..	M.	Aug. 14, '62	Ret. from hosp. Nov. 10, 63. Trans. to Co. D.
Young, John...........	30	New Portland	M.	Aug. 14, '62	Transferred to Co. I.

SIXTEENTH MAINE REGIMENT.   257

COMPANY A—Continued.

NAMES.	Age.	RESIDENCE.	Married or Single.	Mustered into the U. S. service.	REMARKS.
Joined Co. since Dec.		1st, 1862			
Barrett, William	22	Portland	S.	Aug. 1, '63	Substitute.
Bovard, John	23	Portland	S.	Aug. 4, '63	Substitute, trans. to Co. I
Blacklock, Archibald	39	Portland	S.	Aug. 8, '63	Substitute, trans. to Co. H.
Berry, Kendrick	40	Troy	M.	Sept. 10, '63	Substitute, trans. to Co. H.
Brackett, Freeman	22	Bradford		Aug. 14, '63	Substitute, trans. to Co. H.
Briggs, Edward	25	Gouldsboro	M.	Sept. 11, '63	Substitute, missing action June 7, trans. to Co. D.
Conway, Hugh	23	Hampden	S.	Sept. 8, '63	Substitute, trans. to Co. I.
Coakley, John	22	Ireland		Aug. 7, '63	Drafted.
Clements, Thomas R.	33	Monroe	M.	Sept. 15, '63	Substitute, trans. to Co. I.
Dorr, Henry A.	23	Orland		Sept. 5, '63	Drafted, trans. to Co. E.
Dolan, Patrick H.	30	Portland		Aug. 7, '63	Substitute, des. ab. in arr., trans. to Co. G.
Downey, John	31	New Haven		Aug. 4, '63	Substitute.
Emery, Solomon G.	26	Northfield	S.	Aug. 13, '63	Substitute.
Fahey, James	20	Bangor	S.	Sept. 10, '63	Substitute, trans. to Co. E.
Ford, Timothy	22	Monroe		Sept. 1, '63	Sub., missing in action Aug. 18, '64.
Fletcher, Benjamin F.	28	Troy	S.	Sept. 1, '63	Substitute.
Gorman, James	23	Calais	S.	Sept. 7, '63	Drafted ab., wd., tr. Co. G.
Hanson, David D.	29	Bangor	M.	Sept. 1, '63	Sub., disc., Dec. 9, '63.
Haley, Ebenezer	23	Baring	S.	Sept. 8, '63	Substitute, trans. to Co. K.
Hill, Charles A.	24	So. Berwick	S.	Sept. 18, '63	Substitute.
Hopkins, Daniel	39	Ft. Fairfield	M.	Sept. 10, '63	Substitute, trans. to Co. K.
Jackson, Jeremiah H.	30			Aug. 5, '63	Drafted.
Johnston, Warren A.	37	Ft. Fairfield	S.	Sept. 19, '63	Sub. Transferred to Co. B.
Knowles, William H.	27	St. Marys		Aug. 7, '63	Sub. Transferred to Co. D.
Lattie, James	24	Matmiscontis	S.	Sept. 10, '63	Substitute. Prisoner.
Lancaster, Willard	22	Hudson		Aug. 15, '63	Draf. Transferred to Co. B.
Linniken, Rufus	25			Aug. 7, '63	Draf. Transferred to Co. D.
Malcomb, John F.	22	Newcastle	S.	Aug. 7, '63	Substitute, trans. to Co. D.
Malcomb, William A.	36	Newcastle	S.	Aug. 4, '63	Substitute, trans. to Co. D.
Malcomb, Simon L.	20	Newcastle	S.	Aug. 4, '63	Substitute.
Moody, David jr.	26			Sept. 5, '63	Drafted, trans. to Co. D.
Martin, Michael	27	Rockland	S.	Sept. 5, '63	Substitute, trans. to Co. D.
Nelson, Frank E.	25	Winslow		July 20, '63	Drafted, trans. to Co. H.
Reed, Benjamin F.	29	Boothbay		July 18, '63	Drafted.
Rider, George A.	26	Washington		July 21, '63	Drafted, disc. to accept com.
Riley, James	38	Saco	S.	Aug. 10, '63	Substitute.
Ricker, Milton W.	22	Bangor	M.	Aug. 24, '63	Substitute, trans. to Co. C.
Smith, William S.	25	Calais		Sept. 5, '63	Substitute.
Smith, Andrew	26	Machias		Aug. 22, '63	Substitute, trans. to Co. F.
Smith, S. Stillman	32	Hodgdon	M.	Sept. 10, '63	Substitute.
Severance, Jefferson	18	Buxton		Aug. 18, '63	Drafted, disc. Dec. 9, '63.
Silver, William S.	38	Trescott		Aug. 10, '63	Drafted.
Steeves, James A.	23	Eastport	M.	Aug. 17, '63	Substitute, trans. to Co. F.
White, Henry A.				Aug. 10, '63	Sub., miss. act. June 7, '64.
Joined Co. since Dec.		1st, 1863			
Choate, Charles E.	21	Fairfield	S.	Sept. 7, '64	Transferred to Co. E.
Hart, George	18	Bangor	S.	Sept. 3, '64	Transferred to Co. E.
Ketch, Richard	27	N. Brunswick	M.	Sept. 2, '64	Transferred to Co. G.
Maulley, Frank	27	Auburn	S.	Sept. 5, '64	Transferred to Co. K.
Reynolds, John				Sept. 2, '64	Not accounted for.
Soule, Richard	26	Bradford	S.	Sept. 2, '64	Transferred to Co. D.
Stewart, Thomas	29	Auburn	M.	Sept. 2, '64	Transferred to Co. F.
Sweem, Israel	22	Van Buren	S.	Sept. 2, '64	Transferred to Co. C.
Taylor, Francis F.	37	Houlton	S.	Sept. 16, '64	Transferred to Co. C.
Watson, Henry	18	Hartland	S.	Sept. 5, '64	Transferred to Co. C.

COMPANY A.—NEW ORGANIZATION.

NAMES.	Age.	RESIDENCE.	Married or Single	Mustered into the U. S. Service.	REMARKS.
SERGEANTS.					
William H. Dudley	30	Pittston	S.	Sept. 23, '64	
Hiram K. Colby	19	Topsham	S.	Sept. 23, '64	
Joseph E. Hooker	20	Gardiner	S.	Sept. 23, '64	Wd. Apr. 1, '65, disc. by order, June 2, '65.
Calvin W. Smith	23	Gardiner	S.	Sept. 23, '64	
Charles H. Martin	24	Gardiner	S.	Sept. 23, '64	Wd. in action Feb. 6, '65.
CORPORALS.					
David S. Stevens	21	Gardiner	S.	Sept. 23, '64	
John S. Dennis	42	Gardiner	M.	Sept. 23, '64	
Charles A. Morse	22	Solon	S.	Sept. 23, '64	Deserted April 1, '65.
Joseph C. Gardiner	25	Vassalboro	S.	Sept. 23, '64	Disc. June 9, '65.
John Ray	35	Gardiner	S.	Sept. 23, '64	Deserted, Oct. 8, '64.
Albion D. Barrett	27	Canaan	S.	Sept. 23, '64	Reduced to the ranks.
Elisha P. Seavey	25	Gardiner	S.	Sept. 23, '64	
Edmund Decelles	20	Brunswick	S.	Sept. 23, '64	Des. Oct. 8, '64.
George H. Baker	20	Gardiner	S.	Sept. 23, '64	Disc.by order June 15, '65.
Alpheus A. Mann	21	Gardiner	S.	Sept. 23, '64	Wd. April 1, '65.
Charles T. Rice	20	Farmingdale	S.	Sept. 23, '64	
Joseph E. Stetson	18	Brunswick	S.	Sept. 23, '64	
Ezekiel Gerald	18	Waterville	S.	Sept. 23, '64	
MUSICIAN.					
George W. Fuller	17	W. Gardiner	S.	Sept. 23, '64	
PRIVATES.					
Annis, Henry A.	18	Sidney	S.	Sept. 23, '64	
Averill, Alvarado	18	Farmingdale	S.	Sept. 23, '64	
Baker, George H.	20	Gardiner	S.	Sept. 23, '64	Promoted Corporal.
Barnes, Darius	22	Canaan	S.	Sept. 23, '64	
Booker, Daniel	19	Gardiner	S.	Sept. 23, '64	
Brawn, William	29	Gardiner	M.	Sept. 23, '64	
Brown, Charles W.	18	Thomaston	S.	Sept. 23, '64	
Brannon, Timothy	24	Madison	S.	Sept. 23, '64	Des. Oct. 4, '64.
Brush, Edward	18	Gardiner	S.	Sept. 23, '64	
Butts, Edward F.	20	Canaan	S.	Sept. 23, '64	
Brawn, Alinander	18	Skowhegan	S.	Sept. 23, '64	
Baker, Horatio B.	29	Moscow	M.	Sept. 23, '64	Wd. in act. Feb. 7, '65.
Coleman, Edmund G.	21	Vassalboro	S.	Sept. 23, '64	
Drinkwater Edward H.	18	Topsham	S.	Sept. 23, '64	
Dunn, John	18	Solon	S.	Sept. 23, '64	
Durgin, Frank W.	19	Gardiner	S.	Sept. 23, '64	
Fairbanks, William H.	21	W. Gardiner	S.	Sept. 23, '64	Disc. by order June 3, '65.
Fairbanks, Charles F.	18				Disc. Oct. 16, '64.
Follett, Francis	18	Searsmont	S.	Sept. 23, '64	Wd. Nov. 26, '64. disc. by order June 6, '65.
Gardiner, Henry W.	18	Vassalboro	S.	Sept. 23, '64	Supposed des. Oct. 8, '64.
Gatchell, Charles C.	18	Durham	S.	Sept. 23, '64	
Gerald, Ezekiel	18	Waterville	S.	Sept. 23, '64	Promoted Corporal.
Gilly, Samuel M	18	Augusta	S.	Sept. 23, '64	Disc. by order June 15, '65.
Gilpatrick, Robert	39	Washington	M.	Sept. 23, '64	Disc. July 20, '65.
Gorden, Charles H.	25	Mt. Vernon	S.	Sept. 23, '64	
Guilford, Lester	18	W. Gardiner	S.	Sept. 23, '64	
Hammond, James jr.	30	Brunswick	M.	Sept. 23, '64	
Hart, William	18	Washington	S.	Sept. 23, '64	
Hodges, William H.	23	Gardiner	M.	Sept. 23, '64	Wd. in act. Feb. 6, '65, disc. by order May 29, '65.
Hodgdon, Benjamin S.	18	Farmingdale	S.	Sept. 23, '64	
Hodgdon, Daniel R.	23	Gardiner	M.	Sept. 23, '64	Wounded in action Feb. 6, '65.
Henderson, John F.	29	Moscow	M.	Sept. 23, '64	Discharged Aug. 9, '65.
Huzzey, Julius H.	20	Canaan	S.	Sept. 23, '64	
Huntoon, William H.	19	Mt. Vernon	S.	Sept. 23, '64	
Huff, Charles H.	18	Mercer	S.	Sept. 23, '64	
Hutchinson, Fred. A.	18	Wayne	S.	Sept. 23, '64	
Jones, Samuel	19	Washington	S.	Sept. 23, '64	
Jones, Zenas	18	Washington	S.	Sept. 23, '64	Discharged June 6, '65.
Kelly, Major	43	Gardiner	M.	Sept. 23, '64	Disc. by order June 15, '65.

SIXTEENTH MAINE REGIMENT. 259

COMPANY A.—NEW ORGANIZATION.—Continued.

NAME.	Age.	RESIDENCE.	Married or Single	Mustered into the U. S. Service.	REMARKS.
Kelly, George W......	24	Gardiner.....	S.	Sept. 23, '64	Des. Oct. 8, '64. Dishon. disc. Dec. 2, '65.
Kelly, Edward.........	24	Gardiner.....	S.	Sept. 23, '64	Des. Oct. 8, '64.
Kenniston, Wilbert W	18	Gardiner.....	S.	Sept. 23, '64	
Lowell, Joseph S......	18	Farmingdale.	S.	Sept. 23, '64	
Leavitt, Charles C.....	21	Brunswick...	S.	Sept. 23, '64	
Martin, Reuben C......	19	Canaan.......	S.	Sept. 23, '64	Disc. June 9, '65.
McLaughlin, Timothy..	44	Waterville...	S.	Sept. 23, '64	Wd. in action Feb. 6, '65.
McNeill, Daniel........	31	P. E. Island..	S.	Sept. 23, '64	
McGilvery, John.......	43	Waterville...	S.	Sept. 23, '64	
Mann, Alfred A........	21	Gardiner.....	S.	Sept. 23, '64	Promoted Corporal.
Morse, Stephen S......	44	Augusta......	M.	Sept. 23, '64	Wd. Nov. 22, '64.
Moulton, George T.....	18	Pittsfield	S.	Sept. 23, '64	
Messer, James B.......	26	Moscow......	S.	Sept. 23, '64	
McCurdy, Christopher .	26	Nobleboro....	M.	Sept. 23, '64	Wd. in action Feb. 6, '65. Wd. April 1, '65.
McCurdy, Lyman......	33	Nobleboro....	S.	Sept. 23, '64	
O'Hara, James	22	Moscow......	M.	Sept. 23, '64	
O'Brien, James........	24	Madison......	S.	Sept. 23, '64	Probable prisoner.
Pierce, Reuben B......	35	Moscow......	M.	Sept. 23, '64	
Partridge, Frederick E.	18	Belgrade.....	S.	Sept. 23, '64	
Porter, John W........	18	Brunswick...	S.	Sept. 23, '64	
Potter, Emerald M.....	18	W. Gardiner.	S.	Sept. 23, '64	
Pinkham, William A..	19	Pittston......	S.	Sept. 23, '64	
Rice, Charles T........	20	Farmingdale.	S.	Sept. 23, '64	Promoted Corporal.
Ricker, Hiram H.......	37	Gardiner.....	M.	Sept. 23, '64	
Rhodes, George E.....	18	Gardiner.....	S.	Sept. 23, '64	
Royal, John F.........	28	Gardiner.....	M.	Sept. 23, '64	
Robinson, George H...	18	Norridgewock	S.	Sept. 23, '64	Disc. May 29, '65.
Ryan, William	28	Madison......	S.	Sept. 23, '64	Des. Oct. 4, '64.
Strout, Leavitt.........	24	Madison......	S.	Sept. 23, '64	
Shay, John............	26	Madison......	S.	Sept. 23, '64	Des. Oct. 4, '64.
Shaw, Llewellyn.......	27	Augusta......	M.	Sept. 23, '64	
Spear, John A	18	W. Gardiner.	S.	Sept. 23, '64	Disc. May 22, '65.
Spear, Joseph F.......	19	W. Gardiner.	S.	Sept. 23, '64	Wd. in action Feb. 6, '65. Disc. Aug. 7, '65.
Spear, Milton C.	18	W. Gardiner.	S.	Sept. 23, '64	
Stetson, Joseph E......	18	Brunswick...	S.	Sept. 23, '64	Promoted Corporal.
Stinson, Frank H.	18	Topsham.....	S.	Sept. 23, '64	
Sheridan, Francis P....	35	Solon.........	S.	Sept. 23, '64	
Stanley, Leander......	18	Gardiner.....	S.	Sept. 23, '64	Disc. by order May 22, '65.
Walker, George A. 1st.	23	Brunswick...	S.	Sept. 23, '64	
Walker, George A. 2d.	18	Canaan.......	S.	Sept. 23, '64	Wd. in action Feb. 6, '65.
White, William	45	Gardiner.....	M.	Sept. 23, '64	
Wentworth, Franklin..	30	Vassalboro...	S.	Sept. 23, '64	
Wentworth, Daniel....	37	Augusta	M.		Disc. by order May 16, '65.
Williams, John	30	Madison......	M.		Deserted Oct. 4, '64.
Warren, Adrastus C....	24	Canaan.......	M.		Wd. April 1, '65.
Joined Co. since organization.					
Eldridge, Albert.......	19	Portland.....		Nov. 16, '64	Substitute.
Hawksley, Samuel.....	19	Houlton......		Oct. 24, '64	Missing in action Feb. 6, '65.
Strout, Levi N........	29	Augusta		Sept. 24, '64	Substitute, wd. Feb. 6, '65.

COMPANY B.

NAMES.	Age.	RESIDENCE.	Married or Single	Mustered into the U. S. Service.	REMARKS.
SERGEANTS.					
Allen Partridge	20	Augusta	S.	Aug. 14 '62	Disc. for dis. Jan. 12, '63.
Fred. H. Beecher	21	Gardiner	S.	Aug. 14, '62	Prom. 2d and 1st Lieut.
William D. Ewer	27	Vassalboro	M.	Aug. 14, '62	Disc. for dis. March 5, '63.
Leonard L. Taylor	37	Gardiner	M.	Aug. 14, '62	Disc. by order June 5, '65.
George R. Parsons	19	Gardiner	S.	Aug. 14, '62	
Melvin C. Wadsworth	20	Pittston	S.	Aug. 14, '62	Prom. 2d Lieutenant.
Reuben M Farrington	18	China	S.	Aug. 14, '62	
Gustavus Moore	19	Gardiner	S.	Aug. 14, '62	
George H. Stone	19	Farmingdale	S.	Aug. 14, '62	
Charles E. Deering	24	Gardiner	S.	Aug. 14, '62	Prom. Q. M. Sergeant.
Thomas E. Smith	22	Gardiner	M.	Aug. 14, '62	Wounded April 1, '65.
CORPORALS.					
Alvin M. C. Heath	33	Gardiner	M.	Aug. 14, '62	Wounded Fred. Dec. 13, '62.
George H. Berry	19	Gardiner	S.	Aug. 14, '62	Wounded Fred. Dec. 13, '62.
Alfred M. Hamlin	19	China	S.	Aug. 14, '62	Disc. for dis. April 2, '63.
Melvin C. Wadsworth	20	Pittston	S.	Aug. 14, '62	Prom. 1st Sergeant.
Daniel W. Hume	23	Augusta	M.	Aug. 14, '62	Missing Fred. Dec. 13, '62.
Charles E. Deering	24	Gardiner	S.	Aug. 14, '62	Prom. 1st Sergeant. Taken prisoner July 1, '63.
George H. Hooker	23	Gardiner	M.	Aug. 14, '62	
Reuben M. Farrington	18	China	S.	Aug. 14, '62	Promoted Sergeant.
Aug. W. McCausland	18	Gardiner	M.	Aug. 14, '62	Wounded July 1, '63. Disc. July 16, '64 on acct. of wd.
Charles O. Wadsworth	22	Gardiner	S.	Aug. 14, '62	Wounded June 21, '64.
Alonzo C. Atkins	18	Manchester	M.	Aug. 14, '62	Wounded Oct. 2, '64.
Hiram W. Campbell	18	Manchester	S.	Aug. 14, '62	
Charles L. Peaslee	33	Enfield	M.	Aug. 14, '63	
Thomas E. Smith	22	Gardiner	M.	Aug. 14, '62	Prom. Sergt. Wd. Apr. 1, '65.
Horace P. Tasker	18	Jackson	S.	Aug. 21, '63	Wounded Feb. 6, '65.
Sewell G. Woodbury	31	Mars Hill	S.	Aug. 15, '63	
Charles Chamberlain	19	Bangor	S.	Sept. 30, '64	Wounded Feb. 7, '65.
Charles B. Chase	25	Belfast	M.	Oct. 5, '64	
MUSICIAN.					
Edward A. Priest	18	Vassalboro	S.	Aug. 14, '62	Disc. for dis. May 2, '63.
WAGONER.					
Luther E. Burgess	23	Turner	M.	Aug. 14, '62	
PRIVATES.					
Adkins, Charles A	18	Turner	S.	Aug. 14, '62	
Atkins, Alonzo C	18	Manchester	S.	Aug. 14, '62	
Austin, Henry D	19	Augusta	M.	Aug. 14, '62	Disc. Mar. 25, '65. Missing battle Get. July 1, '63.
Benson, James S	29	Gardiner	M.	Aug. 14, '62	
Braun, Charles P	20	Gardiner	S.	Aug. 14, '62	
Braun, Emery M	19	Gardiner	S.	Aug. 14, '62	Wounded Dec. 13, '62. Disc. April 22, '63.
Britt, James	18	Augusta	S.	Aug. 14, '62	
Brookings, Edmund J	23	Farmingdale	S.	Aug. 14, '62	Disc. by order June 8, '65.
Brooks, James D	29	Augusta	M.	Aug. 14, '62	Wounded Dec. 13, '62. Disc. Feb. 17, '63.
Bruce, William W	32	Augusta	M.	Aug. 14, '62	Mustered out May 18, '65. Missing Get. July 1, '63.
Campbell, Hiram W	18	Manchester	S.	Aug. 14, '62	Promoted Corporal.
Chenery, George W	29	Gardiner	M.	Aug. 14, '62	
Crowell, John H	22	Gardiner	S.	Aug. 14, '62	
Dana, Stephen W	23	Gardiner	M.	Aug. 14, '62	Disc. for dis. Jan. 8, '63.
Davis, Charles F	19	Gardiner	S.	Aug. 14, '62	
Devine, George H	18	Augusta	S.	Aug. 14, '62	Deserted Sept. 21, 62.
Doyle, Thomas	19	Augusta	S.	Aug. 14, '62	
Douglass, John W	36	Gardiner	M.	Aug. 14, '62	Missing. Discharged for disability Jan. 30, '63.
Eldridge, Randall	18	Gardiner	S.	Aug. 14, '62	Wounded Aug. 18, '64. Missing. Disc. Jan. 13, '65.
Ewer, Henry A	18	Vassalboro	S.	Aug. 14, '62	Wounded Get. July 1, '63. Mustered out May 18, '65.
Folger, Edward C	18	Augusta	S.	Aug. 14, '62	Wd. Aug. 18, '64. In Hosp.

COMPANY B.—Continued.

NAMES.	Age.	RESIDENCE.	Married or Single	Mustered into the U. S. Service.	REMARKS.
Follett, Ephraim B.	21	Gardiner	S.	Aug. 14, '62	Deserted Dec. 13, '62.
Ford, Everett G.	22	Turner	S.	Aug. 14, '62	Discharged for disability.
Gardiner, George W.	18	Gardiner	S.	Aug. 14, '62	
Garry, Charles F.	19	Gardiner	S.	Aug. 14, '62	Deserted June 10, '64.
Glidden, Samuel S.	19	Farmingdale	S.	Aug. 14, '62	
Haines, David	44	Gardiner	M.	Aug. 14, '62	Discharged April 21, '63.
Hinkley, Ora K.	30	Gardiner	M.	Aug. 14, '62	Discharged Nov. 28, '62.
Holbrook, Israel W.	35	Gardiner	M.	Aug. 14, '62	Missing 1862.
Holt, Valentine	43	Augusta	M.	Aug. 14, '62	
Huntington, Wm. H.	33	Gardiner	S.	Aug. 14, '62	Wounded at Gettysburg.
Kirk, John P.	19	Gardiner	S.	Aug. 14, '62	Discharged Jan. 16, '63.
Lacchaus, Vedal	28	Waterville	M.	Aug. 14, '62	
Little, Arno	18	Vienna	S.	Aug. 14, '62	
Lovejoy, A. Judson	24	Augusta	S.	Aug. 14, '62	Left in rear Oct. 25, '62. Supposed prisoner.
Maury, Joseph	19	Waterville	S.	Aug. 14, '62	Miss. bat. Spotts. May '64.
McCausland, Aug. W.	18	Gardiner	S.	Aug. 14, '62	Prom. Corp. Wounded in action July 1, '63.
McDonley, John	21	Augusta	M.	Aug. 14, '62	
McFarland, Albert	24	Gardiner	M.	Aug. 14, '62	Wounded Dec. 13, '62.
Moore, Gustavus	19	Gardiner	S.	Aug. 14, '62	Promoted 2d Lieut. Co. E. Prom.Sergt.Prls.July1,'63.
Murray, Lewis	41	Waterville	M.	Aug. 14, '62	Missing since Dec. 13, '62. Supposed dead.
Nary, Thomas J.	32	Augusta	S.	Aug. 14, '62	Discharged June 8, '63.
Norcross, Albert H.	21	Augusta	S.	Aug. 14, '62	
Palmer, Ambrose H.	20	Winslow	S.	Aug. 14, '62	Missing Spottsylvania, 1864.
Phillips, Charles M.	29	Augusta	M.	Aug. 14, '62	Wd. in action July 1, '63.
Phillips, Joseph P.	36	Augusta	M.	Aug. 14, '62	Discharged Aug. 31, '63.
Plummer, Evarts P.	21	Augusta	S.	Aug. 14, '62	
Palmer, John	18	Winslow	S.	Aug. 14, '62	Prls. July 1. Paroled.
Pooler, Joseph	26	Waterville	M.	Aug. 14, '62	Deserted Feb. 7, '65.
Pullen, Elias	44	Winthrop	M.	Aug. 14, '62	Discharged Aug. 31, '63.
Savage, William K.	26	Gardiner	S.	Aug. 14, '62	
Smith, Charles D.	19	Gardiner	S.	Aug. 14, '62	Pris. Weldon R.R., Aug., '64.
Smith, James P.	28	Waterville	S.	Aug. 14, '62	
Smith, Thomas E.	22	Gardiner	M.	Aug. 14, '62	Pro. Corp.&Ser. Wd. Apr 1, '65. Disc. May 30, '65.
Spear, Nahum	21	Gardiner	S.	Aug. 14, '62	
Sprague, Charles	18	Gardiner	S.	Aug. 14, '62	
Stackpole, Aaron	24	Gardiner	M.	Aug. 14, '62	
Starrett, Samuel C.	18	China	S.	Aug. 14, '62	Discharged April 16, '63.
Stone, George H.	19	Farmingdale	S.	Aug. 14, '62	Promoted Sergeant.
Strong, George F.	25	Gardiner	M.	Aug. 14, '62	
Richardson, Joseph W.	32	Turner	S.	Aug. 14, '62	Disc. for dis. Sept. 15, '64.
Robie, John G.	36	Litchfield	S.	Aug. 14, '62	
Robinson, William H.	29	Gardiner	S.	Aug. 14, '62	Pris. July 1, '63. Paroled. Wd. Disc. Feb. 18, '65.
Tabor, Charles H.	25	Gardiner	M.	Aug. 14, '62	
Tabor, Franklin P.	18	Vassalboro	S.	Aug. 14, '62	
Tallow, Martin	22	Waterville	S.	Aug. 14, '62	
Thayer, Adin B.	18	Waterville	S.	Aug. 14, '62	Miss. bat. Gettys. Capt'd Weldon R. R. Aug., '64.
Tinkham, Alonzo F.	23	Gardiner	M.	Aug. 14, '62	Missing in action Dec.13,'62.
Turner, Henry	21	Rome	S.	Aug. 14, '62	
Turner, Samuel W.	23	Augusta	S.	Aug. 14, '62	Discharged July 18, '64.
Wadsworth, Charles O.	22	Gardiner	S.	Aug. 14, '62	Promoted Corporal.
Wakefield, William O.	22	Gardiner	S.	Aug. 14, '62	Discharged May 12, '63.
Washburn, Charles A.	23	Gardiner	M.	Aug. 14, '62	Discharged Nov. 18, '62.
Waterhouse, John W.	22	Farmingdale	S.	Aug. 14, '62	
Waterhouse, Warren C.	24	Gardiner	M.	Aug. 14, '62	Discharged March 27, '63.
Webber, Samuel L.	43	Richmond	M.	Aug. 14, '62	Discharged Jan. 8, '63.
Webber, Wesley	22	Gardiner	M.	Aug. 14, '62	
Welch, Joseph W.	38	Gardiner	M.	Aug. 14, '62	Discharged Feb. 27, '65.
Welch, Warren E.	18	Gardiner	S.	Aug. 14, '62	
Wentworth, George M.	39	Gardiner	M.	Aug. 14, '62	

COMPANY B.—Continued.

NAMES.	Age.	RESIDENCE.	Married or Single	Mustered into the U. S. Service.	REMARKS.
Joined Company since		Dec. 1, 1862.			
Bean, Milton A	23			July 16, '63	Disc by order June 15, '65.
Blair, John	25	Waterville	M.	July 29, '63	Drafted.
Beal, Sewall G	18	Portland	M.	Sept. 18, '63	Drafted.
Bagley, George A	27	Greenbush	M.	Aug. 18, '63	Draft Mus. out May 14, '65.
Brown, Byron B	18	Patten	S.	Sept. 19, '63	Drafted.
Cross, Joseph	22	Waterville	S.	July 30, '63	Drafted. Des. Oct. 25, '63.
Davis, Clinton A	24	Denmark	S.	Aug. 31, '63	Drafted. Par. Pris. Discharged May 24, '65.
Foster, Benjamin G	28	Amherst	M.	Sept. 8, '63	Drafted. Pris. July 1, '63.
Gray, Joseph A	28	Sidney	S.	July 25, '63	Con. Des. Oct. 25, '63.
Hutchinson, Benj. F	21	Lewiston	S.	Aug. 10, '63	Con. Wounded July 24, '64.
Lord, Elijah	32	So. Berwick	M.	Sept. 17, '63	Con. Par. Pris.
Lawrence, Gilman	33	Newport	M.	Aug. 13, '63	Con. Discharged.
Lurvey, Joseph H	26	Patten	M.	Aug. 15, '63	Con.
Lampher, Asa C	24	Bradford	S.	Aug. 3, '63	Con. Wounded July 24, '64. Discharged May 19, '65.
Maloon, Stephen	32	Detroit	M.	July 20, '63	Con.
Minnack, William	28	Bath	S.	Aug. 4, '63	Con.
Mallett, Horace N	26	Houlton	M.	Aug. 15, '63	Con.
Mansfield, Henry	29	Greenbush	M.	Sept. 8, '63	Con.
Monroe, William B	23	Greenfield	M.	Aug. 13, '63	Con. Wounded.
Miller, Frank B	21	Orono	S.	Sept. 7, '63	Con. Wounded.
Maddocks, Henry	32	Dartmouth	M.	Aug. 30, '63	Con. Missed at Weldon R. R. Aug. 18, '64.
Peaslee, Charles L	33	Enfield	M.	Aug. 14, '63	Con. Promoted Corporal.
Rose, Moses	27	Presque Isle	M.	Aug. 15, '63	Con.
Smith, Oliver P	38	Presque Isle	M.	Sept. 7, '63	Con.
Silfkey, Hiram H	37	Winthrop	M.	Aug. 3, '63	Con. Discharged Apr. 2, '65.
Smith, Hiram R	18	Starks	S.	July 30, '63	Con.
Twist, George	26	Bridgewater	M.	Sept. 8, '63	Con.
Thomas, Benjamin P	44	Woodstock	M.	Sept. 5, '63	Con.
Turner, Alden	18	Palermo	S.	Sept. 1, '63	Con. Prisoner.
Tasker, Horace P	18	Jackson	S.	Aug. 21, '63	Con. Promoted Corporal.
Trimble, Richard	24	Calais	S.	Sept. 1, '63	Con.
Wilson, Joseph	43	Hudson	M.	Aug. 31, '63	Con. Disc. March 25, '65.
West, Joseph A	20	Carmel	S.	Aug. 13, '63	Con. Wounded Laurel Hill.
Wight, William L	37	Presque Isle	M.	Aug. 31, '63	Con.
Woodbury, Suel G	30	Mars Hill	S.	Aug. 15, '63	Con. Promoted Corporal.
Weeks, Theodore	34	Fremont Plan	S.	Aug. 15, '63	Con.
Williams, John	22	Brooksville	S.	Sept. 10, '63	Con. Deserted Oct. 26, '63.
Williams, George	25	Eastport	S.	Sept. 8, '63	Con. Deserted Feb. 20, '65.
Webb, Daniel M	24	Fort Fairfield		Aug. 15, '63	Con.
Whittaker, Zebulon	27	Clifton	S.	Aug. 12, '63	Con.
Wilson, James	25	Portland	S.	Aug. 4, '63	Con. Deserted Nov. 26, '63.
Wolff, Thomas	20	Litchfield	S.	July 25, '63	Con.
Joined Company since		Dec. 1, 1863.			
Brown, Jeremiah	18	Augusta	M.	Sept. 8, '64	Substitute.
Brown, Daniel B	21	Portland	M.	Oct. 7, '64	Con.
Bacon, Joseph A	24	Belfast	M.	Sept. 28, '64	Con. Wounded Feb. 7, '65. Discharged June 28, '65.
Bither, Rufus	32	Belfast	M.	Sept. 28, '64	Con.
Bowers, William	29	Augusta	S.	Oct. 7, '64	Con.
Boyd, John	25	Portland	S.	Oct. 7, '64	
Bull, Peter	34	Bangor		Oct. 13, '64	Con. Wounded Feb. 6, '65.
Chamberlain, Charles	19	Bangor	S.	Sept. 30, '64	Con. Promoted Corporal.
Chamberlain, Walter R	22	Bangor	S.	Sept. 30, '64	Con. Discharged by order June 15, '65.
Clapp, Leonard H	29	Bangor	M.	Sept. 30, '64	Con.
Clough, Llewellyn	18	Augusta		Nov. 28, '63	
Cookson, Thomas P	33	Belfast	M.	Sept. 28, '64	Con.
Chase, Charles B	25	Belfast	M.	Oct. 5, '64	Substitute. Prom. Corp.
Cockland, John	22	Belfast	M.	Oct. 6, '64	Substitute.
Davis, Stillman P	36	Bangor	M.	Oct. 6, '64	Substitute. Hung himself Jan. 4, '65.
Day, Alson L	27	Bangor	S.	Sept. 30, '64	Con.

COMPANY B.—*Continued.*

NAMES.	Age.	RESIDENCE.	Married or Single	Mustered into the U. S. Service.	REMARKS.
Dickey, Howard	42	Belfast	S.	Sept. 27, '64	Con.
Douglas, Chester R.	29	Belfast	M.	Sept. 22, '64	Con.
Dexter, Henry E.	29	Vienna	M.	Aug. 14, '62	Trans. from Co. A. Disc. July 24, '65.
Emery, Cyrus	21	Bangor	S.	Oct. 4, '64	Substitute.
Hubbard, Frank	21	Augusta	S.	Sept. 3, '64	Substitute.
Hall, Abner E.	18	Bangor	S.	Sept. 7, '64	Substitute.
Hacket, Alden	18	Patten	S.	Aug. 14, '62	Trans. from Co. A. Died of dis. Dec. 17, '64.
Jackson, Jeremiah H.	30	Belfast		Aug. 5, '63	Con. Wounded May 10, '64.
Johnston, Warren A.	34	Fort Fairfield		Sept. 19, '63	Sub. Transferred from Co. A. Discharged Mar. 25, '65.
Kelley, James	18	Bangor	S.	Aug. 29, '64	Substitute.
Kelley, John	18	Auburn	S.	Sept. 8, '64	Substitute. Wd. Feb. 6, '65.
Kelley, William D. Jr.	29	Bangor	M.	Sept. 3, '64	Substitute.
Knowlton, Frank	20	Portland		Sept. 7, '64	Substitute. Des. Oct. 3, '64.
Knights, Charles F.	18	Augusta	S.	Sept. 3, '64	Substitute. Wounded. Feb. 6, '65.
Kealiher, John	31	Moose Riv. Pl.	S.	Aug. 11, '62	Transferred from Co. A.
Lancaster, Willard	32	Golden Ridge		Aug. 15, '63	Con. Wounded Mar. 31, '65. Gravelly Run.
Libby, Richard	18	Auburn	M.	Sept. 2, '64	Substitute.
Mallion, Joseph H.	40	Skowhegan	M.	Aug. 14, '62	Joined as Capt. from Co. G.
McCollor, Phineas	24	Moose Riv. Pl.		Aug. 14, '62	Sergt. from Co. A. Wd. at Laurel Hill.
Minnick, John	36	Portland		Feb. 21, '64	Discharged to enter Navy.
Pelkey, Joseph E.	24	Bangor		Oct. 13, '64	Disc. by order May 20, '65.
Porter, Richard D.	23	Bangor		Oct. 13, '64	
Powers, Nelson A.	31	Medway		Aug. 13, '63	Wounded Aug. 5, '64.
Rainer, Albert	21	Bangor	S.	Aug. 29, '64	Substitute.
Reed, Charles G.	32	Bangor		Oct. 13, '64	
Watson, John W.	21	New Portland		Aug. 14, '62	Transferred from Co. A.
Whitman, Jones	18	Turner	S.	Aug. 14, '62	Joined as 2d Lieut. from Co. E. Promoted 1st Lieut.
Warren, Harrison	34	New Portland		Aug. 14, '62	Trans. from Co. A. In Hosp. since '63. Supposed dead.
Wilbur, Daniel A.	18	Augusta	S.	Sept. 1, '64	Substitute. Disc. Dec. 4, '64.

COMPANY C.

NAMES.	Age.	RESIDENCE.	Married or Single	Mustered into the U. S. Service.	REMARKS.
SERGEANTS.					
George D. Bisbee	21	Peru	S.	Aug. 14, '62	Wd. Dec. 13, '62. Pr. 2d Lieut.
Cherbury F. Lothrop	23	Chesterville	S.	Aug. 14, '62	Prom. Sergt.-Major. Taken prisoner at Gettysburg.
William L. Whitney	26	Presque Isle	S.	Aug. 14, '62	Transferred to Co. I.
John C. Thompson	24	Strong	S.	Aug. 14, '62	Wd. Dec. 13, '62. Disc.
Charles N. Adams	21	Wilton	S.	Aug. 14, '62	Prom. 1st Sergt. Pris. Gett. Wounded May 23, '63. Discharged March 20, '65.
Charles C. Small	23	Wilton	S.	Aug. 14, '62	Drowned August 16, '63.
William Farnham	30	Wilton	M.	Aug. 14, '62	Prisoner Aug. 19, '64. Exchanged. Prom. 1st Sergt.
Edwin C. Jones	36	Fayette	M.	Aug. 14, '62	Pris. Aug. 19, '64. Paroled.
Henry D. Fiske	36	Presque Isle	M.	Aug. 14, '62	
Rice Brown	18	Vienna	S.	Aug. 14, '62	
James Ridley	26	E. Livermore	M.	Aug. 14, '62	
Madison J. Grindle	21	Maysville	S.	Aug. 14, '62	Wounded February 6, '65. Discharged May 3, '65.
CORPORALS.					
William Farnham	30	Wilton	M.	Aug. 14, '62	Promoted Sergeant.
James N. Brown	24	E. Livermore	S.	Aug. 14, '62	Deserted Feb. 11, '63.
Edwin C. Jones	36	Fayette	M.	Aug. 14, '62	Promoted Sergeant.
Henry D. Fisk	36	Presque Isle	M.	Aug. 14, '62	Promoted Sergeant.
William N. Yeaton	22	Farmington	S.	Aug. 14, '62	
Cyrus J. Foster	24	Phillips	S.	Aug. 14, '62	Wounded Feb. 2, '63.
Josiah Mitchell	20	Jay	M.	Aug. 14, '62	Disc. for dis. Feb. 4, '63.
Warren G. Powers	21	Wilton	S.	Aug. 14, '62	Wounded Dec. 13, '62. Discharged March 17, '64.
Rice Brown	18	Vienna	S.	Aug. 14, '62	Promoted Sergeant.
Robinson Fairbanks	18	New Sharon	S.	Aug. 14, '62	Wounded August 19, '64. Discharged May 25, '65.
George H. Farnham	18	Wilton	S.	Aug. 14, '62	Wounded July 1, '63.
Dorrillus Hobbs	22	E. Livermore	S.	Aug. 14, '62	Prisoner July 1, '63.
John M. Keene	22	Phillips	S.	Aug. 14, '62	Pris. July 1, '63. Paroled. Discharged June 20, '65.
James Ridley	26	E. Livermore	M.	Aug. 14, '62	Prisoner July 1, '63. Prom. Sergt. Retu'ed Aug. 12,'63.
Charles F. Soule	20	Mapleton	S.	Aug. 14, '62	
Charles M. Blanchard	21	Phillips	S.	Aug. 14, '62	
Orville Brown	29	E. Livermore	S.	Aug. 14, '62	Discharged June 21, '65.
Alphonso L. Chandler	21	Mapleton	S.	Aug. 14, '62	
John W. Dillingham	27	Hermon	M.	Aug. 11, '62	Wounded Feb. 6, '65.
Madison J. Grindle	21	Maysville	S.	Aug. 14, '62	Promoted Sergeant.
Albion W. Stratton	19	Washburn	S.	Aug. 14, '62	Wounded Feb. 6, '65. Disc. by order May 31, '65.
Francis A. Crane	21	Fayette			Prisoner Gettysburg.
MUSICIANS.					
Hartson W. McKenney	19	Phillips	S.	Aug. 14, '62	
James A. Barrows	21	Peru	S.	Aug. 14, '62	
John B. Hall	31	Washburn	M.	Aug. 14, '62	
WAGONER.					
Columbus A. Whitney	32	Turner	M.	Aug. 14, '62	Disc. for dis. Dec. 21, '63.
PRIVATES.					
Adams, Alonzo B.	19	Wilton	S.	Aug. 14, '62	Wounded December 13, '62. Discharged May 20, '63.
Adams, George G. B.	28	Wilton	M.	Aug. 14, '62	
Adams, Melvin	20	Wilton	S.	Aug. 14, '62	
Ally, Alexander	24	Maysville	M.	Aug. 14, '62	
Bartlett, Nathan, Jr.	28	Livermore	S.	Aug. 14, '62	Prisoner in Richmond since July 1, '63.
Bates, John S.	21	Wilton	S.	Aug. 14, '62	Wd. Dec. 13, '62. Disc.
Beal, Simeon P.	32	Temple	M.	Aug. 14, '62	Discharged April 17, '64.
Beals, Calvin	21	E. Livermore	S.	Aug. 14, '62	Wounded May 25, '64. Discharged May 11, '65.
Bean, Albion S.	26	Wilton	M.	Aug. 14, '62	Discharged Oct. 29, '62.
Bean, Shepard B.	18	Maysville	S.	Aug. 14, '62	

SIXTEENTH MAINE REGIMENT.

COMPANY C.—*Continued.*

NAMES.	Age.	RESIDENCE.	Married or Single	Mustered into the U. S. Service.	REMARKS.
Bessee, Charles G.	25	Wilton	M.	Aug. 18, '62	Discharged Feb. 6, '63.
Blanchard, Charles M.	21	Phillips	S.	Aug. 14, '62	Promoted Corporal.
Blanchard, Samuel A.	44	Phillips	M.	Aug. 14, '62	Discharged Jan. 7, '63.
Blackwell, William T.	26	Jay	M.	Aug. 14, '62	Capt. July 1, '63. Paroled.
Brackley, Enoch A.	27	Freeman	M.	Aug. 14, '62	Discharged in Jan., '63.
Brown, Addison J.	18	Washburn	S.	Aug. 14, '62	Discharged Nov. 28, '62.
Brown, Orville	29	E. Livermore	S.	Aug. 14, '62	Wd. Gett. Wd. Mar. 31, '63. Pro. Cor. Disc. June 21, '65.
Brown, Rice	18	Vienna	S.	Aug. 14, '62	Promoted Corporal.
Bryant, Francis A.	31	Washburn	M.	Aug. 14, '62	
Burrows, Silas M.	29	Wilton	M.	Aug. 18, '62	Missing since Dec. 13, '62.
Butterfield, Henry J.	21	Bethel	S.	Aug. 14, '62	
Butterfield, Martin	28	Mapleton	M.	Aug. 14, '62	Pris. Gettysburg. Paroled.
Carpenter, William	29	Jay	M.	Aug. 14, '62	Discharged Oct. 30, '62.
Chaney, Farwell	44	Wilton	M.	Aug. 14, '62	Pris. Gettysburg. Paroled.
Chandler, Alphonso L.	21	Mapleton	S.	Aug. 14, '62	Pris. Gett. Returned to Co. Promoted Corporal.
Chandler, Josiah H.	27	Mapleton	S.	Aug. 14, '62	Discharged Dec. 15, '62.
Church, Charles	18	Phillips	S.	Aug. 14, '62	Wd. Dec. 13, '62. Disc.
Clark, Martin V. B.	21	Weld	S.	Aug. 14, '62	Wd. Dec. 13, '62.
Cook, Cyrus L. J.	26	Freeman	M.	Aug. 14, '62	Transferred to Co. D.
Curtis, Sylvanus	20	Salem	S.	Aug. 14, '62	Missing Dec. 13, '62.
Crane, Francis A.	21	Fayette	M.	Aug. 14, '62	Pris Gett. Prom. Corp.
Duscomb, Thomas A.	27	Wilton	M.	Aug. 14, '62	
Davis, Colamore P.	19	Freeman	S.	Aug. 14, '62	Pris. July 1, '63. Returned to Co. Disc. Mar. 1, '65.
Day, Willard	32	Sedgwick	M.	Aug. 14, '62	Disc. for dis. Jan. 9, '63.
Drury, George F.	18	Wilton	S.	Aug. 14, '62	
Estey, William H.	21	Washburn	S.	Aug. 14, '62	Disc. for dis. Aug. 12, '63.
Evans, George W.	21	Washburn	S.	Aug. 14, '62	Prisoner Weldon R. R. Aug. 19, '64.
Fairbanks, Robinson	18	New Sharon	S.	Aug. 14, '62	Promoted Corporal.
Farnham, George H.	18	Wilton	S.	Aug. 14, '62	Promoted Corporal.
Fifield, Samuel H.	27	Fayette	S.	Aug. 14, '62	Wounded Dec. 13, '62.
Fisk, William H.	28	Fayette	M.	Aug. 14, '62	Discharged Nov. 28, '63.
Greaton, Harrison M.	21	Madrid	S.	Aug. 14, '62	Transferred from Co. D.
Grindle, Madison J.	21	Maysville	S.	Aug. 14, '62	Promoted Corporal.
Grindle, Robert	35	Maysville	M.	Aug. 14, '62	Wounded Dec. 13, '62.
Grover, Joel D.	30	Avon	M.	Aug. 14, '62	Discharged March 26, '63.
Hackett, Granville	28	Mapleton	M.	Aug. 14, '62	Wounded Dec. 13, '62. Discharged June 3, '63.
Hall, John B.	31	Washburn	M.	Aug. 14, '62	
Harris, Chauncy A.	26	Washburn	M.	Aug. 14, '62	
Hinds, David H.	18	E. Livermore	S.	Aug. 14, '62	Wounded July 1, '63. Prisoner Aug. 19, '64.
Hobbs, Dorrillus	22	E. Livermore	S.	Aug. 14, '62	Promoted Corporal.
Hopkins, Thomas S.	18	Mt. Vernon	S.	Aug. 14, '62	Adjutant's Clerk.
Huff, Leonard	21	Norridgew'k	S.	Aug. 14, '62	
Keen, John M.	22	Phillips	S.	Aug. 14, '62	Promoted Corporal.
King, Alburn C.	18	Dixfield	S.	Aug. 14, '62	
Lovell, Israel F.	30	Fremont Pl.	M.	Aug. 14, '62	
Luce, Augustus	18	Freeman	S.	Aug. 14, '62	Wounded Dec. 13, '62.
Lufkin, Loren	28	Phillips	S.	Aug. 14, '62	
Mitchell, Joseph	18	Jay	S.	Aug. 14, '62	
Moulton, Joel D.	37	Phillips	M.	Aug. 14, '62	
Newton, Abraham	..	Canton	M.	Aug. 14, '62	Prisoner July 1, '63. Discharged May 22, '64.
Newton, Walter S.	24	Peru	M.	Aug. 14, '62	Discharged Feb. 13, '63.
Oakes, Charles	21	Mt. Vernon	S.	Aug. 14, '62	
Phinney, Archibald	23	Washburn	S.	Aug. 14, '62	Pris. Aug. 19,'64. Weldon R. R. Discharged June 19,'65.
Quinby, Daniel R.	37	Phillips	S.	Aug. 14, '62	
Rafford, James C.	28	Maysville	M.	Aug. 14, '62	
Reed, Elias	19	Wilton	S.	Aug. 14, '62	Wounded July 1, '63.
Reed, John W.	26	Jay	S.	Aug. 14, '62	Wounded Dec. 13, '62.
Ridley, James	26	E. Livermore	M.	Aug. 14, '62	Promoted Corporal.

COMPANY C.—Continued.

NAMES.	Age.	RESIDENCE.	Married or Single	Mustered into the U. S. Service	REMARKS.
Rowe, A. Winthrop	18	Phillips	S.	Aug. 14, '62	Orderly Reg. Headquarters.
Royall, John F.	25	Wilton	M.	Aug. 14, '62	Discharged Jan. 28, '63.
Sanborn, Job L.	23	Fryeburg	S.	Aug. 14, '62	Missing Dec. 13, '62.
Sharp, Henry A.	29	Lyndon	S.	Aug. 14, '62	Prisoner Aug. 19, '64.
Small, Charles C.	23	Wilton	S.	Aug. 14, '62	Trans. from Co. I. Pro. Serg.
Soper, Joel	18	Freeman	S.	Aug. 14, '62	Wounded Dec. 13, '62.
Soule, Charles F.	20	Mapleton	S.	Aug. 14, '62	Promoted Corporal.
Stickney, John H.	21	Phillips	S.	Aug. 14, '62	
Stratton, Albion W.	19	Washburn	S.	Aug. 14, '62	Wd. Gett. Prom. Corp.
Trefethen, A. B.	25	Wilton	M.	Aug. 14, '62	Discharged Dec. 20, '62.
Tuck, Warren	18	Avon	S.	Aug. 14, '62	Missing Dec. 13, '62.
Tuttle, John	43	Freeman	M.	Aug. 14, '62	
Whitney, David C.	27	Industry	S.	Aug. 14, '62	Disc. for dis. March 14, '63.
Winship, Enoch L.	21	Phillips	S.	Aug. 14, '62	
Witham, Sidney T.	37	Chesterville	M.	Aug. 14, '62	
Joined Company since Dec. 1, 1862.					
Allen, Jonathan	26	Vienna	S.	July 31, '63	Con.
Allen, John O.	21	Lowell	S.	Sept. 1, '63	Con.
Anderson, John	33	Letter B, R. 2.	M.	July 15, '63	Con. Prisoner Aug. 19, '64.
Adams, Lyman H.	20	Wilton	S.	Aug. 15, '63	Con. Wd. Disc. Mar. 20, '65.
Allen, Charles W.	25	Mapleton	M.	July 28, '63	Con. Disc. for dis. Jan. 11, '64.
Black, Moses B.	44	Palermo	M.	Sept. 4, '63	Con.
Brackett, James H.	21	Alton	S.	Aug. 15, '63	Con.
Brown, Albert C.	20	Houlton	S.	Aug. 15, '63	Con.
Brawn, Reuben W.	19	Windsor	S.	July 18, '63	Con. Prisoner May 5. '64.
Brawn, Franklin	18	Palermo	S.	Aug. 26, '63	Con. Wounded Feb. 7, '65.
Coy, Joseph	20	Scarboro	S.	Aug. 4, '63	Deserted Nov. 25, '63.
Coombs Isaac N.	22	Parkman	S.	July 14, '63	Con. Pris. Aug. 19, '64.
Cole, Ezekiel L.	26	China		July 14, '63	Con. Pris. Aug. 19, '64.
Chase, Miles O.	21	Chelsea	S.	July 24, '63	Con.
Dumare, Octave	20	Portland	S.	Aug. 5, '63	Con. Disc. June 28, '64.
Doe, James	23	Portland	S.	Aug. 4, '63	Con. Deserted Nov. 25, '63.
Doherty, William	22	N. Orleans, La	S.	July 31, '63	Con.
Debleux, Louis	29	Harmony	S.	Aug. 5, '63	Con.
Davis, Ambrose C.	23	Windsor	M.	July 4, '63	Con.
Davis, Lendall C.	20	Vienna	S.	Aug. 4, '63	Con.
Davis, James	24	Augusta	S.	July 31, '63	Con.
Dillingham John W.	27	Hermon	M.	Aug. 12, '63	Con. Promoted Corporal.
Dillingham Andrew J.	35	Hermon	M.	Sept. 18, '63	Con.
Dunn, Rufus R.	32	Dixfield	M.	Sept. 16, '63	Con.
Erskine, Thomas G.	23	Alton	M.	Sept. 4, '63	Con.
Freeman, Thomas O.	33	Greenbush	M.	Aug. 13, '63	Con. Wounded May 10, '64.
Foster, Edwin R.	33	Sherman	S.	Sept. 11, '63	Con. Prisoner June 5, '64.
Farrar, William	25	Oldtown	M.	Aug. 12, '63	Con. Prisoner Aug. 19, '64.
Grant, William D.	24	New Sharon	S.	July 15, '63	Con. Paroled Prisoner.
Getchell, Otis	20	Alton	S.	Sept. 15, '63	Con. Wounded Aug. 18, '64.
Graves, John D.	31	Hermon	M.	Aug. 13, '63	Con. Wounded.
Gross, Leonard	22	Oldtown	S.	Aug. 12, '63	Con.
Gilman, Charles H.	21	Patten	S.	Aug. 14, '63	Con. Par. Pris. Wd. Feb. 6, '65.
Gordan, John H.	32	Greenbush	M.	Aug. 13, '63	Con. Wounded May 8, '64. Discharged Mar. 7, '65.
Hamilton, George	21	Portland	S.	Aug. 4, '63	Con.
Hathorn, Robert H.	20	Medford	S.	Sept. 8, '63	Con.
Humphrey, Elias	27	Hampden	M.	Aug. 10, '63	Con. Pris. Aug. 19, '64.
Hinkley, John C. Jr.	29	Oldtown	M.	Aug. 12, '63	Con.
Huntley, Isaac S.	22	Merrill Pl.	S.	Sept. 11, '63	Con.
Hanson, Charles W.	18	Lincoln	S.	Sept. 2, '63	Con.
Kitchen, Charles A.	32	China	M.	July 14, '63	Con.
Lamb, Nathaniel	27	Greenbush	S.	Aug. 13, '63	Con.
Lawrence, Almond	34	Orneville	M.	Aug. 14, '63	Con.
Miller, William H.	38	Lewiston	M.	Sept. 9, '63	Con. Deserted Oct. 8, '63.
McGowell, William	22	Portland	S.	Aug. 4, '63	Con.
Marston, Daniel W.	15	Phillips	S.	Sept. 20, '61	Con. From Co. D. 9th Me. Regt. Disc. Sept. 20, '64.
Shorey, Appleton W.	25	China	M.	July 14, '63	Con. Pris. Aug. 19, '64.
Smith, Robert M.	23	Oldtown	M.	Aug. 18, '63	Con.

COMPANY C.—Continued.

NAMES.	Age.	RESIDENCE.	Married or Single	Mustered into the U. S. Service.	REMARKS.
Tracy, William A	34	Wilton	M.	July 15, '63	Con.
Wright, Charles W	42	Wilton	S.	July 31, '63	Con. Pris. Aug. 19, '64.
Warren, George	20	Whitefield	S.	Sept. 10, '63	Con.
Joined Company since Dec. 1, 1863.					
Allen, Seth	40	Patten	M.	Sept. 7, '64	Substitute.
Avery, James P	18	Winterport	S.	Sept. 1, '64	Sub. Wd. Feb. 7, '65.
Acherson, Martin	18	S.Step'u,N.B.	S.	Sept. 6, '64	Substitute.
Atkinson, Alonzo P	18	Portland	S.	Sept. 5, '64	Substitute.
Averill, Eben G	18	Orneville	S.	Oct. 5, '64	Substitute.
Billington, Enoch M	18	N. Vineyard	S.	Sept. 8, '64	Sub. Wd. Feb. 7, '65.
Bishop, Alfred	38	Bangor		Oct. 13, '64	Sub.
Bishop, Joseph	19	Madawaska	S.	Sept. 7, '64	Substitute. Wounded Feb. 7, '65. Disc. June 14, '65.
Brown, William	21	Bangor	S.	Oct. 5, '64	Substitute.
Bishop, Frederick	36	Bangor		Oct. 13, '64	Con.
Cyr, Joseph	18	Madawaska	S.	Sept. 6, '64	Substitute.
Cook, Edward C	29	Bangor		Oct. 13, '64	Con.
Cahill, Francis	21	N. Brunswick	S.	Aug. 30, '64	Substitute.
Clements, Lyman W	18	Winterport	S.	Sept. 2, '64	Sub. Disc. June 24, '65.
Davies, Edward F	27	Castine	M.	Aug. 14, '62	Joined as Capt. from Co. K.
Downes, Charles N	18	Mexico	S.	Apr. 12, '64	Wounded Feb 6, '65.
Davis, William L	18	Wellington	S.	Sept. 6, '64	Substitute. Disc. by order May 10, '65.
Duffee, James	27	Lawrence,Ms.	S.	Sept. 8, '64	Sub. Wd. March 31, '65.
Driscoll, John	24	Auburn		Oct. 19, '64	Substitute.
Dean, Avery	27	Lincolnville	M.	Sept. 27, '64	Con.
Dean, Lewis Jr	32	Lincolnville	M.	Sept. 27, '64	Con.
English, William J	22	Portland		Jan. 13, '65	
Franquire, Andrew	38	Madawaska	S.	Sept. 4, '64	Substitute.
Frost, Hazen W	18	Milo	S.	Sept. 3, '64	Sub. Disc. June 21, '65.
Fogg, Simon	21	Nort'ton,N.H	S.	Oct. 7, '64	Substitute.
Ferguson, Francis	23	Augusta	S.	Oct. 6, '64	Substitute.
Grant, Simon T	19	New Sharon	S.	Mar. 14, '64	
Glidden, Calvin A	21	Plymouth	M.	Oct. 5, '64	Sub. Wd. Feb. 6, '65.
Graffam, Silas	34	Baldwin	S.	Sept. 19, '64	Con. Discharged by order June 2, '65.
Green, George S	25	Bridgton	S.	Sept. 20, '64	Con.
Grant, John	25	Portland	S.	Oct. 5, '64	Substitute.
Hanning, Frank	26	E. I	S.	Oct. 5, '64	Substitute.
Harmon, Martin	24	Winn	S.	Oct. 21, '64	Sub. Wd. Feb. 6, '65.
Johnson, Benjamin	34	Monroe	S.	Oct. 27, '64	Con.
Kellogg, Horace	18	Patten	S.	Sept. 13, '64	Substitute.
Murray, Charles	18	Lewiston	S.	Mar. 21, '64	
Mitchell, Otis F	25	Casco	M.	Sept. 27, '64	Con.
Rowe, William T	18	Phillips	S.	Dec. 19, '63	
Royal, Russell D	18	Patten	S.	Sept. 3, '64	Substitute.
Reed, William H	24	Stetson	S.	Aug. 14, '64	Sub. Trans. from Co. A.
Ricker, Milton W	22	Bangor	M.	Aug. 22, '63	Sub. Disc. May 20, '65.
Seavey, John	20	Portland		Nov. 2, '64	
Scudder, Silas H	30	Mars Hill	M.	Jan. 8, '64	
Stinneford, Oliver R	32	Harmony	M.	Aug. 14, '62	Transferred from Co. A.
Sweeno, Israel	22	Van BurenPl.	S.	Sept. 2, '64	Transferred from Co. A.
Taylor, Francis F	37	Houlton	S.	Sept. 16, '64	Trans. from Co.A. Wounded Feb. 6, '65.
Varney, Charles T	26			Sept. 2, '63	
Wilson, John F	27	N. Brunswick	S.	Sept. 7, '64	Sub.
Watson, Henry	18	Hartland	S.	Sept. 5, '64	Transferred from Co. A.
West, Aratus H	28	New Portland	M.	Aug. 14, '62	Transferred from Co. A.

COMPANY D.

NAMES.	Age.	RESIDENCE.	Married or Single.	Mustered into the U. S. Service.	REMARKS.
SERGEANTS.					
S. Harrison Plummer..	21	Waterford....	S.	Aug. 14, '62	Prom. 1st Lieut.
William B. Etter......	26	Waterford....	M.	Aug. 14, '62	Wd. Fred. Dec. 13, '62.
John M. Webster......	19	Waterford....	S.	Aug. 14, '62	Pro. 1st Sergt., pris. July 1, '63, died of dis. July 11, '64.
Jesse A. Cross.........	24	Bethel.......	M.	Aug. 14, '62	Discharged Nov. 24, '62.
Charles A. Locke......	27	Bethel.......	M.	Aug. 14, '62	Reduced to ranks at own request.
William F. Lombard...	29	Peru.........	M.	Aug. 14, '62	Prisoner.
Joseph H. Hamilton...	24	N. Yarmouth.	S.	Aug. 14, '62	Pris. Wd. Spotts., May 8, '64. Wd. Feb. 6, '65.
Wm. H. Broughton...	21	Portland.....	S.	Aug. 14, '62	Prom. 2d Lieut.
Walter E. Stone.......	22	Waterford....	S.	Aug. 14, '62	Reduced to ranks.
Edwin R. Bowie......	21	Portland.....	S.	Aug. 14, '62	
Joseph Dunnells......	18	Newfield.....	S.	Aug. 14, '62	
William H. Small.....	20	Dixfield.....	S.	Aug. 14, '62	
Fordyce P. Twitchell..	18	Bethel.......	S.	Aug. 14, '62	
James Parsons........	26	Lexington....	M.	Aug. 14, '62	
CORPORALS.					
Benjamin F. Walton...	22	Peru.........	S.	Aug. 14, '62	Discharged March 23, '63.
David J. Parsons......	20	Mexico.......	S.	Aug. 14, '62	Prisoner Dec. 13, '62.
Edwin Farrar.........	26	Bethel.......	M.	Aug. 14, '62	Wd. Fred. Dec. 26, '62.
Isaac F. Jewett.......	18	Waterford....	S.	Aug. 14, '62	Wd. Fred. Dec. 13, '62.
Chelsea C. Abbott.....	23	Dixfield.....	S.	Aug. 14, '62	
Walter E. Stone.......	22	Waterford...	S.	Aug. 14, '62	
Sanford M. Reed......	21	Mexico.......	S.	Aug. 14, '62	Missing in bat. July 1, '63.
Joseph H. Hamilton...	24	N. Yarmouth.	S.	Aug. 14, '62	Promoted Sergeant.
Benjamin F. Fuller....	22	Brunswick...	S.	Aug. 14, '62	Wd. July 1, '63. In hosp.
Laforest Kimball......	22	Waterford...	S.	Aug. 14, '62	Wd. July 1, '63, disc. Mar. 28, '64.
Charles H. Putnam ...	21	Bethel.......	S.	Aug. 14, '62	Pris. July 1, '63, died in Richmond, Nov. 22, '63.
Edwin Bailey.........	18	Lovell.......	S.	Aug. 14, '62	
Peter T. Bean........	30	Bethel.......	S.	Aug. 14, '62	
Edwin R. Bowie......	21	Portland.....	S.	Aug. 14, '62	Promoted Sergeant.
Charles Conture.......	19	Quebec.......	S.	Aug. 14, '62	Pris. Aug. 19, '64.
Nelson A. Lane.......	18	Poland.......	M.	Aug. 14, '62	
Charles D. Ryder.....	18	N. Yarmouth.	M.	Aug. 14, '62	Wd. Feb. 7, '65.
William H. Small.....	20	Dixfield.....	S.	Aug. 14, '62	Promoted Sergeant.
Horatio G. Townsend..	18	Newfield.....	S.	Aug. 14, '62	Disc. June 28, '65.
Fordyce P. Twitchell...	18	Bethel.......	S.	Aug. 14, '62	Promoted Sergeant.
William F. Lombard...	29	Peru.........	M.	Aug. 14, '62	Promoted Sergeant.
MUSICIANS.					
George P. Hall........	25	Bethel.......	M.	Aug. 14, '62	
Cyrus L. J. Cook......	26	Madrid.......	M.	Aug. 14, '62	From Co. C. Des. Jan 4, '63.
Charles A. Locke......	27	Bethel.......	M.	Aug. 14, '62	
WAGONER.					
Oliver H. McKeen.....	29	Waterford ...	M.	Aug. 14, '62	
PRIVATES.					
Adams, Hazen.........	18	Stoneham....	S.	Aug. 14, '62	Pris. July 1, '63, died in Richmond, Nov. 5, '63.
Adkins, Moses D......	27	Cumberland .	M.	Aug. 14, '62	Deserted before muster.
Andrews, Henry F.....	18	Lowell.......	S.	Aug. 14, '62	
Bailey, Edwin, ...	18	Lowell.......	S.	Aug. 14, '62	Promoted Corporal.
Bailey, Stillman W....	19	Peru.........	S.	Aug. 14, '62	Promoted.
Bancroft, Columbus...	28	Dixfield.....	M.	Aug. 14, '62	Prisoner July 1, '63.
Bean, Peter T........	30	Bethel.......	S.	Aug. 14, '62	Pris. July 1, '63; pro. corp.
Beard, Lewis C.......	19	Bethel.......	S.	Aug. 14, '62	
Broughton, Wm. H....	21	Portland.....	S.	Aug. 14, '62	Promoted Sergeant.
Buck, Franklin.......	32	Greenwood...	M.	Aug. 14, '62	
Butters, Levi.........	37	Fryeburg....	M.	Aug. 14, '62	Disc. Nov. 10, '62.
Butters, James M.....	24	Lovell.......	M.	Aug. 14, '62	
Butters, Timothy.....	38	Waterford...	M.	Aug. 14, '62	Pris. Aug. 19, '64, died Nov. 29, '64.
Bowie, Edwin R......	21	Portland.....	S.	Aug. 14, '62	Promoted Corporal.
Chapman, Milton.....	31	Bethel.......	M.	Aug. 14, '62	

COMPANY D—Continued.

NAMES.	Age.	RESIDENCE.	Married or Single.	Mustered into the U. S. Service.	REMARKS.
Coffin, Stephen	24	Lovell	S.	Aug. 14, '62	Hospital nurse.
Coture, Charles	19	Quebec	S.	Aug. 14, '62	Promoted Corporal.
Downey, John	19	Windsor, N.S.	S.	Aug. 14, '62	Miss. in action July 1, '63.
Downes, Theo. S.	38	Mexico	M.	Aug. 14, '62	Wd. Nov. 4, '62, Disc. Dec. 13, 62.
Dunnells, Joseph	18	Newfield	S.	Aug. 14, '02	Promoted Sergeant.
Eastman, Sylvester M.	20	Lovell	S.	Aug. 14, '62	
Fish, Lorenzo S.	25	Dixfield	S.	Aug. 14, '62	Miss. since Dec. 13, '62, supposed killed.
Foster, John F.	19	Gray	S.	Aug. 14, '62	Miss. since July 1, '63, disc. Sept. 24, '64.
Foy, Almerin A.	19	Sumner	S.	Aug. 14, '62	
Fuller, Benjamin F.	22	Brunswick	S.	Aug. 14, '62	Promoted Corporal.
Gray, Enoch P.	20	Lovell	S.	Aug. 14, '62	
Gray, Jeremiah P.	18	Lovell	S.	Aug. 14, '62	
Gray, Samuel jr.	33	Stoneham	M.	Aug. 14, '62	
Greaton, Harrison M.	21	Brunswick	S.	Aug. 14, '62	Transferred to Co. C.
Hamilton, Joseph H.	24	N. Yarmouth	S.	Aug. 14, '62	Promoted to Corporal.
Hamblen, Alpheus S.	24	Lovell	S.	Aug. 14, '62	Wd. Dec. 13, '62, disc. for dis. Mar. 18, '64.
Hamlin, Edwin L.	21	Waterford	S.	Aug. 14, '62	Wd. Dec. 13, '62.
Harriman, Abel H.	18	Lovell	S.	Aug. 14, '62	Guard at headquarters.
Hayes, Edward E.	24	Mexico	M.	Aug. 14, '62	
Hayes, Erastus	21	Mexico	S.	Aug. 18, '62	
Herriman, George M.	18	Lovell	S.	Aug. 14, '62	
Hill, Wilson	31	Stoneham	M.	Aug. 14, '62	Disc. Nov. 24, '62.
Hilton, Smith	26	Lewiston	M.	Aug. 14, '62	
Hobart, Austin W.	32	Bethel	S.	Aug. 14, '62	Pris. Aug. 19, '64.
Holt, George S.	22	Portland	S.	Aug. 14, '62	Wd. Fred. Dec. 13, '62.
Hubbard, James	27	Dixfield	M.	Aug. 14, '62	Miss. in action May 8, '64.
Huston, James T.	18	Roxbury	S.	Aug. 14, '62	
Irish, Stephen	20	Lovell	S.	Aug. 14, '62	Disc. March 23, '63.
Jones, Greenfield T.	18	Pownal	S.	Aug. 14, '62	
Kenniston, Amos H.	18	Lovell	S.	Aug. 14, '62	Disc. Mar. 23, '63.
Kilgore, Dean A.	45	Waterford	M.	Aug. 14, '62	Disc. Mar. 10, '63.
Kimball, Andrew	24	Waterford	S.	Aug. 14, '62	
Kimball, Laforest	22	Waterford	S.	Aug. 14, '62	Promoted Corporal.
Lane, Nelson A.	18	Poland	S.	Aug. 14, '62	Promoted Corporal.
Lovejoy, John H.	18	Norway	S.	Aug. 14, '62	Disc. Mar. 5, '63.
Manning, Michael	35	Portland	M.	Aug. 14, '62	Disc. Feb. 27, '63.
Mason, James S.	44	Portland	M.	Aug. 14, '62	Disc. March 10, '63.
Mason, Thomas	36	Lewiston	M.	Aug. 14, '62	
McKeen, Lyman R.	32	Lovell	M.	Aug. 14, '62	Miss. since Dec. 13, '62, supposed killed.
Milliken, Sullivan O.	18	Waterford	S.	Aug. 14, '62	Never mustered.
Murphy, James	30	Portland	M.	Aug. 14, '62	Deserted Aug. 19, '62.
Park, Silas H.	26	Dixfield	S.	Aug. 14, '62	Pris. Getts. July 1, '63.
Parsons, Joseph A.	18	Mexico	S.	Aug. 14, '62	Miss. in action Dec. 13, '62.
Pingree, Asa B.	43	Albany	M.	Aug. 14, '62	Disc. Dec. 15, '62.
Plummer, Charles	36	Waterford	M.	Aug. 14, '62	Pro. Com. Serg. Nov. 11, '64.
Putnam, Charles H.	21	Bethel	S.	Aug. 14, '62	Promoted Corporal.
Richards, Prentiss M.	29	Roxbury	S.	Aug. 14, '62	Pris. Getts. July 1, '63.
Rider, Charles D.	18	N. Yarmouth	S.	Aug. 14, '62	Wd.Getts.July1,'63,pro.cor.
Roberts, Adrian G.	29	Minot	M.	Aug. 14, '62	Disc. Jan. 14, '63.
Roberts, Albert W.	18	Falmouth	S.	Aug. 14, '62	Pris. July 1, '63.
Rolfe, Henry A. J.	20	Rumford	S.	Aug. 14, '62	Disc. Nov. 13, '62.
Rourke, Lorenzo	18	Lewiston	S.	Aug. 14, '62	Disc. Mar. 6, '63.
Russell, Ceylon	40	Bethel	S.	Aug. 14, '62	
Seavey, Seth E.	18	Albany	S.	Aug. 14, '62	Accidentally Wd. Oct.19,'62.
Small, William H.	20	Dixfield	S.	Aug. 14, '62	Promoted Corporal.
Smith, Charles	21	Phila'phia, Pa	S.	Aug. 14, '62	Wd. July 1, '63.
Stevens, Charles H.	23	Waterford	S.	Aug. 14, '62	Missing since July 1, '63. Supposed killed.
Stone, Moody R.	32	Waterford	S.	Aug. 14, '62	Absent sick.
Townsend, Horatio G.	18	Newfield	S.	Aug. 14, '62	Promoted Corporal.
Twitchell, Fordyce P.	18	Bethel	S.	Aug. 14, '62	Pris. Getts. Prom. Corp.

COMPANY D.—Continued.

NAMES.	Age.	RESIDENCE.	Married or Single.	Mustered into the U. S. Service.	REMARKS.
Warren, Jonathan	36	Lovell	M.	Aug. 14, '62	Pris. Getts. Wd in action June 18, '64.
Washburn, Hiram K.	18	Dixfield	S.	Aug. 14, '62	Disc. Feb. 27, '63.
Wells, Edward	24	Lovell	S.	Aug. 14, '62	Des. Aug. 18, '62.
Wentworth, Leonidas	27	Hope	S.	Aug. 14, '62	
White, Barnard H.	27	Dixfield	S.	Aug. 14, '62	Disc. Feb. 5, '63.
Whitman, Gilbert M. L.	18	Woodstock	S.	Aug. 14, '62	
Wood, Isaac W.	26	Waterford	S.	Aug. 14, '62	
Yeaton, James A.	35	Dixfield	M.	Aug. 14, '62	
Joined Co. since Dec. 1st, 1862.					
Brown, Charles	22	Portland	S.	July 31, '63	Conscript.
Brown, George	28	Portland	M.	July 28, '63	Con. Wd. In hospital.
Bodson, William	40	Portland	S.	Aug. 8, '63	Con. Paroled Prisoner.
Bryan, George	22	Lewiston	M.	July 30, '63	Con. Paroled Pris.
Bell, George W.	20	Saco	S.	July 30, '63	Con. Pris. May 5, '64.
Burns, David	25	Portland	S.	Aug. 7, '63	Con.
Bartlett, Jonathan C.	29	Litchfield	M.	Aug. 4, '63	Sub. miss. act. May 8, '64.
Bryant, Johnson F.	20	Paris	S.	Aug. 5, '63	Con. Disc. May 25, '65.
Barrett, Michael J.	37	Lewiston	M.	Aug. 8, '63	Con. Disc. dis. Jan. 11, '64.
Blake, William	42	Portland	M.	Aug. 10, '63	Con.
Coffin, Albert M.	28	Carroll	S.	Aug. 13, '63	Con. Disc. dis. May 30, '64.
Cutts, Oliver W.	18	Milo	S.	Sept. 8, '63	Con. Pris. May 19, '64.
Dee, Nicholas	23	Sarsfield	S.	Sept. 8, '63	Con.
Daggett, Albion K.	44	Bangor	M.	Aug. 27, '63	Con. Disc. Dec. 12, '63.
Farris, Daniel jr.	23	Charlotte	M.	Sept. 10, '63	Con.
Grant, Benjamin F.	25	Bangor	M.	Sept. 5, '63	Con. Wd. In hospital.
Glover, Sylvanus G.	23	Lewiston	S.	Aug. 8, '63	Con. Miss. ac'n June 6, '64.
Gould, William A.	21	Brownville	S.	Aug. 22, '63	Con.
Houlahan, James H.	44	Lewiston	S.	Aug. 21, '63	Con. Paroled Pris.
Inman, Horatio W.	20	Lee	S.	Aug. 13, '63	Con. Disc. by order May 22, '65.
Jones, William G.	28	Belfast	S.	Sept. 10, '63	Con. Paroled Pris.
Kneeland, Charles H.	28	Lee	M.	Aug. 10, '63	Con.
Lee, Israel	27	Bancroft	M.	Aug. 14, '63	Con.
Leathers, Emery R.	33	Presque Isle	M.	Aug. 13, '63	Con. Disc. by order June 15, '65.
Leaker, George	27	Portland	M.	Sept. 11, '63	Con. Paroled Pris.
Lowell, Oliver H.	32	Gorham	S.	Aug. 14, '62	Prom. Capt. from 1st Lieut. Co. F.
Meader, Isaac	20	Litchfield	S.	Aug. 3, '63	Con. Par. Pris. Disc. by order June 5, '65
McKenney, Nicholas	22	Sarsfield	S.	Aug. 15, '63	Con. Wd. May 6, '64.
McKenney, James	18	Sarsfield	S.	Sept. 9, '63	Con. Disc. order May 25, '65.
McPherson, James	21	Alva P'l	S.	Sept. 11, '63	Con.
Moody, Frank	18	Weston	S.	Sept. 11, '63	Con. Wd. May 8, '64.
Martin, Richard H	26	Molunkus	S.	Aug. 15, '63	Con. Absent sick.
Mallett, Howard	25	Lee	M.	Aug. 13, '63	Con.
Mitchell, Peleg	44	Peru	M.	Sept. 11, '63	Con.
Malaghan, Thomas	36	Portland	S.	Aug. 18, '63	Con. Wd. May 6, '64.
Pollard, Frederick	22	Greene	S.	Aug. 3, '63	Con. Wd. Disc. by order June 5, '65.
Pray, George H.	28	Portland	M.	Aug. 8, '63	Con.
Pollard, Andrew J.	34	Linneus	M.	Aug. 14, '63	Con. Wd. In hospital.
Parsons, Joseph W.	30	Hermon	S.	Aug. 15, '63	Con. Pris. May 5, '64.
Parsons, Almond	18	Sebec	S.	Sept. 10, '63	Con.
Putnam, Daniel G.	31	Dover	M.	Aug. 14, '63	Con. Pris. May 5, '64.
Rich, Charles H.	28	Strong	S.	Aug. 14, '63	Con. Disc. dis. April 26, '64.
Robertson, Stephen S.	18	Bethel	S.	Sept. 15, '63	Con. Pris. Aug. 19, '64.
Seavey, Ezra S.	33	Mars Hill	M.	Sept. 10, '63	Con. Pris. Aug. 19, '64.
Sibley, Edward P	18	Lowell	S.	Sept. 18, '63	Con. Par. Pris. Disc.
Stackpole, Edmund F.	22	Yarmouth	M.	Sept. 10, '63	Con. Des. Nov. 23, '63.
Smith, John	23	Portland	S.	Sept. 10, '63	Con. Des. Oct. 26, '63.
Summers, Alga	23	Whitneyville	S.	Sept. 5, '63	Con. Wd. May 8, '64.
Thompson, Amos S.	19	Portland	S.	July 30, '63	Con. Disc. dis. Dec. 19, '63.
Joined Co. since Dec. 1st, 1863.					
Belongey, Morris	19	Portland	S.	Nov. 11, '64	Con.

COMPANY D.—Continued.

NAME.	Age.	RESIDENCE.	Married or Single.	Mustered into the U. S. service.	REMARKS.
Briggs, Edward	25	Gouldsboro	M.	Sept. 11, '63	Con. From Co. A.
Darby, Isaac H	23	Belfast		Mar. 21, '65	Conscript.
Fitch, Atwood	19	Damariscotta	S.	Aug. 14, '62	From Co. K. as 2d L't.
Hunt, Charles H	32	Eastport	S.	Sept. 3, '64	Con. Disc. April 26, '65.
Holt, Samuel	30	Belfast	M.	Oct. 5, '64	Conscript.
Jacobs, George T	28	Belfast	M.	Sept. 22, '64	Conscript.
Kingsbury, Marcus D	19	Bradford	S.	Oct. 6, '64	Substitute.
Knowles, William H	27	St. Marys		Aug. 7, '63	Sub. from Co. A. Missing in action Aug. 19, '64.
Liniken, Rufus	25		S.	Aug. 7, '63	Con. from Co. A.
Moody, David jr	26		S.	Aug. 5, '63	Con. from Co. A.
Malcomb, William A	21	Newcastle	S.	July 28, '63	Sub. from Co. A. Prisoner.
Malcomb, John F	22	Newcastle	S.	Aug. 7, '63	Sub. from Co. A. Wounded. Disc. April 21, '65.
Marshall, Charles	19	Bangor	S.	Oct. 13, '64	Conscript.
Mathews, Edward H	40		M.	Sept. 27, '64	Substitute. Missing in action Feb. 6, '65.
Morrell, William	21	Portland	M.	Oct. 9, '64	Sub. Par. Pris. Discharged by order June 5, '65.
Mahoney, John	25	Bangor	S.	Oct. 5, '64	Substitute.
Mahoney, Dennis	44	Augusta	S.	Oct. 6, '64	Substitute.
Meader, George W	18	Belfast		Oct. 26, '64	Substitute. Discharged by order May 29, '65.
Mylne, Alexander F	29	Bangor	M.	Oct. 7, '64	Substitute.
Martin, Michael	27	Rockland	S.	Sept. 5, '63	Substitute from Co. A.
Mann, George R	30	Bangor	M.	Sept. 30, '64	Con. Wd. Feb. 7, '65. disc. by order May 19, '65.
Mansfield, Joseph D	22	Foxcroft	M.	Sept. 24, '64	Conscript.
Monk, Alfred K	18	Belfast	S.	Oct. 6, '64	Substitute.
Malone, Theodore	22	Bangor	S.	Sept. 20, '64	Con. Disc. July 19, '65.
Maxey, William H	24	Belfast	M.	Sept. 21, '64	Con. Wd. Feb. 7, '65.
Newcomb, Alonzo	18	Belfast	S.	Oct. 6, '64	Substitute. Wd. Feb. 7, '65.
Newcomb, Henry G	19	Belfast	S.	Oct. 6, '64	Substitute. Missing in action Feb. 6, '65.
Potter, Gabriel	21		S.	Oct. 24, '64	Substitute.
Pillsbury, Charles E	26	Belfast	S.	Sept. 21, '64	Sub. Wd. Feb. 7, '65, disc. by order June 6, '65.
Parlin, Charles H	24	Skowhegan		Dec. 3, '64	Joined as 2d Lt. from N.C.S.
Parsons, James	26	Lexington		Jan. 14, '62	From Co. A. Prom. Sergt.
Soule, Richard	26	Bradford	S.	Sept. 21, '64	From Co. A.
Smitte, Franklin	25	Belfast	M.	Sept. 22, '64	Conscript.
Townsend, Lysander P	33	Portland		July 14, '63	Conscript. Discharged by order June 17, '65.
Tendell, William	38	Auburn	M.	July 7, '64	Substitute. Discharged by order May 29, '65.
Wyman, James R	37	Harmony		July 7, '63	From Co. A. Prisoner.

COMPANY E.

NAMES.	Age	RESIDENCE.	Married or Single.	Mustered into the U. S. service.	REMARKS.
SERGEANTS.					
Lincoln K. Plummer	19	Jefferson	S.	Aug. 14, '62	Pro. 2d Lieut. and 1st Lieut.
Edwin C. Stevens	20	Waterville	S.	Aug. 14, '62	Prom. 1st Sergt. and Sergt.-Major. Pris. July 1, '63.
Aubrey Leavitt	23	Turner	M.	Aug. 14, '62	Pro. 1st Lieut. and 2d Lieut. Wounded July 1, '63.
Lewis B. Doe	40	Vassalboro	M.	Aug. 14, '62	
Hiram H. Houston	27	Newport	M.	Aug. 14, '62	
Jones Whitman	18	Turner	S.	Aug. 14, '62	Pro. 1st Sergt. and 2d Lieut. and 1st Lieut. Co. B.
Warren Seaward	27	Vassalboro	S.	Aug. 14, '62	Discharged July 20, '65.
Joseph G. Lamb	21	Leeds	S.	Aug. 14, '62	Disc. by order May 29, '65.
Martin B. Soule	24	Waterville	S.	Aug. 14, '62	Wd. July 1, '63, disc. June 15, '64.
William Balentine	23	Waterville	S.	Aug. 14, '62	Wounded.
Luther Bradford	22	Turner	S.	Aug. 14, '62	Wd. Aug. 18, '64; Wd. Feb. 6, '65.
Clement C. Williams	19	New Portland	S.	Aug. 14, '62	Pris. Aug. 19, '64; disc. July 31, '65.
Bray Wilkins	18	Fairfield	S.	Aug. 14, '62	
CORPORALS.					
Jones Whitman	18	Turner	S.	Aug. 14, '62	Promoted Sergeant.
Samuel K. Doe	36	Vassalboro	M.	Aug. 14, '62	Disc. for dis. Dec. 17, '62.
Warren Seaward	20	Vassalboro	S.	Aug. 14, '62	Promoted Sergeant.
Daniel F. Houghton	21	Weld	M.	Aug. 14, '62	Disc. for dis. May 15, '63.
Winslow E. Packard	24	Jay	M.	Aug. 14, '62	Red. to ranks; acc. wd.
Charles E. Cross	25	Waterville	S.	Aug. 14, '62	Reduced to ranks.
Joseph G. Lamb	21	Leeds	S.	Aug. 14, '62	Pro. Sergt. Pris. July 1, '63.
George W. Williams	27	Newport	M.	Aug. 14, '62	
Charles H. George	27	Hebron	M.	Aug. 14, '62	Disc. for dis. Jan. 31, '63.
Martin B. Soule	24	Waterville	M.	Aug. 14, '62	Promoted Sergeant.
William Balentine	23	Waterville	S.	Aug. 14, '62	Promoted Sergeant.
Consider F. Blaisdell	25	Jay	M.	Aug. 14, '62	Disc. by order May 29, '65.
Eben Curtis, 2d	26	Leeds	S.	Aug. 18, '62	Red. to ranks at own request.
Sampson A. Thomas	21	Turner	S.	Aug. 14, '62	Pris. July 1, '63; paroled.
Octavius H. Tubbs	18	Hebron	S.	Aug. 14, '62	Disc. by Secretary War Jan. 4, '64.
Luther Bradford	22	Turner	S.	Aug. 14, '62	Promoted Sergeant.
Henry F. Judkins	24	Fairfield	M.	Aug. 14, '62	Prisoner Aug. 19, '64.
Harrison Merchant	20	Weld	M.	Aug. 14, '62	Pris. July 1, '63; paroled.
Daniel A. Soule	19	Waterville	S.	Aug. 14, '62	
Thomas D. Staples	34	Castine	M.	Sept. 16, '62	
Henry A. Dorr	23	Brewer	S.	Sept. 5, '63	
Pascal P. Gilmore	19	Dedham	S.	Sept. 5, '63	
Bray Wilkins	18	Fairfield	S.	Aug. 14, '62	Promoted Sergeant.
Benjamin F. Worth	18	Vassalboro	S.	Aug. 14, '62	Wounded Aug. 18, '64.
MUSICIANS.					
Frank E. Hitchings	18	Waterville	S.	Aug. 14, '62	Disc. for dis. March 9, '63.
James S. Priest	25	Vassalboro	S.	Aug. 14, '62	Reduced to ranks.
Charles H. Ring	18	Newport	S.	Aug. 14, '62	
Frank M. Merrill	19	Turner	S.	Aug. 14, '62	
WAGONER.					
Otis Hood jr	26	Turner	S.	Aug. 14, '62	
PRIVATES.					
Abbott, Charles	25	Newport	M.	Aug. 14, '62	Acc. wd. Oct. 20, '62; Pris. July 1, '63.
Andrews, James M.	29	Plymouth	M.	Aug. 14, '62	
Alden, Seth H.	21	Turner	S.	Aug. 14, '62	Wounded Dec. 13, '62.
Allen, Sidney A.	18	Turner	S.	Aug. 14, '62	Disc. by civil authority.
Balentine, William	23	Waterville	S.	Aug. 14, '62	Promoted Corporal.
Bates, William T.	23	Waterville	S.	Aug. 14, '62	Hospital nurse, Dec. 16, '62.
Bearce, Isaac P.	18	Hebron	S.	Aug. 14, '62	Disc. for dis. Dec. 6, '62.
Berry, Charles R.	24	Leeds	S.	Aug. 14, '62	Wounded Dec. 13, '62.
Blaisdell, Consider F.	25	Jay	M.	Aug. 14, '62	Pro. Corp. Pris. July 1, '63.
Bolton, Horace W.	22	Newport	M.	Aug. 14, '62	Disc. for dis. Dec. 6, '62.

COMPANY E.—Continued.

NAMES.	Age.	RESIDENCE.	Married or Single	Mustered into the U. S. Service.	REMARKS.
Bradford, Luther	22	Turner	S.	Aug. 14, '62	Wd. Dec. 13, '62; pris. July 1, '63.
Braun, Robert C.	32	Vassalboro	M.	Aug. 14, '62	
Bumpus, Franklin L.	27	Belgrade	M.	Aug. 14, '62	Disc. for dis. Jan. 15, '63.
Burgess, Ambrose	43	Vassalboro	M.	Aug. 14, '62	Wd. Dec. 13, '62.
Burnham, John A.	28	Leeds	S.	Aug. 14, '62	Disc. for dis. Sept. 23, '63.
Curtis, Eben, 2d	26	Leeds	S.	Aug. 18, '62	Prom. Corporal.
Cushman, Phyletus F.	18	Hebron	S.	Aug. 14, '62	
Daniels, Lorrain A.	18	Newport	S.	Aug. 14, '62	
Emerson, John	20	China	S.	Aug. 14, '62	Disc. for dis. Jan. 20, '63.
Fales, Curtis V.	20	Turner	S.	Aug. 14, '62	Prisoner July 1, '63.
Fossett, Robert M.	30	Vassalboro	M.	Aug. 14, '62	
Foster, Charles H.	20	Pittsfield	S.	Aug. 14, '62	Disc. for dis. Jan. 1, '63.
Foster, William G.	18	Pittsfield	S.	Aug. 14, '62	Wd. July 2, '63; disc. Nov. 24, '63.
Freeman, Charles A.	21	Vassalboro	S.	Aug. 14, '62	Disc. for dis. Sept. 25, '62.
George, Charles H.	27	Hebron	M.	Aug. 14, '62	Prom. Corporal Dec. 1, '62.
George, Francis	21	Leeds	S.	Aug. 14, '62	Hospital nurse.
Greenwood, Geo. H.	18	Hebron	S.	Aug. 14, '62	
Grindell, Jeremiah jr.	28	Newport	M.	Aug. 14, '62	Disc. for dis. Feb. 2, '63.
Harmond, George C.	18	Turner	S.	Aug. 14, '62	Prisoner July 1, '63. Paroled.
Heath, John	33	Jay	M	Aug. 14, '62	
Heywood, Calvin M.	18	Turner	S.	Aug. 14, '62	Disc. for dis. Feb. 20, '63.
Hodsdon, Samuel L.	21	Byron	S.	Aug. 14, '62	
Hoyt, Stephen A.	42	Vassalboro	S.	Aug. 14, '62	Prisoner July 1, '63.
Hussey, George G., jr.	20	Leeds	S.	Aug. 14, '62	
James, Charles E.	31	Jay	M.	Aug. 14, '62	Wounded Dec. 13, '62.
Jennings, Rollin F	25	Leeds	M.	Aug. 14, '62	
Johnson, Benjamin W.	27	Jay	M.	Aug. 14, '62	Promoted Musician.
Johnson, Frank B.	22	Pittsfield	S.	Aug. 14, '62	Wounded Dec. 13, '62.
Judkins, Henry F	24	Fairfield	M.	Aug. 14, '62	Comp. Clerk, wd. Dec. 13, '62.
Knight, Joseph F	21	Newport	S.	Aug. 14, '62	
Littlefield, Asel A.	18	Belgrade	S.	Aug. 14, '62	
Lyford, Charles F	19	Waterville	S.	Aug. 14, '62	Wounded Dec. 13, '62.
Lyford, James N.	18	Waterville	S.	Aug. 14, '62	Prisoner July 1, '63; Exch.
Lyon, Charles C	24	Newport	M.	Aug. 14, '62	Wd. July 1, '63; dis. June 3, '64.
Merchant, Harrison	20	Weld	M.	Aug. 14, '62	Prisoner July 1, '63. Paroled.
Merrill, Frank M	19	Turner	S.	Aug. 14, '62	Detailed for Drummer.
Mills, Albion B.	18	Vassalboro	S.	Aug. 14, '62	Wounded July 1, '63.
Monk, Isaac J	24	Turner	M.	Aug. 14, '62	Prisoner July 1, '63. Paroled.
Peare, George H.	21	Leeds	M.	Aug. 14, '62	Disc. for dis. Mar. 14, '63.
Pettengill, Samuel W.	20	Leeds	S.	Aug. 14, '62	
Pratt, Sarson C	19	Turner	S.	Aug. 14, '62	
Priest, Hiram T	18	Vassalboro	S.	Aug. 14, '62	
Pulsifer, Alexander W.	29	Weld	S.	Aug. 14, '62	Wd. May 5, '64; dis. Jan. 10, '65.
Richardson, Orson F.	18	Vassalboro	S.	Aug. 14, '62	
Richmond, Granville	35	Leeds	M.	Aug. 14, '62	Disc. for dis. Jan. 9, '65.
Riggs, Jerry W	21	Jay	S.	Aug. 14, '62	Wd. May 4, 64; disc. June 5, '65.
Robinson, John F.	36	Rome	M.	Aug. 14, '62	Disc. for dis. July 16, '63.
Spaulding, Melb'ne C.	21	Newport	S.	Aug. 14, '62	Deserted Dec. 1, '62.
Soule, Daniel A	19	Waterville	S.	Aug. 18, '62	
Soule, Martin B.	24	Waterville	S.	Aug. 14, '62	Promoted Corporal.
Thomas, David S.	18	Byron	S.	Aug. 14, '62	Pris. July 1, '63; paroled.
Thomas, Sampson A.	21	Turner	S.	Aug. 14, '62	Promoted Corporal.
Tibbetts, Andrew J.	27	Newport	M.	Aug. 14, '62	Prisoner July 1, '63.
Tibbetts, William A.	21	Belgrade	S.	Aug. 14, '62	Disc. for dis. June 10, '63.
Towle, Clark L	18	Newport	S.	Aug. 14, '62	Wounded Dec. 13, '62.
Towle, Mark	18	Newport	S.	Aug. 14, '62	Pris. Aug. 19, '64; paroled.
Townsend, Roscoe B.	24	Jay	S.	Aug. 14, '62	
Trask, Ezra W	38	Belgrade	M.	Aug. 14, '62	Wounded May 5, '64.
Tubbs, Octavius H.	18	Hebron	S.	Aug. 14, '62	Prom. Corp.; pris. July 1, '63.
Ward, George W	18	Vassalboro	S.	Aug. 14, '62	Disc. for dis. Nov. 1, '62.
Webber, Gustavus V.	28	Vassalboro	M.	Aug. 14, '62	Wd. July 1, '63; disc. Dec. 16, '63

COMPANY E.—Continued.

NAMES.	Age.	RESIDENCE.	Married or Single	Mustered into the U. S. Service.	REMARKS.
Webber, Virgil H	25	Vassalboro	S.	Aug. 14, '62	
Weymouth, Timothy	36	Pittsfield	S.	Aug. 14, '62	
Wheeler, William W	18	Leeds	S.	Aug. 14, '62	Disc. for dis. May 20, '63.
White, Charles S	33	Jay	M.	Aug. 14, '62	Disc. for dis. Mar. 14, '63.
White, Frank J	18	Palmyra	S.		Rejected at Final Muster, Aug. 14, '62.
Winship, Charles P	18	Turner	S.	Aug. 14, '62	Pris. Dec. 13, '62; exch.; wd. July 1, '63.
Worth, Benjamin F	18	Vassalboro	S.	Aug. 14, '62	Wd. at Weldon R. R. Aug. 18, '64; pro. corp.
Worth, Francis	44	Vassalboro	M.	Aug. 14, '62	
Weber, John W	21	Belgrade	S.	Aug. 14, '62	Disc. for dis. Dec. 10, '62.
Joined Company since Dec. 1, 1862.					
Achorn, Orlando R	18	Augusta	S.	July 17, '63	Con. Wounded Feb. 7, '65.
Arnold, Isaac	39	Bradford	M.	Sept. 9, '63	Con.
Arnold, Joseph T	41	Bradford	M.	Sept. 15, '63	Con.
Baron, Alfred	22	Portland	S.	Aug. 1, '63	Con. Des. Sept. 6, '63.
Blodgett, Lorenzo D	21	Portland	S.	Aug. 1, '63	Con.
Blodgett, Hamlin L	20	Portland	S.	July 13, '63	Con.
Bickmore, Daniel O	27	Oldtown	M.	Aug. 12, '63	Con. Wd. May 10, '64.
Babcock, Luther J	29	Edinburg	M.	Aug. 14, '63	Con.
Burnham, William O	20	Oldtown	S.	Aug. 12, '63	Con.
Buswell, Stephen	20	Presque Isle	S.	Sept. 5, '63	Con. Miss. in action Aug. 19, 64.
Bryant, Charles F	23	Presque Isle	M.	Aug. 15, '63	Con. Pris. June 21, '64.
Berry, John	26	Bridgewater	S.	Sept. 1, '63	Con.
Cooley, Elisha	44	Augusta	M.	July 17, '63	Con. Wounded Aug. 18, '64.
Cotton, Charles	28	Portland	S.	Aug. 5, '63	Con. Deserted Sept. 1, '63.
Cobb, Amasa	18	Parkman	S.	Aug. 10, '63	Con.
Cookson, Christopher C	25	Linneus	M.	Aug. 14, '63	Con.
Christophers, Joseph	29	Alvah Plan.	S.	Sept. 11, '63	Con. Miss in action, June 6, '64.
Crocker, Elbridge P	23	Lowell	M.	Aug. 14, '63	Con.
Crabb, William H	22	Bangor	S.	Sept. 16, '63	Con.
Cole, Lemuel N	19	Hampden	M.	Sept. 11, '63	Con.
Chambers, Benj. W	19	Linneus	S.	Sept. 17, '63	Con. Miss. in action, May 8, '64.
Davis, Alvah M	21	Jefferson	S.	July 31, '63	Con. Wounded May 6, '64.
Davis, Daniel	40	Oldtown	M.	Aug. 12, '63	Con. Miss. in action, June 1, '64.
Davis, Daniel, 2d	33	Winn	M.	Sept. 3, '63	Con.
Davis, George T	21	Turner	M.	July 17, '63	Con.
Davis, Henry L	22	Portland	S.	Sept. 17, '63	Con.
Dane, Francis S	32	Dedham	M.	Aug. 27, '63	Con.
Dickey, William	25	Oldtown	S.	Sept. 14, '63	Con. Des. Sept. 26, '64.
Decker, Greenlief E	21	Smithfield	S.	July 28, '63	Con. Disc. June 26, '65.
Douns, Ezekiel C	36	Portland	M.	Aug. 5, '63	Con.
Dudley, Ambrose	22	Augusta	S.	Aug. 4, '63	Con. Disc. Nov. 26, '63.
Ellis, John	21	Lewiston	S.	Sept. 18, '63	Con. Des. Nov. 2, '63.
Fairbrother, Isaac H	21	Orono	S.	Aug. 26, '63	Con.
Hale, Charles	25	No. 4 R. L.	M.	Aug. 13, '63	Con. Disc. Feb. 13, '64.
Hall, Lucius W	27	Anson	M.	July 27, '63	Con. Des. May 4, '64.
Hatch, George W	29	Exeter	M.	Sept. 7, '63	Con. Wounded June, '64; wounded Apr. 1, '65.
Howard, James Jr	20	Medway	S.	Aug. 13, '63	Con.
Hutchins, Charles L	34	Augusta	M.	July 14, '63	Con. Disc. Dec. 8, '63.
Hartwell, John	21	St. Albans	S.	Aug. 31, '63	Con.
Imhoff, Oscar	21	Augusta	S.	Aug. 8, '63	Con. Deserted Sept. 8, '63.
Jewell, Benjamin F	24	Troy	M.	Aug. 31, '63	Con. Wounded May 10, '64.
Jewell, Edwin M	22	Wales	S.	July 16, '63	Con. Deserted Nov. 27, '63.
Kay, John M	28	Portland	S.	July 31, '63	Con.
Keefe, John	21	Portland	S.	July 28, '63	Con. Deserted Sept. 17, '63.
Kelly, James	22	Calais	M.	Aug. 5, '63	Con. Deserted Nov. 28, '63.

COMPANY E—Continued.

NAMES.	Age.	RESIDENCE.	Married or Single.	Mustered into the U. S. Service.	REMARKS.
Lewis, Benjamin	30	Calais	M.	July 31, '63	Con.
Lyon, John	30	Portland	S.	Aug. 4, '63	Con. Deserted May 4, '64.
McKillop, Donald	33	Portland	S.	July 31, '63	Con.
McNulty, George	22	Portland	S.	July 29, '63	Con. Wounded April 1, '65; discharged May 30, '65.
Manson, Frederic	23	Calais	S.	Aug. 10, '63	Con.
Montague, Frederic	28	Augusta	S.	Aug. 1, '63	Con.
Neal, David C	21	Monticello	S.	Sept. 1, '63	Con.
O'Dea, Thomas	18	Portland	S.	Sept. 19, '63	Con.
Partridge, Samuel	21	Hampden	S.	Sept. 16, '63	Con. Miss. in act. May 7, '64.
Peters, John	18	Portland	S.	July 29, '63	Con. Deserted Sept. 8, '63.
Reed, Jacob	31	Dixfield	M.	July 30, '63	Con. Deserted Sept. 6, '63.
Runnells, Andrew J	25	Pattagumpus	M.	Aug. 13, '63	Con. Wounded Feb. 6, '65.
Schmit, John	32	Augusta	S.	Aug. 8, '63	Con. Deserted Sept. 6, '64.
Staples, Thomas D	34	Castine	M.	Sept. 16, '63	Con.
Ward, Sylvanus H	18	Greenbush	S.	Sept. 17, '63	Con.
Weed, Alonzo S	20	Augusta	S.	July 22, '63	Con.
Westfal, William	29	Portland	S.	Aug. 1, '63	Con. Deserted Sept. 6, '64.
Witherell, Daniel	40	Lewiston	M.	July 30, '63	Con.
Joined Cmpany since Dec. 1, 1863.					
Baston, Franklin N	35	Bangor		Oct. 13, '64	Con.
Bell, James	18	Houlton		Nov. 24, '64	Substitute.
Choate, Charles E	18	Fairfield	S.	Sept. 7, '64	Transferred from Co. A.
Dorr, Henry A	23	Brewer	S.	Sept. 5, '63	Trans. from Co. A; pr. corp.
Downing, George A	21	Skowhegan	S.	Aug. 14, '62	Trans. from Co. A.
Fahay, James	20	Bangor		Sept. 10, '63	Substitute; transferred from Co A; disc. May 29, '65.
Gilmore, Pascal P	19	Dedham	S.	Sept. 5, '63	Substitute; prom. corp.
Greenlow, George W	18	Presque Isle	S.	Sept. 8, '63	Substitute.
Greenlow, Aaron R	24	Presque Isle	S.	Oct. 13, '64	Con. Disc. May 30, '65.
Getchell, Andrew	18	Portland	S.	Aug. 18, '63	Substitute.
Gardiner, Enoch R	24	Mapleton Pl	S.	Oct. 13, '64	Con.
Hart, George	18	Bangor	S.	Sept. 3, '64	Transferred from Co. A.
Hair, George	22	Fremont Pl	S.	Nov. 10, '64	Con. Wounded Mar. 31, '65; discharged May 30, '65.
Hanscom, William H	19	Orono	S.	Sept. 5, '63	Substitute.
Hayden, John	25	Bangor	S.	Sept. 13, '64	Substitute; wd. Feb. 6, '65.
Haskins, Moses	44	Oldtown	M.	Sept. 7, '64	Substitute.
Kelly, Hugh	30	Bangor	S.	Sept. 9, '64	Substitute.
Kimball, Charles	19	Harmony	S.	Sept. 9, '64	Substitute; disc. June 6, '65.
Kimball, Sylvester E	18	Harmony	S.	Sept. 9, '64	Substitute.
Kenney, George	22	Augusta	S.	Oct. 7, '64	Substitute; wounded Feb. 6, '65; discharged May 17, '65.
Mahony, William R	18	Saco	S.	Sept. 9, '64	Substitute.
Moore, Gustavus	19	Gardiner	S.	Aug. 14, '62	Joined as 2d Lieut. from Co. B.
Murch, Albert J	24	Starks	S.	Aug. 14, '62	Transferred from Co. A.
Newell, Albert M	27	Portland	M.	Oct. 6, '64	Substitute; disc. June 5, '65.
Newell, James N	33	Portland	M.	Oct. 6, '64	Substitute.
O'Brien, Dennis	28	Augusta	S.	Oct. 7, '64	Substitute.
Page, Samuel W	21	Orono	S.	Sept. 30, '64	Con.
Phillips, Reuel	36	Bangor	M.	Sept. 30, '64	Con.
Perkins, Abner W	37	Bangor		Sept. 5, '64	Con.
Roberts, Frank A	26	Bangor	S.	Oct. 6, '64	Substitute; disc. June 14, '65.
Reynolds, Hiram	38	Belfast	M.	Sept. 28, '64	Con.
Ricker, Isaiah	37	Belfast	S.	Sept. 27, '64	Con.
Richards, Anson N	37	Belfast	M.	Sept. 27, '64	Con. Disc. July 13, '65.
Riley, John	21	Augusta	S.	Oct. 7, '64	Sub.; miss. in act. Dec. 10, '64.
Rowe, Charles A	30	Portland	M.	Oct. 7, '64	Substitute.
Royal, Darius N	37	Belfast	M.	Sept. 27, '64	Con.
Sedeau, Paul	22	Bangor	S.	Oct. 5, '64	Substitute.
Smith, Henry J	23	Bangor	S.	Sept. 30, '64	Con.
Smith, William W	35	Bangor	S.	Oct. 1, '64	Con.

COMPANY E.—Continued.

NAME.	Age.	RESIDENCE.	Married or Single.	Mustered into the U. S. service.	REMARKS.
Smith, Aaron G.	22	Belfast	S.	Sept. 27, '64	Conscript.
Sumner, Samuel S.	39	Orono	M.	Sept. 30, '64	Substitute; disc. May 20, '65.
Thompson, John F.	18	New Portland	S.	Aug. 14, '62	Transferred from Co. A; discharged May 3, '65.
Williams, Clement C.	19	New Portland	S.	Aug. 14, '62	Sergt.; trans. from Co. A; pris. Aug 19, '64; disc. July 31, '65.
Wilkins, Bray	18	Fairfield	S.	Aug. 14, '62	Corp.; Trans. from Co. A; promoted Sergeant.
Waite, John P.	24	Cushing		Oct. 10, '64	Substitute.

COMPANY F.

NAMES.	Age.	RESIDENCE.	Married or Single.	Mustered into the U. S. Service.	REMARKS.
SERGEANTS.					
Daniel L. Warren	22	Standish	S.	Aug. 14, '62	Promoted 2d Lieutenant.
Isaac R. Whitney	22	Windham	S.	Aug. 14, '62	Prom. 1st Sergt.; 2d Lieut. Co. G.
Charles H. McKenney	25	Bridgton	M.	Aug. 14, '62	Discharged June 19, '65.
James Locke	44	Buxton	M.	Aug. 14, '62	Reduced to ranks at own request; disc. Mar. 26, '64.
Charles W. Ross	32	Biddeford	M.	Aug. 14, '62	Prisoner July 1, '63.
James P. Hamblen	33	Limington	M.	Aug. 14, '62	Acting Ordnance Sergeant.
John McPhee	32	Gorham	M.	Aug. 14, '62	Pris. July 1, '63. Exch'ged.
Alpheus S. Harmon	18	Standish	S.	Aug. 14, '62	
Frank J. Leavitt	19	Buxton	S.	Aug. 14, '62	
Charles L. Seavey	18	Saco	S.	Aug. 14, '62	
Frank L. Tarbox	21	Hollis	S.	Aug. 14, '62	
CORPORALS.					
George A. Gatchell	34	Buxton	M.	Aug. 14, '62	Discharged June 6, '65.
Lorenzo Hooper	26	Waterboro	S.	Aug. 14, '62	Reduced to ranks Aug. 13, '62 and detailed teamster.
Edward L. Varney	21	Brunswick	S.	Aug. 14, '62	Prisoner July 1, '63.
Charles H. Goodridge	22	Westbrook	S.	Aug. 14, '62	Red. to r'ks; disc. Jun.23,'65.
William Cannell	27	Gorham	M.	Aug. 14, '62	Prisoner July 1, '63.
Benjamin F. Metcalf	19	Gorham	M.	Aug. 14, '62	Discharged Nov. 29, '62.
Samuel P. Burnell	19	Bridgton	S.	Aug. 14, '62	
John McPhee	32	Gorham	M.	Aug. 14, '62	Promoted Sergeant.
Ephraim H. Floyd	27	Saco	M.	Aug. 14, '62	
Jacob T. Locke	27	Dayton	M.	Aug. 14, '62	Disc. for dis. July 15, '63.
William Manchester jr.	23	Standish	S.	Aug. 14, '62	
John Arkit	19	Paris	S.	Sept. 7, '63	
Benjamin Dalton	32	Bridgton	M.	Aug. 14, '62	
Charles H. Goodridge	22	Westbrook	S.	Aug. 14, '62	
Alpheus S. Harmon	18	Standish	S.	Aug. 14, '62	Promoted Sergeant.
Frank J. Leavitt	19	Buxton	S.	Aug. 14, '62	Pro. Serg.; pris. Aug. 19,'64.
Thomas D. Page	24	Burlington	S.	Aug. 14, '63	
Charles L. Seavey	18	Saco	S.	Aug. 14, '62	Promoted Sergeant.
Sumner C. Swett	19	Standish	S.	Aug. 14, '62	
Frank L. Tarbox	21	Hollis	S.	Aug. 14, '62	Promoted Sergeant.
MUSICIANS.					
Henry C. Crockett	18	Westbrook	S.	Aug. 14, '62	
Larkin E. Barker	21	Bridgton	S.	Aug. 14, '62	
Sidney E. Swett	18	Standish	S.	Aug. 14, '62	Reduced to ranks.
William A. Follett	18	Scarboro	S.	Aug. 14, '62	
WAGONERS.					
Gideon M. Tucker	32	Standish	M.	Aug. 14, '62	Promoted to wagon master.
Thomas J. Dorset	18	Standish	S.	Aug. 14, '62	
John D. March	31	Bridgton	S.	Aug. 14, '62	
Frank Rhodes	26	Dayton	S.	Aug. 14, '62	
Charles A. Warren	20	Waterboro	S.	Aug. 14, '62	
PRIVATES.					
Andrews, Abram S.	20	Gorham	S.	Aug. 14, '62	Prisoner July 1, '63.
Barker, Levi D.	18	Sweden	S.	Aug. 14, '62	Prisoner July 1, '63.
Benson, Oran	26	Waterboro	S.	Aug. 14, '62	Wounded Feb. 6, '65.
Bickford, Warren C.	18	Parsonsfield	S.	Aug. 14, '62	Wounded December 13, '62.
Blair, Samuel	18	Gorham	S.	Aug. 14, '62	
Bowden, Charles A.	18	Waterboro	S.	Aug. 14, '62	Rejected at final muster.
Brocklebank, Nathan C.	26	Bridgton	M.	Aug. 14, '62	
Burnham, George R.	20	Hollis	M.	Aug. 14, '62	Wounded July 1, '63; disc. May 13, '65.
Burnham, John M.	19	Parsonsfield	S.	Aug. 15, '62	
Cleaves, Royal L.	18	Bridgton	S.	Aug. 14, '62	Nurse in Regt. Hospital. Prom. Hospital Steward.
Crediford, Oliver	18	Biddeford	S.	Aug. 14, '62	
Cross, Aaron	22	Bridgton	S.	Aug. 14, '62	
Davis, Josiah B.	28	Saco	S.	Aug. 14, '62	Pris. Dec. 13, '62. Wd.

COMPANY F.—*Continued.*

NAMES.	Age.	RESIDENCE.	Married or Single.	Mustered into the U. S. Service.	REMARKS.
Dalton, Benjamin	32	Bridgton	M.	Aug. 14, '62	Asst. Q. M. Sergeant, '62. Wd. Aug. 18, '64; pro. Cor.
Dorset, Thomas J	18	Standish	S.	Aug. 14, '62	Detailed regt. wagoner.
Fenderson, Benjamin	34	Saco	S.	Aug. 14, '62	Wd. July 1, '63; disc. June 6, '65.
Floyd, Ephraim H	27	Saco	M.	Aug. 14, '62	Promoted Corporal.
Follett, William A	18	Scarboro	S.	Aug. 14, '62	Promoted Musician.
Giles, Charles H	27	Waterboro	S.	Aug. 14, '62	Disc. for dis. Oct. 16, '63.
Green, Joseph	32	Saco	M.	Aug. 14, '62	Pris. July 1, '63; exch.
Green, William F	30	Gorham	M.	Aug. 14, '62	
Guilford, Hiram	25	Saco	M.	Aug. 14, '62	
Hamblen, James P	33	Limington	M.	Aug. 14, '62	Detailed Ordnance Sergeant.
Harding, George	18	Gorham	S.	Aug. 14, '62	Discharged Feb. 1, '63.
Harding, John F	20	Dover, N. H.	S.	Aug. 14, '62	Pris. July 1, '63; wd. Feb. 6, '65.
Harding, John M	30	Saco	M.	Aug. 14, '62	Discharged Nov. 13, '62.
Harmon, Alpheus S	18	Standish	S.	Aug. 14, '62	Promoted Corporal.
Harmon, Benjamin	42	Buxton	M.	Aug. 14, '62	Discharged April 14, '63.
Hodgdon, Abram B	21	Hollis	S.	Aug. 14, '62	Disc. Sept. 21, '63.
Howe, William G	20	Standish	S.	Aug. 14, '62	Des. Sept. 28, '62.
Johnson, Albion	33	Gorham	M.	Aug. 14, '62	
Jordan, Granville B	18	Sweden	S.	Aug. 14, '62	Wounded Aug. 19, '64.
Lancaster, Bradford F	23	Anson	S.	Aug. 14, '62	Wd. Disc. Sept. 17, '63.
Leavitt, Frank J	19	Buxton	S.	Aug. 14, '62	Promoted Corporal.
Libby, Lorenzo D	34	Windham	M.	Aug. 14, '62	
Livingston, Luther D. 2d	32	Saco	M.	Aug. 14, '62	
Locke, Edward A	25	Waterboro	S.	Aug. 14, '62	Wd. Disc. Dec. 24, '63.
Locke, Jacob T	27	Dayton	M.	Aug. 14, '62	Promoted to Corporal.
Locke, James F	18	Buxton	S.	Aug. 14, '62	Disc. for dis. Mar. 26, '64.
Locke, William P	20	Buxton	S.	Aug. 14, '62	
Lowd, William R	39	Denmark	M.	Aug. 14, '62	Disc. June 17, '65.
Manchester, William jr.	23	Standish	S.	Aug. 14, '62	Promoted Corporal.
March, John C	20	Kennebunk't	S.	Aug. 14, '62	Wd. Disc. May 15, '65.
March, John D	31	Bridgton	S.	Aug. 14, '62	Detailed as Wagoner.
Mayo, Gardner G	26	Bridgton	M.	Aug. 14, '62	Deserted Oct. 6, '62.
McCann, Charles M	23	Saco	S.	Aug. 14, '62	
McGrath, Charles E	21	Brownfield	S.	Aug. 14, '62	
Merrill, George E	18	Saco	S.	Aug. 14, '62	
Palmer, George	21	Saco	M.	Aug. 14, '62	Wounded July 1, '63.
Pelton, La Roy	18	Anson	S.	Aug. 14, '62	
Pierce, Charles R	21	Wareham, Ms	S.	Aug. 14, '62	
Pike, Benjamin F	18	Hollis	S.	Aug. 14, '62	
Powers, Albert	18	Windham	S.	Aug. 14, '62	Pris. July 1, '63; exch.; pris. Aug. 18, '64.
Reynolds, Charles	23	Saco	M.	Aug. 14, '62	Wd. May 5, '64; disc. May 22, '65.
Richardson, Joseph	28	Sweden	M.	Aug. 14, '62	
Richardson, Osborn	19	Denmark	M.	Aug. 14, '62	
Ricker, Hiram	21	Waterboro	S.	Aug. 14, '62	Absent; sick since Nov. '62.
Rhoades, Frank	26	Dayton	S.	Aug. 14, '62	Detailed as asst. wagoner.
Robinson, James	38	Sebago	M.	Aug. 14, '62	Discharged Jan. 12, '63.
Rogers, Cyrus 2d	34	Anson	M.	Aug. 14, '62	Discharged March 9, '63.
Rogers, James	40	Buxton	M.	Aug. 14, '62	Discharged Oct. 7, '62.
Savage, Eugene	18	Anson	S.	Aug. 14, '62	Absent. Unknown.
Sawyer, Freeman C	19	Saco	S.	Aug. 14, '62	
Seavey, Charles L	18	Saco	S.	Aug. 14, '62	Promoted Corporal.
Smith, David	18	Waterboro	S.	Aug. 14, '62	Discharged Aug. 21, '65.
Smith, Francis L	22	Buxton	S.	Aug. 14, '62	
Smith, George W	18	Saco	S.	Aug. 14, '62	Pris. July 1, '63; exch.; pris. Aug. 18, '64.
Smith, Melville B	18	Hollis	S.	Aug. 14, '62	Wd. Aug. 18, '64; disc. Feb. 27, '65.
Swett, Sidney E	13	Standish	S.	Aug. 14, '62	Detailed as drummer.

COMPANY F.—*Continued.*

NAMES.	Age.	RESIDENCE.	Married or Single	Mustered into the U. S. service.	REMARKS.
Swett, Sumner C.	19	Standish	S.	Aug. 14, '62	Promoted Corporal.
Strout, James A.	20	Standish	S.	Aug. 14, '62	
Tarbox, Frank L.	21	Hollis	S.	Aug. 14, '62	Promoted Corporal.
Thompson, John E.	21	Standish	M.	Aug. 14, '62	Supposed discharged.
Thorpe, David H.	32	Saco	M.	Aug. 14, '62	
Tibbetts, Sheldron	29	Saco	M.	Aug. 14, '62	Wounded July 1, '63.
Tyler, Abram	21	Buxton	M.	Aug. 14, '62	
Tyler, George	18	Buxton	S.	Aug. 14, '62	
Tyler, John A.	18	Buxton	S.	Aug. 14, '62	Discharged Nov. 10, '62.
Ward, William W.	18	Gorham	S.	Aug. 14, '62	
Warren, Charles A.	20	Waterboro	S.	Aug. 14, '62	Det. as wagoner Sept. 7, '62.
Walker, Eben J.	39	Anson	M.	Aug. 14, '62	
Webster, John W.	18	Man'ter, N.H.	S.	Aug. 14, '62	Pris. Aug. 18,'64 to May 4,'65.
Whitney, Alonzo M.	18	Gorham	S.	Aug. 14, '62	
Joined Company since Dec. 1, 1862.					
Allen, Benjamin F.	22	Belfast	S.	Aug. 14, '63	Drafted.
Arkit, John	19	Paris	S.	Sept. 7, '63	Substitute. Prom. Corp.
Atwood, George H.	23	Otisfield	S.	Sept. 18, '63	Substitute.
Bishop, James C.	18	Wayne	S.	Sept. 9, '63	Sub. Disc. by order May 22, '65.
Blake, Frederic W. C.	39	Portland	S.	Sept. 12, '63	Substitute.
Butters, Warren	28	Exeter	M.	Aug. 15, '63	Drafted. Wd.; disc. April 21, '65.
Bussell, Theodore E.	26	Hudson	M.	Aug. 13, '63	Drafted. Miss. since Aug. 19, '64.
Bradford, Abraham	25		M.	Aug. 6, '63	Drafted. Wd.; disc. Jan. 16, 65.
Chadbourne, John W.	23	Oxford	M.	Sept. 9, '63	Substitute. Wounded.
Cunningham, Samuel	44	Washington	M.	Aug. 26, '63	Sub. Disc. May 19, '65.
Douglass, Ashbell S.	29	Sebec	M.	Aug. 14, '63	Drafted.
Dow, John E.	19	Buchanan Pl.	S.	Sept. 17, '63	Substitute.
Dunton, Wilmot W.	44	Liberty	M.	Aug. 27, '63	Sub. Missing since Aug. 19. '64.
Evans, Hiram F.	25	Washington	S.	Aug. 26, '63	Sub. Wd. Feb. 6, '65.
Fenderson, Joseph P.	27	Saco	M.	Sept. 10, '63	Drafted.
Gammon, Levi	22	Buckfield	S.	Sept. 7, '63	Sub. Disc. Jan. 27, '64.
Gould, Thomas J.	21	Dixmont	M.	Sept. 10, '63	Sub. Disc. Sept. 6, '64.
Grant, Benjamin F.	18	Bradford	S.	Sept. 5, '63	Substitute.
Glasier, George A.	40	Boston, Mass.	M.	Aug. 12, '63	Sub. Des. Oct. 16, '63.
Haley, Dennis	19	Saco	S.	Sept. 9, '63	Substitute.
Hammond, Edwin G.	26	Lincoln	M.	Aug. 14, '63	Drafted.
Mark, Andrew	22	Biddeford	S.	Sept. 15, '63	Substitute. Paroled pris.
Merritt, Edmund W.	22	Bridge'r, Ms.	M.	Aug. 14, '63	Drafted. Wd. June 17, '64; Disc. May 25, '65.
Page, Thomas D.	22	Burlington	S.	Aug. 14, '63	Drafted. Promoted Corp.
Paul, Frank	28	Gorham	S.	Aug. 29, '63	Substitute.
Perry, Clark E.	44	Hebron	S.	Aug. 14, '63	Drafted.
Pickering, Ansel	21	Wakef'd, N.H	S.	Aug. 14, '63	Draf. Disc. May 18, '65.
Pierce, Samuel	25	Hudson	S.	Aug. 13, '63	Drafted.
Powers, William T.	27	Marion	M.	Aug. 13, '63	Drafted.
Rowe, Cyrus A.	29	Sumner	M.	Aug. 13, '63	Drafted. Wd. May 5, '64; disc. Feb. 18, '65.
Rowe, Lloyd D.	18	Springfield	S.	Aug. 28, '63	Substitute.
Rogers, Charles E.	19	Veazie	S.	Sept. 5, '63	Substitute.
Reeves, Samuel	35	Augusta	M.	Aug. 31, '63	Sub. Disc. for dis. Dec. 29, '63.
Reeves, Stephen H.	32	Windsor	M.	Aug. 4, '63	Sub. Disc. for dis.Dec.29,'63.
Speed, William H.	21	Charleston.	S.	Sept. 1, '63	Substitute.
Tucker, George M.	18	Lee	M.	Sept. 10, '63	Sub. Des. Nov. 29, '63.
Joined Company since Dec. 1, 1863.					
Berry, Levi	40	Embden	M.	Aug. 14, '62	Transferred from Co. A.
Crossman, Alfred M.	25	Alton		Nov. 3, '64	Conscript.
Dean, Daniel	21	Belfast	S.	Oct. 5, '64	Deserted April 1, '65.

COMPANY F.—Continued.

NAMES.	Age.	RESIDENCE.	Married or Single	Mustered into the U. S. Service.	REMARKS.
Inman, Stewart M.	30	Orono	M.	Sept. 30, '64	Wounded April 1, '65.
Keisser, Charles	25	Kenduskeag	S.	Sept. 30, '64	
Lothrop, Cherbury F.	25	Chesterville	S.	Aug. 14, '62	Joined as 2d Lieut. from Sergeant-Major; prom. 1st Lieut. and Adjutant.
Murphy, John F.	19	Bangor	S.	Sept. 6, '64	
Merrill, Hiram A.	26	New Portland	M.	Aug. 14, '62	Transferred from Co. A; discharged June 14, '65.
O'Connell, Michael	26	Bangor	M.	Sept. 2, '64	
Okan, Henry	21	Oldtown	S.	Sept. 9, '64	
Oliver, Seth	41	Appleton	M.	Aug. 14, '62	Transferred from Co. A; discharged May 20, '65.
Pickering, Albert	24	Holden		Oct. 5, '64	
Plonde, Joseph	21	Sarsfield Pl.		Oct. 24, '64	
Rowell, Haniff	34	Anson	M.	Aug. 14, '62	Transferred from Co. A; discharged June 6, '65.
Small, Daniel	29		M.	Sept. 28, '64	
Smith, Andrew	26	Machias		Aug. 23, '63	Sub. Trans. from Co. A.
Spear, Asa	44		M.	Sept. 22, '64	
Steeves, James A.	23	Eastport	M.	Aug. 17, '63	Sub. Trans. from Co. A.
Sylvester, Martin B.	42		M.	Sept. 27, '64	
Spearin, Daniel A.	20	Skowhegan		Aug. 14, '62	Joined as 2d Lieut. fr. Co. A.
Sullivan, James	22	Trenton	S.	Oct. 5, '64	Wd. Feb. 7, '65.
Spaulding, Chauncy	19	Monroe	S.	Oct. 6, '64	
Soule, Charles C.	21	Lincolnville	S.	Oct. 6, '64	
Stevens, James A.	23	Belfast	M.	Aug. 27, '63	Trans. from Co. A; des. March, '65.
Stewart, Thomas	29	Bath	M.	Sept. 2, '64	Transferred from Co. A.
Smith, Andrew J.	26	Bangor	M.	Aug. 22, '63	Transferred from Co. A; disc. May 18, '65.
Tibbetts, Joel	35	Bangor	M.	Oct. 7, '64	
Thomas, Norris J.	29			Sept. 30, '64	
Veancour, Desira S.	19	Orono	S.	Oct. 5, '64	
Withee, Alonzo S.	33	Glenburn	M.	Sept. 30, '64	
Woodward, Solomon	18	Mass.	S.	Oct. 7, '64	
Wilson, Charles	33	Portland	S.	Oct. 7, '64	
Young, James B.	31	Lincolnville	M.	Sept. 27, '64	

SIXTEENTH MAINE REGIMENT. 281

COMPANY G.

NAMES.	Age.	RESIDENCE.	Married or Single.	Mustered into the U. S. Service.	REMARKS.
SERGEANTS.					
James U. Childs	21	Farmington	S.	Aug. 14, '62	Pro. 2d Lieut. Co. H. Pris. July 1, '63.
Thomas H. B. Lenfest	21	Palmyra	S.	Aug. 14, '62	
Benjamin F. Watson	27	Farmington	S.	Aug. 14, '62	Disc. for dis. Jan. 4, 1863.
Cyrus Bosworth	44	Skowhegan	M.	Aug. 14, '62	Wd. Mar. 13, '63. Disc.
William H. Towers	24	Calais	M.	Aug. 14, '62	
John H. Frain	21	Madison	S.	Aug. 14, '62	Prs. Aug. 19, 64; disc. Sep. 4, 65.
Byron D. Babcock	19	Palmyra	S.	Aug. 14, '62	Discharged by W. D.
Joseph A. Ricker	18	Chesterville	S.	Aug. 14, '62	
Joseph P. Austin	19	Skowhegan	S.	Aug. 14, '62	
Luke Emery	22	Anson	S.	Aug. 14, '62	Wd. Feb. 6, '65.
Alonzo Smith	21	Anson	S.	Aug. 14, '62	
Boardman Williamson	19	New Sharon	S.	Aug. 14, '62	
CORPORALS.					
Joseph P. Austin	19	Skowhegan	S.	Aug. 14, '62	Prom. Sergt.
Gardner B. Wade	18	Farmington	S.	Aug. 14, '62	Wd. in action May 8, '64.
Gorham Lord	19	Detroit	S.	Aug. 14, '62	Pris. July 1, '63; wd. My. 10, '64
Thomas W. Luce	38	Farmington	M.	Aug. 14, '62	
Darius Sawyer	25	Madison	M.	Aug. 14, '62	
David McCleary	39	Farmington	M.	Aug. 14, '62	Disc. Jan. 7, '63.
William T. Symons	22	Skowhegan	S.	Aug. 14, '62	Wd. Feb. 20, '63. Disc.
William W. Hardy	29	N. Vineyard	S.	Aug. 14, '62	Discharged Dec. 29, '62.
Benjamin Norton	29	New Sharon	M.	Aug. 14, '62	
John H. Frain	21	Madison	S.	Aug. 14, '62	Pro. 1st. Sergt. Prisoner.
Byron D. Babcock	19	Palmyra	S.	Aug. 14, '62	Promoted Sergeant.
Joseph A. Ricker	18	Chesterville	S.	Aug. 14, '62	Prom. Sergt.; pris.; exch.
Benjamin T. Roberts	31	Skowhegan	S.	Aug. 14, '62	
Luke Emery	22	Anson	S.	Aug. 14, '62	Promoted Sergeant.
Samuel T. Farnham	21	Palmyra	S.	Aug. 14, '62	Prisoner Aug. 19, '64.
John W. Lake	18	N. Vineyard	S.	Aug. 14, '62	
Sylvanus Lowe	27	Sebec	M.	Aug. 14, '63	
Levi M. Moore	18	New Sharon	S.	Aug. 14, '62	
Eugene M. Ryder	18	Belfast	S.	Aug. 31, '63	
Alonzo Smith	21	Anson	S.	Aug. 14, '62	Promoted Sergeant.
Boardman Williamson	19	New Sharon	S.	Aug. 14, '62	Promoted Sergeant.
Albion Bailey	18	Harmony	S.	Aug. 14, '62	
Hiram R. Brackett	21	Detroit	S.	Aug. 14, '62	Disc. by order May 24, '65.
MUSICIANS.					
Peletiah Coolbroth	31	Standish	M.	Aug. 14, '62	Prom. principal musician.
James S. Thomas	28	Gorham	S.	Aug. 14, '62	Disc. for dis. June 18, '64.
WAGONER.					
Elisha G. Baker	20	New Sharon	S.	Aug. 14, '62	
PRIVATES.					
Austin, Joseph P.	19	Skowhegan	S.	Aug. 14, '62	Promoted Corporal.
Babcock, Byron D.	19	Palmyra	S.	Aug. 14, '62	Pro. Cor.; wd. pris. Jly. 1, '63.
Babcock, Charles L.	23	Palmyra	M.	Aug. 14, '62	Wd. Dec. 13, 62; disc. Mar. 5, 63.
Bachelder, Isaac P.	21	Palmyra	S.	Aug. 14, '62	Disc. Jan. 13, '63.
Baker, Amos	26	Hartland	S.	Aug. 14, '62	
Bickford, Reuel	33	Skowhegan	M.	Aug. 14, '62	Deserted Jan. 21, '63.
Bigelow, William H.	19	Skowhegan	S.	Aug. 14, '62	Wd. Dec. 13, '62.
Blake, Willard L.	18	Pittsfield	S.	Aug. 14, '62	Wd. Dec. 13, '62.
Blunt, David F.	19	Skowhegan	S.	Aug. 14, '62	
Boston, Jason L.	33	Hartland	S.	Aug. 14, '62	Miss. in action May 10, '64.
Bragg, Edward S.	29	Farmington	M.	Aug. 14, '62	Disc. for dis. Nov. 11, '62.
Brawn, Wilson	28	Skowhegan	S.	Aug. 14, '62	Wd. Dec. 13, '62; both arms amputated.
Chamberlain, Wm. H.	18	Skowhegan	S.	Aug. 14, '62	Disc. by order May 26, '65.
Chase, William	18	Palmyra	S.	Aug. 14, '62	Disc. Jan. 19, '63.
Cleveland, Joseph L.	27	Skowhegan	M.	Aug. 14, '62	Wounded Dec. 13, '62.
Corbett, Chas. P.	19	Farmington	S.	Aug. 14, '62	Died Smoketown, Oct. 24, '62.
Crocker, Abner	18	Strong	S.	Aug. 14, '62	
Crocker, Hiram jr.	19	Strong	S.	Aug. 14, '62	Discharged April 25, '63.
Crocker, Sylvester	22	Strong	S.	Aug. 14, '62	Wounded May 5, '64.
Cross, Josiah W.	27	Detroit	M.	Aug. 14, '62	
Day, James W.	19	New Sharon	S.	Aug. 14, '62	Discharged Nov. 1, '62.

20

COMPANY G.—*Continued.*

NAMES.	Age.	RESIDENCE.	Married or Single.	Mustered into the U. S. Service.	REMARKS.
Demon, Edward	31	Skowhegan	M.	Aug. 14, '62	
Dow, Joseph B	37	Farmington	M.	Aug. 14, '62	Promoted Hospital Steward.
Dow, Joshua R	26	Farmington	S.	Aug. 14, '62	Wd. Dec.13,62; disc. Ap.2,'63.
Doyen, Joseph P	19	New Sharon	S.	Aug. 14, '62	Deserted Dec. 11, '62.
Dyer, Aaron H	18	Farmington	S.	Aug. 14, '62	Disc. for dis. Feb. 26, '63.
Dyer, Israel F	19	Farmington	S.	Aug. 14, '62	Wounded Dec. 13, '62.
Emery, Luke	22	Anson	S.	Aug. 14, '62	Pris. July 1, '63; wounded Aug. 18, '64; prom. Corp.
Fairbrother, Frank	19	Palmyra	S.	Aug. 14, '62	Wounded July 1, '63.
Farnham, Samuel T	21	Palmyra	S.	Aug. 14, '62	Pris. July 1,'63; prom. Corp.
Fenderson, John H	21	Madison	S.	Aug. 14, '62	Deserted Jan. 21, '63.
Fisher, Roswell	33	Detroit	M.	Aug. 14, '62	Wd.Dec.13,'62; dis.My.4,'63.
Furbush, William A	18	N. Vineyard	S.	Aug. 14, '62	Wounded Dec. 13, '62.
Gibbs, Thomas A	22	Skowhegan	S.	Aug. 14, '62	Prisoner July 1, '63.
Gleason, Sumner A	18	Farmington	S.	Aug. 14, '62	
Goodrich, Eben	18	Skowhegan	S.	Aug. 14, '62	Discharged Jan. 27, '63.
Gray, Andrew	21	Palmyra	S.	Aug. 14, '62	Discharged Aug. 7, '65.
Hodgkins, Jacob T	26	New Sharon	S.	Aug. 14, '62	Wd. and pris., July 1, '63.
Houston, Lorenzo C	32	Detroit	M.	Aug. 14, '62	Missing since Dec. 13, '62; wounded Fredericksburg.
Judkins, Sumner S	26	Skowhegan	S.	Aug. 14, '62	Discharged Jan. 9, '63.
Lake, John W	18	N. Vineyard	S.	Aug. 14, '62	Promoted Corporal.
Locke, William T	26	Temple	M.	Aug. 14, '62	Discharged Mar. 11, '63.
Lovejoy, Leonard R	42	Farmington	M.	Aug. 14, '62	Discharged Mar. 31, '63.
Mace John W	24	Farmington	M.	Aug. 14, '62	
Mace, Wilson J	22	Farmington	S.	Aug. 14, '62	Discharged June 4, '63.
Maddocks, Alanson C	18	Farmington	S.	Aug. 14, '62	Deserted Dec. 11, '62.
Merrow, John E	30	Skowhegan	M.	Aug. 14, '62	
Moody, Converse	44	Farmington	M.	Aug. 14, '62	Discharged Oct. 31, '62.
Moore, Levi M	18	New Sharon	S.	Aug. 14, '62	Wd. May 8, '64; prom. Corp.
Neal, Andrew	39	New Sharon	M.	Aug. 14, '62	
Norton, Shepley W	40	N. Vineyard	M.	Aug. 14, '62	Discharged Apr. 2, '63.
Paine, Leonard	18	Anson	S.	Aug. 14, '62	Deserted Jan. 20, '63.
Phelps, Lewis G	27	Skowhegan	S.	Aug. 14, '62	
Pollard, Lyman B	26	Palmyra	S.	Aug. 14, '62	Discharged Mar. 31, '63.
Pratt, James W	23	Palmyra	S.	Aug. 14, '62	Discharged Nov. 19, '62.
Prince, Edward M	20	New Sharon	S.	Aug. 14, '62	
Pullen, Harrison	18	Anson	S.	Aug. 14, '62	Wd. at Gettysburg July, '63.
Quinby, Manley L	27	Skowhegan	M.	Aug. 14, '62	Discharged Dec. 4, '62.
Quint, Andrew J	23	Anson	S.	Aug. 14, '62	Wd.Dec.13,'62; disc.Ap.9,63.
Quint, George R	18	Anson	S.	Aug. 14, '62	Wd.Getts.,'63; wd.May 8,'64.
Quint, William F	24	Anson	S.	Aug. 14, '62	Pris. July 1, '63; wd. May 8, '64; disc. Feb. 25, '65.
Ramsdell, Hiram B	21	New Sharon	S.	Aug. 14, '62	Wounded Dec. 13, '62.
Ricker, Joseph A	18	Chesterville	S.	Aug. 14, '62	Promoted Corporal.
Roberts, Benjamin T	31	Skowhegan	S.	Aug. 14, '62	Promoted Corporal.
Roby, Benjamin C	27	New Sharon	M.	Aug. 14, '62	Des. Sept. 20, '62; ret. under Pre. Proc.; wd. Aug.18,'64.
Sawyer, Thomas D	39	New Sharon	M.	Aug. 14, '62	
Smith, Alonzo	21	Anson	S.	Aug. 14, '62	Wd. Dec.13,'62; prom. Corp.
Smith, E. Crosby	27	Presque Isle	S.	Aug. 14, '62	Deserted Dec. 9, '62.
Smith, Llewellyn C	19	Skowhegan	S.	Aug. 14, '62	
Snow, Daniel B	20	Skowhegan	S.	Aug. 14, '62	Pris. July 1, '63; exch. Wd. May 5, '64.
Shea, John	36	Anson	M.	Aug. 14, '62	Pro. principal musician.
Taylor, James C	40	Palmyra	M.	Aug. 14, '62	Discharged Jan. 8, '63.
Tibbetts, Isaac F	26	Palmyra	S.	Aug. 14, '62	Wounded Dec. 13, '62.
Titcomb, William H	21	Palmyra	S.	Aug. 14, '62	
Wade, Gardner B	18	Farmington	S.	Aug. 14, '62	Pris.July 1,'63; Pro. Corp.
Wellman, Joseph F	44	Tempic	M.	Aug. 14, '62	Discharged Aug. 20, '63.
Wheeler, John M	20	Skowhegan	S.	Aug. 14, '62	Wounded Dec. 13, '62.
Wyman, Clarence L	20	Skowhegan	S.	Aug. 14, '62	Deserted Dec. 9, '62.
Williamson, Boardman	19	New Sharon	S.	Aug. 14, '62	Wd. Gettysburgh July, '63; wd. May 8, '64; prom. corp.
Wilson, Edward	22	Skowhegan	S.	Aug. 14, '62	
Works, Lewis	31	New Sharon	M.	Aug. 14, '62	Pris. July 1, '63; paroled.

COMPANY G.—Continued.

NAMES.	Age.	RESIDENCE.	Married or Single	Mustered into the U. S. Service.	REMARKS.
Joined Company since		Dec. 1, '62.			
Boyle, Barney	28	Portland	S.	Aug. 5, '63	Conscript.
Coharn, Timothy	20	Lewiston	S.	Aug. 10, '63	Con.; paroled prisoner.
Collins, George	21	Portland	S.	Aug. 4, '63	Conscript.
Condon, Wm. H.	20	Baileyville	S.	Sept. 18, '63	Con.; pris. May 21, '64.
Doyle, Michael	20	Brewer	S.	Sept. 18, '63	Conscript.
Eaton, John	27	Waldo	M.	Aug. 27, '63	Conscript; wounded.
Field, George A	18	Brewer	S.	Aug. 29, '63	Con. disc. by ord. June 5,'65.
Green, James	27	Portland	S.	Aug. 7, '63	Con.; disc. by special order 108, April, '64.
Green, William H	21	Barnard	S.	Sept. 15, '63	Conscript.
Hall, Joseph A	24	Damariscotta	S.	Aug. 7, '63	Con.; wd. Feb. 7, '65.
Holbrook, Isaac	28	Plymouth	M.	Aug. 13, '63	Conscript.
Hewitt, Philo	29	Ft. Fairfield	M.	Aug. 15, '63	Conscript.
Jones, Frank	21	Parkman	M.	Aug. 28, '63	Conscript.
Judkins, Alonzo	30	Orneville	M.	Aug. 14, '63	Conscript.
Low, Sylvanus	27	Sebec	M.	Aug. 14, '63	Con.; promoted Corporal.
Libby, Amasa P	20	Lincoln	S.	Sept. 2, '63	Con.; disc. Aug. 26, '64.
Love, William	19	Norridgew'k	S.	July 29, '63	Conscript.
Lyons, Isaiah	21	Springfield	S.	Sept. 3, '63	Conscript.
Mardin, Edwin	21	Atkinson	S.	Sept. 5, '63	Conscript.
Merritt, Samuel	43	Bangor	M.	Sept. 5, '63	Conscript.
Morgan, Bowman S	22	Orneville	M.	Aug. 14, '63	Con.; disc. by ord. June 2,'65.
Mullin, John	24	Portland	S.	Aug. 8, '63	Con.; disc. by order Apr. 19, '64, to enter Navy.
McGinley, John	23	Houlton	S.	Aug. 15, '63	Conscript.
Nelson, Chester	20	Lincoln	S.	Aug. 14, '63	Conscript.
Parkman, Russell F	20	Corinna	S.	Aug. 12, '63	Con.; wounded May 8, '64; discharged March 1, '65.
Porter, Lewis M	18	Orneville	S.	Sept. 5, '63	Con.; paroled prisoner.
Piper, Merrill J	20	Portland	S.	Sept. 5, '63	Conscript; disc. for disability Dec. 22, '63.
Rankin, Charles H	19	Monticello	S.	Aug. 15, '63	Conscript.
Rogers, Erastus C	21	Ft. Fairfield	S.	Aug. 15, '63	Conscript.
Rogers, John L	29	Ft. Fairfield	S.	Sept. 5, '63	Conscript.
Rogers, William S	29	Carmel	M.	Aug. 13, '63	Con.; miss. in action June 5, '64; disc. Sept. 4, '65.
Rogers, William S. B	22	Brownville	M.	Aug. 14, '63	Con.; wounded in action.
Redd, Henry J	18	Brooks	S.	Aug. 10, '63	Conscript.
Ryder, Eugene M	18	Belfast	S.	Aug. 31, '63	Con.; promoted Corporal.
Robbins, Samuel S	21	Anson	S.	Aug. 25, '63	Conscript; prisoner.
Scott, David S	21	Chester	S.	Aug. 13, '63	Conscript.
Sanders, Richard	22	Portland		Aug. 7, '63	Con.; disc. April 19, '64, to enter Navy.
Saunders, Francis E	21	Parkman	S.	Aug. 21, '63	Con.; paroled prisoner.
Senegne, Charles	30	Hallowell	M.	Aug. 5, '63	Conscript.
Shaw, Erastus M	20	China	S.	July 22, '63	Conscript.
Shaff, Charles P	34	Portland	M.	July 1, '63	Conscript.
Sidney, John	42	Portland	M.	Aug. 3, '63	Con.; disc. Apr. 19, '64.
Slavin, John	33	Portland	M.	Aug. 5, '63	Con.; disc. May 18, '65.
Smith, James	21	Portland	S.	July 28, '63	Con.; paroled prisoner.
Smith, James A	25	Portland	S.	Aug. 5, '63	Con.; disc. for dis. Jan. 7, '64.
Smith, Joseph B	35	Mt. Vernon	S.	Aug. 1, '63	Conscript.
Smith, William	30	Portland		Aug. 3, '63	Con.; discharged for disability, Nov. 12, '63.
Snow, George A	18	Augusta		July 25, '63	Con.; disc. for dis. Dec. 12,'63.
Spearin, Charles W	24	Sebec	S.	Sept. 2, '63	Conscript.
Stone, Edwin F	18	Augusta	S.	July 25, '63	Conscript.
Stubbs, Zoeth E	21	Corinna	S.	Aug. 31, '63	Con.; wd. May 21, '64.
Sullivan, Harriman P.	21	Clinton	S.	Aug. 3, '63	Con.; wd. Aug. 18, '64.
Sutherland, Aug. A	20	Lisbon	S.	July 30, '63	Conscript.
Taylor, Howard W	22	Byron	M.	July 28, '63	Conscript.
Thompson, Charles E	28	Starks	M.	July 30, '63	Con.; deserted Oct. 4, '64.
Walsh, John	30	Portland		Aug. 3, '63	Con.; deserted Sept. 9, '63.
Welch, John E	38	Canaan	S.	Aug. 4, '63	Conscript.
Welch, Robert	42	Temple	M.	July 28, '63	Conscript.

COMPANY G.—Continued.

NAMES.	Age.	RESIDENCE.	Married or Single	Mustered into the U. S. Service.	REMARKS.
Webber, George L.	25	Winslow	....	Aug. 4, '63	
West, Allen	32	Waltham	....	Aug. 10, '63	Returned to 1st Me. Cav.
Withee, Amos P.	23	Skowhegan	S.	Aug. 4, '63	Paroled prisoner.
Winslow, John	21	Biddeford	S.	Aug. 10, '63	Wd. June 18, '64; disc.
Joined Company since	c	Dec. 1, '63.			
Alden, Adelbert	24	Drew Pl.	....	Oct. 13, '64	Conscript.
Ball, Franklin	23	Mapleton Pl.	....	Oct. 13, '64	Conscript.
Buzzell, Hannibal D.	33	Castle Hill Pl.	....	O t. 13, '64	Con.; disc. by ord. June 6,'65.
Beckwith, Joel	24	Maysville	....	Oct. 13, '64	Conscript.
Bickford, Stephen D.	27	Pittsfield	....	Nov. 4, '64	Substitute.
Barnes, William B.	38	Hartland	....	Sept. 21, '64	Conscript.
Bailey, Albion	18	Harmony	S.	Aug. 14, '62	Tr. from Co. A; prom. corp.
Brackett, Hiram R.	21	Detroit	S.	Aug. 14, '62	Corp. from Co. A; disc. by order May 24, '65.
Carville, Benjamin	36	N. Portland	M.	Aug. 14, '62	Transferred from Co. A.
Dolan, Patrick H.	30	Portland	....	Aug. 7, '63	Transferred from Co. A.
Davis, Nathan	41	No. 2, R. 2	....	Sept. 22, '64	
Dyer, William	31	No. 2, R. 3	....	Oct. 13, '64	
Faulkner, James E.	27	Weston	....	Oct. 12, '64	
Furbush, Jairus H.	36	N. Portland	M.	Aug. 14, '62	Transferred from Co. A.
Gifford, LaForest F.	18	Bangor	S.	Aug. 14, '62	Transferred from Co. A.
Gould, Benjamin F.	31	Belfast	S.	Sept. 7, '63	Con.; disc. by ord. June 6,'65.
Gorman, James	23		S.	Sept. 9, '63	Sub.; trans. from Co. A.
Gould, Edmund	22		....	Dec. 22, '63	
Goodwin, Lyman O.	21	Palmyra	S.	Aug. 14, '62	Transferred from Co. A.
Goodridge, Noah	36	Sarsfield Pl.	....	Oct. 13, '64	
Hughes, James	21	Hartland	....	Nov. 10, '64	Wd. April 1, '65; Disc. June 21, '65.
Holmes, Wallace L.	18	Levant	....	Sept. 2, '64	
Hendrix, Martin K.	42	Forestv'le Pl.	....	Oct. 13, '64	
Ketch, Richard	27		M.	Sept. 2, '64	Trans. from Co. A; sub.
Levenseller, John	26	Sebec	....	Dec. 21, '63	
Leavitt, Rodney	32	Drew Pl.	....	Oct. 13, '64	
Lyons, Thomas G.	24	Ft. Fairfield	....	Oct. 26, '64	Disc. by order June 6, '65.
Larry, Peter	27	Sebec	....	Dec. 21, '63	
Libby, James	18		S.	Sept. 2, '64	Substitute.
Lawrence, Henry B.	18		S.	Sept. 3, '64	Substitute.
Linton, Robert	21		S.	Sept. 3, '64	Sub.; wd. at Gravelly Run, March 31, '65.
Leavitt, Zachary	18		S.	Sept. 6, '64	Substitute.
Lougee, David B.	18	Plymouth	S.	Sept. 8, '64	Substitute.
Lang, Patrick	21		S.	Sept. 7, '64	Substitute.
Mack, George	18	Wells	S.	Sept. 6, '64	Sub.; par. pris.; discharged June 19, '65.
McBrien, William	27	Oldtown	S.	Aug. 31, '64	Substitute.
Mehegan, William	22	Sebec	S.	Sept. 21, '64	Substitute.
Matchett, Edward J.	20	Madison	S.	Sept. 3, '64	Substitute.
McGlauflin, James	35	Mapleton Pl.	....	Oct. 13, '64	Conscript.
Orr, John	44	Buchanan Pl.	....	Oct. 13, '64	Discharged July 21, '65.
Perham, William	35	Sebec	....	Dec. 22, '63	
Richards, Lewis G.	26	Limerick	M.	Aug. 14, '62	Joined as 1st Lieut. from Co. H; muster revoked; disc. Feb. 4, '65.
Stevens, John	20	Portland	....	Nov. 14, '64	
Thorn, John H.	27	Island F'ls pl.	....	Oct. 13, '64	Conscript.
Treat, Albert	18	Bradford	....	Dec. 15, '63	Par. pris.; disc. July 22, '65.
Whitcomb, Tilson T.	27	Concord	M.	Aug. 14, '62	Trans. from Co. A; prisoner.
Wiggin, Frank	27	Limestone Pl.	M.	Aug. 14, '62	Joined as 1st Lt. from Co. H.
Whitney, Isaac R.	22	Windham	S.	Aug. 14, '62	Joined as 2d Lt. from Co. F; not mustered.
Williams, John	18	Bridgton	....	Nov. 2, '64	
Wright, James	34	Sebago	....	Nov. 3, '64	
Whittemore, Samuel H.	20	Sebec	....	Dec. 22, '63	

SIXTEENTH MAINE REGIMENT.

COMPANY H.

NAMES.	Age.	RESIDENCE.	Married or Single	Mustered into the U. S. Service.	REMARKS.
SERGEANTS.					
John D. Conley	33	Bangor	S.	Aug. 14, '62	Prom. to 2d Lieut. and Capt.
John McDonald	21	Calais	S.	Aug. 14, '62	Red. to ranks; discharged by order June 2, '65.
Joel S. Stevens	40	Frankfort	M.	Aug. 14, '62	Red. to ranks; discharged for dis. Jan. 13, 65.
George K. Shadduck	37	Limerick	M.	Aug. 14, '62	Deserted Nov. 8, '62.
David Dresser	30	Princeton	M.	Aug. 14, '62	Discharged for disability.
Lewis G. Richards	26	Limerick	M.	Aug. 14, '62	Prom. 1st Sergt., prom. 2d Lieut.; not mus.; pris.; prom. 1st Lieut. Co. G.
Frank Wiggin	27	Limestone Pl.	M.	Aug. 14, '62	Red. to ranks to join band; prom. 1st Lieut. Co. G.
George H. Fisher	26	Winterport	S.	Aug. 14, '62	Prom. 1st Sergt.; par. pris.
William Fennelly	23	Mt. Desert	S.	Aug. 14, '62	Par. pris.; disc. June 30, '65.
Thomas D. Witherly	20	Bangor	S.	Aug. 14, '62	Paroled prisoner.
Dudley B. Bean	20	Passadumk'g	S.	Aug. 14, '62	
David Phillips	24	Pittsfield	M.	Aug. 14, '62	
Samuel C. Adams	19	Mayfield	S.	Aug. 14, '62	
CORPORALS.					
Thomas D. Witherly	20	Bangor	S.	Aug. 14, '62	Promoted Sergeant.
Nelson Hewey	24	Veazie	M.	Aug. 14, '62	Disc. for dis. July 14, '63.
Lewis G. Richards	26	Limerick	M.	Aug. 14, '62	Promoted to Sergeant.
Enoch A. Rogers jr	27	Pittsfield	M.	Aug. 14, '62	Discharged June 16, '63.
George H. Fisher	26	Winterport	S.	Aug. 14, '62	Promoted to Sergeant.
Charles J. Hayes	27	Limerick	M.	Aug. 14, '62	Redured to ranks; missing since battle of Gettysburg.
William C. Atwater	36	Winterport	M.	Aug. 14, '62	Red. to ranks and disc. for disability June 15, '63.
Fred L. Ladd	20	Kenduskeag	S.	Aug. 14, '62	Red. to ranks. Disc. Nov. 16, '62 for disability.
Charles L. Favour	20	Limerick	S.	Aug. 14, '62	Wd. Dec. 13, '62 and July 1, '63; disc. Nov. 12, '63.
Isaac C. Dow	24	Tremont	S.	Aug. 18, '62	Disc. for dis. Mar. 13, '63.
Stephen Hines	22	Bangor	S.	Aug. 14, '62	Disc. for dis. June 13, '63.
Charles R. Atkins	21	Pittsfield	S.	Aug. 14, '62	
William E. Annis	24	Herman	S.	Aug. 13, '63	
George F. Dearborn	21	Monson	S.	Aug. 14, '62	
Amasa Gregory	22	Montville	S.	Aug. 14, '62	Discharged March 23, '65.
Albert Hoyt	18	Bangor	S.	Aug. 21, '63	Discharged May 21, '65.
James Maloney	18	Bangor	S.	Aug. 17, '63	
David Phillips	24	Pittsfield	M.	Aug. 14, '62	Promoted Sergeant.
Thomas Potts	19	Biddeford	S.	Aug. 14, '62	
Bradford Winn	28	Portland	S.	Sept. 15, '63	
George W. Varney	18	Pittsfield	S.	Aug. 14, '62	
Samuel C. Adams	19	Mayfield	S.	Aug. 14, '62	Promoted Sergeant.
Dudley B. Bean	20	Passadumk'g	S.	Aug. 14, '62	Promoted Sergeant.
MUSICIANS.					
Samuel R. Garey	31	Limerick	M.	Aug. 14, '62	
Stephen Clark	25	Winterport	M.	Aug. 14, '62	Disc. for dis. Dec. 13, '62.
PRIVATES.					
Atkins, Charles R	21	Pittsfield	S.	Aug. 14, '62	Par. Pris.; Prom. Corp.
Banks, Ezekiel M	28	Kenduskeag	M.	Aug. 14, '62	
Bean, Dudley B	20	Passadumk'g	S.	Aug. 14, '62	Promoted Corporal.
Bean, Watson D	40	Passadumk'g	M.	Aug. 14, '62	Disc. for dis. Aug. '63.
Chick, Winfield S	18	Thorndike	S.	Aug. 14, '62	Wounded July 1, '63.
Christophers, Christ'r	24	Washburn	S.	Aug. 14, '62	
Clement, Samuel H	19	Winterport	S.	Aug. 14, '62	Miss. in battle Gettysburgh.
Cobb, Daniel	32	Pittsfield	M.	Aug. 14, '62	
Curtis, Frederick A	20	Winterport	S.	Aug. 14, '62	Missing in battle Fred. Dec. 13, '62.
Day, Calvin	26	Cornish	M.	Aug. 14, '62	Wounded July 1, '63.
Day, Darius	24	Cornish	S.	Aug. 14, '62	

COMPANY H—Continued.

NAMES.	Age.	RESIDENCE.	Married or Single	Mustered into the U. S. Service.	REMARKS.
Dearborn, George F....	21	Monson......	S.	Aug. 14, '62	Promoted Corporal.
Dearborn, George J....	21	Limerick.....	S.	Aug. 14, '62	
Deuplisea, Charles H...	18	Princeton.....	S.	Aug. 14, '62	
Dow, Isaac C..........	24	Tremont......	S.	Aug. 18, '62	
Durgin, John M........	19	Veazie.......	S.	Aug. 14, '62	
Dyer, George F........	18	Biddeford....	S.	Aug. 14, '62	
Everett, John H.......	21	Kenduskeag...	S.	Aug. 14, '62	
Farrar, Benton........	20	Topsfield.....	S.	Aug. 14, '62	Missing in action June 4, '64; disc. July 31, '65.
Favour, Charles L.....	20	Limerick.....	S.	Aug. 14, '62	Promoted Corporal.
Fennelly, William.....	23	Mt. Desert...	S.	Aug. 18, '62	
Fife, Nathan J........	21	Tremont......	S.	Aug. 14, '62	
Foss, James C.........	41	Winterport...	M.	Aug. 14, '62	
Foster, John M........	35	Pittsfield.....	M.	Aug. 14, '62	Disc. for dis. Jan. 12, '63.
George, Timothy A.....	32	Holden.......	S.	Aug. 14, '62	Disc. for dis. July 31, '65.
Goodwin, Charles......	29	Cornish......	S.	Aug. 14, '62	
Gowell, John B........	23	Calais........	M.	Aug. 14, '62	
Gregory, Amasa.......	22	Montville.....	S.	Aug. 14, '62	Promoted Corporal.
Griffin, Roscoe T......	20	Bangor.......	S.	Aug. 14, '62	Disc. for dis. in April, '63.
Hagan, John..........	32	Calais........	S.	Aug. 14, '62	
Hatch, Horace J.......	32	Mapleton Pl..	M.	Aug. 14, '62	
Haley, John E.........	24	Rockland.....	S.	Aug. 14, '62	
Hathorn, Charles......	19	Veazie.......	S.	Aug. 14, '62	
Hines, Stephen........	22	Bangor.......	S.	Aug. 14, '62	
Hodsdon, Clarence L...	18	Bangor.......	S.	Aug. 14, '62	
Holmes, Robert........	22	Ellsworth.....	S.	Aug. 14, '62	
Howes, Charles E......	31	Washburn.....	M.	Aug. 14, '62	Dropped as des. Nov. 15, '62.
Hurd, Luther..........	20	Sanford.......	S.	Aug. 14, '62	Wd. Dec. 13, '62; disc.
Kenniston, Leonard E..	25	Kenduskeag...	S.	Aug. 14, '62	
Kenniston, Thomas E..	24	Kenduskeag...	S.	Aug. 14, '62	
Kingdon, John.........	30	Maysville.....	S.	Aug. 14, '62	
Lang, Charles A.......	20	Pittsfield.....	S.	Aug. 14, '62	Discharged Aug. 25, '63.
Libby, Minot C........	32	Winterport...	S.	Aug. 14, '62	Disc. Mar. 16, '63 for dis.
Libby, Otis J..........	22	Winterport...	S.	Aug. 14, '62	Wd. & disc. Mar. 27, '63 for dis.
Lovely, Danforth......	26	Mapleton Pl..	S.	Aug. 14, '62	Prisoner Aug. 19, '64.
Maddox, John H.......	18	Limerick.....	S.	Aug. 14, '62	
McAnulty, James......	32	Calais........	M.	Aug. 18, '62	Disc. for dis. Dec. 18, '62.
McCollum, John.......	23	Ellsworth.....	S.	Aug. 14, '62	Disc. March 5, '64.
McGinley, John........	38	Biddeford....	M.	Aug. 14, '62	
Middleton, Thomas....	26	Ellsworth.....	S.	Aug. 14, '62	Prisoner.
Moore, William L......	23	Princeton.....	M.	Aug. 14, '62	Cattle guard.
Mudge, Parker........	18	Cornish......	S.	Aug. 14, '62	Acc. Wd.; disc. April 21, '63.
Nason, William B......	24	Kenduskeag...	S.	Aug. 14, '62	Supposed disc. Jan. 6, '63.
Neal, Adam J.........	30	Waite Plan...	S.	Aug. 14, '62	Miss. in action July 1, '63.
O'Conners, Patrick....	19	Tremont......	S.	Aug. 14, '62	Discharged March 18, '64.
Patten, George W......	22	Pittsfield.....	S.	Aug. 14, '62	
Patten, Jacob M.......	28	Pittsfield.....	S.	Aug. 14, '62	
Phillips, David........	24	Pittsfield.....	M.	Aug. 14, '62	Promoted Corporal.
Pierce, James S.......	18	Limerick.....	S.	Aug. 14, '62	Missing in action May 8, '64.
Potts, Thomas.........	19	Biddeford....	S.	Aug. 14, '62	Promoted Corporal.
Pugsley, Francis......	32	Scarboro.....	M.	Aug. 14, '62	
Rhoades, William F....	40	Whitefield....	M.	Aug. 14, '62	Disc. for dis. Nov. 15, '62.
Redding, George F.....	18	Calais........	S.	Aug. 14, '62	Pris. since July 1, '63.
Reed, Samuel M.......	19	Tremont......	S.	Aug. 18, '62	Wd. Dec. 13, '62; disc. in Sept., '63.
Rich, Tyler F..........	19	Tremont......	S.		
Rideout, Eben.........	28	Mars Hill....	S.	Aug. 14, '62	
Rubert, Moses J.......	23	Passadumk'g..	S.	Aug. 14, '62	
Sally, Hiram S.........	25	Pittsfield.....	M.	Aug. 14, '62	
Sally, William S.......	21	Pittsfield.....	S.	Aug. 14, '62	Disc. for dis. Nov. 15, '62.
Sawyer, John I........	31	Passadumk'g..	S.	Aug. 14, '62	
Simpson, Joseph......	32	Corinth......	S.	Aug. 14, '62	Cattle guard.
Sius, Joseph E........	21	Washington..	S.	Aug. 14, '62	

COMPANY H.—*Continued*.

NAMES.	Age.	RESIDENCE.	Married or Single	Mustered into the U. S. Service	REMARKS.
Smith, George	18	Limerick	S.	Aug. 14, '62	Disc. by order June 2, '65.
Smith, George W	18	Princeton	S.	Aug. 14, '62	
Smith, Lyman	26	Mt. Desert	S.	Aug. 14, '62	Wounded Dec. 13, '62.
Smith, William H	21	Portland	S.	Aug. 14, '62	Paroled prisoner.
Stetson, Ephraim H	21	Embden	S.	Aug. 14, '62	
Thompson, James H	33	Princeton	M.	Aug. 14, '62	Wounded May 1, '64.
Whitten, Martin L	30	Etna	M.	Aug. 14, '62	Paroled prisoner.
Wiggin, Frank	27	Limestone Pl.	M.	Aug. 14, '62	Promoted Sergeant.
Wilson, George W	28	Parsonsfield	M.	Aug. 14, '62	Andersonville prison.
Varney, George W	18	Pittsfield	S.	Aug. 14, '62	Wd. Dec. 13, '62 on duty; promoted Corporal.
Yeaton, James P	21	Waite Plan	S.	Aug. 14, '62	Disc. for dis. in July, '63.
Joined Company since Dec. 1, 1862.					
Annis, William E	24	Hermon	S.	Aug. 13, '63	Con.; par. pris.; pro. corp.
Bodge, Bradford S	20	Augusta	S.	Aug. 3, '63	Conscript.
Chandler, Henry A	20	Augusta	S.	July 31, '63	Conscript. Prisoner.
Crampton, Charles	31	Portland	S.	July 31, '63	Con. Pris. Aug. 18, '64.
Chandler, Josiah H	24	Mapleton Pl.	M.	Aug. 13, '63	Conscript.
Chase, Wilbur F	21	Chester	S.	Aug. 13, '63	Conscript.
Clark, John	23	Lewiston	S.	Sept. 11, '63	Conscript.
Carey, Michael	37	Bangor	S.	Sept. 8, '63	Conscript. Wd. Feb. 6, '65.
Dore, Charles B	21	Hermon	S.	Aug. 13, '63	Conscript. Paroled pris.
Dugan, Martin W	20	Bangor	S.	Sept. 9, '63	Conscript.
Engels, Louis	35	Belfast	S.	Aug. 20, '63	Conscript. Prisoner.
Felker, George W	23	Bangor	S.	Aug. 13, '63	Con. Disc. May 20, '65.
Fogg, Abel	32	Belfast	M.	Aug. 13, '63	Con. Wd. April 1, '65; disc. May 18, '65.
Farley, John	38	Bangor	M.	Sept. 9, '63	Conscript. Paroled pris.
Freeze, Retire Jr	24	Lagrange	S.	Aug. 31, '63	Conscript.
Fisher, Charles	21	Lewiston	S.	Sept. 15, '63	Con. Des. Oct. 21, '63.
Garrow, Solomon	20	Portland	S.	July 31, '63	Conscript. Deserted Nov. 27, '63. In arr.
Giles, Charles	32	Augusta	M.	July 14, '63	Con. Deserted Dec. 18, '64.
Gammon, Ralph	20	Portland	S.	Aug. 10, '63	Conscript.
Galvin, John	21	Augusta	S.	July 29, '63	Conscript.
Graham, John R	22	Portland	S.	July 10, '63	Conscript.
Gray, Joseph A	28	Plymouth	S.	July 25, '63	Con. Des. Nov. 23, '63.
Gilbert, Lewis	22	Portland	S.	July 30, '63	Conscript. Paroled pris.
Garland, Albert	23	Bangor	S.	Aug. 13, '63	Conscript.
Gardner, Grindal	18	Belfast	S.	Sept. 17, '63	Con. Disc. Feb. 20, '65.
Gould, Charles H	22	Portland	S.	Sept. 15, '63	Conscript.
Haley, John	25	Portland	S.	July 29, '63	Conscript.
Hartnett, William	30	Portland	S.	July 31, '63	Conscript.
Henderson, James A	21	Augusta	S.	July 30, '63	Con. Missing in action May 19, '64.
Hart, Michael	23	Augusta	S.	July 29, '63	Conscript.
Hoyt, Lemuel T	24	Portland	S.	July 14, '63	Con. Paroled prisoner.
Hoyt, Albert	18	Bangor	S.	Aug. 21, '63	Con. Promoted Corporal.
Heal, Henry A	20	Bangor	S.	Aug. 28, '63	Con. Paroled prisoner.
Hamilton, Edwin W	19	Bangor	S.	Sept. 8, '63	Conscript.
Harriman, Frank S	27	Manchester	S.	July 15, '63	Conscript.
Hatch, Charles E	24	Bangor	S.	Sept. 9, '63	Con. Paroled prisoner.
Jenkins, Dennis A	33	Woodville	S.	Aug. 13, '63	Con. Paroled prisoner.
Jones, Frank	28	Portland	S.	Aug. 3, '63	Conscript.
Johnson, George	21	Portland	S.	Aug. 10, '63	Conscript.
Knapp, Walter	20	Portland	S.	Aug. 3, '63	Con. Des. Jan. 1, '65.
Kingsbury, James J	30	Holden	S.	Aug. 3, '63	Conscript.
Kaehner, August	27	Augusta	S.	Aug. 24, '63	Con. Paroled prisoner.
Linsicomb, William J	28	Lewiston	S.	Sept. 9, '63	Con. Des. Oct. 21, '63.
Marston, John J	19	Bangor	S.	Sept. 18, '63	Con. Pris. in Richmond, Va.
Maloney, James	18	Bangor	S.	Aug. 17, '63	Con. Promoted Corporal.
Nason, William H	27	Portland	S.	Aug. 5, '63	Conscript.
Nash, Jasper H	18	Bangor	M.	Aug. 2, '63	Conscript.

COMPANY H.—Continued.

NAMES.	Age.	RESIDENCE.	Married or Single	Mustered into the U. S. Service.	REMARKS.
Page, Prince B.........	21	Belfast.......	S.	Aug. 17, '63	Con. Deserted Jan. 1, '65.
Robbins, John..........	22	Augusta......	S.	July 28, '63	Conscript.
Tobin, John............	22	Portland.....	S.	July 29, '63	Conscript.
Thayer, James H.......	18	Bangor	S.	Sept. 9, '63	Conscript.
Winn, Bradford........ Joined Company since	28	Portland..... Dec. 1, 1863.	M.	Sept. 15, '63	Con. Promoted Corporal.
Adams, Samuel C......	19	Mayfield.....	S.	Aug. 14, '62	Tr. from Co. A; pro. corp.
Adams, Philip C.......	21	Solon........	S.	Aug. 14, '62	Trans. from Co. A; disc. by order May 22, '65.
Boyce, Daniel..........	32		....	Nov. 19, '64	Con. Disc. May 29, '65.
Brackett, Freeman.....	22	Bradford.....	S.	Aug. 14, '62	Con. Tr. from Co. A; pris.
Bailey, Isaiah..........	43	Alexander....	....	Oct. 5, '64	Conscript.
Berry, Kendrick.......	40	Troy..........	S.	Sept. 10, '63	Sub. Trans. from Co. A; des. Dec. 10, '64.
Bradbury, John C.....	22	No. Limerick.	....	Oct. 12, '64	Conscript.
Blacklock, Archibald..	30	Milltown.....	S.	Aug. 8, '63	Transferred from Co. A.
Colson, Ansley........	37	Waltham.....	....	Nov. 3, '64	Discharged April 26, '65.
Connelly, John........	23	Brunswick...	S.	Aug. 26, '64	Substitute.
Campbell, William....	18	E. Machias...	....	Oct. 12, '64	Substitute.
Donaghe, Andrew.....	33	Belfast.......	S.	Sept. 3, '64	Substitute.
Dufour, Francis.......	33	Bridgton.....	....	Nov. 11, '64	Substitute.
Dill, Albert E.........	18	Matawamk'g.	S.	Sept. 6, '64	Substitute.
Damon, Joshua.......	31	Presque Isle..	....	Oct. 13, '64	Conscript.
Despres, John.........	25	Sebec........	....	Nov. 16, '64	Conscript.
Fisher, William P.....	26	Bangor	S.	Aug. 31, '64	Substitute.
Freeze, Fred W.......	18	Otis..........	....	Sept. 2, '64	Sub. Disc. May 17, '65.
Frazier, James........	26	Bremen......	S.	Aug. 26, '64	Sub. Disc. May 25, '65.
Gould, George H.....	18	Lewiston.....	S.	Aug. 14, '62	Transferred from Co. A.
Goodwin, Charles 2d..	23	Digby, N. S..	S.	Aug. 2, '64	Substitute.
Hall, Simeon W.......	18	Clinton.......	S.	Aug. 2, '64	Substitute.
Harrington, Edwin W.	18	Charles'n, Ms.	S.	Aug. 6, '64	Substitute.
Irish, Simeon.........	22		....	Oct. 13, '64	Conscript.
Leslie, James W......	28	Portland.....	....	Nov. 22, '64	Discharged Jan. 25, '65.
Lagin, Hugh..........	25	Calais........	M.	Aug. 6, '64	Substitute.
Leighton, George W...	21	Cornish......	....	Aug. 14, '62	Deserted Aug. 20, '62.
Martin, Alvin C......	43	Waltham.....	....	Oct. 21, '64	Conscript.
Martin, John.........	25	Macwahoc Pl.	....	Oct. 13, '64	Conscript.
Mahar, Simon........	20	Harrington...	....	Oct. 24, '64	Substitute.
McElroy, David.......	29	Bangor	....	Nov. 21, '64	Discharged June 17, '65.
Nelson, Frank E......	25	Winslow.....	M.	July 30, '63	Con. Trans. from Co. A.
Philpot, Samuel D....	34	No. Limerick.	....	Oct. 13, '64	Conscript.
Randall, Charles......	38	Wade Plan...	....	Oct. 13, '64	Conscript.
Smith, Frank.........	26	Reed Plan ...	....	Oct. 20, '64	Conscript.
Sutter, Earnest.......	22	Kennebunk't	....	Oct. 12, '64	Substitute.
True, Edward W......	27	Belfast,Ac.Gt	....	Oct. 14, '64	Conscript.
Whittaker, Isaac......	25	Presque Isle..	....	Oct. 13, '64	Conscript. Disc. by order June 6, '65.

SIXTEENTH MAINE REGIMENT.

COMPANY I.

NAMES.	Age.	RESIDENCE.	Married or Single	Mustered into the U. S. Service.	REMARKS.
SERGEANTS.					
Edwin E. Hall	30	Lewiston	M.	Aug. 14, '62	Disc. Dec. 1, '62.
E. Freeman Higgins	22	Lewiston	S.	Aug. 14, '62	
Albert N. Potter	36	Webster	M.	Aug. 14, '62	Reduced to ranks and discharged June 2, '65.
Zelotes Rowe	33	Lisbon	S.	Aug. 14, '62	Promoted 1st Sergeant; prisoner in Richmond, Va.
Charles C. Small	23	Wilton	S.	Aug. 14, '62	Transferred to Co. C.
Wm. L. Whitney	36	C'ntr'b'y N.H.	S.	Aug. 14, '62	Red. to ranks for phy. dis.
Wilbur F. Mower	20	Greene	S.	Aug. 14, '62	Promoted 2d Lieutenant.
Jabez P. Parker	18	Greene	S.	Aug. 14, '62	Pro. 1st Sergt. and 2d Lieut., and 1st Lieut. Co. K; wd. May, '64.
Geo. B. Haskell	25	Webster	S.	Aug. 14, '62	Disc. by order June 5, '65.
Geo. D. Marston	28	Auburn	M.	Aug. 14, '62	Disc. June 19, '65.
Thomas W. Foley	24	Corinth	M.	Aug. 14, '62	
Thomas J. Gould	21	Lisbon	S.	Aug. 14, '62	
Leonard P. Martin	28	Bangor	S.	Jan. 5, '64	Disc. by order May 23, '65.
Hosea D. Manley	21	Auburn	S.	Aug. 14, '62	Promoted Sergeant-Major.
CORPORALS.					
Hosea D. Manley	21	Auburn	S.	Aug. 14, '62	Prom. Sergt.; missing since battle of Gettysburgh.
George D. Marston	28	Auburn	M.	Aug. 14, '62	Prom. Sergt.; missing since battle of Gettysburgh.
Wilbur F. Mower	20	Greene	S.	Aug. 14, '62	Promoted Sergeant.
Africa P. Cutton	36	Lisbon	M.	Aug. 14, '62	
George W. Jordan	26	Webster	M.	Aug. 14, '62	Incapable of duty.
George B. Haskell	25	Webster	S.	Aug. 14, '62	Promoted Sergeant.
Jabez P. Parker	18	Greene	S.	Aug. 14, '62	Promoted Sergeant.
Lowell Butterfield	18	Augusta	S.	July 31, '63	Wounded Feb. 6, '65.
Nath'l Gilpatrick	38	Lisbon	M.	Aug. 14, '62	Missing battle of Fredericksburgh, Dec. 13, '62.
Arannah Briggs	21	Greene	S.	Aug. 14, '62	Prisoner at Salisbury, N. C.
William Davis	28	Durham	M.	Aug. 14, '62	Wounded July 1, '63; prisoner Aug. 19, '64.
John Dunn	21	Portland	M.	July 31, '63	
Thomas W. Foley	24	Corinth	M.	Aug. 14, '62	Promoted Sergeant.
Thomas J. Gould	21	Lisbon	S.	Aug. 14, '62	Promoted Sergeant.
Ephraim L. Jordan	21	Webster	S.	Aug. 14, '62	
Samuel Peabody	38	Canton	M.	Aug. 14, '62	Par. pris.; disc. June 26, '65.
Albert N. Potter	36	Webster	M.	Aug. 14, '62	Disc. by order June 2, '65.
Daniel Small	23	Lisbon	S.	Aug. 14, '62	
John S. Brown	39	Augusta	M.	Aug. 14, '62	Prisoner in Richmond, Va.
MUSICIANS.					
Noah Jordan	44	Auburn	M.	Aug. 14, '62	Discharged April 8, '63.
John K. Bumps	32	Knox	M.	Aug. 18, '62	
WAGONER.					
Wm. W. Marston	25	Buckfield	M.	Aug. 14, '62	
PRIVATES.					
Allen, Charles W.	27	Livermore	M.	Aug. 20, '62	Discharged Dec. 30, '63.
Allen, Lorenzo D.	36	Canton	M.	Aug. 20, '62	
Allen, Osborne	24	Canton	S.	Aug. 14, '62	Discharged Dec. 18, '63.
Allen, William	21	Presque Isle	S.	Aug. 14, '62	
Anderson, Charles R.	21	Lewiston	S.	Aug. 14, '62	Not mustered.
Anderson, George W.	25	Byron	M.	Aug. 14, '62	Missing in battle of Gettysburgh, July 1, '63.
Batchelder, Wm. H.	26	Wilton	M.	Aug. 14, '62	Hosp. att.; wd. July 1, '63.
Beale, James P.	18	Durham	S.	Aug. 14, '62	Discharged Feb. 4, '63.
Bisbee, Lewis C.	28	Canton	M.	Aug. 20, '62	Promoted 1st Lieutenant.
Blake, Isaac A.	21	Lisbon	S.	Aug. 14, '62	Missing in action Dec. 13, '62.
Briggs, Arannah	21	Greene	S.	Aug. 14, '62	Promoted Corporal.
Brown, John S.	39	Augusta	M.	Aug. 14, '62	Prom. Corp.; pris. at Gettysburgh, July, '63.

21

COMPANY I—Continued.

NAMES.	Age.	RESIDENCE.	Married or Single.	Mustered into the U. S. Service.	REMARKS.
Bumps, John K	33	Knox	M.	Aug. 18, '62	
Campbell, Alonzo	31	Manchester	M.	Aug. 14, '62	Discharged Jan. 13, '63.
Churchill, Charles C	21	Bucklield	S.	Aug. 14, '62	
Cloudman, Octavius	20	Webster	S.	Aug. 14, '62	Discharged Mar. 13, '63.
Cotton, Andrew J	23	Lisbon	S.	Aug. 14, '62	
Cotton, Blanchard	18	Lisbon	S.	Aug. 14, '62	
Crockett, Benjamin B	37	Webster	M.	Aug. 14, '62	
Cushman, Stephen L	26	Canton	M.	Aug. 20, '62	Discharged in '63.
Davis, Robert	21	Gardiner	S.	Aug. 14, '62	Wd. at Gettys., July, '63.
Davis, William	28	Durham	M.	Aug. 14, '62	Wd. at Gettys., July, '63.
Doble, Alden	44	Hartland	M.	Aug. 20, '62	Discharged Mar. 14, '63.
Dyer, Edward P	21	Greene	S.	Aug. 14, '62	Discharged Jan. 20, '63.
Ellis, Albert A	18	Hartford	S.	Aug. 20, '62	Discharged Mar. 1, '63.
Estes, Jeremiah	18	Durham	S.	Aug. 14, '62	Prisoner at Gettysburgh. '63.
Farris, Freeman H	37	Turner	M.	Aug. 14, '62	Wounded at Gettysburgh.
Farrar, Benjamin F	22	Lisbon	S.	Aug. 14, '62	
Flagil, George B	18	Monmouth	S.	Aug. 14, '62	Deserted from 7th Regt.
Foley, Thomas W	24	Corinth	M.	Aug. 14, '62	Promoted Corporal.
Frost, George W	18	Greene	S.	Aug. 14, '62	
Galvin, John	44	Lewiston	M.	Aug. 14, '62	
Garcelon, Benjamin F	24	Webster	S	Aug. 14, '62	Pris. at Gettys., July 1, '63.
Gilbert, Roscoe	27	Greene	M.	Aug. 14, '62	Deserted before muster.
Gordon, James R	19	Augusta	S.	Aug. 14, '62	Rep. deserter Sept. 21, '62.
Gould, Thomas J	21	Lisbon	S.	Aug. 14, '62	Promoted Corporal.
Gould, Silas C	20	Lisbon	S.	Aug. 14, '62	Missing in action Dec.13,'62.
Hackett, Henry	44	Durham	M.	Aug. 14, '62	Disc. by order June 2, '65.
Hackett, Orison W	32	Greene	M.	Aug. 14, '62	Discharged June 19, '63.
Hayes, Edward	24	Lewiston	M.	Aug. 14, '62	Wd. at F'd'k'g, Dec. 13, '62.
Holmes, Stewart	21	Turner	S.	Aug. 14, '62	Miss. since bat. Gettysb'gh.
Howard, Elias	35	Manchester	M.	Aug. 14, '62	
Howland, Enoch	31	Topsham	M.	Aug. 14, '62	Wd. in action Feb. 6, '65.
Hutchins, George A	21	Canton	S.	Aug. 14, '62	Disc. for dis. Dec. 23, '64.
Jewett, Warren	18	Clinton	S.	Aug. 14, '62	Discharged Jan. 6, '63.
Johnson, William	22	Greene	S.	Aug. 14, '62	
Jones, Orlando A	18	Turner	S.	Aug. 14, '62	Missing in battle of Fredericksburgh, Dec. 13, '62.
Jordan, Ephraim L	21	Webster	S.	Aug. 14, '62	Promoted Corporal.
Lane, Newman B	18	Augusta	S.	Aug. 14, '62	
Leavens, George G	18	Durham	S.	Aug. 14, '62	Discharged Feb. 18, '63.
Lewis, John F	21	Auburn	S.	Aug. 14, '62	Discharged Dec. 14, '63.
Littlefield, Thomas C	18	Hallowell	S.	Aug. 14, '62	Not in Company.
Loring, Hiram W	19	Lewiston	S.	Aug. 14, '62	Discharged Jan. 6, '63.
Marshall, David	26	Yarmouth	S.	Aug. 14, '62	
McCausland, Alonzo D	19	Farmingdale	S.	Aug. 14, '62	Discharged Dec. 15, '62.
McKinney, Francis A	25	Webster	M.	Aug. 14, '62	Discharged Dec. 11, '62.
Michaels, William H	18	Greene	S.	Aug. 14, '62	
Mower, Eugene S	18	Greene	S.	Aug. 14, '62	
Murphy, Jeremiah	18	Augusta	S.	Aug. 14, '62	
Murphy, Thomas	19	Augusta	S.	Aug. 14, '62	Wd. at F'k'b'g, Dec. 13, '62.
Nason, Edwin H	18	Greene	S.	Aug. 14, '62	Discharged Jan. 19, '63.
Nevins, Amos	44	Lewiston	M.	Aug. 14, '62	Discharged Jan. 18, '63.
Niles, Adon A	21	Webster	S.	Aug. 14, '62	Discharged Feb. 23, '63.
O'Neil, Patrick	43	Lewiston	M.	Aug. 14, '62	
Parmenter, Joseph W	34	Lewiston	M.	Aug. 14, '62	Discharged Dec. 23, '63.
Peabody, Samuel	38	Canton	S.	Aug. 14, '62	Promoted Corporal; pris.
Perry, Daniel	36	Minot	M.	Aug. 14, '62	
Piper, George T	19	Turner	S.	Aug. 14, '62	Missing at Gettysburgh.
Powers, Roderick	21	Presque Isle	S.	Aug. 14, '62	
Richards, Moses	26	Augusta	M.	Aug. 14, '62	
Roberts, Mathew	25	Lewiston	S.	Aug. 14, '62	
Roberts, Thomas L	37	Turner	M.	Aug. 14, '62	Discharged April 15, '63.
Sinclair, Charles W	18	Manchester	S.	Aug. 14, '62	Discharged Mar. 9, '63.
Small, Daniel	23	Lisbon	S.	Aug. 14, '62	Promoted Corporal.

COMPANY I.—Continued.

NAMES.	Age.	RESIDENCE.	Married or Single	Mustered into the U. S. Service.	REMARKS.
Smith, James O.	18	Gardiner	S.	Aug. 14, '62	Discharged June 26, '65.
Sparrow, John R.	34	Knox	M.	Aug. 14, '62	Disc. for dis. Dec. 23, '64.
Staples, William B.	42	Turner	M.	Aug. 14, '62	Discharged April 2, '63.
Stover, Oliver	41	Webster	M.	Aug. 14, '62	Pris. at Gettys.; missing.
Sullivan, Dennis	43	Portland	M.	Aug. 14, '62	Cattle guard; wd. Mar. 31, '65, at Gravelly Run, disc. June 10, '65.
Shurtliff, William D.	25	Portland		Aug. 14, '62	Not in Company.
Vose, Sebastian S.	24	Lewiston	M.	Aug. 14, '62	
Wade, Nelson	42	Lisbon	M.	Aug. 14, '62	
Waterman, Rinaldo N.	24	Webster	S.	Aug. 14, '62	Discharged in Mar., '63.
Wescott, Charles	18	Lisbon	S.	Aug. 14, '62	Disc. for dis. May 25, '63.
Whitney, William L.	26	C'ntrb'y, N.H.	S.	Aug. 14, '62	Transferred from Co. C; acting Orderly Sergt.
Young, Charles H.	20	Peru	S.	Aug. 20, '62	
Patten, Lora S.	21	Greene	S.	Aug. 14, '62	Missing at Gettysburgh.
Joined Company since Dec. 1, 1862.					
Boyd, John	21	Lewiston	S.	Aug. 4, '63	Con. Deserted Nov. 27, '63.
Barrows, Albert C.	36	Augusta	S.	Aug. 1, '63	Con. Disc. Aug. 2, '63.
Butterfield, Lowell	18	Augusta	S.	July 31, '63	Con. Promoted Corporal.
Born, William	28	Lewiston	S.	Aug. 4, '63	Con. Missing in action at Mine Run, Va.
Blagden, William D.	28	Hudson	M.	Aug. 13, '63	Con. Disc. by ord. May 31, '65.
Banks, Jeremiah	28	Woodville	M.	Aug. 13, '63	Con. Prisoner.
Brann, Peter B.	34	Bangor	M.	Sept. 2, '63	Con.
Booker, Wesley	25	Dover	S.	Aug. 14, '63	Con.; miss. in act. Aug. 19, '64.
Booker, Asa	24	Exeter	M.	Aug. 13, '63	Con.
Bryer, Andrew J.	23	Bangor	M.	Aug. 10, '63	Con.
Barnes, Ira	22	Lee	M.	Aug. 13, '63	Con.
Carr, George	21	Portland	M.	Aug. 4, '63	Con. Deserted Nov. 25, '63.
Clark, William, Jr.	20	Portland	S.	Aug. 4, '63	Con. Miss. in action, May 4, '64; disc. Aug. 23, '65.
Cleveland, John S.	25	Augusta	M.	July 30, '63	Con.
Clifford, Herman	21	Portland	S.	Aug. 3, '63	Con. Wd. May 8, '64.
Corson, Joseph	20	Portland	S.	July 28, '63	Con.
Crosby, Thomas	43	Jay	S.	July 15, '63	Con. Paroled prisoner.
Curtis, John	21	Augusta	M.	Aug. 1, '63	Con. Pris. at Richmond, Va.
Chandler, Roscoe	20	Lewiston	S.	July 16, '63	Con. Pris. Belle Isle, Va.
Colby, Benjamin F.	37	Augusta	S.	Aug. 3, '63	Con. Pris. Aug. 19, '64.
Campbell, Thomas	21	Portland	S.	July 31, '63	Con. Prisoner.
Corlis, John S.	25	Fort Fairfield	M.	Aug. 15, '63	Con. Wd. May 23, '64.
Cleaves, Wm. H. H.	25	Presque Isle	S.	Aug. 15, '63	Con.
Cornish, Josiah	19	Medway Pl.	S.	Aug. 13, '63	Con. Paroled prisoner.
Collins, Josiah	31	Lee	M.	Aug. 13, '63	Con.
Chase, Wesley C.	34	Fort Fairfield	S.	Aug. 15, '63	Con.
Cummings, Charles L.	20	Bangor	S.	Sept. 1, '63	Con. Des. from hospital.
Clark, George	33	Bangor	M.	Sept. 10, '63	Con. Wounded May 6, '64; deserted from hospital.
Dilling, James T.	23	Bangor	M.	Sept. 8, '63	Con. Prisoner.
Dutton, James W.	31	Woodville	S.	Aug. 15, '63	Con. Prisoner.
Dunn, John	21	Portland	M.	July 31, '63	Con. Promoted Corporal.
French, Stephen L.	18	Augusta	S.	July 31, '63	Con.
Frasier, William, Jr.	20	Herman	S.	Aug. 3, '63	Con. Disc. by ord. May 29, '65.
Hart, James	27	Belfast	M.	Aug. 7, '63	Con. Wd. May 8, '64.
Lincoln, Augustus C.	20	Bangor	S.	Aug. 22, '63	Con. Prisoner.
McGowan, Charles	22	Lewiston	S.	Aug. 4, '63	Con. Des. Nov. 27, '63.
Penthand, James	21	Burlington	S.	Sept. 7, '63	Con. Deserted.
Sentien, James	21	Burlington	S.	Sept. 8, '63	Con.
Servus, Frank	30	Belfast	M.	Aug. 25, '63	Con. Deserted Oct. 20, '63.
Spencer, Moses	28	Corinna	M.	Aug. 15, '63	Con. Wd. Feb. 7, '65.
Tarbox, Moses, Jr.	31	Bangor	M.	Sept. 18, '63	Con.
Troop, Andrew	23	Portland	S.	Sept. 15, '63	Con. Deserted Oct. 20, '63.
Thompson, Charles H.	19	Lewiston	S.	Sept. 19, '63	Con. Prisoner.

COMPANY I.—*Continued.*

NAMES.	Age.	RESIDENCE.	Married or Single.	Mustered into the U. S. Service.	REMARKS.
Varney, Alfred W	22	Belfast	M.	Sept. 10, '63	Conscript.
Walker, George H	20	Portland	S.	Aug. 10, '63	Conscript.
West, Fred W	21	Lewiston	S.	Sept. 5, '63	Conscript.
Winship, Andrew J	27	Swanville	M.	Aug. 14, '63	Con. Miss. in act. May 8, '64
Wentworth, John B	34	Orrington	M.	Aug. 12, '63	Con. Disc. April 22. '64.
Whittier, Rael M	21	Herman	S.	Aug. 13, '63	Conscript.
Wyman, Ralph	28	Bangor	M.	Aug. 13, '63	Conscript.
Worcester, John W	21	Bangor	S.	Aug. 10, '63	Conscript.
Young, Lewis P	34	No. 5, R. 3		Aug. 14, '63	Con. Disc. Dec., '63.
Joined Company since Dec., 1863.					
Butts, Isaac H	20	New Portland	S.	Aug. 14, '62	Transferred from Co. A.
Bovard, John	23	Boston	S.	Aug. 4, '63	Transferred from Co. A.
Brown, Hiram R	29	Harmony	S.	Aug. 14, '62	Transferred from Co. A.
Barry, James	21	London, Eng.	S.	Oct. 4, '64	Deserted Dec. 8, '64.
Cleaves, Samuel B	38	Presque Isle		Oct. 13, '64	Conscript.
Corrigan, Thomas	21	Milford	S.	Sept. 7, '64	Sub.; wd. Feb. 7, '65.
Clark, Henry R	18	Solon	S.	Aug. 14, '62	Trans. from Co. A; disc. by order, May 23, '65.
Carville, Benjamin	36	New Portland	M.	Aug. 14, '62	Transferred from Co. A.
Chamberlain, Stephen	21	Mayfield	S.	Aug. 14, '62	Trans. from Co. A; disc. by order, May 29, '65.
Clements, Thomas R	33	Monson	S.	Sept. 15, '63	Sub.; trans. from Co. A; disc.
Conway, Hugh	23	St. Johns, N.B.	S.	Sept. 8, '63	Sub.; Trans. from Co. A.
Cleaves, James R	34	Presque Isle		Oct. 13, '64	Conscript.
Delaney, Thomas	24	Cork, Ire	S.	Oct. 4, '64	Conscript.
Farnclough, Joshua	27	England	M.	Oct. 6, '64	Substitute.
Ford, Timothy	44	Belfast		Sept. 1, '63	Sub; disc.byord.June22,'65.
Gorman, Frank	20	Cork, Ire	S.	Oct. 6, '64	Sub.; disc. July 12. '65.
Hammond, Lowell F	18	Paris	S.	Sept. 7, '64	Substitute.
Hanley, John	21	St. Johns, N.B.	S.	Oct. 5, '64	Con. Deserted Dec. 13, '64.
Kelley, Patrick	34	Eaton Grant		Oct. 15, '64	Conscript.
Lyshom, Albert	21	Oldtown	S.	Sept. 30, '63	Conscript.
Lee, George	26	Ireland	S.	Oct. 8, '63	Sub.; deserted Jan. 28, '65.
McDonald, John	23	Liverpool	S.	Oct. 4, '63	
McPheters, Gorham	21	Orono	S.	Sept. 30, '64	Conscript.
Miller, Charles	18		M.	Nov. 15, '64	Con. Discharged by order. May 24, '65.
McPheters, John S	26	Orono	S.	Nov. 15, '64	Conscript.
McNeal, Daniel	31	Bangor	M.	Nov. 7, '64	Substitute; paroled pris.
Miles, Barnard	31	Massachusetts	M.	Nov. 8, '64	Substitute; discharged May 18, '65; order W. D.
Martin, Leonard P	28	Bangor	S.	Jan. 5, '64	Promoted 1st Sergeant.
Metcalf, John	18	New Vineyard	S.	Sept. 7, '64	Sub.; disc.by ord.May 23,'65.
Murphy, John	19	Boston		Sept. 7, '64	Substitute.
McLaughlin, William	26			Oct. 4, '64	Conscript.
Noland, Mathew	19	Montville	S.	Oct. 4, '64	Deserted Dec. 13, '64.
Nason, Dexter	20	Sangerville	M.	Oct. 1, '64	Con.; wd. Feb. 7, '65.
Parker, William B	24	Bloomfield	S.	Oct. 7, '64	Sub.; wd. Mar. 31, '65; disc. June 12, '65.
Purrington, Leonard H	18	Farmington	S.	Sept. 2, '64	Sub.; disc. by ord.May 23,'65.
Patterson, John	28	Milltown	M	Sept. 2, '64	Substitute.
Parshley, Frank B	19	R'ch'st'r, N.H.	S.	Sept. 6, '64	
Robbins, William W	18	Patten	S.	Sept. 3, '64	
Spearin, Jeremiah	35			Oct. 3, '64	Con. Disc.byord.May23,'65.
Tierney, Michael	21	Halifax	S.	Oct. 4, '64	
Thompson, Isaac H	24	Anson	M.	Aug. 14, '62	Joined as 1st Lieut. from 2d Lieut. Co. G.
Thompson, James	33	England	M.	Aug. 1, '64	Substitute.
Tripp, Simeon	27	Embden	M.	Aug. 14, '62	Trans. from Co. A; pris.
Williams, Thomas	23	England	S.	Oct. 6, '64	Substitute.
Warren, Augustus W	18	Boston	S.	Sept. 2, '64	Substitute.
Walter, Thomas G	41			Oct. 13, '64	Substitute.
Young, John	30	New Portland	M.	Aug. 14, '62	Transferred fromr. Co. A.

SIXTEENTH MAINE REGIMENT. 293

COMPANY K.

NAMES.	Age.	RESIDENCE.	Married or Single.	Mustered into the U. S. Service.	REMARKS.
SERGEANTS.					
Joseph O. Lord	31	Biddeford	M.	Aug. 14, '62	Promoted 1st Lieutenant.
Marcus M. L. Hussey	29	Newcastle	M.	Aug. 14, '62	Disc. for dis. Feb. 19, '63.
Freeman K. McIntire	34	Sedgwick	M.	Aug. 14, '62	Disc. for dis. Feb. 5, '63.
Edward F. Davies	27	Castine	M.	Aug. 14, '62	Promoted 2d Lieutenant.
Atwood Fitch	19	Bristol	S.	Aug. 14, '62	Promoted 2d Lieut. Co. D, Dec. 1, '63.
Wilmot H. Chapman	18	Nobleboro	S.	Aug. 14, '62	Pro. 1st Serg. Pro. 2d Lieut.
Walter Dunbar	20	Nobleboro	S.	Aug. 14, '62	Wounded May 10, '64; promoted 1st Sergt.
Francis C. Mayo	24	Bluehill	S.	Aug. 14, '62	Disc. by order June 5, '65.
Joseph B. Varnum	36	Castine	M.	Aug. 14, '62	
Reuel W. Higgins	27	Deer Isle	M.	Aug. 14, '62	
Charles P. Allen	18	Brooklin	M.	Aug. 14, '62	
Henry B. Butler	30	Castine	M.	Aug. 14, '62	Wd. in action Feb. 6, '65.
Joseph Peacock	18	Bluehill	S.	Aug. 14, '62	
CORPORALS.					
Benjamin W. Cole	24	Brooklin	M.	Aug. 14, '62	Wd. Fredk'g. Dec. 13, '62.
Reuel W. Higgins	27	Deer Isle	M.	Aug. 14, '62	
George W. Houdlett	25	Newcastle	M.	Aug. 14, '62	Disc. for dis. Feb. 14, '63.
Johnson H. Lufkin	29	Deer Isle	S.	Aug. 14, '62	
George H. Dority	26	Brooklin	S.	Aug. 14, '62	
Wilmot H. Chapman	18	Nobleboro	S.	Aug. 14, '62	Promoted Sergeant.
Samuel Hooper	18	Castine	S.	Aug. 14, '62	Disc. for dis. Feb. 5, '63.
David R. Lane	21	Jefferson	S.	Aug. 14, '62	Disc. for dis. Jan. 16, '63.
John J. Blodgett	21	Castine	S.	Aug. 14, '62	
Charles T. Choate	18	Bluehill	S.	Aug. 14, '62	Wounded June 13; disc. Jan. 23, '65.
Frank Devereux	21	Castine	S.	Aug. 14, '62	
Charles A. Devereux	18	Penobscot	S.	Aug. 14, '62	
Albert C. Stevens	20	Bluehill	S.	Aug. 14, '62	
Charles F. Palmer	20	Fayette	S	July 28, '63	Conscript.
Charles P. Allen	18	Brooklin	S.	Aug. 14, '62	Promoted Sergeant.
Henry B. Butler	30	Castine	M.	Aug. 14, '62	Promoted Sergeant.
Silas C. Doble	18	Lincoln	S.	Sept. 3, '63	
Roscoe Doble	19	Lincoln	S.	Sept. 1, '63	
Daniel Emerson	34	Boothbay	M.	July 18, '63	
Eli C. Lyons	18	Bangor	S.	Sept. 5, '63	
Alonzo B. Sanborn	23	Brooklin	M.	Aug. 14, '62	
Henry B. Wescott	24	Castine	S.	Aug. 14, '62	Wounded Feb. 7, '65.
Francis M. Willins	21	Bluehill	S.	Aug. 14, '62	
Freeman T. Knowles	18	Skowhegan	S.	Aug. 14, '62	
MUSICIAN.					
Melville D. Brown	21	Harmony	S.	Aug. 14, '62	Disc. Jan. 24, '65.
PRIVATES.					
Allen, Charles P.	18	Brooklin	S.	Aug. 14, '62	Promoted Corporal.
Anderson, John H.	19	Brooklin	S.	Aug. 14, '62	Disc. for dis. Apr. 25, '63.
Babson, Charles L.	21	Brooklin	S.	Aug. 14, '62	Disc. for dis. Oct. 16, '63.
Bettel, Robert	37	Sedgwick	S.	Aug. 14, '62	
Bickford, Elisha F.	18	Castine	S.	Aug. 14, '62	
Bickford, Isaac B.	27	Pittsfield	M.	Aug. 18, '62	Prisoner July 1, '63; wounded May 10, '64.
Blodgett, John J.	21	Castine	S.	Aug. 14, '62	Promoted Corporal.
Bowden, Christopher	29	Brooklin	M.	Aug. 14, '62	
Bowden, Frank M.	18	Castine	S.	Aug. 14, '62	Wounded July 1, '63.
Bowden, Lorenzo D.	24	Castine	M.	Aug. 14, '62	
Brown, William	18	Newcastle	S.	Aug. 14, '62	
Butler, Henry B.	30	Castine	M.	Aug. 14, '62	Pris. July 1, '63; prom. corp.
Byard, John J.	36	Sedgwick	M.	Aug. 14, '62	
Carter, Leander A.	20	Brooklin	S.	Aug. 14, '62	Miss. Fredk'g. Dec. 13, '62.
Chapman, John W.	29	Newcastle	M.	Aug. 14, '62	Disc. for dis. Mar. 10, '63.
Chase, Seth K.	26	Bluehill	M.	Aug. 14, '62	
Choate, Charles T.	18	Bluehill	S.	Aug. 14, '62	Pro. corp.; Pris. July 1, '63.

COMPANY K.—Continued.

NAMES.	Age.	RESIDENCE.	Married or Single	Mustered into the U. S. Service.	REMARKS.
Clark, Benjamin F.	36	Damariscotta.	M.	Aug. 14, '62	
Coligan, Daniel	20	Washington.	S.	Aug. 14, '62	
Cousins, Timothy D.	35	Sedgwick	S.	Aug. 14, '62	
Cunningham, Edward	34	Jefferson	S.	Aug. 14, '62	Prisoner July 1, '63.
Curtis, Daniel M.	24	Deer Isle.	S.	Aug. 14, '62	
Davis, Alvah M.	20	Jefferson	S.	Aug. 14, '62	Disc. for dis. Nov. 10, '62.
Devereux, Charles A.	18	Penobscot	S.	Aug. 14, '62	Prom. Corp.; wd. July 1, '63.
Devereux, Frank	21	Castine.	S.	Aug. 14, '62	Promoted Corporal.
Dodge, Frank	18	Newcastle.	S.	Aug. 14, '62	
Dow, Reuben A.	21	Brooklin.	S.	Aug. 14, '62	Wd. Gettysburgh July, '63.
Dunbar, Walter	20	Nobleboro.	S.	Aug. 14, '62	Promoted Sergeant.
Fox, James E.	18	Washington.	S.	Aug. 14, '62	Transferred to Co. A.
Gregory, John	21	Bluehill.	S.	Aug. 14, '62	
Grey, Judson	44	Sedgwick	M.	Aug. 14, '62	Discharged April 22, '64.
Grindle, Daniel E.	18	Bluehill.	S.	Aug. 14, '62	Wounded Fred. Dec. 13, '62; disc. Aug. 13, '64.
Grindle, James W.	30	Bluehill.	M.	Aug. 14, '62	
Hatch, Mark E.	28	Castine.	M.	Aug. 14, '62	Disc. April 22, '64.
Hiscock, William S.	18	Damariscotta.	S.	Aug. 14, '62	
Jarvis, Andrew J.	32	Castine.	S.	Aug. 14, '62	Disc. for dis. Dec. 15, '62.
Jenkins, Robert	44	Rockland	M.	Aug. 14, '62	Disc. for dis. Dec. 27, '62.
Jones, John R.	18	Damariscotta.	S.	Aug. 14, '62	Miss. Fred. Dec. 13, '62.
Jones, Medbury	24	Washington.	S.	Aug. 14, '62	Wounded Dec. 13, '62.
Jordan, Hollis J.	18	Trenton	S.	Aug. 14, '62	Disc. for dis. Mar. 9, '63.
Joyce, Moses S.	28	Deer Isle.	M.	Aug. 14, '62	Disc. for dis. Sept. 21, '63.
Lambert, Gregory	44	Bluehill.	M.	Aug. 14, '62	
Lane, David R.	21	Jefferson.	S.	Aug. 14, '62	Promoted Corporal.
Lane, John T.	19	Deer Isle.	M.	Aug. 14, '62	
Leach, Henry	18	Penobscot.	S.	Aug. 14, '62	
Macomber, Otis	31	Bluehill.	M.	Aug. 14, '62	
Marks, Calvin B.	20	Bluehill.	M.	Aug. 14, '62	Prisoner.
Marks, James B.	22	Sedgwick	S.	Aug. 14, '62	Prisoner July 1, '63.
Mayo, Francis C.	24	Bluehill.	S.	Aug. 14, '62	Pro. Sergt.; pris. July 1, '63.
McNear, Alfred	21	Newcastle.	S.	Aug. 14, '62	Disc. for dis. Dec. 2, '62.
Morgrage, Andrew J.	31	Castine.	M.	Aug. 14, '62	Prisoner July 1, '63.
Osgood, Rodolphus W.	25	Bluehill.	S.	Aug. 14, '62	Disc. for dis. Jan. 4, '64.
Page, Ira	21	Sedgwick	S.	Aug. 14, '62	Wd.; disc. May 19, '65.
Parlin, Charles H.	25	Skowhegan	S.	Aug. 14, '62	Prom. Commissary Sergt.
Peacock, Joseph	18	Bluehill.	S.	Aug. 14, '62	Promoted Sergeant.
Pearson, Charles	19	Bluehill.	S.	Aug. 14, '62	
Pierce, John H.	18	Bath.	S.	Aug. 14, '62	Miss. Fred. Dec. 13, '62.
Peters, Charles F.	24	Bluehill.	S.	Aug. 14, '62	Wounded Fredericksburgh.
Powers, Harlon P.	20	Deer Isle.	S.	Aug. 14, '62	Miss. Fred. Dec. 13, '62.
Reaves, Isaac G.	28	Jefferson.	M.	Aug. 14, '62	Disc. for dis. April 1, '64.
Sanborn, Alonzo B.	23	Brooklin.	M.	Aug. 14, '62	Wd. Gettysburgh July 1, '63; Promoted Corporal.
Sargent, Benj. W.	36	Sedgwick	M.	Aug. 14, '62	
Savage, Hiram	25	Washington.	S.	Aug. 14, '62	Prisoner Gettysburgh.
Sherman, Samuel	44	Newcastle.	M.	Aug. 14, '62	Hospital attendant.
Spaulding, Daniel	26	Pittsfield.	M.	Aug. 18, '62	Wounded in action.
Stevens, Albert C.	20	Bluehill.	S.	Aug. 14, '62	Prom. Corp.; wd. July 1, '63.
Varnum, Joseph B.	36	Castine.	M.	Aug. 14, '62	Pro. Sergt.; pris. July 1, '63.
Veazie, James A.	18	Penobscot.	S.	Aug. 14, '62	Miss. Fred. Dec. 13, '62.
Webber, Cyrus K.	21	Limerick.	M.	Aug. 14, '62	
Wescott, Henry B.	24	Castine.	S.	Aug. 14, '62	Pris. July 1, '63; exch.; pro. Corporal.
Willens, Francis M.	21	Bluehill.	S.	Aug. 14, '62	Promoted Corporal.
Willens, Walter J.	41	Bluehill.	M.	Aug. 14, '62	Promoted Corporal.
Wilson, Isaac M.	18	Sedgwick	S.	Aug. 14, '62	Wd. Fred. Dec. 13, '62.
Wilson, Thomas J.	22	Sedgwick	S.	Aug. 14, '62	Pris. July 1, '63; exch.
Joined Company since Dec. 1, 1862.					
Abbott, Orson	20	Bucksport.	S.	Sept. 10, '63	Con. Wd. May 8, '64.

COMPANY K.—Continued.

NAMES.	Age.	RESIDENCE.	Married or Single	Mustered into the U. S. Service.	REMARKS.
Bisbee, Robert	26	Calais	M.	Aug. 10, '63	Con. Missing in action; discharged Aug. 8, '65.
Brown, Walter M	23	Lee	S.	Sept. 18, '63	Con.
Brown, Hezekiah	18	Lee	S.	Sept. 11, '63	Con.
Berry, William	28	Saco	S.	Sept. 16, '63	Con. Wd. in action.
Barnby, John B	18	Orono	S.	Aug. 22, '63	Con.
Bell, Daniel	22	Orono	S.	Sept. 8, '63	Con. Disc. for dis. Jan. 7, '64.
Bell, Joseph, jr	18	Orono	S.	Aug. 22, '63	Con. Disc. Jan. 14, '64; Arm amputated.
Carney, James	20	Portland	S.	Aug. 1, '63	Con. Des. Sept. 17, '63.
Cloyes, John F	28	Bangor	S.	Aug. 16, '63	Con.
Doble, Silas C	18	Lincoln	S.	Sept. 3, '63	Con. Promoted Corporal.
Doble, Roscoe	19	Lincoln	S.	Sept. 1, '63	Con. Wd. May 10, '64. Promoted Corporal.
Drew, Isaac	34	Lincoln	M.	Aug. 14, '63	Con.
Emery, Joseph F	21	Clinton	S	Aug. 15, '63	Con. Wounded Feb. 7, '65. Disc. by order May 20, '65.
Emerson, Charles	18	Orono	S.	Sept. 1, '63	Con. Disc. by ord. May 29, '65.
Emerson, Daniel	34	Boothbay	M	July 18, '63	Con. Prom. Corporal.
Fowler, Timothy	28	Canaan	M.	Aug. 15, '63	Con. Wd. in action.
Foster, Samuel A	30	Hampden	M.	Sept. 4, '63	Con. Prisoner of war.
Fisher, George W	18	Brewer	S.	Sept. 4, '63	Con. Disc. for dis. May 24, '65.
Gray, Levi R	21	Oldtown	S.	Sept. 4, '63	Con. Miss. in action, June 5, '64; disc. June 26, '65.
Gliddon, Lewis	21	Freedom	S.	Aug. 13, '63	Con.
Green, Benjamin P	18	Barnard	S.	Sept. 7, '63	Con. Disc. for dis. Jan. 19, '64.
Grover, George R	34	Lewiston	S.	Aug. 14, '63	Con. Disc. by ord. June 2, '65.
Ham, Herbert J	18	Foxcroft	S.	Sept. 5, '63	Con. Des. June 12, '65.
Hopkinson, Henry M	23	New Sharon	S.	Aug. 15, '63	Con.
Hamlin, James H	26	Castine	M.	Sept. 7, '63	Con. Disc. April 22, '64.
Hines, Augustus	37	Etna	M.	Aug. 21, '63	Con. Wd. and absent on furlough Oct. 22, '64.
Haney, Thomas	21	Houlton	S.	Aug. 14, '63	Con. Wounded Feb. 7, '65.
Jordan, Charles A	31	Gardiner	M.	Aug. 27, '63	Con. Par. pris.; Discharged by order May 29, '65.
Joseph, Angel	28	Portland	M.	Aug. 3, '63	Con. Deserted May 4, '64.
Logan, John	30	Portland	M.	July 31, '63	Con. Discharged for dis. May 10, '65.
Lyons, Eli C	18	Bangor	S.	Sept. 5, '63	Con. Prom. Corporal.
McGuire, James	21	Biddeford	S.	Sept. 16, '63	Con. Disc. April 22, '64.
McGuire, James	42	Portland	S.	July 28, '63	Con. Disc. April 21, '65 for disability.
McMahan, Bernhard	32	Augusta	S.	Aug. 1, '63	Con. Miss. in action, June 5, '64.
Moffatt, Hudson	22	Portland	S.	July 29, '63	Con. Disc. April 22, '64.
Nason, John T	22	Bradley	S.	Aug. 12, '63	Con.
Olscamp, Joseph	20	Portland	S.	July 29, '63	Con. Paroled prisoner.
Palmer, Charles F	20	Fayette	S.	July 28, '63	Con. Promoted Corporal.
Pazzie, George	27	Portland	S.	Aug. 3, '63	Con. Deserted Oct. 25, '63.
Peterson, Hans	23	Portland	S.	Aug. 5, '63	Con. Disc. Apr. 22, '64.
Pooler, Frank	20	Bangor	M.	July 23, '63	Con. Discharged for disability Dec. 9, '63.
Poole, Benjamin F	18	Mt. Vernon	S.	July 31, '63	Con. Wd. in action.
Phillips, John	31	Kittery	S.	Sept. 16, '63	Con. Disc. April 22, '64.
Quirk, John	21	Portland	S.	July 28, '63	Con. Paroled prisoner.
Rankins, Albert	29	Portland	S.	July 30, '63	Con. Des. Dec. 6, '63.
Ranker, Joseph	25	Portland	M.	Aug. 30, '63	Con. Disc. for dis. Ap. 1, '64.
Simons, Gilbert	27	Bangor	M.	Aug. 5, '63	Con. Disc. Apr. 22, '64.
Stevens, David H	33	Lewiston	M.	Sept. 18, '63	Con. Disc. for dis. Jan. 4, '64.
St. John, William	44	Portland	M.	Aug. 10, '63	Con.
Shaw, Hazen M	26	Orono	M.	Sept. 1, '63	Con. Dis. by order May 29, '65.
Shuman, James M	19	Belfast	S.	Aug. 27, '63	Conscript.

COMPANY K.—Continued.

NAMES.	Age.	RESIDENCE.	Married or Single	Mustered into the U. S. Service.	REMARKS.
True, William A.	19	Freeman	S.	Sept. 7, '63	Con. Wounded Feb. 7, '65.
Thing, Everard	21	Mt. Vernon	S.	Aug. 3, '63	Con. Wd.; arm amputated; disc. Mar. 22, '65.
Tarr, Hiram M.	28	Salem	M.	Aug. 13, '63	Con. Wd. in action; disc. Dec. 10, '64.
Winslow, Hiram	24	Portland	S.	Aug. 3, '63	Con. Joined Company since Dec. 1, 1863.
Brady, James	26	Bridgton		Oct. 21, '64	Substitute.
Burr, George C.	18	Bangor	S.	Sept. 6, '64	Substitute.
Bennett, Edwin A.	24	No. 2 R 3		Oct. 13, '64	Con.
Conden, Alfred	18	Brooksville	S.	Jan. 3, '63	
Cole, George L.	18	Bangor	S.	Sept. 7, '64	Discharged June 12, '65.
Curran, John	18	Bangor	S.	Sept. 12, '64	Substitute.
Dunham, Hosea A.	24	Madrid		Oct. 26, '64	Conscript.
Dakin, James T.	43	Amity		Oct. 12, '64	Conscript.
Foster, Stephen H.	34	Danforth		Oct. 3, '64	Conscript.
Gilbert, William	25	Bangor	S.	Sept. 9, '64	Sub. Wounded in action.
Greene, William	18	Rockport		Sept. 2, '64	Substitute.
Graham, Henry		Brighton		Nov. 4, '64	Substitute.
Greenleaf, Daniel	38	Washburn		Oct. 13, '64	Conscript.
Heath, Calvin W.	18	Bangor	S.	Sept. 5, '64	Substitute.
Hill, George F.	18	Bangor	S.	Sept. 8, '64	Sub. Wd. Feb. 7, '65. Disc. by order May 19, '65.
Howard, Augustus A.	18	Brownsville		Feb. 18, '65	
Haley, Ebenezer	23	Belfast		Sept. 8, '63	Substitute.
Hopkins, Daniel	39	Belfast	S.	Sept. 6, '63	Sub. Wounded in action.
Howard, Anson H.	18	Brownville		Feb. 1, '65	
Hurd, Joel B.	20	Harmony		Aug. 14, '62	Trans. from Co. A. Disc. July 19, '65.
Henderson, William	35	Brownfield		Nov. 2, '64	
Holbrook, Abel C.	33	Embden		Aug. 14, '62	Transferred from Co. A.
Holmes, John		N. Yarmouth		Aug. 7, '63	Substitute.
Johnson, Martin A.	19	Limington		Nov. 2, '64	Conscript.
Johnson, Charles	18	Kenneb'kp't		Nov. 14, '64	Sub. Wounded April 1, '65.
Knowles, Freeman T.	18	Skowhegan	S.	Aug. 14, '62	Tr. from Co. A. Promoted Corp. Paroled prisoner.
Knowles, William H.	27	Lexington		Aug. 7, '63	Substitute. Prisoner.
Moulton, Daniel W.	32	Madrid		Oct. 26, '64	Conscript.
Mortimer, Richard	21	Kenneb'kp't		Oct. 26, '64	Sub. Wounded April 1, '65.
Maulley, Frank	27	Auburn	S.	Sept. 5, '64	Sub. Trans. from Co. A. Missing in action.
Page, John L.	18	Sedgwick	S.	Dec. 28, '64	Vet. Disc. by order May 29, '65.
Parker, Jabez P.	18	Greene	S.	Aug. 14, '62	Prom. 1st Lieut. from 2d Lieut. Co. I.
Page, Rufus E.	18	Sedgwick	M.	Jan. 4, '64	
Place, Benjamin H.	40			Oct. 31, '64	Discharged June 12, '65
Robinson, Fred. C.	18	Bangor	S.	Sept. 1, '64	Substitute.
Russell, Joshua	41	Danforth		Oct. 3, '64	Con. Disc. by order June 6, '65.
Redding, Ebenezer	43	Calais		Oct. 25, '64	
Spearin, Daniel A.	21	Skowhegan	S.	Aug. 14, '62	1st Sergt. from Co. A. Promoted 2d Lieut. Co. F.
Stinchfield, Thomas F.	29	Clinton Gore		Oct. 21, '64	
Smith, William	40	Washburn		Oct. 13, '64	
Tripp, Simeon	27	New Portland	M.	Aug. 14, '62	Tr. fr. Co. A. Pris. of war.
Twist, John A.	27	Bridgewater		Aug. 24, '64	
Webster, George W.	40	Kenneb'kp't		Nov. 1, '64	
Wilson, John	25	Mayfield		Oct. 21, '64	

SIXTEENTH MAINE REGIMENT.

OFFICERS AND ENLISTED MEN ON DETACHED SERVICE.

NAMES.	Co.	DUTY.	DATE.
COLONEL			
Charles W. Tilden.....	....	Com. 3d Brig., 3d Div., 5th A.C.	1864
LIEUT.-COLONEL			
Aug. B. Farnham.....	....	Inspector Gen. and Chief of Staff 2d Div. 5th A. C.............	May 8, '64
SURGEON			
Charles Alexander...	....	Surg.-in-Chief 1st Brig. 3d Div. 5th A. C.....................	July 16, '64
ASST. SURGEON.			
Joseph B. Baxter.....	....	In charge 2d Div. Hospital......	Aug., 1863
ADJUTANT			
Abner R. Smail.......	....	A.D.C. 1st Brig. 2d Div. 1st A.C.	Dec. 13, '62
		A.A.A.G. 1st Bri. 2d Div. 1st AC.	July 1, '63
QUARTERMASTER			
George W. Brown....	....	A.A.Q.M. 2d Bri. 3d Div. 5th A.C.	Feb., 1865
CAPTAIN			
Lincoln K. Plummer.	E	A.D.C. 2d Brig. 3d Div. 5th A.C.	Dec., 1864
FIRST LIEUTENANT			
Aubrey Leavitt.......	E	A.D.C. 2d Brig. 3d Div. 5th A.C.	Dec., 1864
		A.D.C. 1st Brig. 2d Div. 5th A.C.	Apr. 12, '64
CAPTAIN			
Joseph H. Malbon....	G	Com. 2d Div. 1st A.C. Amb. Corps	1863
LIEUTENANT			
Charles A. Garcelon..	I	Com. 1st Brig. 2d Div. 1st A. C. Amb. Corps................	1863
PRIVATES			
John Kealigher.......	A	Second Maine Battery.........	Dec., 1862
James Leavitt........	A	Second Maine Battery.........	Dec., 1862
John H. McKeen.....	A	Second Maine Battery.........	Dec., 1862
Charles P. Brann.....	B	Second Maine Battery.........	Dec., 1862
Charles F. Davis......	B	Second Maine Battery.........	Dec., 1862
George W. Gardiner..	B	Second Maine Battery.........	Dec., 1862
Arno Little..........	B	Second Maine Battery.........	Dec., 1862
John McDonley......	B	Second Maine Battery.........	Dec., 1862
William K. Savage ...	B	Second Maine Battery.........	Dec., 1862
Nahum Spear........	B	Second Maine Battery.........	Dec., 1862
Henry Turner.......	B	Second Maine Battery.........	Dec., 1862
John W. Waterhouse.	B	Second Maine Battery.........	Dec., 1862
Melvin Adams.......	C	Second Maine Battery.........	Dec., 1862
John W. Reed.......	C	Second Maine Battery.........	Dec., 1862
Enoch P. Gray.......	D	Second Maine Battery.........	Dec., 1862
Smith Hilton.........	D	Second Maine Battery.........	Dec., 1862
Charles Smith........	D	Second Maine Battery.........	Dec., 1862
Rollin F. Jennings. ...	E	Second Maine Battery.........	Dec., 1862
Charles E. McGrath..	F	Second Maine Battery.........	Dec., 1862
Osborne Richardson..	F	Second Maine Battery.........	Dec., 1862
Lorenzo D. Allen.....	I	Second Maine Battery.........	Dec., 1862
Newman B. Lane	I	Second Maine Battery.........	Dec., 1862
Jeremiah Murphy....	I	Second Maine Battery.........	Dec., 1862
Mathew Roberts......	I	Second Maine Battery.........	Dec., 1862
William Brown.......	K	Second Maine Battery.........	Dec., 1862
Frank Dodge.........	K	Second Maine Battery.........	Dec., 1862
Amos Baker..........	G	Fifth Maine Battery............	
Christ'er Christophers	H	Fifth Maine Battery............	
John B. Gowen......	H	Fifth Maine Battery............	
Charles Hathorn.....	H	Fifth Maine Battery............	
John Kingdon........	H	Fifth Maine Battery............	
John McCollum......	H	Fifth Maine Battery............	
John McGinley......	H	Fifth Maine Battery............	
John L. Sawyer......	H	Fifth Maine Battery............	

OFFICERS AND ENLISTED MEN ON DETACHED SERVICE.—
Continued.

NAME.	RANK.	Co.	DUTY.	DATE.
Allen, Charles W	Priv.	I	Brig. Com. Dept	
Bartlett, Nathan jr	Priv.	C	Ambulance Corps	1862
Beals, Calvin	Priv.	C	Cattle Guard	1863
Brann, Robert C	Sergt.	E	Pioneer Corps	1862
Burnham, John M	Priv.	F	Cattle Guard	1863
Cross, Aaron	Priv.	F	Guard Brig. Hd. Qrts.	1863
Coligan, Daniel	Priv.	K	Brig Teamster	1862
Chase, Seth K	Priv.	K	Guard Brig. Hd. Qrts.	1863
Curtis, Daniel M	Priv.	K	Ambulance	1863
Dorset, Thomas J	Priv.	F	Div. Teamster	1863
Downing, George A	Priv.	A	Ambulance Corps	1863
Follett, Ephraim B	Priv.	B	Ambulance Corps	1862
Folger, Edward C	Priv.	B		1863
Floyd, Ephraim H	Corp.	F	In Maine	
Farrar, Benton	Priv.	H	Guard Corps Hd. Qrts.	1863
Goodrich, Ira H	Priv.	A	Div. Teamster	Oct. 31,'62
Green, William F	Priv.	F	Div. Teamster	
Gray, Judson	Priv.	K	Ambulance Corps	1862
Hackett, Henry	Priv.	I	Ambulance Corps	
Hayes, Edward E	Priv.	D	Div. Teamster	
Hayes, Erastus	Priv.	D	Div. Teamster	
King, Alburn C	Priv.	C	Cattle Guard	1863
Lovell, Israel F	Priv.	C	Ambulance Corps	1863
Littlefield, Asel A	Priv.	E	Ambulance Corps	1862
Lowd, William R	Priv.	F	Ambulance Corps	1862
Libbey, Lorenzo D	Priv.	F	Div. Teamster	
Macomber, Otis	Priv.	K	Ambulance Corps	1862
Moore, William L	Priv.	H	Cattle Guard	
Marston, William W	Priv.	I	Div. Teamster	
Merrill, Hiram A	Priv.	F		
Norcross, Albert H	Priv.	B		1863
Nelson, Chester	Priv.	G	Pioneer Corps	1864
Quinby, Daniel R	Priv.	C	Cook in Div. Hospital	1863
Richardson, Joseph W	Priv.	B	Pioneer Corps	
Robie, John G	Priv.	B	Ambulance Corps	
Riggs, Jerry W	Priv.	E	Pioneer Corps	1862
Richmond, Granville	Priv.	E	Brig. Com. Dept	1863
Rowell, Haniff	Priv.	A		1863
Simpson, Joseph	Priv.	H	Cattle Guard	
Sullivan, Dennis	Priv.	I	Cattle Guard	
Stone, George H	Priv.	B	Ambulance Corps	
Soule, Charles F	Priv.	C		1863
Soule, Daniel A	Priv.	E	Brig. Com. Dept	
Stickney, John H	Priv.	C	Cattle Guard	
Tyler, Abram	Priv.	F	Res. Brig. Battery	
Townsend, Roscoe B	Priv.	E	Div. Teamster	1863
Tibbetts, Sheldron H	Priv.	F	Div. Teamster	
Watson, John W	Priv.	A	In Maine	1863
Willens, Francis M	Priv.	A	Cattle Guard	1863
Willens, Walter J	Priv.	K	Guard Corps Hd. Qrts	
Wentworth, George M	Priv.	B		1864
Worth, Francis	Priv.	E	Ambulance Corps	1863
Young, Charles H	Priv.	I	Guard Corps Hd. Qrts	
Young, John	Priv.	A	Div. Teamster	1863

SIXTEENTH MAINE REGIMENT. 299

ENLISTED MEN, whose term of service had not expired at muster-out of Sixteenth regiment, June 5, 1865, transferred to TWENTIETH MAINE VOLUNTEER INFANTRY.

NAME.	RANK.	Co.	
Gerald, Ezekiel	Corporal.	A	
Kenniston, Wilbert W	Private.	A	
McLaughlin, Timothy	Private.	A	
McNeill, Daniel	Private.	A	
McGilvery, John	Private.	A	
Eldridge, Albert	Private.	A	
Strout, Levi N	Private.	A	
Blair, John	Private.	B	
Beal, Sewell G	Private.	B	
Brown, Byron B	Private.	B	
Foster, Benjamin G	Private.	B	
Lord, Elijah	Private.	B	
Mansfield, Henry	Private.	B	Disc. July 21, 1865.
Monroe, William B	Private.	B	Disc. July 31, 1865.
Miller, Frank B	Private.	B	
Peaslee, Charles L	Corporal.	B	
Smith, Oliver P	Private.	B	
Smith, Hiram R	Private.	B	
Twist, George W	Private.	B	
Turner, Alden	Private.	B	
Tasker, Horace P	Corporal.	B	
Trimble, Richard	Private.	B	
West, Joseph A	Private.	B	
Woodbury, Sewell G	Corporal.	B	
Webb, Daniel M	Private.	B	
Wolff, Thomas	Private.	B	
Brown, Jeremiah	Private.	B	
Brown, Daniel B	Private.	B	
Bowers, William	Private.	B	
Bull, Peter	Private.	B	
Clough, Llewellyn	Private.	B	Disc. June 30, 1865.
Chase, Charles B	Corporal.	B	
Cockland, John	Private.	B	
Emery, Cyrus	Private.	B	
Hubbard, Frank	Private.	B	
Jackson, Jeremiah H	Private.	B	
Kelley, John	Private.	B	
Kelley, William D. Jr	Private.	B	
Lancaster, Willard	Private.	B	Disc. July 22, 1865.
Porter, Richard D	Private.	B	
Powers, Nelson A	Private.	B	
Reed, Charles G	Private.	B	
Alley, Alexander	Private.	C	
Allen, Jonathan	Private.	C	
Anderson, John	Private.	C	
Allen, Seth	Private.	C	
Avery, James P	Private.	C	
Acherson, Martin	Private.	C	

ENLISTED MEN, whose term of service had not expired at muster-out of Sixteenth Regiment, June 5, 1865, transferred to TWENTIETH MAINE VOLUNTEER INFANTRY.—*Continued.*

NAME.	RANK.	Co.	
Averill, Eben G...............	Private.	C	
Brackett, James H.............	Private.	C	
Brown, Albert C...............	Private.	C	
Brawn, Reuben W..............	Private.	C	
Brawn, Franklin...............	Private.	C	Disc. June 6, 1865.
Billington, Enoch N............	Private.	C	
Bishop, Alfred.................	Private.	C	
Brown, William................	Private.	C	
Bishop, Frederick..............	Private.	C	
Cyr, Joseph...................	Private.	C	
Cook, Edward C...............	Private.	C	
Downes, Charles N.............	Private.	C	Disc. June 30, 1865.
Duffee, James.................	Private.	C	Disc. July 18, 1865.
Driscoll, John.................	Private.	C	
Debleux, Louis................	Private.	C	
Davis, Lendell C...............	Private.	C	
Dillingham, John W............	Private.	C	
Freeman, Thomas O............	Private.	C	
English, William J.............	Private.	C	
Franquire, Andrew.............	Private.	C	
Ferguson, Francis..............	Private.	C	
Grant, William D..............	Private.	C	
Graves, John D................	Private.	C	
Gilman, Charles H.............	Private.	C	
Grant, Simon T................	Private.	C	
Glidden, Calvin A..............	Private.	C	Disc. June 6, 1865.
Grant, John...................	Private.	C	
Hanning, Frank................	Private.	C	
Harmon, Martin...............	Private.	C	
Hinkley, John C. Jr............	Private.	C	
Huntley, Isaac S...............	Private.	C	
Murray, Charles...............	Private.	C	
Rowe, William T...............	Private.	C	
Seavey, John..................	Private.	C	
Sweeno, Israel.................	Private.	C	
Taylor, Francis F..............	Private.	C	
Tracy, William A..............	Private.	C	
Varney, Charles T.............	Private.	C	
Warren, George................	Private.	C	
Brown, George.................	Private.	D	
Bryan, George.................	Private.	D	
Bell, George W................	Private.	D	
Blake, William................	Private.	D	
Belongey, Morris...............	Private.	D	
Briggs, Edward................	Private.	D	
Darby, Isaac H................	Private.	D	
Farris, Daniel, Jr..............	Private.	D	
Grant, Benjamin F.............	Private.	D	

SIXTEENTH MAINE REGIMENT. 301

ENLISTED MEN, whose term of service had not expired at muster-out of Sixteenth Regiment, June 5, 1865, transferred to TWENTIETH MAINE VOLUNTEER INFANTRY.—*Continued.*

NAME.	RANK.	Co.	
Houlahan, James H.	Private.	D	
Holt, Samuel.	Private.	D	
Jones, William G.	Private.	D	Disc. June 20, 1865.
Kneeland, Charles H.	Private.	D	
Kingsbury, Marcus D.	Private.	D	
Linniken, Rufus.	Private.	D	
Lee, Israel.	Private.	D	
Leaker, George.	Private.	D	
McKenney, Nicholas.	Private.	D	
McPherson, James.	Private.	D	
Moody, Frank.	Private.	D	
Martin, Richard H.	Private.	D	
Moody, David, Jr.	Private.	D	
Marshall, Charles.	Private.	D	
Mahoney, John.	Private.	D	
Mahoney, Dennis.	Private.	D	
Mylne, Alexander F.	Private.	D	
Monk, Alfred K.	Private.	D	Disc. June 26, 1865.
Newcomb, Alonzo.	Private.	D	
Pray, George H.	Private.	D	Disc. June 26, 1865.
Pollard, Andrew J.	Private.	D	
Parsons, Almond.	Private.	D	
Potter, Gabriel.	Private.	D	
Robertson, Stephen S.	Private.	D	
Seavey, Ezra S.	Private.	D	
Summers, Alger.	Private.	D	
Soule, Richard.	Private	D	
Achorn, Orlando R.	Private.	E	
Arnold, Isaac.	Private.	E	
Arnold, Joseph T.	Private.	E	
Baston, Franklin N.	Private.	E	
Bickmore, Daniel O.	Private.	E	
Burnham, William O.	Private.	E	
Berry, John.	Private.	E	
Cooley, Elisha.	Private.	E	Disc. June 20, 1865.
Cookson, Christopher C.	Private.	E	Disc. June 20, 1865.
Crocker, Elbridge P.	Private.	E	Disc. June 30, 1865.
Dorr, Henry A.	Corporal.	E	
Davis, Alvah M.	Private.	E	
Davis, Daniel, 2d.	Private.	E	
Davis, George T.	Private.	E	
Davis, Henry L.	Private.	E	
Downs, Ezekiel C.	Private.	E	
Fairbrother, Isaac H.	Private.	E	
Greenlow, George W.	Private.	E	
Getchell, Andrew.	Private.	E	
Gardiner, Enoch R.	Private.	E	
Hayden, John.	Private.	E	

ENLISTED MEN, whose term of service had not expired at muster-out of Sixteenth Regiment, June 5, 1865, transferred to TWENTIETH MAINE VOLUNTEER INFANTRY.—*Continued.*

NAME.	RANK.	Co.	
Hatch, George W	Private.	E	
Howard, James, Jr	Private.	E	
Jewell, Benjamin F	Private.	E	
Kelley, Hugh	Private.	E	
Kay, John M	Private.	E	
Kelley, James	Private.	E	
McKillop, Donald	Private.	E	
Manson, Frederick	Private.	E	
Montague, Frederick	Private.	E	
O'Brien, Dennis	Private.	E	
Rowe, Charles A	Private.	E	
Runnels, Andrew J	Private.	E	
Staples, Thomas D	Corporal.	E	
Sedeau, Paul	Private.	E	
Waite, John P	Private.	E	
Arkit, John	Corporal.	F	
Chadbourne, John W	Private.	F	
Crossman, Alfred M	Private.	F	
Douglass, Ashbell S	Private.	F	
Evans, Hiram F	Private.	F	
Fenderson, Joseph P	Private.	F	
Haley, Dennis	Private.	F	
Hammond, Edwin G	Private.	F	
Mark, Andrew	Private.	F	
Oban, Henry	Private.	F	
Page, Thomas D	Corporal.	F	
Pierce, Samuel	Private.	F	
Pickering, Albert	Private.	F	
Ploude, Joseph	Private.	F	
Sullivan, James	Private.	F	Disc. July 6, 1865.
Spaulding, Chauncey	Private.	F	
Soule, Charles C	Private.	F	
Stewart, Thomas	Private.	F	
Tibbetts, Joel	Private.	F	
Veancour, Desira S	Private.	F	
Woodward, Solomon	Private.	F	
Wilson, Charles	Private.	F	
Alden, Adelbert	Private.	G	
Beckwith, Joel	Private.	G	
Bickford, Stephen D	Private.	G	
Coharn, Timothy	Private.	G	
Doyle, Michael	Private.	G	
Dolan, Patrick H	Private.	G	
Dyer, William	Private.	G	
Faulkner, James E	Private.	G	
Gorman, James	Private.	G	
Goodridge, Noah	Private.	G	Died in Prison.
Hughes, James	Private.	G	Disc. June 21, 1865.

SIXTEENTH MAINE REGIMENT. 303

ENLISTED MEN, whose term of service had not expired at muster-out of Sixteenth Regiment, June 5, 1865, transferred to TWENTIETH MAINE VOLUNTEER INFANTRY.—*Continued.*

NAME.	RANK.	Co.	
Hall, Joseph A	Private.	G	
Hewett, Philo	Private.	G	
Jones, Frank	Private.	G	
Low, Sylvanus	Private.	G	
Levanseller, John	Private.	G	Disc. July 3, 1865.
Leavitt, Rodney	Private.	G	
Libbey, James	Private.	G	
Linton, Robert	Private.	G	
Leavitt, Zachary	Private.	G	
McGinley, John	Private.	G	
Mehegan, William	Private.	G	
McGauflin, James	Private.	G	
Nelson, Chester	Private.	G	
Orr, John	Private.	G	Disc. July 21, 1865.
Perham, William	Private.	G	Disc. June 10, 1865.
Porter, Lewis N	Private.	G	Disc. July 10, 1865.
Rogers, John L	Private.	G	
Rogers, William S. B	Private.	G	
Ryder, Eugene M	Corporal.	G	
Stevens, John	Private.	G	
Scott, David S	Private.	G	
Saunders, Francis E	Private.	G	
Seneque, Charles	Private.	G	
Shaw, Erastus M	Private.	G	Disc. July 6, 1865.
Shaff, Charles P	Private.	G	
Smith, James	Private.	G	Disc. July 20, 1865.
Smith, Joshua B	Private.	G	
Stone, Edwin F	Private.	G	
Stubbs, Zoeth E	Private.	G	
Sutherland, Augustus A	Private.	G	
Thorne, John H	Private.	G	Disc. June 8, 1865.
Treat, Albert	Private.	G	Disc. July 22, 1865.
Williams, John	Private.	G	
Wright, James	Private.	G	
Withee, Amos P	Private.	G	
Annis, William E	Corporal.	H	
Bailey, Isaiah	Private.	H	
Bradbury, John C	Private.	H	
Blacklock, Archibald	Private.	H	
Crampton, Charles	Private.	H	
Chandler, Josiah H	Private.	H	
Chase, Wilbur F	Private.	H	
Carey, Michael	Private.	H	
Connelly, John	Private.	H	
Campbell, William	Private.	H	
Donaghe, Andrew	Private.	H	
Dufour, Francis	Private.	H	
Dill, Albert E	Private.	H	

ENLISTED MEN, whose term of service had not expired at muster-out of Sixteenth Regiment, June 5, 1865, transferred to TWENTIETH MAINE VOLUNTEER INFANTRY.—*Continued.*

NAME.	RANK.	Co.	
Damon, Joshua	Private.	H	
Despres, John	Private.	H	
Dore, Charles B	Private.	H	
Fisher, William P	Private.	H	
Farley, John	Private.	H	
Garron, Solomon	Private.	H	
Gammon, Ralph H	Private.	H	
Galvin, John	Private.	H	
Graham, John R	Private.	H	
Gilbert, Lewis	Private.	H	
Gould, Charles H	Private.	H	
Goodwin, Charles, 2d	Private.	H	
Harrington, Edwin W	Private.	H	
Haley, John	Private.	H	
Hartnett, William	Private.	H	
Hart, Michael	Private.	H	
Heal, Henry A	Private.	H	
Hatch, Charles E	Private.	H	Disc. June 12, 1865.
Irish, Simeon	Private.	H	
Jenkins, Dennis A	Private.	H	
Jones, Frank	Private.	H	
Kaehner, Augustus	Private.	H	Disc. June 19, 1865.
Lagin, Hugh	Private.	H	
Martin, Alvin C	Private.	H	Disc. June 21, 1865.
Martin, John	Private.	H	
Maloney, James	Corporal.	H	
Nason, William H	Private.	H	
Nash, Jasper H	Private.	H	
Mahar, Simon	Private.	H	
McElroy, David	Private.	H	Disc. June 17, 1865.
Nelson, Frank E	Private.	H	
Philpot, Samuel D	Private.	H	
Randall, Charles	Private.	H	
Smith, Frank	Private.	H	
Sutter, Earnest	Private.	H	
True, Edward W	Private.	H	Disc. June 26, 1865.
Bovard, John	Private.	I	
Butterfield, Lowell	Corporal.	I	
Bryer, Andrew J	Private.	I	
Barnes, Ira	Private.	I	
Cleaves, Samuel B	Private.	I	
Conway, Hugh	Private.	I	
Cleaves, James R	Private.	I	
Cleveland, John S	Private.	I	
Clifford, Herman	Private.	I	
Corson, Joseph	Private.	I	
Crosby, Thomas	Private.	I	
Corliss, John S	Private.	I	

SIXTEENTH MAINE REGIMENT. 305

ENLISTED MEN, whose term of service had not expired at muster-out of Sixteenth Regiment, June 5, 1865, transferred to TWENTIETH MAINE VOLUNTEER INFANTRY.—*Continued.*

NAME.	RANK.	Co.	
Cleaves, William H. H.	Private.	I	
Cornish, Josiah	Private.	I	
Collins, Josiah	Private.	I	
Delaney, Thomas	Private.	I	
Dunn, John	Corporal.	I	
French, Stephen L.	Private.	I	
Farnclough, Joshua	Private.	I	
Gorman, Frank	Private.	I	Disc. July 12, 1865.
Hart, James	Private.	I	
Kelley, Patrick	Private.	I	
McDonald, John	Private.	I	
McLaughlin, William	Private.	I	
Parker, William B.	Private.	I	Disc. June 12, 1865.
Patterson, John	Private.	I	
Parshley, Frank B.	Private.	I	
Tiernay, Michael	Private.	I	
Thompson, James	Private.	I	
Williams, Thomas	Private.	I	
Walter, Thomas G.	Private.	I	
Abbott, Orson	Private.	K	
Berry, William	Private.	K	
Barnby, John B.	Private.	K	
Brady, James	Private.	K	
Bennett, Edwin A.	Private.	K	
Condon, Alfred	Private.	K	Disc. June 21, 1865.
Curran, John	Private.	K	Disc. June 12, 1865.
Cloyes, John F.	Private.	K	
Doble, Silas C.	Corporal.	K	
Doble, Roscoe	Corporal.	K	
Dunham, Hosea A.	Private.	K	
Dakin, James T.	Private.	K	
Emerson, Daniel	Corporal.	K	
Fowler, Timothy	Private.	K	
Foster, Stephen H.	Private.	K	
Graham, Henry	Private.	K	
Greenlief, Daniel	Private.	K	
Gliddon, Lewis	Private.	K	
Ham, Herbert J.	Private.	K	Disc. June 12, 1865.
Hopkinson, Henry M.	Private.	K	Disc. June 28, 1865.
Haney, Thomas	Private.	K	
Howard, Augustus A.	Private.	K	
Haley, Ebenezer	Private.	K	
Hopkins, Daniel	Private.	K	Disc. June 28, 1865.
Howard, Anson H.	Private.	K	
Henderson, William	Private.	K	
Holmes, John	Private.	K	
Johnson, Charles	Private.	K	
Lyons, Eli C.	Corporal.	K	

ENLISTED MEN, whose term of service had not expired at muster-out of Sixteenth Regiment, June 5, 1865, transferred to TWENTIETH MAINE VOLUNTEER INFANTRY.—*Continued.*

NAME.	RANK.	Co.	
Molton, Daniel W	Private.	K	
Mortimer, Richard	Private.	K	Disc. June 29, 1865.
Nason, John T	Private.	K	
Olscamp, Joseph B	Private.	K	
Poole, Benjamin F	Private.	K	
Page, Rufus E	Private.	K	
Quirk, John	Private.	K	
Robinson, Fred C	Private.	K	
Redding, Ebenezer	Private.	K	
Stinchfield, Thomas F	Private.	K	
Smith, William	Private.	K	
St. John, William	Private.	K	
Shuman, James M	Private.	K	
True, William A	Private.	K	
Twist, John A	Private.	K	
Webster, George W	Private.	K	
Wilson, John	Private.	K	

Transferred to the INVALID CORPS from Sixteenth Maine Regiment.

NAME.	Rank.	Co.	No. of Order.	Date of order.
Blake, Willard L................	Private.	G	202	July 1, '63
Benson, James S................	Private.	B	221	July 16, '63
Bickford, Warren C.............	Private.	F	283	Aug. 11, '63
Butters, James M...............	Private.	D	302	Sept. 7, '63
Bumps, John K.................	Private.	I	319	Sept. 25, '63
Buck, Franklin.................	Private.	D	320	Sept. 26, '63
Bowden, Lorenzo D.............	Private.	K	358	Nov. 6, '63
Bryant, Francis A..............	Private.	C	358	Nov. 6, '63
Bailey, Albion..................	Private.	A	394	Dec. 12, '63
Bettel, Robert..................	Private.	K	394	Dec. 12, '63
Blodgett, John J................	Corporal.	K	324	Dec. 12, '63
Cotton, Andrew J...............	Private.	I	202	July 1, '63
Churchill, Charles C............	Private.	I	358	Nov. 6, '63
Clement, Charles W............	Private.	A	394	Dec. 12, '63
Crockett, Benjamin B..........	Private.	I	394	Dec. 12, '63
Davis, Norman A...............	Private.	I	202	July 1, '63
Dorritt, George H...............	Private.	K	202	July 1, '63
Drury, George F................	Private.	C	216	Sept. 3, '63
Everett, Jonas H................	Private.	H	202	July 1, '63
Fox, James E...................	Private.	A	302	Sept. 7, '63
Farrar, Benjamin F.............	Corporal.	I	320	Sept. 26, '63
Grindall, Robert................	Private.	C	202	Sept. 7, '63
Galvin, John....................	Private.	I	365	Nov. 13, '63
Gleason, Sumner A.............	Private.	G	370	Nov. 18, '63
Glidden, Samuel S..............	Private.	B	370	Nov. 18, '63
Hussey, B......................	Corporal.	A	289	Aug. 19, '63
Harris, Chauncy A..............	Private.	C	296	Sept. 3, '63
Hamlin, Edward L..............	Private.	D	302	Sept. 7, '63
Hodsden, Clarence L............	Private.	H	302	Sept. 7, '63
Hooker, George H...............	Corporal.	B	394	Dec. 12, '63
Jewett, Isaac F..................	Corporal.	D	307	Sept. 12, '63
Lane, John T...................	Private.	K	221	July 16, '63
Lancaster, Bradford F...........	Private.	F	302	Sept. 7, '63
Lufkin, Johnson H..............	Corporal.	K	302	Sept. 7, '63
Locke, Edward A...............	Private.	F	312	Sept. 16, '63
Livingstone, L. D...............	Private.	F	365	Nov. 13, '63
McDonley, John................	Private.	B	302	Sept. 7, '63
McFarland, Albert..............	Private.	B	302	Sept. 7, '63
Mace, J. W.....................	Private.	G	358	Nov. 6, '63
Plummer, William S............	Corporal.	A	221	July 16, '63
Phelps, Lewis G................	Private.	G	235	July 27, '63
Pike, F.........................	Private.	F	235	July 27, '63
Prince, Edward M..............	Private.	A	296	Sept. 3, '63
Pratt, Henry L..................	Private.	A	302	Sept. 7, '63
Pratt, Sarson C.................	Private.	E	302	Sept. 7, '63
Russell, Ceylon.................	Private.	D	358	Nov. 6, '63
Sibley, John F..................	Private.	A	271	Aug. 5, '63
Smith, Lyman..................	Private.	H	302	Sept. 7, '63
Stackpole, Aaron...............	Private.	B	302	Sept. 7, '63
Sargent, Benjamin W...........	Private.	G	312	Sept. 16, '63
Smith, James O.................	Private.	I	394	Dec. 12, '63

Transferred to the INVALID CORPS from Sixteenth Maine Regiment.
—*Continued.*

NAME.	Rank.	Co.	No. of Order.	Date of order.
Simms, Joseph	Private.	H	394	Dec. 12, '63
Turner, John C	Corporal.	A	394	Dec. 12, '63
Wade, Nelson H	Private.	I	302	Sept. 7, '63
Winship, Enoch L	Private.	C	370	Nov. 18, '63
Whitney, William L	Sergeant.	I	394	Dec. 12, '63
Yeaton, James A	Private.	D	307	Sept. 12, '63
Young, E. M	Sergeant.	A	358	Nov. 6, '63

ENLISTED MEN, transferred from Sixteenth Maine Regiment to U. S. NAVY, April 22, 1864.

NAME.	RANK.	COMPANY
Achorn, Jacob B	Private.	A
Barrett, William	Private.	A
Downey, John	Private.	A
Fletcher, Benjamin F	Private.	A
Hill, Charles A	Private.	A
Reed, Benjamin F	Private.	A
Riley, James	Private.	A
Smith, William S	Private.	A
Silver, William S	Private.	A
Minnack, William	Private.	B
Norcross, Albert H	Private.	B
Minnick, John	Private.	B
Doherty, William	Private.	C
Hamilton, George	Private.	C
McGowell, William	Private.	C
Dane, Francis S	Private.	E
Lewis, Benjamin	Private.	E
Mullin, John	Private.	G
Sanders, Richard	Private.	G
Sidney, John	Private.	G
Johnson, George	Private.	H
Tobin, John	Private.	H
Wentworth, John B	Private.	I
Grey, Judson	Private.	K
Hatch, Mark E	Private.	K
Hamlin, James H	Private.	K
McGuire, James	Private.	K
Moffit, Hudson	Private.	K
Peterson, Hans	Private.	K
Phillips, John	Private.	K
Simons, Gilbert	Private.	K

SIXTEENTH MAINE REGIMENT. 309

ENLISTED MEN, transferred from Sixteenth Maine Regiment to the
VETERAN RESERVE CORPS.

NAME.	RANK.	Co.	DATE.
Allen, Charles W	Private.	I	February 16, 1865.
Allen, Benjamin F	Private.	F	March 15, 1864.
Allen, William	Private.	I	August 29, 1864.
Bryant, Francis A	Private.	C	
Brann, Emery M	Private.	B	September 21, 1863.
Black, Moses B	Private.	C	
Balentine, William	Sergeant.	E	January 1, 1865.
Blodgett, John J	Corporal.	K	December 15, 1863.
Bethel, Robert	Private.	K	
Bowden, Lorenzo D	Private.	K	
Crowell, John H	Private.	B	
Choate, Charles E	Corporal.	E	
Collins, George	Private.	G	March 15, 1865.
Churchill, Charles C	Private.	I	November 15, 1863.
Cotton, Andrew J	Private.	I	July 1, 1863.
Crockett, Benjamin B	Private.	I	December 15, 1864.
Davis, Robert	Private.	I	January 15, 1864.
Devereaux, Charles A	Corporal.	K	February 15, 1864.
Dow, Reuben A	Private.	K	
Farnham, George H	Corporal.	C	February 11, 1863.
Farrar, Benjamin F	Private.	I	September 30, 1864.
Griffin, Roscoe T	Private.	H	September 4, 1863.
Gliddon, Samuel S	Private.	B	
Gross, Leonard	Private.	C	
Galvin, John	Private.	I	May 15, 1863.
Hooker, George H	Corporal.	B	
Holbrook, Israel W	Private.	B	
Hopkins, Thomas S	Private.	C	May 31, 1864.
Heath, John	Private.	E	March 16, 1864.
Hodgkins, Jacob T	Private.	G	November 28, 1864.
Holmes, Wallace L	Private.	G	March 18, 1864.
Holmes, Robert	Private.	H	
Howard, Elias	Private.	I	April 23, 1864.
Johnson, Benjamin W	Musician.	E	September 30, 1864.
Lyon, Charles C	Private.	E	February 15, 1865.
Lombard, William F	Sergeant.	D	March 28, 1865.
Lane, John T	Private.	K	July 1, 1863.
Maloon, Stephen	Private.	B	
Mulayhan, Thomas	Private.	D	
Merritt, Samuel	Private.	G	March 15, 1865.
Pollard, Lyman B	Private.	G	August 24, 1863.
Pettengill, Samuel W	Private.	E	December 15, 1864.
Pratt, Sarson C	Private.	E	September 28, 1864.
Powers, Roderick	Private.	I	May 1, 1865.
Pierson, Charles	Private.	K	
Reed, Elias	Private.	C	July 11, 1864.
Ricker, Joseph A	Sergeant.	G	November 26, 1864.
Smith, Robert M	Private.	C	
Shadduck, George H	Private.	H	
Salley, Hiram S	Private.	H	

ENLISTED MEN, transferred from Sixteenth Maine Regiment to the
VETERAN RESERVE CORPS.—*Continued.*

NAME.	Rank.	Co.	Date.
Simms, Joseph E	Private.	H	
Stevens, Albert C	Corporal.	K	March 15, 1864.
Sargent, Benjamin W	Private.	K	
Tebbetts, William A	Private.	E	March 19, 1864.
Tuttle, John	Private.	C	June 15, 1864.
Tibbetts, Sheldron H	Private.	F	January 22, 1864.
Tibbetts, Isaac F	Private.	G	
Varney, Alfred W	Private.	I	May 1, 1865.
Varnum, Joseph B	Sergeant.	K	December 30, 1864.
Witham, Sidney	Private.	C	
Ward, Sylvanus H	Private.	E	January 1, 1865.
Witherell, Daniel	Private.	E	April 20, 1863.
Wade, Nelson H	Private.	I	September 29, 1863.
Webber, Cyrus K	Private.	K	

BURIAL PLACE OF THE MARTYRED DEAD.
NATIONAL CEMETERIES AT WASHINGTON, D. C.

The U. S. M. Asylum Cemetery is situated about two miles northeast of the city. The Harmony Cemetery is about one mile and a half from city on Bladensburg road. The Arlington Cemetery is on the Lee Estate, in Virginia, three miles from city.

NAMES.	Co.	DIED.	PLACE OF BURIAL.	
Burgess, A...........	E	Dec. 26, '62	U. S. M. Asylum.	Wounds.
Brown, Charles.......	D	May 2, '64	U. S. M. Asylum.	
Babcock, L. J........	E	Nov. '64	National, Arlington	
Clark, M. V. B.......	C	Dec. 30, '62	U. S. M. Asylum.	Wounds.
Cobb, Daniel.........	H	Feb. 6, '63	U. S. M. Asylum.	
Chase, M. O..........	C	Dec. 22, '63	U. S. M. Asylum.	
Cole, L. H...........	E	Mar. 29, '64	U. S. M. Asylum.	
Cousins, T. D........	K	Sept. 5, '62	U. S. M. Asylum.	
Dow, J. E............	F	April 26, '64	Harmony.	
Davis, A. C..........	C	Aug. 6, '64	National, Arlington	
Eaton, J.............	G	July 8, '64	National, Arlington	
Farrar, Edwin C......	D	Dec. 26, '62	U. S. M. Asylum.	Wounds.
Furbush, William.....	G	Jan. 13, '63	U. S. M. Asylum.	
Goodridge, Noah......	G	Feb. 14, '63	U. S. M. Asylum.	
Garland, A...........	H	Feb. 6, '64	U. S. M. Asylum.	
Green, W. H..........	G	Feb. 4, '64	U. S. M. Asylum.	
Getchell, O..........	C	Aug. 30, '64	National, Arlington	
Hutchinson, F........	A	Dec. 24, '64	National, Arlington	
Hart, G..............	E	May 5, '65	National, Arlington	
Hendrix, M. K........	G	May 14, '65	National, Arlington	
Johnson, William.....	I	Oct. 23, '62	U. S. M. Asylum.	
James, Charles E.....	E	Jan. 3, '63	U. S. M. Asylum.	Wounds.
Jones, M.............	K	Jan. 16, '63	U. S. M. Asylum.	
Kingsbury, J. J......	H	May 10, '64	U. S. M. Asylum.	
Luce, Thomas.........	C	Nov. 17, '62	U. S. M. Asylum.	
Lurvey, J. H.........	B	Mar. 19, '64	U. S. M. Asylum.	
Love, William........	G	May 26, '64	National, Arlington	
Leavitt, Arch. D.....	Maj.	May 31, '64	National, Arlington	
Lawrence, H. B.......	G	Dec. 6, '64	National, Arlington	
Mann, A. A...........	A	April 23, '65	National, Arlington	
Norton, Benjamin.....	G	Oct. 21, '62	U. S. M. Asylum.	
Palmer, Corp. Chas. F.	K	May 22, '64	National, Arlington	
Pierce, C. R.........	F	June 14, '64	National, Arlington	
Reed, John W.........	C	Jan. 6, '63	U. S. M. Asylum.	
Ramsdell, H..........	C	Jan. 10, '63	U. S. M. Asylum.	
Smith, James.........	A	Dec. 14, '62	U. S. M. Asylum.	
Soper, Joel..........	C	Dec. 26, '62	U. S. M. Asylum	
Scott, William A.....	K	Jan. 5, '63	U. S. M. Asylum.	
Sweatt, John.........	A	Jan. 22, '63	U. S. M. Asylum.	
Spaulding, D.........	K	May 29, '64	National, Arlington	
Taylor, H. W.........	G	Oct. 27, '63	U. S. M. Asylum.	
Warren, H. S.........	A	Oct. 26, '63	U. S. M. Asylum.	
Worth, Francis.......	E	Jan. 14, '64	U. S. M. Asylum.	
Wentworth, F.........	A	Jan. 6, '65	National, Arlington	
Whitaker, Z. P.......	B	Feb. 24, '65	National, Arlington	
Young, L. P..........	I	Dec. 28, '63	U. S. M. Asylum.	

NATIONAL CEMETERY, ALEXANDRIA, VA.

Contains 3,691 graves. Situated in the southwestern suburbs of the city; has been laid off into blocks and ranges similar to the National Cemetery in Washington. Well kept gravel walks traverse the grounds. The graves have been sodded, and white tablets lettered in black are placed at the head of each, giving name, rank, regiment, and date of death.

No. of Grave.	NAME.	Co.	DIED.	PLACE OF BURIAL.
619	Bigelow, W. H.	G	Dec. 24, '62	National, Alexan'a.
1049	Chase, Wesley C.	I	Nov. 11, '63	National, Alexan'a.
642	Cole, Benjamin W.	K	Dec. 9, '62	National, Alexan'a.
643	Coston, Samuel L. C.	A	Dec. 30, '62	National, Alexan'a.
3261	Day, Alson L.	B	June 24, '65	National, Alexan'a.
633	Dyer, Israel F.	G	Dec. 21, '62	National, Alexan'a.
655	Jewett, Warren	I	Jan. 2, '63	National, Alexan'a.
1767	Kyle, James S.	A	Apr. 21, '64	National, Alexan'a.
699	Luce, Augustus	C	Jan. 24, '63	National, Alexan'a.
1074	Perry, Clark E.	F	Nov. 30, '63	National, Alexan'a.
657	Towers, William H.	G	Jan. 3, '63	National, Alexan'a.

BURIED FROM LIBBY AND CAMP LAWTON PRISONS,

AT CITY POINT, AND IN THE FIELD BEFORE PETERSBURGH AND RICHMOND, VA.

Belle Isle: This cemetery has been fenced in by the U. S. C. C., but the head-boards remain as when the city was occupied, the names being carved in, not painted.

NAME.	Co.	DIED.	PLACE OF BURIAL.
Bartlette, Nathaniel.	C	Dec. 10, '63	Belle Isle.
Brown, W*	A	Feb. 1, '64	Depot Field Hosp., City Point.
Cobb, A.	E	July 25, '64	Depot Field Hosp., City Point.
Crane, F. A.	C	Jan. 13, '65	Depot Field Hosp., City Point.
Frost, G. W.	I	Nov. 3, '64	Depot Field Hosp., City Point.
Gilbert, William	K	Feb. 7, '65	In Mrs. Cummings' lot, Gardiner, Maine.
Huff, C. H.	A	Jan. 2, '64	Depot Field Hosp., City Point.
Howland, E.	I	Feb. 21, '65	Depot Field Hosp., City Point.
Libby, Richard	B	Jan. 29, '65	Near Aiken's House.
Shender, B†	I	Jan. 9, '64	Belle Isle.
Warren, C. A.	F	Oct. 7, '6	Camp Lawton, Millen, Georgia.
Allen, J. O.	C	April 27, '65	Hampton, Virginia.

* John S. of Company I (?).
† Oliver Stover, Company I, Dec. 9, 1864 (?).

NATIONAL CEMETERY, GETTYSBURGH.

This cemetery occupies seventeen acres on Cemetery Hill. In laying out the grounds a semi-circular form was adopted; the head of each body pointing toward a common center, the National Monument. The work of disinterring and reinterring the Union dead was begun October 7th, 1863, and completed in about five months. Many of the bodies then in unmarked graves we identified by means of papers, letters, photographs, etc., and marks found on their clothing. The cemetery was dedicated Nov. 19th, 1863.

No. of Grave.	NAME.	Co.	DIED.	PLACE OF BURIAL.
Sec. A, 1	Corp. Frank Devereux.	K	July 1, '63	National Cemetery.
Sec. A, 17	Frank Fairbrother	G	July 9, '63	National Cemetery.
Sec. A, 3	George D. Marston	I	July 9, '63	National Cemetery.
Sec. A, 4	Unknown		July 9, '63	National Cemetery.
Sec. D, 8	Wm. H. Huntingdon	B	July 9, '63	National Cemetery.
Sec. D, 9	Harrison Pullen	G	July 18, '63	National Cemetery.
Sec. G,	Albion B. Mills	B	Oct. 7, '63	National Cemetery.

NATIONAL CEMETERY, ANDERSONVILLE, GEORGIA.

Contains the graves of the "martyred dead" at Andersonville, Georgia, and is about three hundred yards distant from the Stockade, where our soldiers were held as prisoners. The graves cover a space of nine acres.

No. of Grave.	NAME.	Co.	DIED.	PLACE OF BURIAL.
12,055	Boren,* W	I	Nov. 13, '64	National Cemetery.
11,980	Bryant, C. F	E	Nov. 13, '64	National Cemetery.
6,950	Condon, William H	G	Aug. 26, '64	National Cemetery.
8,625	Curtis, John	I	Sept. 13, '64	National Cemetery.
12,367	Cutts, O. M	D	Jan. 1, '65	National Cemetery.
8,145	Foster, E. R	C	Sept. 8, '64	National Cemetery.
7,073	Foster, Samuel A	K	Aug. 28, '64	National Cemetery.
7,301	Grant, B. Frank	F	Aug. 30, '64	National Cemetery.
5,355	Ingalls, L†	H	Aug. 11, '64	National Cemetery.
7,967	Lincoln, A	I	Sept. 6, '64	National Cemetery.
709	Malcom, H. M‡	A	April 24, '64	National Cemetery.
2,131	O'Brien, W§	A	June 18, '64	National Cemetery.
7,979	Parsons, James W	D	Sept. 6, '64	National Cemetery.
8,441	Pulverman, G‖	D	Sept. 11, '64	National Cemetery.
3,639	Wilson, G. W	H	July 20, '64	National Cemetery.
2,095	Wyman, W¶	A	June 17, '64	National Cemetery.

* Probably Borne.
† Does not appear on rolls.
‡ Probably W. A. Malcomb, Company D.
§ Probably James O'Brien.
‖ Does not appear on rolls.
¶ Probably James R. Wyman, Company D.

BURIED IN MAINE, NEW YORK, AND MARYLAND.

No. of Grave.	NAME.	Co.	DIED.	PLACE OF BURIAL.
2	Booker, Asa..........	I	May 23, '64	Davids Island, N. Y.
16	Davis, Stillman P.....	B	May 4, '65	Augusta, Maine.
471	Fales, Curtis V.......	E	Oct. 12, '63	Annapolis, Maryland.
661	Hatch, Horace J......	H	Feb. 3, '63	Annapolis, Maryland.
1,145	Patten, Lora S........	I	March 3, '64	Annapolis, Maryland.
507	Phelps, Lewis G......	G	July 29, '63	Dept. of the East.
1,336	Scudder, Silas H......	C	Mar. 14, '64	Annapolis, Maryland.
1,511	Tabor, C. H..........	B	Sept. 17, '63	Annapolis, Maryland.
1,605	Ward, W. W..........	F	Oct. 10, '63	Annapolis, Maryland.
430	Whitten, M. L........	H	April 7, '63	Camp Parole, Annap.

LIST OF DECEASED SINCE MUSTER-IN.

List of members of Sixteenth Maine Regiment deceased from date of organization to date of muster-out, June 5, 1865.

NAMES.	Co.	Date.	Cause.	
MAJOR.				
Arch. D. Leavitt............		May 31, '64	Wounds.	Hospital, Wash'n.
CAPTAINS.				
Charles A. Williams....	A	Nov. 10, '62	Disease.	Rhorersville, Md.
Charles K. Hutchins....	B	Dec. 13, '62	Killed.	Fredericksb'h, Va.
Moses W. Rand	D	Dec. 8, '62	Disease.	
Oliver H. Lowell.......	D	July 1, '63	Killed.	Gettysburgh, Pa.
William A. Stevens....	E	June 17, '64	Killed.	Front of Petersburgh, Virginia.
John Ayer.............	H	Feb. 22, '63	Wounds.	Libby Prison, Richmond, Virginia.
Stephen C. Whitehouse	K	July 1, '63	Killed.	Gettysburgh, Pa.
FIRST LIEUTENANTS.				
Nathaniel W. Coston...	A	May 27, '64	Wounds.	
George W. Edwards....	B	May 27, '63	Wounds.	Richmond, Va.
SECOND LIEUTENANT.				
Henry P. Herrick......	D	Dec. 13, '62	Killed.	Fredericksb'h, Va.
SERGEANT-MAJOR.				
Edwin C. Stevens.........		Aug. 18, '6	Killed.	Weldon Railroad.
PRIVATES.				
Atkinson, Alonzo P....	C	Nov. 7, '64	Disease.	
Allen, J. O	C	Apr. 27, '65	......	Hampton, Va.
Adams, Melvin........	C	Dec. 13, '62	Killed.	
Adams, Hazen.	D	Nov. 5, '63	......	
Adkins, Charles A.....	B	Dec. 5, '62	Disease.	
Andrews, James M.....	E	Dec. 13, '62	Killed.	
Andrews, Abram S.....	F	Nov. 2, '63	......	Prisoner.
Banks, Ezekiel H.......	H	Dec. 16, '62	......	Falmouth, Va.
Banks, Jeremiah.......	I	Dec. 17, '64	......	Prisoner.
Babcock, Luther J.....	E	Nov. '64		
Bailey, Stillman W.....	D	Dec. 13, '62	Killed.	
Barrows, Silas M.......	C	Dec. 13, '62	Killed.	
Barnes, Darius........	A	Jan. 15, '64	......	
Bartlett, Nathan jr.....	C	Dec. 10, '63	......	Prisoner.
Barker, Levi D........	F	Dec. 18, '63	......	Prisoner.
Bates, William T.......	E	July 1, '63	Killed.	
Batchelder, William H..	I	Sept. 25, '64	Wounds.	
Bean, Shepard B.......	C	Dec. 13, '62	Killed.	
Bell, James............	E	Apr. 17, '65	Disease.	
Benson, Oran..........	F	May 7, '65	Wounds.	
Berry, Charles R.......	E	Dec. 25, '62	Wounds.	
Berry, George H.......	B	Dec. '62	Wounds.	
Bickford, Elisha F.....	K	July 1, '63	Killed.	
Bigelow, William H....	G	Dec. 23, '62	Wounds.	
Blanchard, Charles M..	C	May 8, '64	Killed.	
Blake, Frederick W. C..	F	Feb. 1, '64	......	
Blackwell, William T...	C	May 9, '64	Disease.	
Blodgett, Lorenzo D ...	E	Nov. 1, '63	Disease.	
Blodgett, Hamlin L....	E	May 15, '65	Disease.	
Bodson, William.......	D	Jan. 7, '65	......	

List of members of Sixteenth Maine Regiment deceased from date of organization to date of muster out, June 5, 1865.—*Continued.*

NAMES.	Co.	DATE.	CAUSE.	
Bodge, Bradford S	H	May 8, '64	Wounds.	
Booker, Asa	I	Apr. 23, '64		
Bowden, Christopher	K	Dec. 24, '62	Wounds.	
Bowden, Frank M	K	July 20, '63	Wounds.	
Boyd, John	B	Dec. 17, '64	Disease.	
Boyle, Barney	G	Apr. 1, '65	Disease.	
Brackett, Freeman	H	Nov. 22, '65		
Brann, Peter B	I	Dec. 1, '63		
Briggs, Araunah	I	Feb. 18, '65	Disease.	Salisbury, N. C.
Brocklebank, Nathan	F	July 30, '63		
Brown, Wilson	G	Dec. 13, '62	Wounds.	
Brown, Charles	D	May 2, '64		Washington.
Brown, John S	I	Nov. '63		Richmond, Va.
Brown, Walter M	K	Dec. 5, '63	Disease.	
Brown, Hezekiah	K	Oct. 18, '64	Disease.	
Born, William	I	1864		Mine Run.
Bryant, Charles F	E	Nov. 13, '64		
Bumps, John K	I	1864		
Burgess, Ambrose	E	Dec. 26, '62		Washington.
Burrows, Silas M	C	Dec. 13, '62	Killed.	
Butterfield, Henry J	C	July 1, '63	Killed.	
Butterfield, Martin	C	Nov. 22, '64	Disease.	
Butters, Timothy	D	Nov. 29, '64		
Butler, Henry B	K	Mar. 2, '65	Wounds.	
Campbell, Thomas	I	Jan. 4, '65		
Canwell, William	F	July 1, '63	Killed.	
Chase, Wesley C	I	Nov. 10, '63		
Chandler, Henry A	H	Mar. 1, '65		
Chandler, Roscoe	I	Apr. 7, '64		Belle Isle, Va.
Chaney, Farwell	C	Mar. 10, '64		
Chase, Miles O	C	Dec. 22, '63	Disease.	Washington.
Clark, Benjamin F	K	Mar. 22, '63	Disease.	
Clark, Martin V. B	C	Dec. 30, '62	Wounds.	Washington.
Clark, John	H	Jan. 7, '64	Disease.	
Coston, Samuel L	A	Dec. 30, '62		
Cousins, T. D	K	Sept. 5, '62		
Cleveland, Joseph L	G	1863		
Coakley, John	A	June 3, '64	Killed.	
Cobb, Daniel	H	Feb. 6, '63		
Cobb, Amasa	E	July 25, '64		City Point, Va.
Cole, Benjamin W	K	Dec. 27, '62	Wounds.	
Cole, Lemuel N	E	Mar. 29, '64		
Cole, Ezekiel L	C	Feb. 18, '65	Disease.	
Condon, William H	G	Aug. 26, '64	Wounds.	
Corbett, Charles P	G	Oct. 24, '62		Smoketown.
Crane, Francis A	I	Jan. 15, '65	Disease.	
Crabb, William H	E	Jan. 21, '64		In Camp.
Cunningham, Owen	A	Dec. 13, '62	Killed.	
Cunningham, Daniel C.	A	Feb. 5, '63	Disease.	
Cunningham, Edward	K	Dec. 15, '63	Disease.	Richmond, Va.

SIXTEENTH MAINE REGIMENT. 317

List of members of Sixteenth Maine Regiment deceased from date of organization to date of muster-out, June 5, 1865.—*Continued*.

NAMES.	Co.	DATE.	CAUSE.	
Curtis, John	I	Sept. 13, '64		Richmond, Va.
Curtis, Sylvanus	C	Dec. 13, '62	Killed.	
Cushman, Phyletus F.	E	Dec. 13, '62	Killed.	
Cutts, Oliver W.	D	Jan. 1, '65		
Damon, Edward	G	Dec. 13, '62	Killed.	
Daniels, Lorrain A.	E	Mar. 6, '63		
Davis, Josiah B.	F	June '63		
Davis, Stillman P.	B	Jan. 4, '65	Suicide.	Cony Hospital, Augusta, Maine.
Davis, Ambrose C.	C	Aug. 25, '64	Wounds.	
Davis, James	C	May 8, '64	Killed.	
Day, Darius	H	Mar. 3, '63		
Dearborn, George J.	H	Mar. 1, '63		
Dee, Nicholas	D	Feb. 21, '64		
Deuphsea, Charles H.	H	Dec. 13, '62	Killed.	
Devereux, Frank	K	July 1, '63	Killed.	
Dilling, James T.	I	Jan. 19, '65		
Dillingham, Andrew J.	C	May 10, '64	Killed.	
Day, Alson L.	B	June 24, '65		
Doe, Lewis B.	E	Jan. 4, '63	Accident.	
Downey, John	D	July 1, '63	Killed.	
Dow, John E.	F	Mar. 26, '64		
Drew, Isaac	K	Jan. 8, '64		
Dugan, Martin W.	H	Jan. 15, '64	Disease.	
Dunn, Rufus R.	C	July 21, '64		Richmond, Va.
Durgin, John M.	H	Mar. 10, '63		
Dutton, James W.	I	Dec. 16, '64		
Dyer, Israel F.	G	Dec. 21, '62	Wounds.	
Eastman, Sylvester	D	Dec. 13, '62	Killed.	
Eaton, John	G	July 8, '64		Washington.
Emery, Solomon G.	A	Dec. 3, '63		Washington.
Engels, Louis	H	Aug. 11, '64		
Erskine, Thomas G.	C	June 26, '64	Wounds.	
Estes, Jeremiah	I	Nov. '64		Annapolis, Md.
Etter, William B.	D	Jan. 23, '63	Wounds.	
Evans, Charles E.	H			
Fairbrother, Frank	G	July 9, '63	Wounds.	
Fales, Curtis V.	E	Oct. 12, '63		
Farrar, Edwin	D	Dec. 26, '62	Wounds.	
Farrington, Reuben	B		Disease.	China, Maine.
Farrar, William	C	Jan. 29, '65		
Fife, Nathan J.	H	Jan. 9, '63		
Fifield, Samuel H.	C	Dec. 29, '62		
Fish, Lorenzo S.	D	Dec. 13, '62	Killed.	
Fiske, Henry D.	C	Jan. 21, '65		
Fogg, Simon	C	Jan. 15, '65	Disease.	
Fossett, Robert M.	E	Oct. 25, '62		
Foster, Cyrus J.	C	1863	Wounds.	
Foster, Edwin R.	C	Sept. 8, '64		
Foss, James C.	H	May 12, '64	Killed.	

List of members of Sixteenth Maine Regiment deceased from date of organization to date of muster-out, June 5, 1865.—*Continued.*

NAMES.	Co.	DATE.	CAUSE.	
Foster, Samuel A	K	Aug. 27, '64		Prisoner.
Freese, Retire jr	H	May 10, '64	Killed.	
Frost, George W	I	Nov. 3, '64	Disease.	
Furbish, William A	G	Jan. 13, '63	Wounds.	
Garland, Albert	H	Feb. 6, '64		Washington.
Garcelon, Benjamin F	I	Nov. 24, '64		Prisoner.
Getchell, Calvin	A	Dec. 13, '62	Killed.	
Getchell, Otis	C	Aug. 30, '64		
Gibbs, Thomas A	G	Dec. 9, '63		
Gilbert, William	K	Feb. 7, '65		
Gould, William A	D	May 10, '64	Killed.	
Gould, Edmund	G	May 10, '64	Killed.	
Gray, Samuel jr	D	July 1, '63	Killed.	
Grant, Benjamin F	F	Aug. 31, '64		Andersonville, Ga.
Greaton, Harrison M	C	Dec. 13, '62	Killed.	
Gregory, John	K	Jan. 12, '63		
Green, William H	G	Feb. 4, '64	Disease.	
Guilford, Hiram	F	Dec. 13, '62	Killed.	
Guilford, Lester	A	Feb. 6, '64	Killed.	
Hackett, Orison W	I			
Hackett, Alden	B	Dec. 17, '64	Disease.	
Hall, Abner E	B	Oct. 16, '64		
Hamilton, Edwin W	H	Feb. 9, '65	Disease.	
Hanks, Jason	A	Jan. 22, '63	Disease.	
Hanson, Charles W	C	Dec. 5, '62		
Harriman, Frank S	H	Jan. 10, '64	Disease.	
Hartwell, John	E		Killed.	Steamer Gen. Lyon
Hart, George	E	May 5, '65		Washington.
Harding, John F	F	Feb. 21, '65	Killed.	
Hatch, Horace J	H	Feb. 3, '63	Wounds.	
Hathorn, Robert H	C	June 20, '64	Killed.	
Heath, Alvan M. C	B	Dec. 13, '62	Killed.	
Hendrix, Martin K	G	May 14, '65		
Higgins, Freeman E	I	Apr. 24, '64		
Hinds, David H	C	Nov. 24, '64		
Hobart, Austin W	D	Dec. 14, '64		
Hobbs, Dorillus	C	Nov. 19, '63		Richmond, Va.
Hodsdon, Samuel L	E	Mar. 9, '64		
Holbrook, Isaac	G	Dec. 17, '63	Disease.	
Houston, Hiram H	E	Jan. 3, '63	Disease.	
Houston, Lorenzo C	G	Dec. 13, '62	Killed.	
Howland, Enoch	I	Feb. 24, '65	Wounds.	
Hoyt, Lemuel T	H	Apr. 1, '65		
Huff, Leonard	C	1863		Alexandria, Va.
Huff, Charles H	A	Jan. 2, '64		
Humphrey, Elias	C	Jan. 9, '65		
Huntington, William H	B	July 9, '63		
Hussey, George G. jr	E	Oct. 28, '62		
Huston, James T	D	Feb. 8, '63		
Hutchinson, Fred'k A	A	Dec. 24, '64		

SIXTEENTH MAINE REGIMENT.

List of members of Sixteenth Maine Regiment deceased from date of organization to date of muster-out, June 5, 1865.—*Continued.*

NAMES.	Co.	DATE.	CAUSE.	
Hutchinson, Benj. F.	B	Feb. 7, '65	Killed.	
James, Charles E.	E	Jan. 26, '63	Wounds.	
Johnson, William	I	Oct. 23, '62		
Johnson, Frank B.	E	Dec. 26, '62	Wounds.	
Johnson, Martin A.	K	Feb. 6, '65	Disease.	
Jones, Greenlief T.	D	Jan. 30, '63		
Jones, Medbury	K	Jan. 16, '63	Wounds.	
Judkins, Henry F.	E	Jan. 5, '65		
Judkins, Alonzo	G	Dec. 14, '63	Disease.	
Kenniston, Leonard E.	H	Jan. 1, '63		
Kenniston, Thomas E.	H	Jan. 23, '63		
Ketch, Richard	G	Feb. 20, '65		
Kingsbury, James J.	H	May 10, '64		Washington.
Kitchen, Charles A.	C	Jan. 13, '64	Disease.	
Knowles, William H.	K	Dec. 10, '64		Prisoner.
Kyle, James S.	A	Oct. 21, '62	Disease.	
Lambert, Gregory	K	Sept. 14, '63		Prisoner.
Lamb, Nathaniel	C	Jan. 23, '64	Wounds.	
Lang, Patrick	G	Mar. 31, '65	Killed.	
Larry, Peter	G	Aug. 19, '64	Disease.	
Lattie, James	A	1864		Prisoner.
Lawrence, Gilman	B	Dec. 30, '63		
Lawrence, Almond	C	June 6, '64	Killed.	Picket.
Lawrence, Henry B.	G	Dec. 6, '64	Disease.	
Leach, Henry	K	Dec. 13, '62	Killed.	
Lenfist, Thomas H. B.	G	May 8, '64	Killed.	
Libbey, Richard	B	Jan. 29, '65	Disease.	
Lincoln, Augustus C.	I	Sept. 6, '64		Prisoner.
Littlefield, Asel A.	E	June 20, '64	Killed.	
Locke, William P.	F	Dec. 13, '62	Killed.	
Longfellow, Kendall	C			
Love, William	G	May 26, '64	Wounds.	
Luce, Augustus	C	Jan. 21, '63	Wounds.	
Luce, Thomas W.	G	Nov. 17, '62		
Lufkin, Loren	C	May 8, '64	Killed.	
Lurvey, Joseph H.	B	Mar. 19, '64	Disease.	
Lyford, Charles F.	E	Dec. 14, '62	Wounds.	
Lyons, Isaiah	G	Jan. 7, '64	Disease.	
Maddox, John H.	H	Dec. 13, '62	Killed.	
Macomber, Otis	K	Mar. 15, '63	Disease.	
Mallett, Howard	D	Nov. 17, '63		
Malcomb, Simon L.	A	June 24, '64	Killed.	Near Petersb., Va.
Mallett, Horace N.	B	Dec. 29, '63		
Malcomb, William A.	D	Apr. 24, '64		Prisoner.
Mann, Alford A.	A	Apr. 22, '65	Wounds.	
Martin, Michael	D	May 8, '64	Killed.	
Mardin, Edwin	G	Jan. 3, '64	Disease.	
Marston, John J.	H	Feb. '64		Richmond.
Marston, William W.	I	June 1, '64		
Marshall, David	I	Jan. 7, '64	Disease.	
Marks, Calvin B.	K	Dec. 12, '64		Prisoner.

List of members of Sixteenth Maine Regiment deceased from date of organization to date of muster-out, June 5, 1865.—*Continued.*

NAMES.	Co.	DATE.	CAUSE.	
Marks, James B.	K	Dec. 5, '64	....	Prisoner.
March, John C.	F	Dec. 13, '62	Killed.	
McCann, Charles M.	F	Mar. 18, '63	....	
McPhee, John.	F	April 1, '65	Killed.	
McKeen, Lyman R.	D	Dec. 13, '62	Killed.	
Merrill, George E.	F	Dec. 13, '62	Killed	
Merrill, Frank M.	E	Dec. 21, '62	Disease.	
Michaels, William H.	I	Feb. 18, '63	....	
Middleton, Thomas	H	Mar. 1, '65	....	Prisoner.
Mills, Albion B.	E	Oct. 7, '63	Wounds.	
Mitchell, Joseph.	C	Oct. 6, '62	....	Smoketown, Md.
Mitchell, Peleg.	D	Dec. 19, '63	....	Washington.
Morrill, Winslow A.	A	1863	Wounds.	
Murray, Lewis A.	B	Dec. 13, '62	Killed.	Supposed.
Murch, Albert J.	E	Jan. 6, '65	....	
Murphy, Thomas.	I	Dec. 13, '62	Killed.	
Newell, James N.	E	Feb. 6, '65	Killed.	
Niles, Adon A.	I	Dec. 26, '63	....	
Norton, Benjamin.	G	Oct. 21, '62	....	
Oakes, Charles.	C	Oct. 7, '62	....	Smoketown, Md.
Packard, Winslow E.	E	Jan. 9, '63	Wounds.	
Palmer, John.	B	Feb. 6, '65	Killed.	
Palmer, Charles F.	K	May 22, '64	Wounds.	
Parsons, George R.	B	Dec. 16, '62	Wounds.	
Parsons, Joseph A.	D	Dec. 13, '62	Wounds.	Supposed.
Parsons, James.	D	Sept. 6, '64	....	Prisoner.
Parsons, Joseph W.	D	Apr. 6, '65	....	
Patten, Lora S.	I	Mar. 2, '64	....	
Paul, Frank.	F	May 10, '64	Killed.	
Pelton, Leroy.	F	Feb. 15, '63	....	
Perry, Daniel.	I	Mar. 28, '63	....	
Perry, Clark E.	F	Nov. 28, '63	....	
Phillips, Charles M.	B	Feb. 19, '64	Disease.	
Pierce, Charles R.	F	June 14, '64	....	
Powers, William T.	F	Jan. 13, '63	....	
Priest, Hiram S.	E	July 1, '63	Killed.	
Pullen, Harrison.	G	July 18, '63	Wounds.	
Putnam, C. H.	D	Nov. 22, '63	....	Richmond, Va.
Putnam, Daniel G.	D	Sept. 11, '64	....	
Ramsdell, Hiram B.	G	Jan. 11, '63	Wounds.	
Rankin, Charles H.	G	May 8, '64	Killed.	
Redding, George F.	H	Feb. 25, '65	....	Prisoner, Richm'd.
Redd, Henry J.	G	April 13, '64	Disease.	Cony Hospital, Augusta, Maine.
Reed, John W.	C	Jan. 6, '63	Wounds.	
Reed, Jacob.	E	Dec. 16, '63	....	Division Hospital.
Richards, Prentiss M.	D	Dec. 11, '63	....	
Rich, Tyler F.	H	May 26, '64	Killed.	
Richardson, Joseph.	F	Dec. 13, '62	Killed.	
Rideout, Eben.	H	April 4, '63	....	In camp.

SIXTEENTH MAINE REGIMENT.

List of members of Sixteenth Maine Regiment deceased from date of organization to date of muster-out, June 5, 1865.—*Continued.*

NAMES.	Co.	DATE.	CAUSE.	
Roberts, Albert W	D	Aug. 9, '64	Disease.	
Robbins, Samuel S	G	Apr. 27, '64		Prisoner.
Roberts, Benjamin T	G	Dec. 13, '62	Killed.	
Rogers, Erastus C	G	Dec. 25, '63	Disease.	
Rogers, Charles E	F	Dec. 3, '63		
Rose, Moses	B	Nov. 24, '63		
Rowe, Lloyd D	F	June 7, '64		
Rowe, Zelotes	I	Sept. 7, '64		Libby Prison.
Sanborn, Job L	C	Dec. 13, '62	Killed.	
Sawyer, Freeman C	F	Dec. 13, '62	Killed.	
Sawyer, Darius	G	Dec. 13, '62	Killed.	
Sawyer, Thomas D	G	Dec. 2, '62		
Scudder, Silas H	C	Mar. 16, '65	Disease.	
Seavey, Seth E	D	May 10, '64	Killed.	
Sharp, Henry A	C	Dec. 11, '64		
Shorey, Appleton W	C	Feb. 5, '65		
Small, Charles C	C	Aug. 6, '63	Drowned.	Rappahannock, Va
Smith, Aaron G	E	Feb. 6, '65	Disease.	
Smith, William H	H	Nov. 29, '63		
Smith, James	A	Dec. 15, '62	Disease.	
Smith, Llewellyn C	G	Jan. 28, '63		Hospital.
Smith, George W	H	Dec. 13, '62	Killed.	
Smith, Francis L	F	Feb. 6, '63		
Smith, James P	B	Nov. 29, '62	Disease.	Brooks Station, Va
Soper, Joel	C	Dec. 26, '62	Wounds.	
Spaulding, Daniel	K	May 20, '64	Wounds.	
Speed, William H	F	Nov. 16, '63		
Sprague, Charles	B	Dec. 13, '62	Killed.	
Stafford, John	A	Dec. 13, '62	Killed.	
Stevens, Charles H	D	July 1, '63	Killed.	Supposed.
Stetson, Ephraim H	H	May 26, '63		
Stone, Walter E	D	June 18, '63	Disease.	
Stover, Oliver	I	Dec. 7, '64		Prisoner.
Sullivan, Harriman A	G	Sept. 26, '64	Wounds.	
Sweat, John	A	Jan. 22, '63	Disease.	
Swett, Sidney E	F	Dec. 23, '63		
Scott, William A	K	Jan. 5, '63		
Tabor, Franklin P	B	1862		Warrenton, Va.
Tabor, Charles H	B	Sept. 17, '63		Annapolis, Md.
Tallow, Martin	B	Oct. 8, '64	Killed.	
Taylor, Howard W	G	Oct. 26, '63		
Thayer, James H	H	June 4, '64	Killed.	
Thomas, Benjamin P	B	Nov. 17, '63		
Thompson, Charles H	I	Nov. 30, '64		Prisoner.
Titcomb, William H	G	Dec. 13, '62	Killed.	
Towers, William H	G	Jan. 1, '63		Prisoner.
Towle, Clark L	E	Dec. 31, '62	Wounds.	
Towle, Mark	E	1864		Prisoner.
Trask, Ezra W	E	Sept. 14, '64	Wounds.	
Tripp, Simeon	I	1864		Prisoner.

List of members of Sixteenth Maine Regiment deceased from date of organization to date of muster-out, June 5, 1865.—*Continued.*

NAMES.	Co.	DATE.	CAUSE.	
Tuck, Warren	C	Dec. 13, '62	Killed.	
Varney, Edward L.	F	Nov. 2, '63		
Wade, Gardner B.	G	May 12, '64	Wounds.	
Walker, Eben J.	F	Oct. 18, '63		Washington.
Walker, George A., 2d.	A	Mar. 1, '65	Wounds.	
Ward, William W.	F	Oct. 20, '63		
Warren, Harrison S.	A	1863	Disease.	
Warren, Charles A.	F	Oct. 27, '64		Andersonville, Ga.
Webster, John M.	D	July 11, '64		
Webber, Virgil H.	E	July 1, '63	Killed.	
Webber, George L.	G	Dec. 24, '63	Disease.	
Weeks, Theodore.	B	Jan. 7, '64		
Weed, Alonzo S.	E	Dec. 24, '63		Richmond, Va.
Welch, Robert.	G	Sept. 29, '63		Hospital.
Welch, John E.	G	May 10, '64	Killed.	
Welch, Warren E.	B	Jan. 26, '65	Disease.	
Wentworth, Franklin.	A	Jan. 6, '64		Washington.
Wentworth, Leonidas.	D	Nov. 6, '62	Disease.	Warrenton, Va.
West, Fred W.	I	Dec. 22, '63		
Weymouth, Timothy.	E	Jan. 11, '63		
Wheeler, John M.	G	Dec. 18, '62	Wounds.	
Whitney, Alonzo M.	F	Dec. 13, '62	Killed.	
Whittaker, Zebulon	B	Feb. 24, '65	Disease.	
Whitcomb, Tilson T.	G	Jan., '65		
Whittemore, Samuel H	G	May 10, '64		
Whitten, Martin L.	H	April 6, '65	Disease.	
Whittier, Reuel M.	I	Dec. 16, '63		
Wight, William L.	B	June 21, '64	Killed.	Skirmish line.
Wilson, John F.	C	Feb. 24, '65	Disease.	
Wilson, George W.	H	July 20, '64		Andersonville, Ga.
Wilson, Thomas J.	K	Jan. 18, '64	Disease.	
Winslow, Hiram.	K	Feb. 23, '65		
Williams, George W.	E	Feb. 17, '63	Disease.	
Wilson, Isaac M.	K	Jan. 7, '63	Wounds.	
Witherly, Thomas D.	H	Mar. 26, '65	Disease.	
Witham, James A.	A	Sept. 30, '62	Disease.	
Worth, Francis.	E	Jan. 14, '64		Washington.
Wright, Charles W.	C	Nov. 15, '64		
Wyman, James R.	D	June 17, '64		
Yeaton, William N.	C	July 1, '63	Killed.	
Young, Lewis P.	I	Dec. 28, '63		

SUMMARY

Showing the Gains and Losses in the Sixteenth Regiment from August 14th, 1862, to June 5th, 1865.

	Officers					Enlisted Men.			Officers.						Enlisted Men.									Mustered out and subsequently discharged.		Wounded in action.	
	Mustered in.	Promoted from the ranks.	Transferred from companies.	Assigned.	From civil life.	Total commissioned.	Mustered in.	Recruits received.	One company assigned.	Transferred.	Total enlisted men.	Resigned.	Discharged for disability.	Discharged for promotion.	Killed in action and died of wounds.	Died of disease.	Total loss of officers.	Discharged by order.	Discharged for disability.	Discharged for promotion.	Transferred.	Killed in action and died of wounds.	Died of disease.	Missing in action.	Deserted.	Total loss of enlisted men.	Loss, Aggregate.	Officers.	Enlisted men.	Officers.	Enlisted men.
Field and Staff	16		16	3	3						14																112	14				
Company A							98	57		25	228							16	20		31	16	12	13	10	134	139	2	136	6	28
Company B							95	79			174							8	8		81	21	25	6	5	154	164	3	44	4	28
Company C							85	92		1	178							14	22		63	21	21	5	12	158	152	3	23		36
Company D							98	73			171							11	25		54	14	21	3	18	146	161	4	24	3	27
Company E							96	98			194							10	34		56	18	27	4	9	157	161	4	37	2	34
Company F							97	58			152							10	29		35	10	25	2	15	125	121	3	40	3	28
Company G							98	100			197							15	25		66	8	23	9	18	141	152	3	25		26
Company H							97	87			179							17	14		61	22	33	3	12	148	152	3	53		36
Company I							96	92			182							10	21		73	12	21	4	14	144	154	2	38	2	12
Company K							96	93			179							14	22		72	21	21	4	21	136	164	6	29	2	27
Totals	29	31	10	3	3		860	829		26	1876	12	17		10	1	57	125	260		541	168	240	52	86	1467	1626	33	469	22	266

www.ingramcontent.com/pod-product-compliance
Lightning Source LLC
Chambersburg PA
CBHW031854220426
43663CB00006B/613